DISCARDED
D0083110

Statistical Analysis of Management Data

Statistical Analysis of Management Data

Hubert Gatignon
The Claude Janssen Chaired Professor of
Business Administration
and Professor of Marketing
INSEAD

KLUWER ACADEMIC PUBLISHERS
BOSTON / DORDRECHT / LONDON

Distributors for North, Central and South America:
Kluwer Academic Publishers
101 Philip Drive
Assinippi Park
Norwell, Massachusetts 02061 USA
Telephone (781) 871-6600
Fax (781) 681-9045
E-Mail <kluwer@wkap.com>

Distributors for all other countries:
Kluwer Academic Publishers Group
Post Office Box 17
3300 AH Dordrecht, THE NETHERLANDS
Telephone +31 (0) 78 657 60 00
Fax +31 (0) 78 657 64 74
E-Mail <services@wkap.nl>

Electronic Services <http://www.wkap.nl>

Gatignon, Hubert; Statistical Analysis of Management Data

ISBN 1-4020-7315-1

Printed on acid-free paper.

Printed in the United States of America

The Publisher offers discounts on this book for course use and bulk purchases. For further information, send email to <kluwer@wkap.com>.
Cover design by Marc Palmer: *http://www.sigildesign.com*

To my daughters, Aline and Valérie

Contents

Preface

I am very indebted to a number of people without whom I would not have envisioned this book. First, Paul Green helped me tremendously in the preparation of the first doctoral seminar I taught at the Wharton School. The orientations and objectives set for that book reflect those he had for the seminar on data analysis which he used to teach before I did. A second individual, Lee Cooper at UCLA, was determinant in the approach I used for teaching statistics. As my first teacher of multivariate statistics, the exercise of having to program all the methods in APL taught me the benefits of such an approach for the complete understanding of this material. Finally, I owe a debt to all the doctoral students in the various fields of management, both at Wharton and INSEAD, who have, by their questions and feedback, helped me develop this approach. I hope it will benefit future students in learning these statistical tools, which are basic to academic research in the field of management especially. Special thanks go to Bruce Hardie who helped me put together some of the data bases and to Frédéric Dalsace who carefully identified sections that needed further explanation and editing. Also, my research assistant at INSEAD, Gueram Sargsyan was instrumental in preparing the examples used in this manual to illustrate the various methods.

1. Introduction

1.1 Overview

This book covers multivariate statistical analyses that are important for researchers in all fields of management whether finance, production, accounting, marketing, strategy, technology or human resources management. Although multivariate statistical techniques such as those described in this book play key roles in fundamental disciplines of the social sciences (e.g., economics and econometrics or psychology and psychometrics), the methodologies particularly relevant and typically used in management research are the center of focus of this study.

This book is especially designed to provide doctoral students with a theoretical knowledge of the basic concepts underlying the most important multivariate techniques and with an overview of actual applications in various fields. The book addresses both the underlying mathematics and *problems of application*. As such, a reasonable level of competence in both statistics and mathematics is needed. This book is not intended as a first introduction to statistics and statistical analysis. Instead, it assumes that the student is familiar with basic statistical techniques. The book presents the techniques in a fundamental way but in a format accessible to students in a doctoral program, to practicing academicians and data analysts. With this in mind, it may be recommended to review some basic statistics and matrix algebra such as provided in the following:

- Green, Paul E. (1978), *Mathematical Tools for Applied Multivariate Analysis*, New York, NY: Academic Press [Chapters 2 to 4].
- Maddala, G. S. (1977), *Econometrics*, New York, NY: McGraw Hill, Inc. [Appendix A].

This book offers a clear, succinct exposition of each technique with emphasis on when each technique is appropriate and how to use it. The focus is on the essential aspects that a working researcher will encounter. In short, the focus is on using multivariate analysis appropriately through understanding of the foundations of the methods to gain valid and fruitful insights into management problems.

This book presents methodologies for analyzing primary or secondary data typically used by academics as well as analysts in management research and provides an opportunity for the researcher to have hands-on experience with such methods.

1.2 Objectives

The main objectives of this book are to:

1. Develop the student's knowledge of the technical details of various techniques for analyzing data.
2. Expose students to applications and "hands-on" use of various computer programs. This experience will make it possible for students to carry out statistical analyses of their own data. Commonly used software is used throughout the book as much as possible across methodologies to avoid having to learn multiple systems with their own, specific data manipulations and instructions. However, not a single data analysis software performs all the analyses presented in the book. Therefore, three basic statistical packages are used: SAS, LIMDEP and LISREL.

1.2.1 Develop the Student's Knowledge of the Technical Details of Various Techniques for Analyzing Data

The first objective is to prepare the researcher with the basic technical knowledge required for understanding the methods, as well as their limitations. This requires a thorough understanding of the fundamental properties of the techniques. Basic knowledge means that the book will not go into the advanced issues of the methodologies. This should be acquired through specialized, more advanced books on the specific topics. Nevertheless, this book should provide enough detail for what is the minimum knowledge expected from a doctoral candidate in management studies. "Basic" should not be interpreted as a lower level of technical expertise. It is used to express the minimum knowledge expected from an academic researcher in management. The objective is to train the reader to understand the technique, to be able to use it and to have the sufficient knowledge to understand more advanced material about the technique that can be found in other books afterwards.

1.2.2 Expose the Students to Applications and "Hand-on" Use of Various Computer Programs for Carrying Out Statistical Analyses of Data

While the basic statistical theories corresponding to the various types of analysis are necessary, they are not sufficient to do research. The use of any technique requires the knowledge of the statistical software corresponding to these analyses. It is indispensable that students learn both the theory *and the practice* of using these methods *at the same time*. A very effective, albeit time consuming way to make sure that the intricacies of a technique are mastered is by programming the software oneself. A quicker way is to make sure that the use of the software coincides with the learning of the theory by associating application examples with the theory and by doing some analysis oneself.

This is why, in this book, each chapter is made of four parts. The first part of any chapter presents the methods from a theoretical point of view with the various properties of the method. The second part shows an example of an analysis with instructions on how to use a particular software program appropriate for that analysis. The third part gives an assignment so that students can actually practice the method of analysis. The data sets for these assignments are described in Appendix C and can be downloaded from the web at: http://www.insead.edu/~gatignon. Finally, the fourth part consists of references of articles which use such techniques appropriately, and which serve as templates. Selected readings could have been reprinted in this book for each application. However, few articles illustrate all the facets of the techniques. By providing a list of articles, each student can choose the applications corresponding best to his or her interests. By accessing multiple articles in the area of interest, the learning becomes richer. All these articles illustrating the particular multivariate techniques used in empirical analysis are drawn from the major research journals in the field of management.

1.3 Types of Scales

Data used in management research are obtained from existing sources (secondary data) such as data published by Ward for automobile sales in the USA or from vendors who collect data such as panel data. Data are also collected for the explicit purpose of the study (primary data): survey data, scanner data, panels.

In addition to this variety of data sources, differences in the type of data which are collected can be critical for their analysis. Some data are continuous measures as, for example, the age of a person, with an absolute starting point at birth or the distance between two points. Some commonly used data do not have such an absolute starting point. Temperature is an example of such a measure. Yet in both cases, i.e., temperatures and distances, multiple units of measurement exist throughout the world. These differences are critical because the appropriateness of data analysis methods varies depending on the type of data at hand. In fact, very often the data may have to be collected in a certain way in order to be able to test hypotheses using the appropriate methodology. Failure to collect the appropriate type of data should prevent performing the test.

In this chapter, we discuss the different types of scales which can be found in measuring variables used in management research.

1.3.1 Definition of Different Types of Scales

Scales are quantitative measures of a particular construct, usually not observed directly. Four basic types of scales can categorize management measurements:

- Ratio
- Interval
- Rank order or ordinal
- Categorical or nominal

1.3.2 The Impact of the Type of Scale on Statistical Analysis

The nature of analysis depends in particular on the scale of the variable(s). Table 1.1 summarizes the most frequently used statistics which are permissible

Table 1.1 Scales of measurement and their properties

Scale	Mathematical group structure	Permissible statistics	Typical examples
Nominal	Permutation group $y = f(x)$ [$f(x)$ means any one-to-one correspondence]	• Frequency distribution • Mode	• Numbering of brands • Assignment of numbers to type of products or models • Gender of consumers • Organization types
Ordinal	Isotonic group $y = f(x)$ [$f(x)$ means any increasing monotonic function]	• Median • Percentiles • Order (Spearman) correlations • Sign test	• Order of entry • Rank order of preferences
Interval	General linear group $y = a + bx$ $b > 0$	• Mean • Average deviation • Standard deviation • Product-moment correlation • t test • F test	• Likert scale items (agree-disagree) • Semantic scale items (ratings on opposite adjectives)
Ratio	Similarity group $y = cx$ $c > 0$	• Geometric mean • Coefficient of variation	• Sales • Market Share • Advertising Expenditures

Sources: Adapted from Stevens (1962), p. 25, Stevens (1959), p. 27, and Green and Tull (1970), p. 181.

Green, P. E. and D. S. Tull (1970), *Research for Marketing Decisions*, Englewood Cliffs, NJ: Prentice-Hall, Inc.

Stevens, S. S. (1962), "Mathematics, Measurement and Psychophysics," in S. S. Stevens, ed., *Handbook of Experimental Psychology*, New York, NY: John Wiley & Sons, Inc.

Stevens, S. S. (1959), "Measurement, Psychophysics and Utility," in C. W. Churchman and P. Ratoosh, eds., *Measurement: Definitions and Theories*, New York, NY: John Wiley & Sons, Inc.

according to the scale type. The order of the scales in the table from Nominal to Ratio is hierarchical in the sense that statistics which are permissible for a scale above are also permissible for the scale in question. For example, a median is a legitimate statistic for an ordinal scale variable but is also legitimate for an interval or ratio scale. The reverse is not true; for example, a mean is not legitimate for an ordinal scale.

1.4 Topics Covered

The methods presented in this book cover the major methods of analysis which have been used in the recent management research literature. A survey of the major journals in the various fields of management was done to identify these methods. This analysis revealed interesting observations.

It is striking that the majority of the analyses involve the estimation of a single equation or of several equations independently of one another. Analyses involving a system of equations represent a very small percentage of the analyses performed in these articles. This appears at first hand surprising given the complexity of management phenomena. Possibly some of the simultaneous relationships analyzed are reflected in methodologies which consider explicitly measurement errors; these techniques appear to have grown over the recent years. Factor analysis is still an important analysis found in a significant proportion of the studies, typically to verify the unidimensionality of the constructs measured. Choice modeling has been an important topic, especially in Marketing but also in the other fields of Management, with studies estimating probit or logit models. A still very small percentage of articles use these models for ordered choice data (i.e., where the data reflects only the order in which brands are preferred from best to worse). Analysis of proximity data concerns few studies.

Therefore, the following topics were selected. They have been classified according to the type of the key variable or variables which is or are the center of the interest in the analysis. Indeed, as discussed in Chapter 2, the nature of the criterion (also called dependent or endogenous) variable(s) determines the type of statistical analysis which may be performed. Consequently, the first issue to be discussed concerns the nature and properties of variables and the process of generating scales with the appropriate statistical procedures. Then, follow the various statistical methods of data analysis.

Introduction to multivariate statistics and tests about means

- Multivariate Analysis of Variance

Multiple item measures

- Reliability

- Factor Analysis

  Principle Component Analysis
  Exploratory Factor Analysis
  Confirmatory Factor Analysis

Single equation econometrics

- Ordinary Least Squares
- Generalized Least Squares
- Pooling Tests

System of equations econometrics

- Seemingly Unrelated Regression
- Two Stage Least Squares
- Three Stage Least Squares

Categorical dependent variables

- Discriminant Analysis
- Quantal choice Models: Logit

Rank ordered data

- Conjoint Analysis
- Ordered Probit

Analysis of covariance structure

- LISREL

Analysis of similarity data

- Multidimensional Scaling

1.5 Pedagogy

There are three key learning experiences necessary to be able to achieve these objectives:

1. the knowledge of sufficient statistical theory to be able to understand the methodologies, when they are applicable, and when they are not appropriate.

2. the ability to perform such analyses with the proper statistical software.
3. the understanding of how these methodologies have been applied in management research.

This book differs from others in that no other book on multivariate statistics or data analysis addresses the specific needs of doctoral education. The three aspects mentioned above are weighted differently. This book emphasizes the first aspect of the methodology itself by providing the mathematical and statistical analyses necessary to fully understand them. This can be contrasted with other books that prefer primarily or exclusively a verbal description of the method.

This book favors the understanding of the rationale for modeling choices, issues and problems. While the verbal description of a method may be better accessible to a wider audience, it is often more difficult to follow the rationale, which is based on mathematics. For example, it is difficult to understand the problem of multicollinearity without understanding the effect on the determinant of the covariance matrix which needs to be inverted. The learning that results from verbal presentation tends, therefore, to be more mechanical.

This book also differs in that, instead of choosing a few articles to illustrate the applications of the methods, as would be found in a book of readings (sometimes with short introductions), a list of application articles is provided from which the reader can choose. Articles tend to be relatively easy to access, especially with services available through the WEB. The list of references covers a large cross section of examples and a history of the literature in this domain.

Finally, the examples of analyses are relatively self explanatory and, although some explanations of the statistical software used are provided with each example, this book does not intend to replace the instruction manuals of those particular software packages. The reader is referred to those for details.

In summary, this book puts the accent on the first aspect of the understanding of the statistical methodology while providing enough information for the reader to develop skills in performing the analyses and in understanding how to apply them to management research problems.

More specifically, the learning of this material involves two parts: the learning of the statistical theory behind the technique and the learning of how to use the technique. Although there may be different ways to combine these two experiences, it is recommended to first learn the theory by reading the sections where the methodologies are presented and discussed. Then, the statistical computer package (e.g., SAS, LIMDEP, LISREL, and other specialized packages) used to apply the methodology is presented in the context of an example. Students can then apply the technique using the data sets available from http://www.insead.edu/~gatignon. Finally, application issues can be illustrated by other applications found in prior research and listed at the end of each chapter.

In addition to the books and articles included with each chapter, the following books are highly recommended to further develop someone's skills in different methods of data analysis. Each of these books is more specialized and covers only a subset of the methods presented in this book. However, they are indispensable complements to become proficient in the techniques used in research.

References

Greene, W. H. (1993), *Econometric Analysis*, New York: MacMillan Publishing Company.

Hanssens, D. M., L. J. Parsons and R. L. Shultz (1990), *Market Response Models: Econometric and Time Series Analysis*, Norwell, MA: Kluwer Academic Publishers.

Judge, G. G., W. E. Griffiths, R. C. Hill, H. Lutkepohl and T.-C. Lee (1985), *The Theory and Practice of Econometrics*, New York, NY: John Wiley & Sons.

2. Multivariate Normal Distribution

In this chapter, we will define the univariate and multivariate normal distribution density functions and then we will discuss the tests of differences of means for multiple variables simultaneously across groups.

2.1 Univariate Normal Distribution

Just to refresh memory, in the case of a single random variable, the probability distribution or density function of that variable x is represented by Equation (2.1):

$$\Phi(x)\frac{1}{\sqrt{2\pi}\sigma}\exp\left\{-\frac{1}{2\sigma^2}(x-\mu)^2\right\} \tag{2.1}$$

2.2 Bivariate Normal Distribution

The bivariate distribution represents the joint distribution of two random variables. The two random variables x_1 and x_2 are related to each other in the sense that they are not independent of each other. This dependence is reflected by the correlation ρ between the two variables x_1 and x_2. The density function for the two variables jointly is:

$$\Phi(x_1,x_2)=\frac{1}{2\pi\sigma_1\sigma_2\sqrt{1-\rho^2}}\exp\left\{-\frac{1}{2(1-\rho^2)}\left[\frac{(x_1-\mu_1)^2}{\sigma_1^2}+\frac{(x_2-\mu_2)^2}{\sigma_2^2}-\frac{2\rho(x_1-\mu_1)(x_2-\mu_2)}{\sigma_1\sigma_2}\right]\right\} \tag{2.2}$$

This function can be represented graphically as in Figure 2.1.

The **Isodensity contour** is defined as the set of points for which the values of x_1 and x_2 give the same value for the density function Φ. This contour is given by Equation (2.3) for a fixed value of C, which defines a constant probability:

$$\frac{(x_1-\mu_1)^2}{\sigma_1^2}+\frac{(x_2-\mu_2)^2}{\sigma_2^2}-2\rho\frac{(x_1-\mu_1)(x_2-\mu_2)}{\sigma_1\sigma_2}=C \tag{2.3}$$

Equation (2.3) defines an ellipse with centroid (μ_1, μ_2). This ellipse is the locus of points representing the combinations of the values of x_1 and x_2 with the same probability, as defined by the constant C (Figure 2.2).

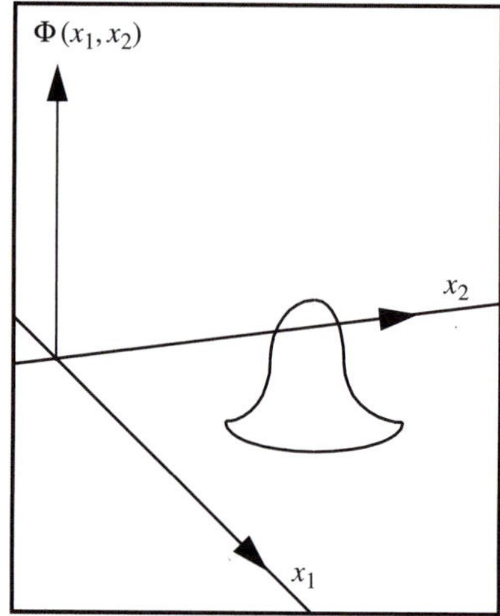

Fig. 2.1 The bivariate normal distribution.

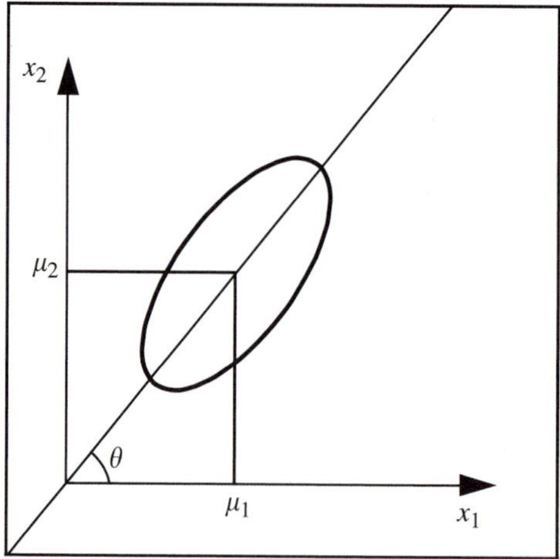

Fig. 2.2 The locus of points of the bivariate normal distribution at a given density level.

For various values of C, we get a family of concentric ellipses (at a different cut, i.e., cross section of the density surface with planes at various elevations) (see Figure 2.3).

The angle θ depends only on the values of σ_1, σ_2 and ρ but is independent of C. The higher the correlation between x_1 and x_2, the steeper the line going through the origin with angle θ, i.e., the bigger the angle.

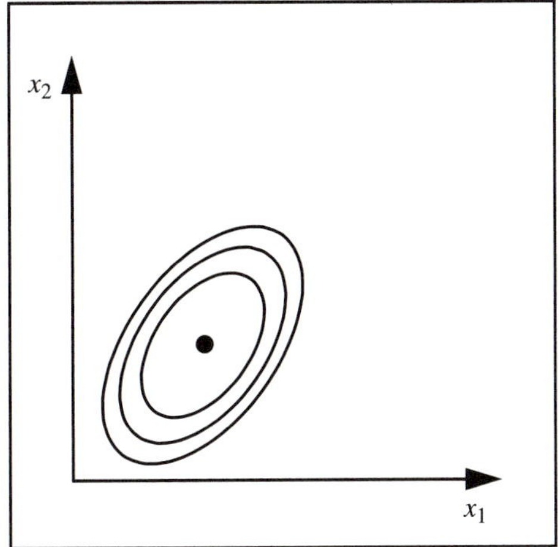

Fig. 2.3 Concentric ellipses at various density levels.

2.3 Generalization to Multivariate Case

Let us represent the bivariate distribution in matrix algebra notation in order to derive the generalized format for more than two random variables.

The covariance matrix of (x_1, x_2) can be written as:

$$\boldsymbol{\Sigma} = \begin{bmatrix} \sigma_1^2 & \rho\sigma_1\sigma_2 \\ \rho\sigma_1\sigma_2 & \sigma_2^2 \end{bmatrix} \tag{2.4}$$

The determinant of the matrix $\boldsymbol{\Sigma}$ is:

$$|\boldsymbol{\Sigma}| = \sigma_1^2\sigma_2^2(1-\rho^2) \tag{2.5}$$

Equation (2.3) can now be re-written as:

$$C = [x_1 - \mu_1, x_2 - \mu_2]\boldsymbol{\Sigma}^{-1} \begin{bmatrix} x_1 - \mu_1 \\ x_2 - \mu_2 \end{bmatrix} \tag{2.6}$$

where

$$\boldsymbol{\Sigma}^{-1} = 1/\left[\sigma_1^2\sigma_2^2(1-\rho^2)\right] \begin{bmatrix} \sigma_2^2 & -\rho\sigma_1\sigma_2 \\ -\rho\sigma_1\sigma_2 & \sigma_1^2 \end{bmatrix} = \frac{1}{1-\rho^2} \begin{bmatrix} \dfrac{1}{\sigma_1^2} & \dfrac{-\rho}{\sigma_1\sigma_2} \\ \dfrac{-\rho}{\sigma_1\sigma_2} & \dfrac{1}{\sigma_2^2} \end{bmatrix} \tag{2.7}$$

Note that $\boldsymbol{\Sigma}^{-1} = |\boldsymbol{\Sigma}|^{-1} \times$ matrix of cofactors.

Let

$$\mathbf{X} = \begin{bmatrix} x_1 - \mu_1 \\ x_2 - \mu_2 \end{bmatrix}$$

then $\mathbf{X}'\mathbf{\Sigma}^{-1}\mathbf{X} = \chi^2$, which is a quadratic form equation and is, therefore, a chi-square variate.

Also, because $|\mathbf{\Sigma}| = \sigma_1^2\sigma_2^2(1-\rho^2)$, $|\mathbf{\Sigma}|^{1/2} = \sigma_1\sigma_2\sqrt{(1-\rho^2)}$, and consequently,

$$\frac{1}{2\pi\sigma_1\sigma_2\sqrt{1-\rho^2}} = (2\pi)^{-1}|\mathbf{\Sigma}|^{-1/2} \tag{2.8}$$

The bivariate distribution function can be now expressed in matrix notation as:

$$\Phi(x_1, x_2) = (2\pi)^{-1}|\mathbf{\Sigma}|^{-1/2}e^{-(1/2)\mathbf{X}'\mathbf{\Sigma}^{-1}\mathbf{X}} \tag{2.9}$$

Now, more generally with p random variables $(x_1, x_2, \ldots, x_p)$, let

$$\mathbf{x} = \begin{bmatrix} x_1 \\ x_2 \\ \vdots \\ x_p \end{bmatrix}; \quad \mu = \begin{bmatrix} \mu_1 \\ \mu_2 \\ \vdots \\ \mu_p \end{bmatrix}.$$

The density function is:

$$\Phi(\mathbf{x}) = (2\pi)^{-p/2}|\mathbf{\Sigma}|^{-1/2}e^{[-(1/2)(\mathbf{x}-\mu)'\mathbf{\Sigma}^{-1}(\mathbf{x}-\mu)]} \tag{2.10}$$

For a fixed value of the density Φ, an ellipsoid is described. Let $\mathbf{X} = \mathbf{x} - \mu$. The inequality $\mathbf{X}'\mathbf{\Sigma}^{-1}\mathbf{X} \leq \chi^2$ defines any point within the ellipsoid.

2.4 Tests About Means

2.4.1 Sampling Distribution of Sample Centroids

2.4.1.1 Univariate distribution

A random variable is normally distributed with mean μ and variance σ^2:

$$x \sim N(\mu, \sigma^2) \tag{2.11}$$

After n independent draws, the mean is randomly distributed with mean μ and variance σ^2/n:

$$\bar{x} \sim N\left(\mu, \frac{\sigma^2}{n}\right) \tag{2.12}$$

2.4.1.2 Multivariate distribution

In the multivariate case with p random variables where $\mathbf{x} = (x_1, x_2, \ldots, x_p)'$, $\mathbf{x}$ is normally distributed following the multivariate normal distribution with mean μ and covariance $\mathbf{\Sigma}$:

$$\mathbf{x} \sim N(\mu, \mathbf{\Sigma}) \tag{2.13}$$

The mean vector for the sample of size n is denoted:

$$\bar{\mathbf{x}} = \begin{bmatrix} \bar{x}_1 \\ \bar{x}_2 \\ \vdots \\ \bar{x}_p \end{bmatrix}.$$

This sample mean vector is normally distributed with a multivariate normal distribution with mean μ and covariance $\mathbf{\Sigma}/n$:

$$\bar{\mathbf{x}} \sim N\left(\mu, \frac{\mathbf{\Sigma}}{n}\right) \tag{2.14}$$

2.4.2 Significance Test: One-sample Problem

2.4.2.1 Univariate test

The univariate test is illustrated in the following example. Let us test the hypothesis that the mean is 150 (i.e., $\mu_0 = 150$) with the following information:

$$\sigma^2 = 256; \quad n = 64; \quad \bar{x} = 154.$$

Then, the z score can be computed:

$$z = \frac{154 - 150}{\sqrt{\frac{256}{64}}} = \frac{4}{\frac{16}{8}} = 2.$$

At $\alpha = 0.05$ (95% confidence interval), $z = 1.96$, as obtained from a normal distribution table. Therefore, the hypothesis is rejected. The confidence interval is

$$\left[154 - 1.96 \times \tfrac{12}{6}, 154 + 1.96 \times \tfrac{12}{6}\right] = [150.08, 157.92]$$

This interval excludes 150. The hypothesis that $\mu_0 = 150$ is rejected. If the variance σ had been unknown, the t statistic would have been used:

$$t = \frac{\bar{x} - \mu_0}{s/\sqrt{n}} \tag{2.15}$$

where s is the observed sample standard deviation.

2.4.2.2 Multivariate test with known Σ

Let us take an example with two random variables:

$$\boldsymbol{\Sigma} = \begin{bmatrix} 25 & 10 \\ 10 & 16 \end{bmatrix} \quad n = 36$$

$$\bar{\mathbf{x}} = \begin{bmatrix} 20.3 \\ 12.6 \end{bmatrix}$$

The hypothesis is now about the mean values stated in terms of the two variables jointly:

$$H: \quad \mu_0 = \begin{bmatrix} 20 \\ 15 \end{bmatrix}$$

At the alpha level of 0.05, the value of the density function can be written as below, which follows a chi-squared distribution at the specified significance level α:

$$n(\mu_0 - \bar{\mathbf{x}})'\boldsymbol{\Sigma}^{-1}(\mu_0 - \bar{\mathbf{x}}) \sim \chi_p^2(\alpha) \tag{2.16}$$

Computing the value of the statistics,

$$|\boldsymbol{\Sigma}| = 25 \times 16 - 10 \times 10 = 300$$

$$\boldsymbol{\Sigma}^{-1} = \frac{1}{300}\begin{bmatrix} 16 & -10 \\ -10 & 25 \end{bmatrix}$$

$$\chi^2 = 36 \times \frac{1}{300}(20 - 20.3, 15 - 12.6)\begin{bmatrix} 16 & -10 \\ -10 & 25 \end{bmatrix}\begin{bmatrix} 20 - 20.3 \\ 15 - 12.6 \end{bmatrix} = 15.72$$

The critical value at an alpha value of 0.05 with 2 degrees of freedom is provided by tables:

$$\chi_{p=2}^2(\alpha = 0.05) = 5.991.$$

The observed value is greater than the critical value. Therefore, the hypothesis that $\mu = \left[\begin{smallmatrix} 20 \\ 15 \end{smallmatrix}\right]$ is rejected.

2.4.2.3 Multivariate test with unknown Σ

Just as in the univariate case, $\boldsymbol{\Sigma}$ is replaced with the sample value $\mathbf{S}/(n-1)$, where $\mathbf{S}$ is the sums-of-squares-and-cross-products (SSCP) matrix, which provides an unbiased estimate of the covariance matrix. The following statistics are then used to test the hypothesis:

$$\text{Hotelling:} \quad T^2 = n(n-1)(\bar{\mathbf{x}} - \mu_0)'\mathbf{S}^{-1}(\bar{\mathbf{x}} - \mu_0) \tag{2.17}$$

where, if

$$\underset{n\times p}{\mathbf{X}^d} = \begin{bmatrix} x_{11} - \bar{x}_1 & x_{21} - \bar{x}_2 & \dots \\ x_{12} - \bar{x}_1 & x_{22} - \bar{x}_2 & \dots \\ \vdots & \vdots & \\ x_{1n} - \bar{x}_1 & x_{2n} - \bar{x}_2 & \dots \end{bmatrix},$$

$$\mathbf{S} = \mathbf{X}^{d'}\mathbf{X}^d$$

Hotelling showed that

$$\frac{n-p}{(n-1)p}T^2 \sim F^p_{n-p} \tag{2.18}$$

Replacing T^2 by its expression given above:

$$\frac{n(n-p)}{p}(\bar{\mathbf{x}} - \mu_0)'\mathbf{S}^{-1}(\bar{\mathbf{x}} - \mu_0) \sim F^p_{n-p} \tag{2.19}$$

Consequently, the test is performed by computing the expression above and comparing its value with the critical value obtained in an F table with p and $n - p$ degrees of freedom.

2.4.3 Significance Test: Two-sample Problem

2.4.3.1 Univariate test

Let us define $\bar{x}_1$ and $\bar{x}_2$ the means of a variable on two unrelated samples. The test for the significance of the difference between the two means is given by

$$t = \frac{(\bar{x}_1 - \bar{x}_2)}{s\sqrt{(1/n_1) + (1/n_2)}} \quad \text{or} \quad t^2 = \frac{(\bar{x}_1 - \bar{x}_2)^2}{s^2[(n_1 + n_2)/(n_1 n_2)]} \tag{2.20}$$

where

$$s = \frac{\sqrt{(n_1 - 1)\frac{\sum_i x_{1i}^2}{n_1 - 1} + (n_2 - 1)\frac{\sum_i x_{2i}^2}{n_2 - 1}}}{(n_1 - 1) + (n_2 - 1)}$$

$$= \sqrt{\frac{\sum_i x_{1i}^2 + \sum_i x_{2i}^2}{n_1 + n_2 - 2}} \tag{2.21}$$

s^2 is the pooled within groups variance. It is an estimate of the assumed common variance σ^2 of the two populations.

2.4.3.2 Multivariate test

Let $\bar{\mathbf{x}}^{(1)}$ be the mean vector in sample 1 $= \begin{bmatrix} \bar{x}_1^{(1)} \\ \bar{x}_2^{(1)} \\ \vdots \\ \bar{x}_p^{(1)} \end{bmatrix}$ and similarly for sample 2.

We need to test the significance of the difference between $\bar{\mathbf{x}}^{(1)}$ and $\bar{\mathbf{x}}^{(2)}$. We will consider first the case where the covariance matrix, which is assumed to be the same in the two samples, is known. Then we will consider the case where an estimate of the covariance matrix needs to be used.

$\boldsymbol{\Sigma}$ is known (the same in the two samples)

In this case, the difference between the two group means is normally distributed with a multivariate normal distribution:

$$\left(\bar{\mathbf{x}}^{(1)} - \bar{\mathbf{x}}^{(2)}\right) \sim N\left(\mu_1 - \mu_2, \boldsymbol{\Sigma}\left(\frac{1}{n_1} + \frac{1}{n_2}\right)\right) \tag{2.22}$$

The computations for testing the significance of the differences are similar to those in section 2.4.2.2. using the chi-squared test.

$\boldsymbol{\Sigma}$ is unknown

If the covariance matrix is not known, it is estimated using the covariance matrices within each group but pooled.

Let $\mathbf{W}$ be the within-groups SSCP (sum of squares cross products) matrix. This matrix is computed from the matrix of deviations from the means on all p variables for each of n_k observations (individuals). For each group k,

$$\underset{n_k \times p}{\mathbf{X}^{d(k)}} = \begin{bmatrix} x_{11}^{(k)} - \bar{x}_1^{(k)} & x_{21}^{(k)} - \bar{x}_2^{(k)} & \cdots \\ x_{12}^{(k)} - \bar{x}_1^{(k)} & x_{22}^{(k)} - \bar{x}_2^{(k)} & \cdots \\ \vdots & \vdots & \\ x_{1n_k}^{(k)} - \bar{x}_1^{(k)} & x_{2n_k}^{(k)} - \bar{x}_2^{(k)} & \cdots \end{bmatrix} \tag{2.23}$$

For each of the 2 groups (each k), the SSCP matrix can be derived:

$$\mathbf{S}_k = \underset{p \times n_k}{\mathbf{X}^{d(k)'}} \underset{n_k \times p}{\mathbf{X}^{d(k)}} \tag{2.24}$$

The pooled SSCP matrix for the more general case of K groups is simply:

$$\underset{p \times p}{\mathbf{W}} = \sum_{k=1}^{K} \underset{p \times p}{\mathbf{S}_k} \tag{2.25}$$

In the case of two groups, K is simply equal to 2.

Then, we can apply Hotelling's T, just as in section 2.4.2.3, where the proper degrees of freedom depending on the number of observations in each group (n_k) are applied.

$$T^2 = (\bar{\mathbf{x}}^{(1)} - \bar{\mathbf{x}}^{(2)})' \left[\frac{\mathbf{W}}{n_1 + n_2 - 2} \frac{n_1 + n_2}{n_1 n_2} \right]^{-1} (\bar{\mathbf{x}}^{(1)} - \bar{\mathbf{x}}^{(2)}) \tag{2.26}$$

$$= \frac{n_1 n_2 (n_1 + n_2 - 2)}{n_1 + n_2} (\bar{\mathbf{x}}^{(1)} - \bar{\mathbf{x}}^{(2)})' \mathbf{W}^{-1} (\bar{\mathbf{x}}^{(1)} - \bar{\mathbf{x}}^{(2)}) \tag{2.27}$$

$$\frac{n_1 + n_2 - p - 1}{(n_1 + n_2 - 2)p} T^2 \sim F^p_{n_1+n_2-p-1} \tag{2.28}$$

2.4.4 Significance Test: *K*-sample Problem

As in the case of two samples, the null hypothesis is that the mean vectors across the K groups are the same and the alternative hypothesis is that they are different.

Let us define Wilk's likelihood-ratio criterion:

$$\Lambda = \frac{|\mathbf{W}|}{|\mathbf{T}|} \tag{2.29}$$

where $\mathbf{T}$ = total SSCP matrix, $\mathbf{W}$ = within-groups SSCP matrix.

$\mathbf{W}$ is defined as in Equation (2.25). The total SSCP matrix is the sum of squared cross products applied to the deviations from the grand means (i.e., the overall mean across the total sample with the observations of all the groups for each variable). Therefore, let the mean centered data for group k be noted as:

$$\underset{n_k \times p}{\mathbf{X}^{d^*(k)}} = \begin{bmatrix} x_{11}^{(k)} - \bar{x}_1 & x_{21}^{(k)} - \bar{x}_2 & \cdots \\ x_{12}^{(k)} - \bar{x}_1 & x_{22}^{(k)} - \bar{x}_2 & \cdots \\ \vdots & \vdots & \\ x_{1n_k}^{(k)} - \bar{x}_1 & x_{2n_k}^{(k)} - \bar{x}_2 & \cdots \end{bmatrix} \tag{2.30}$$

where $\bar{x}_j$ is the overall mean of the j's variate.

Bringing the centered data for all the groups in the same data matrix leads to:

$$\underset{n \times p}{\mathbf{X}^{d^*}} = \begin{bmatrix} \mathbf{X}^{d^*(1)} \\ \mathbf{X}^{d^*(2)} \\ \vdots \\ \mathbf{X}^{d^*(K)} \end{bmatrix} \tag{2.31}$$

The total SSCP matrix T is then defined as:

$$\underset{p\times p}{\mathbf{T}} = \underset{p\times n}{\mathbf{X}^{d^{*\prime}}} \underset{n\times p}{\mathbf{X}^{d^{*}}} \tag{2.32}$$

Intuitively, if we reduce the space to a single variate so that we are only dealing with variances and no covariances, Wilk's lambda is the ratio of the pooled within variance to the total variance. If the group means are the same, the variances are equal and the ratio equals one. As the group means differ, the total variance becomes larger than the pooled within group variance. Consequently, the ratio lambda becomes smaller. Because of the existence of more than one variate, which implies more than one variance and covariances, the within SSCP and Total SSCP matrices need to be reduced to a scalar in order to derive a scalar ratio. This is the role of the determinants. However, the interpretation remains the same as for the univariate case.

Based on Wilk's lambda, we will present two statistical tests: Bartlett's V and Rao's R.

Let n = total sample size across samples, p = number of variables, K = number of groups (number of samples).

Bartlett's V is approximately distributed as a chi-square when $n - 1 - (p + K)/2$ is large:

$$V = -[n - 1 - (p + K)/2]\,\mathrm{Ln}_{\Lambda} \sim X^2_{p(K-1)} \tag{2.33}$$

Bartlett's V is relatively easy to calculate and can be used when $n - 1 - (p + K)/2$ is large.

Another test can be applied, as Rao's R is distributed approximately as an F variate. It is calculated as follows:

$$R = \frac{1 - \Lambda^{1/s}}{\Lambda^{1/s}} \frac{ms - (p(K-1)/2) + 1}{p(K-1)} \approx F^{\nu_1 = p(K-1)}_{\nu_2 = ms - p(K-1)/2 + 1} \tag{2.34}$$

where

$$m = n - 1 - ((p + K)/2)$$

$$s = \sqrt{\frac{p^2(K-1)^2 - 4}{p^2 + (K-1)^2 - 5}}$$

2.5 Examples

2.5.1 Test of the Difference Between Two Mean Vectors – One-Sample Problem

In this example, the file "MKT_DATA" contains data about the market share of a brand over seven periods, as well as the percentage of distribution coverage and the price of the brand. These data correspond to one market, Norway. The question is to know whether the market share, distribution coverage and prices are similar or different from the data of that same brand for the rest of Europe, i.e., with values of market share, distribution coverage and price respectively of 0.17, 32.28 and 1.39. The data are shown below in Table 2.1.

The SAS file showing the SAS code to compute the necessary statistics is shown below in Figure 2.4. The first lines correspond to the basic SAS instructions to read the data from the file. Here, the data file was saved as a text file from Excel. Consequently, the values in the file corresponding to different data points are separated by commas. This is indicated as the delimiter ("dlm"). Also, the data (first observation) starts on line 2 because the first line is used for the names of the variables (as illustrated in Table 2.1). The variable called period is dropped so that only the three variables needed for the analysis are kept in the SAS working data set. The procedure IML is used to perform matrix algebra computations.

This file could easily be used for the analysis of different data bases. Obviously, it would be necessary to adapt some of the instructions, especially the file name and path and the variables. Within the IML subroutine, only three things would need to be changed: (1) the variables used for the analysis, (2) the values for the null hypothesis (m_o) and (3) the critical value of the F statistic with the proper degrees of freedom.

The results are printed in the output file shown below in Figure 2.5. The critical F statistic with 3 and 4 degrees of freedom at the 0.05 confidence level is 6.591 while the computed value is 588.7, indicating that the hypothesis of no difference is rejected.

Table 2.1 Data example for the analysis of three variables

Period	M_Share	Dist	Price
1	0.038	11	0.98
2	0.044	11	1.08
3	0.039	9	1.13
4	0.03	9	1.31
5	0.036	14	1.36
6	0.051	14	1.38
7	0.044	9	1.34

```
/* ************ Example2-1.sas ************** */

OPTIONS LS=80;
DATA work;
INFILE
"C:\SAMD\Chapter2\Examples\Mkt_Data.csv"
dlm = ',' firstobs=2;
INPUT PERIOD M_SHARE DIST PRICE;

data work;
        set work (drop = period) ;
run;

/* Chapter 2, IV.2.3 Multivariate Test with Unknown Sigma */

proc iml;

print " Multivariate Test with Unknown Sigma " ;
print "---------------------------------------" ;

use work;                /* Specifying the matrix with raw market data for Norway */
read all var {M_Share Dist Price} into Mkt_Data;

start SSCP;                        /* SUBROUTINE for calculation of the SSCP matrix */
        n=nrow(x);                         /* Number of rows */
        mean=x[+,]/n;                      /* Column means   */
        x=x-repeat(mean,n,1);              /* Variances      */
        sscp = x'*x;                       /* SSCP matrix    */

finish sscp;                               /* END SUBROUTINE */

x=Mkt_Data;                                /* Definition of the data matrix */
p=ncol(Mkt_Data);
run sscp;                                  /* Execution of the SUBROUTINE   */

print SSCP  n p;

Xbar = mean;                               /* Definition of the mean vector */
m_o = { 0.17 32.28 1.39 };                 /* Myu zero: the mean vector for Europe */

dX = Xbar - m_o;                           /* Matrix of deviations */
dXt = dX';                                 /* Calculation of the transpose of dX */

print m_o;
print Xbar;
print dX;

sscp_1 = inv(sscp);                    /* Calculation of the inverse of SSCP matrix */

T_sq = n*(n-1)*dX*sscp_1*dXt;              /* Calculation of the T_square    */
F    = T_sq*(n-p)/((n-1)*p);               /* Calculation of the F statistic */
```

```
Df_num = p;
Df_den = n-p ;
F_crit = finv(.95,df_num,df_den);        /* Critical F for .05 for df_num, df_den */
Print F F_crit;
quit;
```

Fig. 2.4 SAS input to perform the test of a mean vector (examp2-1.sas).

```
                Multivariate Test with Unknown Sigma
               --------------------------------------

          SSCP                                N          P

     0.0002734      0.035 0.0007786           7          3
         0.035         30      0.66
     0.0007786       0.66 0.1527714

                                M_O

                     0.17      32.28       1.39

                               XBAR

               0.0402857          11 1.2257143

                                DX

               -0.129714     -21.28 -0.164286

                               F     F_CRIT

                     588.72944 6.5913821
```

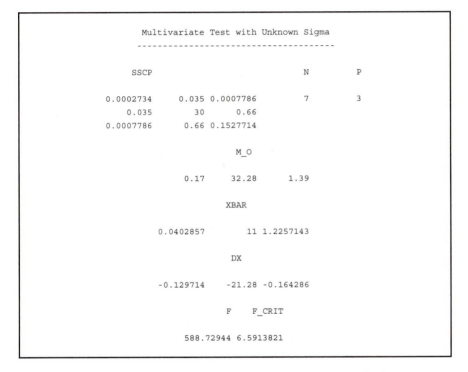

Fig. 2.5 SAS output of analysis defined in Figure 2.4 (examp2-1.lst).

2.5.2 Test of the Difference Between Several Mean Vectors – *K*-sample Problem

The next example considers similar data for three different countries (Belgium, France and England) for seven periods, as shown in Table 2.2. The question is to know whether the mean vectors are the same for the three countries or not.

Table 2.2 Data example for three variables in three countries (groups)

Cntryno	Cntry	Period	M_Share	Dist	Price
1	BELG	1	0.223	61	1.53
1	BELG	2	0.22	69	1.53
1	BELG	3	0.227	69	1.58
1	BELG	4	0.212	67	1.58
1	BELG	5	0.172	64	1.58
1	BELG	6	0.168	64	1.53
1	BELG	7	0.179	62	1.69
2	FRAN	1	0.038	11	0.98
2	FRAN	2	0.044	11	1.08
2	FRAN	3	0.039	9	1.13
2	FRAN	4	0.03	9	1.31
2	FRAN	5	0.036	14	1.36
2	FRAN	6	0.051	14	1.38
2	FRAN	7	0.044	9	1.34
3	UKIN	1	0.031	3	1.43
3	UKIN	2	0.038	3	1.43
3	UKIN	3	0.042	3	1.3
3	UKIN	4	0.037	3	1.43
3	UKIN	5	0.031	13	1.36
3	UKIN	6	0.031	14	1.49
3	UKIN	7	0.036	14	1.56

```
/*  ****************** Examp2-2.sas ******************  */
OPTIONS LS=80;
DATA work;
INFILE
"C:\SAMD\CHAPTER2\EXAMPLES\Mkt_Dt_K.csv"
dlm = ',' firstobs=2;
INPUT CNTRYNO CNTRY $ PERIOD M_SHARE DIST PRICE;
data work;
        set work (drop = cntry period) ;
proc print;
proc freq;
tables cntryno / out = Nk_out (keep = count);
run;
/* Chapter 2, IV.4 Significance Test: K-Sample Problem */
proc iml;
reset center;
print " Multivariate Significance Test: K-Sample Problem " ;
print "-----------------------------------------------" ;
use work ;        /* Specifying the matrix with raw data */
read all var { CNTRYNO M_SHARE DIST PRICE}  into Mkt_Data;
use Nk_out;
read all var {count} into Nk_new;
                        /* Number of observations within each group          */
```

```
n_tot = nrow(Mkt_Data);
K=max(Mkt_Data[,1]);            /* Number of groups (samples) */
p=ncol(Mkt_Data)-1;             /* Number of variables */
print n_tot "    " K "    " p;
start SSCP;                     /* SUBROUTINE for calculation of the SSCP matrix        */
        n=nrow(x);
        mean=x[+,]/n;           /* Column means (mean vector)                           */
        x=x-repeat(mean,n,1);   /* Matrix of variances                                  */
        SSCP = x`*x;            /* SSCP matrix                                          */
print i "      " mean;
finish SSCP;                    /* END SUBROUTINE                                       */
S = J(p,p,0);                   /* Definition of a p x p square matrix with zeros       */
do i = 1 to K;
if i = 1 then a = 1;
else
a=1+(i-1)*nk_new[i-1];
b=a+nk_new[i]-1;
x = Mkt_Data[a:b,2:4];
run SSCP;                       /* Execution of the SUBROUTINE for each group           */
S = S + SSCP;                   /* Accumulation of the sum of SSCP matrices             */
end;                            /* in order to calculate W (within-the-groups SSCP)     */
W = S; DetW = Det(W);
print W "      " DetW;
x=Mkt_Data[,2:4];               /* Definition of the data matrix (dropping the first column: CNTRYNO) */
run SSCP;                       /* Execution of the SUBROUTINE for total data           */
T=SSCP;
DetT = Det(T);
print T "      " DetT;
Lmbd = Det(W) / Det(T);
m = n_tot-1-(p+K) / 2;
reset noname fw=5 nocenter;
print "Lambda =" Lmbd [format=10.6];
print "m =" m [format=2.0]
               "  Use Bartlett's V for large m's and Rao's R otherwise " ;
V = -m*Log(Lmbd);
s = sqrt((p*p*(K-1)**2-4)/(p*p+(K-1)**2-5));
R = (1-Lmbd**(1/s))*(m*s-p*(K-1)/2 + 1)/(Lmbd**(1/s)*p*(K-1));
Df_num = p*(K-1);                       Df_den = m*s-Df_num/2 +1 ;
Chi_crit = CINV(0.95,Df_num);                   F_crit = finv(.95,df_num,df_den);
print "Bartlett's V = " V [format=9.6] "   DF =" DF_num [format=2.0]   ;
print "     Chi_crit =" Chi_crit [format=9.6];
print "Rao's R ="  R [format=9.6]
                      "   DF_NUM =" Df_num [format=2.0]
                      "   DF_DEN ="  Df_den [format=2.0] ;
print "     F_crit =" F_crit [format=9.6];
quit;
```

Fig. 2.6 SAS input to perform a test of difference in mean vectors across K groups (examp2-2.sas).

The SAS file which derived the computations for the test statistics is shown in Figure 2.6. The results are shown in the SAS output below (Figure 2.7). These results indicate that the Bartlett's V statistic of 82.54 is larger than the critical chi square with 6 degrees of freedom at the 0.05 confidence level (which is 12.59). Consequently, the hypothesis that the mean vectors are the same is rejected. The same conclusion could be derived from the Rao's R statistic with its value of 55.10, which is larger than the corresponding F value with 6 and 32 degrees of freedom which is 2.399.

```
                  Multivariate Significance Test: K-Sample Problem
                  ------------------------------------------------

                            N_TOT              K             P
                               21              3             3

                            I           MEAN
                            1       0.2001429 65.142857 1.5742857

                            I           MEAN
                            2       0.0402857        11 1.2257143

                            I           MEAN
                            3       0.0351429 7.5714286 1.4285714

                            W                                 DETW
                   0.0044351 0.2002857 -0.002814          0.246783
                   0.2002857 288.57143 1.8214286
                   -0.002814 1.8214286 0.2144286

                            I           MEAN
                            4       0.0918571 27.904762 1.4095238

                            T                                 DETT
                   0.1276486 42.601714 0.1808686         31.691145
                   42.601714  14889.81 63.809048
                   0.1808686 63.809048 0.6434952

Lambda =    0.007787

m = 17   Use Bartlett's V for large m's and Rao's R otherwise

Bartlett's V =  82.539814     DF =  6
     Chi_crit = 12.591587

Rao's R = 55.104665    DF_NUM =  6     DF_DEN = 32
     F_crit =  2.399080
```

Fig. 2.7 SAS output of analysis defined in Figure 2.6 (examp2-2.lst).

2.6 Assignment

In order to practice with these analyses, you will need to use the data bases INDUP and PANEL described in Appendix C. These data bases provide market share and marketing mix variables for a number of brands competing in five market segments. You can test the following hypotheses:

1. The market behavioral responses of a given brand (e.g., awareness, perceptions or purchase intentions) are different across segments,
2. The marketing strategy (i.e., the values of the marketing mix variables) of selected brands is different (perhaps corresponding to different strategic groups).

Figure 2.8 shows how to read the data within a SAS file and how to create new files with a subset of the data saved in a format which can be read easily using the examples provided throughout this chapter. Use the model described in the examples above and adapt them to the data base to perform these tests.

```
/****************************************************************************
 Assign2.sas
 Creation of additional data files for Chapter2 assignments.
****************************************************************************/
option ls=120 ;
/*---------------------------------------------------------------------------
 Creating the dataset PANEL by reading data from c:\...\panel.csv
---------------------------------------------------------------------------*/
data panel;
  infile 'C:\SAMD\Chapter2\Assignments\panel.csv' firstobs=2  dlm = ',' ;
  input period   segment  segsize  ideal1-ideal3
         brand $  adv_pct   aware    intent shop1-shop3
         perc1-perc3 dev1-dev3 share ;
run;
proc sort data=panel;
        by period brand;
run;
/*---------------------------------------------------------------------------
 Creating the dataset INDUP by reading data from c:\...\indup.csv
---------------------------------------------------------------------------*/
data indup;
  infile 'C:\SAMD\Chapter2\Assignments\indup.csv' firstobs=2  dlm = ',' ;
  input  period  firm  brand $ price  advert
         char1-char5 salmen1-salmen3
         cost dist1-dist3 usales  dsales  ushare dshare  adshare  relprice ;
run;
proc sort data =indup;
        by period brand;
run;
/*---------------------------------------------------------------------------
 Merging PANEL and INDUP into ECON
---------------------------------------------------------------------------*/
```

```
data econ;
        merge panel indup;
        by period brand;
if segment<5 then delete;
run;
proc means noprint;
var intent share ;
output out = econmean mean=IntMean ShrMean;
run;
/*---------------------------------------------------------------------------------
 Writing EconMean to a CSV file (easily opened by Excel)
---------------------------------------------------------------------------------*/
data _NULL_;
  set EconMean (keep = IntMean ShrMean);
  by IntMean ;
  TAB = ',' ;
  FN = "C:\SAMD\CHAPTER2\ASSIGNMENTS\Mean1grp.CSV";
  file PLOTFILE filevar=FN;
  if ( FIRST.IntMean ) then
  do;
    put "IntMean" TAB "ShrMean" ;
  end;
    put  IntMean  TAB  ShrMean  ;
run;
/*---------------------------------------------------------------------------------
 Creating a new dataset EconNew with selected variables from ECON
---------------------------------------------------------------------------------*/
data EconNew;
set  Econ   ;
keep segment period brand intent share ;
where brand = 'salt';
run;
proc sort ;
by Brand Segment Period ;
run;
/*---------------------------------------------------------------------------------
 Writing EconNew to a CSV file (easily opened by Excel)
---------------------------------------------------------------------------------*/
data _NULL_;
  set EconNew;
  by BRAND Segment ;
  TAB = ',' ;
  FN = "C:\SAMD\CHAPTER2\ASSIGNMENTS\DatKgrp.CSV";
  file PLOTFILE filevar=FN;
  if ( FIRST.Brand ) then
  do;
    put "SEGMENT" TAB "BRAND" TAB "PERIOD" TAB "INTENT" TAB "SHARE" ;
  end;
    put  SEGMENT  TAB  BRAND  TAB   PERIOD TAB  Intent  TAB  Share  ;
run;
```

Fig. 2.8 Example of SAS file for reading data sets INDUP and PANEL and creating new data files (assign2.sas).

References

Basic Technical Readings

Tatsuoka, M. M. (1971), *Multivariate Analysis: Techniques for Educational and Psychological Research*, New York, NY: John Wiley & Sons, Inc.

Application Readings

Cool, K. and I. Dierickx (1993), "Rivalry, Strategic Groups and Firm Profitability," *Strategic Management Journal*, 14, 47–59.

Long, R. G., W. P. Bowers, T. Barnett, et al. (1998), "Research Productivity of Graduates in Management: Effects of Academic Origin and Academic Affiliation," *Academy of Management Journal*, 41, 6, 704–714.

3. Measurement Theory: Reliability and Factor Analysis

In this chapter, we will discuss the issues involved in building measures or scales. We focus the chapter on two types of analysis: (1) the measurement of reliability with Cronbach's alpha and (2) the verification of unidimensionality using factor analysis. In this chapter, we concentrate on Exploratory Factor Analysis and we only introduce the notion of Confirmatory Factor Analysis. Although an important step in the construction and the evaluation of scales, the analysis required is a special case of the Analysis of Covariance Structures presented in Chapter 8. Consequently, we postpone the estimation of the parameters of Confirmatory Factor Analysis, as well as the examination of convergent and discriminant validity issues to this chapter.

3.1 Notions of Measurement Theory

3.1.1 Definition of a Measure

If T is the true score of a construct and e represents the error associated to the measurement, the measure X is expressed as:

$$X = T + e \tag{3.1}$$

3.1.2 Parallel Measurements

Measures Y_1 and Y_2 are parallel if they meet the following characteristics:

$$Y_1 = T + e_1 \tag{3.2}$$

$$Y_2 = T + e_2 \tag{3.3}$$

$$E[e_1] = E[e_2] = 0 \tag{3.4}$$

$$V[e_1] = V[e_2] = \sigma_e^2 \tag{3.5}$$

$$\rho(e_1, e_2) = 0 \tag{3.6}$$

3.1.3 Reliability

The reliability of a measure is the squared correlation between the measure and the true score: $\rho^2(X, T)$, also noted ρ_{XT}^2. It is also the ratio of the true score variance to the measure variance:

$$\rho_{XT}^2 = \frac{\sigma_T^2}{\sigma_X^2} \tag{3.7}$$

This can be demonstrated as follows:

$$\begin{aligned}
\sigma(X,T) &= E[(X - E[X])(T - E[T])] \\
&= E[XT - E[X]T + E[X]E[T] - XE[T]] \\
&= E[XT] - E[X]E[T] + E[X]E[T] - E[X]E[T] \\
&= E[XT] - E[X]E[T] \\
&= E[(T+e)T] - E[T+e]E[T] \\
&= E[T^2 + eT] - (E[T])^2 \\
&= E[T^2] - (E[T])^2 \\
&= E[(T - E[T])^2]
\end{aligned} \tag{3.8}$$

This last equality can be shown as follows:

$$(T - E[T])^2 = T^2 + (E[T])^2 - 2TE[T] \tag{3.9}$$

$$= T^2 + (E[T])^2 - 2(E[T])^2 \tag{3.10}$$

$$= T^2 - (E[T])^2 \tag{3.11}$$

but $E[(T-E[T])^2] = \sigma_T^2$, which is the numerator of the reliability expression.

Let us now express the correlation between the true score and the measure:

$$\rho_{XT} = \frac{\sigma(X,T)}{\sigma(X)\sigma(T)} = \frac{\sigma_T^2}{\sigma_X \sigma_T} = \frac{\sigma_T}{\sigma_X} \tag{3.12}$$

$$\Rightarrow \rho_{XT}^2 = \frac{\sigma_T^2}{\sigma_X^2} \tag{3.13}$$

Therefore, the reliability can be expressed as the proportion of the observed score variance that is true score variance. The problem with the definition and formulae above is that the variance of the true score is not known since the true score is not observed. This explains the necessity to use multiple measures and to form scales.

3.1.4 Composite Scales

A composite scale is built from using multiple items or components measuring the constructs. This can be represented graphically as in Figure 3.1. Note that by convention, circles represent unobserved constructs and squares identify observable variables or measures.

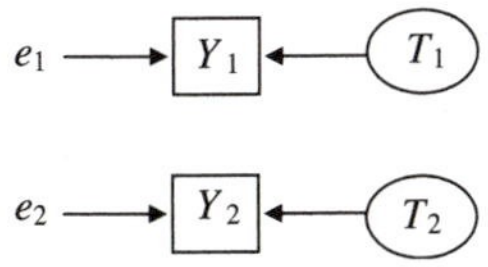

Fig. 3.1 A graphical representations of measures.

3.1.4.1 Reliability of a two-component scale

In this section, we show that the reliability of a composite scale has a lower bound. This lower bound is coefficient alpha. The two components of the scale are:

$$Y_1 = T_1 + e_1 \tag{3.14}$$

$$Y_2 = T_2 + e_2 \tag{3.15}$$

The composite scale corresponds to a formative index:

$$\begin{aligned} X = Y_1 + Y_2 &= \underbrace{T_1 + T_2}_{} + \underbrace{e_1 + e_2}_{} \\ &= \quad T \quad + \quad e \end{aligned} \tag{3.16}$$

Although, a priori, T_1 and T_2 appear as different true scores, we will see that they must be positively correlated and we will show the impact of that correlation on the reliability of the scale. As a consequence, it is best to think of these scores as corresponding to different items of a single construct.

Computation of coefficient α

From Equation (3.16), the composite scale defined as:

$$X = Y_1 + Y_2 \tag{3.17}$$

$$T = T_1 + T_2 \tag{3.18}$$

$$\sigma_T^2 = \sigma^2(T_1) + \sigma^2(T_2) + 2\sigma(T_1, T_2) \tag{3.19}$$

However, because

$$[\sigma(T_1) - \sigma(T_2)]^2 \geq 0$$

(equality if parallel test), then it follows that:

$$\sigma^2(T_1) + \sigma^2(T_2) \geq 2\sigma(T_1, T_2). \tag{3.20}$$

This last inequality results from developing the inequality above it:

$$[\sigma(T_1) - \sigma(T_2)]^2 = [\sigma(T_1)]^2 + [\sigma(T_2)]^2 - 2[\sigma(T_1)\sigma(T_2)]$$

Since, given a positive correlation between T_1 and T_2,

$$\sigma(T_1, T_2) = \rho(T_1, T_2)\sigma(T_1)\sigma(T_2) \leq \sigma(T_1)\sigma(T_2).$$

It follows that:

$$[\sigma(T_1)]^2 + [\sigma(T_2)]^2 - 2[\sigma(T_1)\sigma(T_2)] \leq [\sigma(T_1)]^2 + [\sigma(T_2)]^2 - 2[\sigma(T_1, T_2)]$$

The left hand side of the inequality above being positive, a fortiori, the right hand side is also positive.

It should be noted that this property is only interesting for cases where the items (components) are positively correlated. Indeed, in the case of a negative correlation, the inequality is dominated by the fact that the left hand side is greater or equal to zero.

Therefore, in cases of positively correlated items:

$$\sigma_T^2 \geq 4\sigma(T_1, T_2) \tag{3.21}$$

Consequently, the reliability has a lower bound which is given by

$$\rho_{XT}^2 = \frac{\sigma_T^2}{\sigma_X^2} \geq \frac{4\sigma(T_1, T_2)}{\sigma_X^2} \tag{3.22}$$

But

$$\begin{aligned} \sigma(Y_1, Y_2) &= E[(T_1 + e_1)(T_2 + e_2)] \\ &= E[T_1 T_2] \\ &= \sigma(T_1, T_2) \end{aligned} \tag{3.23}$$

Therefore,

$$\rho_{XT}^2 \geq \frac{4\sigma(Y_1, Y_2)}{\sigma_X^2} \tag{3.24}$$

But since

$$\sigma_X^2 = E[(Y_1 + Y_2)^2] = E[Y_1^2] + E[Y_2^2] + E[2Y_1 Y_2] \tag{3.25}$$

$$= \sigma^2(Y_1) + \sigma^2(Y_2) + 2\sigma(Y_1, Y_2) \tag{3.26}$$

Then

$$2\sigma(Y_1, Y_2) = \sigma_X^2 - \sigma^2(Y_1) - \sigma^2(Y_2) \tag{3.27}$$

and therefore

$$\rho_{XT}^2 \geq 2\left[\frac{\sigma_X^2 - \sigma^2(Y_1) - \sigma^2(Y_2)}{\sigma_X^2}\right] = 2\left[1 - \frac{\sigma^2(Y_1) + \sigma^2(Y_2)}{\sigma_X^2}\right] \tag{3.28}$$

This demonstrates that there is a lower bound to the reliability. If this lower bound is high enough, this means that the actual reliability is even higher and therefore, the scale is reliable. It is also clear from Equation (3.28) that as the (positive) correlation between the two items or components increases, the portion that is substracted from one decreases so that coefficient alpha increases. If the correlation is zero, then coefficient alpha is zero.

3.1.4.2 Generalization to composite measurement with K components

For a scale formed from K components or items:

$$X = \sum_{k=1}^{K} Y_k \tag{3.29}$$

The reliability coefficient alpha is a generalized form of the calculation above:

$$\alpha = \frac{K}{K-1}\left[1 - \frac{\sum_{k=1}^{K} \sigma^2(Y_k)}{\sigma_X^2}\right] \tag{3.30}$$

α is a lower bound estimate of the reliability of the composite scale X, that is of ρ_{XT}^2.

3.2 Factor Analysis

Factor analysis can be viewed as a method to discover or confirm the structure of a covariance matrix. However, in the case of exploratory factor analysis, the analysis attempts to discover the underlying unobserved factor structure. In the case of confirmatory factor analysis, a measurement model is specified and tested against the observed covariance matrix.

Exploratory factor analysis is a special type of rotation. Consequently, rotations are first reviewed in the general context of space geometry.

3.2.1 Axis Rotation

Let us consider Figure 3.2, which shows a set of orthogonal axes X_1 and X_2. The vector Y_1 shows an angle θ relative to X_1. Similarly, the vector Y_2 forms an angle θ with X_2.

The rotation corresponds to a linear transformation of $\mathbf{x}$ to $\mathbf{y}$. If $\mathbf{x}$ is a p-dimensional vector and $\mathbf{V}$ is a square matrix of size p by p (which represents the linear weights applied to vector $\mathbf{x}$), then $\mathbf{y}$, the linear transformation of $\mathbf{x}$,

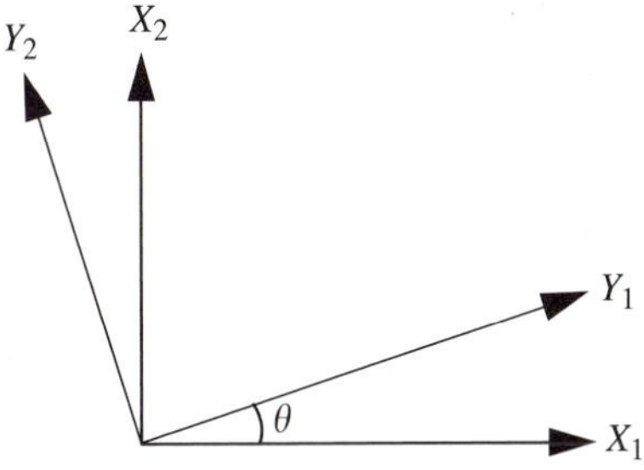

Fig. 3.2 Axis rotation.

is also with dimension p. However, orthogonality conditions must be met so that $\mathbf{V}$ cannot be any matrix. Therefore, the rotation can be expressed in the following equations:

$$\underset{p\times 1}{\mathbf{y}} = \underset{p\times p}{\mathbf{V}'}\ \underset{p\times 1}{\mathbf{x}} \tag{3.31}$$

$$\text{s.t. } \mathbf{V}'\mathbf{V} = \mathbf{I} \tag{3.32}$$

so that conditions be met for orthogonal rotation.

An example of a rotation in a two-dimensional space is given below:

$$y_1 = (\cos\theta)x_1 + (\sin\theta)x_2 \tag{3.33}$$

$$y_2 = (-\sin\theta)x_1 + (\cos\theta)x_2 \tag{3.34}$$

These weights represented in Equations (3.33) and (3.34) are appropriate for an orthogonal rotation because the constraints of orthogonality expressed in Equation (3.32) are respected. Indeed,

$$(\cos\theta)^2 + (\sin\theta)^2 = 1 \tag{3.35}$$

$$(-\sin\theta)^2 + (\cos\theta)^2 = 1 \tag{3.36}$$

$$(\cos\theta)(-\sin\theta) + (\sin\theta)(\cos\theta) = 0 \tag{3.37}$$

These constraints can be expressed in matrix notations as:

$$\begin{bmatrix} \cos\theta & \sin\theta \\ -\sin\theta & \cos\theta \end{bmatrix} \begin{bmatrix} \cos\theta & -\sin\theta \\ \sin\theta & \cos\theta \end{bmatrix} = \begin{bmatrix} 1 & 0 \\ 0 & 1 \end{bmatrix} \tag{3.38}$$

This corresponds to the constraint expressed more generally in Equation (3.32).

3.2.2 Variance Maximizing Rotations (Eigenvalues/vectors)

The advantage of an orthogonal rotation is that it enables to represent the same points in a space using different axes but without affecting the covariance matrix which remains unchanged. The idea is now going to be to find a specific rotation or linear transformation which will maximize the variance of the linear transformations.

3.2.2.1 The objective

The objective is, therefore, to find the linear transformation of a vector which maximizes the variance of the transformed variable (of the linear combination) i.e., to find the weights $\mathbf{v}'$ such that if for one observation, the transformation is

$$\underset{1\times 1}{\mathbf{y}_i} = \underset{1\times p}{\mathbf{v}'}\underset{p\times 1}{\mathbf{x}_i}$$

and for all N observations

$$\underset{1\times N}{\mathbf{y}'} = \underset{1\times p}{\mathbf{v}'}\underset{p\times N}{\mathbf{X}'},$$

the variance of the transformed variable, which is proportional to

$$\underset{1\times 1}{\mathbf{y}'\mathbf{y}} = \sum_{i=1}^{N} \mathbf{y}_i^2 = \mathbf{v}'\mathbf{X}'\mathbf{X}\mathbf{v} = \underset{1\times p}{\mathbf{v}'}\underset{p\times p}{\mathbf{S}}\underset{p\times 1}{\mathbf{v}}$$

is maximized.

In other words, the problem is:

$$\text{Find } \mathbf{V}|\text{Max } \mathbf{y}'\mathbf{y} \tag{3.39}$$

$$\text{s.t.} \quad \underset{1\times 1}{\mathbf{v}'\mathbf{v}} = \sum_{j=1}^{p} v_j^2 = 1 \tag{3.40}$$

This is equivalent, by replacing $\mathbf{y}$ with its expression as a linear combination of $\mathbf{X}$, to:

$$\text{Max } \mathbf{v}'\mathbf{S}\mathbf{v} \tag{3.41}$$

$$\text{s.t.} \quad \mathbf{v}'\mathbf{v} = 1 \tag{3.42}$$

This can be resolved by maximizing the Lagrangian $\mathbf{L}$:

$$\text{Max } \mathbf{L} = \mathbf{v}'\mathbf{S}\mathbf{v} - \lambda(\mathbf{v}'\mathbf{v} - 1) \tag{3.43}$$

Using the derivative rule $\delta\mathbf{x}'\mathbf{A}\mathbf{x}/\delta\mathbf{x} = 2\mathbf{A}\mathbf{x}$:

$$\frac{\delta\mathbf{L}}{\delta\mathbf{v}} = 2\mathbf{S}\mathbf{v} - 2\lambda\mathbf{v} = 0 \tag{3.44}$$

$$= \Big(\underset{p\times p}{\mathbf{S}} - \underset{p\times p}{\lambda\mathbf{I}}\Big)\underset{p\times 1}{\mathbf{v}} = \underset{p\times 1}{0} \tag{3.45}$$

Solving these equations provides the eigenvalues and eigenvectors. First we show how to derive the eigenvalues. Then, we will proceed with the calculation of the eigenvectors.

Finding the eigenvalues

We need to resolve the following system of equations for $\mathbf{v}$ and λ:

$$(\mathbf{S} - \lambda\mathbf{I})\mathbf{v} = 0 \tag{3.46}$$

A trivial solution is $\mathbf{v} = 0$. Pre-multiplying by $(\mathbf{S} - \lambda\mathbf{I})^{-1}$,

$$\mathbf{v} = (\mathbf{S} - \lambda\mathbf{I})^{-1}0 = 0 \tag{3.47}$$

This implies also that, for a non-trivial solution to exist, $(\mathbf{S} - \lambda\mathbf{I})$ must not have an inverse because, if it does, $\mathbf{v} = 0$ and gives a trivial solution.

Therefore, a first condition for a non-trivial solution to Equation (3.46) to exist is that the determinant is zero because the operation shown in Equation (3.47) cannot then be performed:

$$|\mathbf{S} - \lambda\mathbf{I}| = 0 \tag{3.48}$$

Equation (3.48) results in a polynomial in λ of degree p and therefore which has p roots. Following is an example. Let us assume that the covariance matrix is:

$$\mathbf{S} = \begin{bmatrix} 16.81 & 0.88 \\ 0.88 & 6.64 \end{bmatrix}$$

Then,

$$|\mathbf{S} - \lambda\mathbf{I}| = \begin{vmatrix} 16.81 - \lambda & 0.88 \\ 0.88 & 6.64 - \lambda \end{vmatrix} = \lambda^2 - 23.45\lambda + 110.844 = 0 \tag{3.49}$$

Resolving this second degree equation gives the two roots:

$$\lambda_1 = 16.8856 \tag{3.50}$$

$$\lambda_2 = 6.5644 \tag{3.51}$$

They are the eigenvalues.

Finding the eigenvectors

Knowing the eigenvalues, the eigenvectors can now be easily computed. For each eigenvalue, there are p equations with p unknown:

$$(\mathbf{S} - \lambda\mathbf{I})\mathbf{v} = 0 \tag{3.52}$$

subject to normality, i.e., $\mathbf{v}'\mathbf{v} = 1$.

The p unknowns are then straightforward to estimate.

3.2.2.2 *Properties of eigenvalues and eigenvectors*

Two properties of eigenvectors and eigenvalues are indispensable in order to understand the implications of this rotation:

1. $\mathbf{V}'\mathbf{V} = \mathbf{I}$, and, therefore, $\mathbf{V}' = \mathbf{V}^{-1}$ (3.52)
2. $\mathbf{V}'\mathbf{S}\mathbf{V} = \mathbf{\Lambda}$, where $\underset{p \times p}{\mathbf{\Lambda}} = \text{diag}\{\lambda_i\}$. (3.53)

It is important to understand the proof of this last property because it shows how the covariance matrix can be reconstituted with the knowledge of eigenvectors and eigenvalues.

From the first order derivative of the Lagrangian ($\delta \mathbf{L}/\delta \mathbf{v} = 2\mathbf{S}\mathbf{v} - 2\lambda\mathbf{v} = 0$), and putting all eigenvectors together)

$$\underset{p\times p}{\mathbf{S}}\underset{p\times p}{\mathbf{V}} = \underset{p\times p}{\mathbf{V}}\underset{p\times p}{\mathbf{\Lambda}} \tag{3.54}$$

Premultiplying each side by $\mathbf{V}'$ gives:

$$\mathbf{V}'\mathbf{S}\mathbf{V} = \underbrace{\mathbf{V}'\mathbf{V}}_{\mathbf{I}}\mathbf{\Lambda} = \mathbf{\Lambda} \tag{3.55}$$

Furthermore, a third property is that the eigenvalue is the variance of the linearly transformed variable y. From Equation (3.51), premultiplying the left-hand side by $\mathbf{v}'$, one obtains for eigenvalue i and eigenvector i:

$$\mathbf{v}_i'(\mathbf{S} - \lambda_i \mathbf{I})\mathbf{v}_i = 0 \tag{3.56}$$

or

$$\mathbf{v}_i'\mathbf{S}\mathbf{v}_i = \lambda_i \mathbf{v}_i'\mathbf{v}_i \tag{3.57}$$

However, the left-hand side of Equation (3.57) is the variance of the transformed variable y_i:

$$\mathbf{v}_i'\mathbf{S}\mathbf{v}_i = \mathbf{v}_i'\mathbf{X}'\mathbf{X}\mathbf{v}_i = \mathbf{y}_i'\mathbf{y}_i = \lambda_i \tag{3.58}$$

Therefore, the eigenvalue represents the variance of the new variable formed as a linear combination of the original variables.

3.2.3 Principal Component Analysis

The problem in Principal Component Analysis is just what has been described in the prior section. It consists in finding the linear combination that maximizes the variance of the linear combinations of a set of variables (the first linear combination, then the second given that it should be perpendicular to the first, etc.) and to reconstitute the covariance matrix $\mathbf{S} = \mathbf{V}\mathbf{\Lambda}\mathbf{V}'$. Therefore, the problem is identical to finding the eigenvalues and eigenvectors of the covariance matrix.

In Principal Component Analysis, new variables ($\mathbf{y}$) are constructed as exact linear combinations of the original variables. Furthermore, it is a data reduction method in the sense that the covariance matrix can be approximated with a number of dimensions smaller than p, the number of original variables.

Indeed, from Equation (3.55):

$$\mathbf{VV'SV} = \mathbf{V\Lambda} \tag{3.59}$$

$$\mathbf{SV} = \mathbf{V\Lambda} \tag{3.60}$$

$$\mathbf{SVV'} = \mathbf{V\Lambda V'} \tag{3.61}$$

$$\mathbf{S} = \mathbf{V\Lambda V'} \tag{3.62}$$

Let $\mathbf{V}^*$ to include the eigenvectors corresponding to the r largest eigenvalues and $\mathbf{\Lambda}^*$ to include the r largest eigenvalues:

$$\underset{p\times p}{\mathbf{S}^*} = \underset{p\times r}{\mathbf{V}^*}\ \underset{r\times r}{\mathbf{\Lambda}^*}\ \underset{r\times p}{\mathbf{V}^{*\prime}} \tag{3.63}$$

Therefore, it can be seen from Equation (3.63) that replacing the small eigenvalues by zero should not affect the ability to reconstitute the variance covariance matrix $\mathbf{S}$ ($\mathbf{S}^*$ should approximate $\mathbf{S}$). Consequently, r data points are needed for each i instead of the original p variables.

Two points can be made which distinguish Principal Component Analysis from Factor Analysis:

1. The new variables $\mathbf{y}$ are determined exactly by the p $\mathbf{x}$ variables. There is no noise introduced which may represent some measurement error, as discussed in the section on measurement theory. Factor Analysis introduces this notion of measurement error.
2. The new unobserved variables $\mathbf{y}$ are built by putting together the original p variables. Therefore, $\mathbf{y}$ is constructed from the original x variables in an index. As opposed to this constitutive index, in Factor Analysis, the observed $\mathbf{x}$ variables reflect from the various unobserved variables or constructs.

This last distinction between reflective indicators and constitutive indices is developed in the next section.

3.2.4 Factor Analysis

Now that we have explained the difference between Principle Component Analysis and Factor Analysis, we need to distinguish between two different types of Factor Analysis: Exploratory Factor Analysis and Confirmatory Factor Analysis. The basic difference lies in the fact that in Confirmatory Factor Analysis, a structure is proposed in which the observed, measurable variables reflect only specific unobserved constructs while Exploratory factor Analysis allows all measurable variables to reflect from each factor. These two types of Factor Analysis can easily be distinguished by the differences in their graphical representation. Then we will examine the differences analytically.

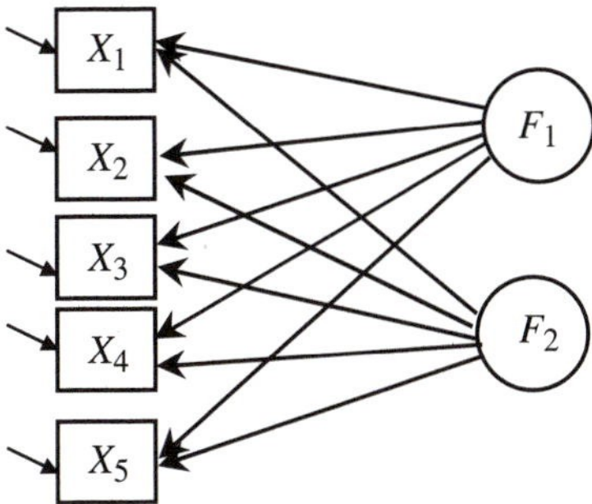

Fig. 3.3 A graphical representation of multiple measures.

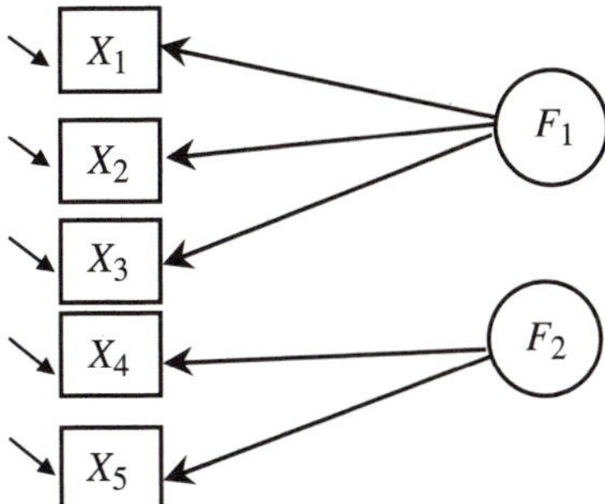

Fig. 3.4 A graphical representation of multiple measures with a confirmatory factor structure.

Exploratory Factor Analysis is graphically represented in Figure 3.3 in an example with two unobserved constructs and five observed variables or measures.

The unobserved constructs are represented with circles while the measures are represented by squares. The arrows on the left side coming into the measured variable boxes indicate the random measurement errors.

In Confirmatory Factor Analysis, only some measures are reflecting specific, individual unobserved constructs, as shown in Figure 3.4.

3.2.4.1 Exploratory Factor Analysis

Exploratory Factor Analysis can be characterized by the fact that it is data driven, as opposed to Confirmatory Analysis which represents a theory of measurement. The purpose of Exploratory Factor Analysis is, in fact, to find or discover patterns which may help understand the nature of the unobserved variables. Consequently, it is a method which, based on patterns of correlations among variables, inductively brings insights into the underlying factors. Considering Figure 4.3, the weights assigned to each arrow linking each factor to each observed variable indicate the extent to which each variable reflects each factor. This can be shown analytically.

As discussed above, each observed variable is a function of all the factors underlying the structure. For example, for two observed variables and two factors:

$$X_1 = \lambda_{11} F_1 + \lambda_{12} F_2 + \varepsilon_1 \tag{3.64}$$

$$X_2 = \lambda_{21} F_1 + \lambda_{22} F_2 + \varepsilon_2 \tag{3.65}$$

where

$$\sigma_1^2 = V[\varepsilon_1]; \quad \sigma_2^2 = V[\varepsilon_2], \quad V[F_1] = V[F_2] = 1 \tag{3.66}$$

The variances are one because they are standardized without imposing additional constraints but which enables the identification. This in a sense simply determines the units of measure of the unobserved construct.

Let us consider now the consequences that these equations impose on the structure of the covariance matrix of the observed variables.

$$V[X_1] = \lambda_{11}^2 + \lambda_{12}^2 + \sigma_1^2 \tag{3.67}$$

Using the property that the factors are orthogonal (uncorrelated with a variance of 1):

$$\mathrm{Cov}[X_1, X_2] = E[(\lambda_{11} F_1 + \lambda_{12} F_2 + \varepsilon_1)(\lambda_{21} F_1 + \lambda_{22} F_2 + \varepsilon_2)] \tag{3.68}$$

$$= \lambda_{11}\lambda_{21} E[F_1^2] + \lambda_{12}\lambda_{22} E[F_2^2] + E[\varepsilon_1 \varepsilon_2] \tag{3.69}$$

$$= \lambda_{11}\lambda_{21} + \lambda_{12}\lambda_{22} \tag{3.70}$$

These equalities follow from the fact that:

$$\mathrm{Cov}[F_1, F_2] = 0 \tag{3.71}$$

$$E[\varepsilon_1 \varepsilon_2] = 0 \tag{3.72}$$

$$V[F_1] = V[F_2] = 1 \tag{3.73}$$

Therefore, the variances in the covariance matrix is composed of two components: commonalities and unique components:

$$V[X_1] = \underbrace{\lambda_{11}^2 + \lambda_{12}^2}_{k_1^2} + \sigma_1^2 \tag{3.74}$$

k_1^2 in Equation (3.74) represents the proportion of variance explained by the common factors while σ_1^2 represents the unique variance.

The commonalities are our center of interest because the error variance or unique variances do not contain information about the data structure. This demonstrates that the noise or measurement error needs to be removed although it only affects the variances (the diagonal of the covariance matrix) but not the covariances.

More generally, we can represent the data structure as:

$$\mathbf{\Sigma} = \mathbf{R} + \mathbf{U} \tag{3.75}$$

where $\mathbf{U} = \text{diag}\{u\}$.

$\mathbf{R}$ is the matrix of common variance and covariances and $\mathbf{U}$ is the matrix of unique variances. In Exploratory factor Analysis, the objective will be to reduce the dimensionality of the $\mathbf{R}$ matrix to understand better the underlying factors driving this structure pattern.

Four steps are involved in Exploratory Factor Analysis. We discuss each step in turn and then we derive the factor loadings and the factor scores.

Estimating commonalities

In this first step, we need to remove the unique component of the variance in order to keep the variance explained by the common factors only. In a typical Exploratory Factory Analysis, $\mathbf{R}$ is specified as the squared multiple correlations of each variable with the remainder of the variables in the set (i.e., the percentage of explained variance obtained in regressing variable j on the $(p-1)$ others). $\mathbf{U}$ is the residual variances from these regressions.

Extracting initial factors

The initial factors are obtained by performing a Principal Component Analysis on $\mathbf{R}$

$$\underset{p\times p}{\mathbf{R}} = \underset{p\times p}{\mathbf{V}} \; \underset{p\times p}{\mathbf{\Lambda}} \; \underset{p\times p}{\mathbf{V}'} \tag{3.76}$$

Determining the number of factors

The issue is to find the number of factors $r < p$ which are necessary to represent the covariance structure. Following from the properties of eigenvalues and eigenvectors,

$$\mathbf{R} = \mathbf{V\Lambda V'} \tag{3.77}$$

Let $\mathbf{V}^*$ to include the eigenvectors corresponding to the r largest eigenvalues and $\mathbf{\Lambda}^*$ to include the r largest eigenvalues:

$$\underset{p\times p}{\mathbf{R}^*} = \underset{p\times r}{\mathbf{V}^*} \; \underset{r\times r}{\mathbf{\Lambda}^*} \; \underset{r\times p}{\mathbf{V}^{*\prime}} \tag{3.78}$$

The problem is about finding r so as to account for most of the matrix $\mathbf{R}$.

A typically used method is the Scree test which consists in plotting the eigenvalues in the order of their decreasing size. The rules to apply are then:

1. $\lambda > 1$: eliminate values less than 1. The rationale for this rule is that each factor should at least account for at least the variance of a single variable.
2. the elbow rule: stop when the curve forms an elbow as shown in Figure 3.5.

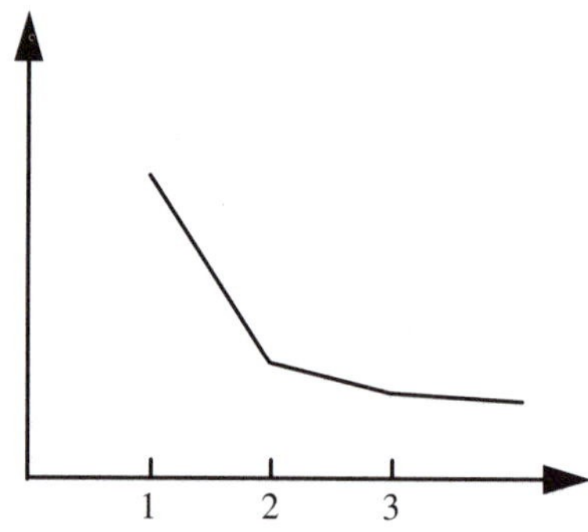

Fig. 3.5 The elbow rule.

None of these methods should be used blindly. Especially, the rule of the eigenvalue greater than one is the default option on most statistical analysis softwares, including SAS. Indeed, the interpretation of the factors is an important criterion for making sense out of the covariance structure.

Rotation to terminal solution

The objective for performing a rotation at this stage, using only the retained factors, is to find more easily *interpretable* factors through rotation.

The most commonly used method is the VARIMAX rotation method. With that method, the rotation searches to give the maximum variance of the *squared* loadings for each factor (in order to avoid problems due to negative loadings). This results in obtaining extreme loadings (very high or very low).

Component loadings (for Principle Component Analysis)

$$\underset{p\times p}{\mathbf{L}} = \underset{p\times p}{\mathbf{V}}\,\underset{p\times p}{\mathbf{\Lambda}}^{1/2} \tag{3.79}$$

because $\mathbf{V\Lambda V'} = \mathbf{V\Lambda}^{1/2}\mathbf{\Lambda}^{1/2}\mathbf{V}'$.

Component scores (for Principle Component Analysis)

$$\underset{N\times p}{\mathbf{Z}} = \underset{N\times p}{\mathbf{X}}\,\underset{p\times p}{\mathbf{V}}\,\underset{p\times p}{\mathbf{\Lambda}}^{-1/2} \tag{3.80}$$

3.2.4.2 *Confirmatory Factor Analysis*

In Confirmatory Factor Analysis, a measurement model is assumed. The objective is to test if the data fit the measurement model. This is, therefore, an ultimate test of the fit of the measurement model to the data.

The figure shown in Figure 3.4 can be expressed by the system of equations.

$$\begin{aligned} X_1 &= \lambda_{11} F_1 + \varepsilon_1 \\ X_2 &= \lambda_{21} F_1 + \varepsilon_2 \\ X_3 &= \lambda_{31} F_1 + \varepsilon_3 \\ X_4 &= \lambda_{42} F_2 + \varepsilon_4 \\ X_5 &= \lambda_{52} F_2 + \varepsilon_5 \end{aligned} \quad (3.81)$$

$$\underset{5\times 1}{\mathbf{X}} = \begin{bmatrix} X_1 \\ X_2 \\ X_3 \\ X_4 \\ X_5 \end{bmatrix} \quad \underset{2\times 1}{\mathbf{F}} = \begin{bmatrix} F_1 \\ F_2 \end{bmatrix} \quad \underset{5\times 2}{\mathbf{\Lambda}} = \begin{bmatrix} \lambda_{11} & \lambda_{12} \\ \lambda_{21} & \lambda_{22} \\ \lambda_{31} & \lambda_{32} \\ \lambda_{41} & \lambda_{42} \\ \lambda_{51} & \lambda_{52} \end{bmatrix} \quad \mathbf{E} = \begin{bmatrix} \varepsilon_1 \\ \varepsilon_2 \\ \varepsilon_3 \\ \varepsilon_4 \\ \varepsilon_5 \end{bmatrix}$$

$$\mathbf{X} = \mathbf{\Lambda F} + \mathbf{E} \quad (3.82)$$

$$E[\mathbf{E}] = 0 \quad (3.83)$$

$$E[\mathbf{EE}'] = \mathbf{D} \quad (3.84)$$

The theoretical covariance matrix of **X** is given by

$$\begin{aligned} \mathbf{E}[\mathbf{XX}'] &= E[(\mathbf{\Lambda F} + \mathbf{E})(\mathbf{\Lambda F} + \mathbf{E})'] && (3.85) \\ &= E[\mathbf{\Lambda FF}'\mathbf{\Lambda}' + \mathbf{EE}'] \\ &= \mathbf{\Lambda} E[\mathbf{FF}']\mathbf{\Lambda}' + E[\mathbf{EE}'] && (3.86) \\ \mathbf{\Sigma} &= \mathbf{\Lambda I \Lambda}' + \mathbf{D} && (3.87) \end{aligned}$$

If the observed covariance matrix estimated from the sample is **S**, we need to find the values of the lambdas which will reproduce a covariance matrix as similar as possible to the observed one.

Maximum Likelihood estimation is used to minimize $\mathbf{S} - \mathbf{\Sigma}$. How many parameters need to be estimated? In the example shown in Figure 4.4, ten parameters must be estimated:

$$5\lambda_{ij}\text{s}' + 5\delta_{ii}\text{s}'$$

The methodology for estimating these parameters is presented in Chapter 8.

3.3 Conclusion – Procedure for Scale Construction

Scale construction involves several steps. Of those steps, this chapter discussed the following statistical analyses which provide a guide in scale construction.

3.3.1 Exploratory Factor Analysis

Exploratory Factor Analysis can be performed separately for each hypothesized factor. This demonstrates the unidimensionality of each factor. One global Factor Analysis can also be performed in order to assess the degree of independence between the factors.

3.3.2 Confirmatory Factor Analysis

Confirmatory factor analysis can be used to assess the overall fit of the entire measurement model and to obtain the final estimates of the measurement model parameters. Although sometimes performed on the same sample as the exploratory factor analysis, when it is possible to collect more data, it is preferable to perform the confirmatory factor analysis on a new sample.

3.3.3 Reliability-Coefficient α

In cases where composite scales are developed, this measure is useful to assess the reliability of the scales. Reliabilities of less than 0.7 for academic research and 0.9 for market research are typically not sufficient to warrant further analyses using these composite scales.

3.4 Application Examples

Figure 3.6 illustrates how to compute means and the correlation matrix for a list of variables in SAS. The output is shown on Figure 3.7. A factor analysis on

```
/*    examp3-1.sas
      computes means and correlation matrix
*/
option ls=120;
data data1;
infile 'c:\SAMD\Chapter3\Examples\product.dat';
input prod rad it1 it2 it3 it4 it5 it6 it7 it8 it9;
if it1=9 then it1=.;
if it2=9 then it2=.;
if it3=9 then it3=.;
if it4=9 then it4=.;
if it5=9 then it5=.;
if it6=9 then it6=.;
if it7=9 then it7=.;
if it8=9 then it8=.;
if it9=9 then it9=.;

proc means;
      var it1 it2 it3 it4 it5 it6 it7 it8 it9;
run;
proc corr;
      var it1 it2 it3 it4 it5 it6 it7 it8 it9;
run;
```

Fig. 3.6 SAS input file example for computing means and correlation matrix (examp3-1.sas).

Variable	N	Mean	Std Dev	Minimum	Maximum
IT1	13	2.9230769	1.8009969	1.0000000	6.0000000
IT2	12	4.9166667	0.9962049	3.0000000	6.0000000
IT3	13	3.0000000	1.7320508	1.0000000	6.0000000
IT4	12	3.3333333	2.0150946	1.0000000	6.0000000
IT5	11	3.1818182	1.6624188	1.0000000	6.0000000
IT6	12	3.7500000	1.6583124	1.0000000	6.0000000
IT7	13	3.6923077	1.7504578	1.0000000	6.0000000
IT8	13	4.2307692	1.4232502	1.0000000	6.0000000
IT9	13	4.3846154	1.7577666	1.0000000	6.0000000

Correlation Analysis

9 'VAR' Variables: IT1 IT2 IT3 IT4 IT5 IT6 IT7 IT8 IT9

Simple Statistics

Variable	N	Mean	Std Dev	Sum	Minimum	Maximum
IT1	13	2.923077	1.800997	38.000000	1.000000	6.000000
IT2	12	4.916667	0.996205	59.000000	3.000000	6.000000
IT3	13	3.000000	1.732051	39.000000	1.000000	6.000000
IT4	12	3.333333	2.015095	40.000000	1.000000	6.000000
IT5	11	3.181818	1.662419	35.000000	1.000000	6.000000
IT6	12	3.750000	1.658312	45.000000	1.000000	6.000000
IT7	13	3.692308	1.750458	48.000000	1.000000	6.000000
IT8	13	4.230769	1.423250	55.000000	1.000000	6.000000
IT9	13	4.384615	1.757767	57.000000	1.000000	6.000000

Correlation Analysis

Pearson Correlation Coefficients / Prob > |R| under Ho: Rho=0 / Number of Observations

	IT1	IT2	IT3	IT4	IT5	IT6	IT7	IT8	IT9
IT1	1.00000	-0.81024	0.98843	-0.80100	-0.66790	-0.85535	-0.90687	-0.67522	-0.41105
	0.0	0.0014	0.0001	0.0017	0.0247	0.0004	0.0001	0.0113	0.1629
	13	12	13	12	11	12	13	13	13
IT2	-0.81024	1.00000	-0.78272	0.80847	0.73283	0.63671	0.77374	0.86405	0.57608
	0.0014	0.0	0.0026	0.0026	0.0159	0.0352	0.0031	0.0003	0.0500
	12	12	12	11	10	11	12	12	12
IT3	0.98843	-0.78272	1.00000	-0.79341	-0.66790	-0.85385	-0.90703	-0.67609	-0.41057
	0.0001	0.0026	0.0	0.0021	0.0247	0.0004	0.0001	0.0112	0.1635
	13	12	13	12	11	12	13	13	13
IT4	-0.80100	0.80847	-0.79341	1.00000	0.51068	0.89776	0.87782	0.59463	0.50232
	0.0017	0.0026	0.0021	0.0	0.1315	0.0001	0.0002	0.0414	0.0961
	12	11	12	12	10	12	12	12	12
IT5	-0.66790	0.73283	-0.66790	0.51068	1.00000	0.35687	0.63479	0.74788	0.44725
	0.0247	0.0159	0.0247	0.1315	0.0	0.3114	0.0359	0.0081	0.1678
	11	10	11	10	11	10	11	11	11

```
IT6 -0.85535  0.63671 -0.85385  0.89776  0.35687  1.00000  0.88462  0.46717  0.31882
      0.0004   0.0352   0.0004   0.0001   0.3114      0.0   0.0001   0.1257   0.3125
          12       11       12       12       10       12       12       12       12

IT7 -0.90687  0.77374 -0.90703  0.87782  0.63479  0.88462  1.00000  0.59951  0.25834
      0.0001   0.0031   0.0001   0.0002   0.0359   0.0001      0.0   0.0303   0.3941
          13       12       13       12       11       12       13       13       13

IT8 -0.67522  0.86405 -0.67609  0.59463  0.74788  0.46717  0.59951  1.00000  0.72770
      0.0113   0.0003   0.0112   0.0414   0.0081   0.1257   0.0303      0.0   0.0048
          13       12       13       12       11       12       13       13       13

IT9 -0.41105  0.57608 -0.41057  0.50232  0.44725  0.31882  0.25834  0.72770  1.00000
      0.1629   0.0500   0.1635   0.0961   0.1678   0.3125   0.3941   0.0048      0.0
          13       12       13       12       11       12       13       13       13
```

Fig. 3.7 SAS output example for computation of means and correlations (examp3-1.lst).

```
/*   examp3-2.sas
     Factor analysis
*/
option ls=120;
data data1;
infile 'c:\SAMD\Chapter3\Examples\product.dat';
input prod rad it1 it2 it3 it4 it5 it6 it7 it8 it9;
if it1=9 then it1=.;
if it2=9 then it2=.;
if it3=9 then it3=.;
if it4=9 then it4=.;
if it5=9 then it5=.;
if it6=9 then it6=.;
if it7=9 then it7=.;
if it8=9 then it8=.;
if it9=9 then it9=.;

proc factor rotate=varimax;
     var it1 it2 it3 it4 it5 it6 it7 it8 it9;
run;
```

Fig. 3.8 SAS input file example for factor analysis (examp3-2.sas).

the same list of variables is requested in Figure 3.8 using the SAS procedure "Factor." The results are shown in Figure 3.9. This factor analysis of the perception of innovations on nine characteristics are summarized by two factors with eigenvalues greater than one (the default option in SAS) and that explain 89.9% of the variance. The rotated factor patterm shows that Factor 1 groups variables IT1, IT3, IT4, IT6 and IT7, while Factor 2 reflects variables IT5, IT8 and IT9. Variable IT2 does not discriminate well between the two factors, as it loads simultaneously on both, although it loads slightly more on Factor 2. The reliability of the scales (corresponding to the two

```
Initial Factor Method: Principal Components
                              Prior Communality Estimates: ONE
                 Eigenvalues of the Correlation Matrix:  Total = 9  Average = 1
           1        2       3       4       5       6       7       8       9
 Eigenvalue   6.3837  1.6888  0.4677  0.1936  0.1446  0.0792  0.0346  0.0078  0.0000
 Difference   4.6949  1.2210  0.2742  0.0490  0.0654  0.0447  0.0267  0.0078
 Proportion   0.7093  0.1876  0.0520  0.0215  0.0161  0.0088  0.0038  0.0009  0.0000
 Cumulative   0.7093  0.8969  0.9489  0.9704  0.9865  0.9953  0.9991  1.0000  1.0000

            2 factors will be retained by the MINEIGEN criterion.
                                Factor Pattern
                                    FACTOR1   FACTOR2
                          IT1       -0.92918   0.26260
                          IT2        0.94032   0.23536
                          IT3       -0.92918   0.26260
                          IT4        0.89699  -0.22064
                          IT5        0.75835   0.42615
                          IT6        0.79402  -0.53485
                          IT7        0.90676  -0.34096
                          IT8        0.76170   0.57319
                          IT9        0.60015   0.73096


                    Variance explained by each factor
                              FACTOR1   FACTOR2
                             6.383698  1.688772

Initial Factor Method: Principal Components
                        Final Communality Estimates: Total = 8.072470
     IT1        IT2        IT3        IT4        IT5        IT6        IT7        IT8        IT9
0.932342   0.939598   0.932342   0.853266   0.756708   0.916530   0.938466   0.908733   0.894485

Rotation Method: Varimax
                  Orthogonal Transformation Matrix
                                   1          2
                       1       0.80559    0.59247
                       2      -0.59247    0.80559

                     Rotated Factor Pattern
                                FACTOR1    FACTOR2
                    IT1        -0.90412   -0.33897
                    IT2         0.61807    0.74672
                    IT3        -0.90412   -0.33897
                    IT4         0.85333    0.35369
                    IT5         0.35844    0.79261
                    IT6         0.95654    0.03956
                    IT7         0.93249    0.26256
                    IT8         0.27402    0.91304
                    IT9         0.05040    0.94443

                   Variance explained by each factor
                            FACTOR1    FACTOR2
                           4.735659   3.336811

                     Final Communality Estimates: Total = 8.072470
     IT1        IT2        IT3        IT4        IT5        IT6        IT7        IT8        IT9
0.932342   0.939598   0.932342   0.853266   0.756708   0.916530   0.938466   0.908733   0.894485
```

Fig. 3.9 SAS output of factor analysis (examp3-2.lst).

```
/*   examp3-3.sas
     Reliability Coefficient Alpha
*/
option ls=120;
data data1;
infile 'c:\SAMD\Chapter3\Examples\product.dat';
input prod rad it1 it2 it3 it4 it5 it6 it7 it8 it9;
if it1=9 then it1=.;
if it2=9 then it2=.;
if it3=9 then it3=.;
if it4=9 then it4=.;
if it5=9 then it5=.;
if it6=9 then it6=.;
if it7=9 then it7=.;
if it8=9 then it8=.;
if it9=9 then it9=.;
it1r=7-it1;
it3r=7-it3;

proc means;
     var it1r it2 it3r it4 it5 it6 it7 it8 it9;
     output out=results mean=m1r m2 m3r m4 m5 m6 m7 m8 m9
                        std=s1r s2 s3r s4 s5 s6 s7 s8 s9;
run;

data data2;
set data1;
if _n_=1 then set results;

it1rs=(it1r-m1r)/s1r;
it2s=(it2-m2)/s2;
it3rs=(it3r-m3r)/s3r;
it4s=(it4-m4)/s4;
it5s=(it5-m5)/s5;
it6s=(it6-m6)/s6;
it7s=(it7-m7)/s7;
it8s=(it8-m8)/s8;
it9s=(it9-m9)/s9;
run;
proc corr alpha;
  var it1rs it3rs it4s it6s it7s;
 run;
proc corr alpha;
  var it2s it5s it8s it9s;
run;
```

Fig. 3.10 SAS input file for reliability coefficient alpha (examp3-3.sas).

```
    Variable   N          Mean        Std Dev        Minimum        Maximum
    -------------------------------------------------------------------------
    IT1R       13     4.0769231     1.8009969      1.0000000      6.0000000
    IT2        12     4.9166667     0.9962049      3.0000000      6.0000000
    IT3R       13     4.0000000     1.7320508      1.0000000      6.0000000
    IT4        12     3.3333333     2.0150946      1.0000000      6.0000000
    IT5        11     3.1818182     1.6624188      1.0000000      6.0000000
    IT6        12     3.7500000     1.6583124      1.0000000      6.0000000
    IT7        13     3.6923077     1.7504578      1.0000000      6.0000000
    IT8        13     4.2307692     1.4232502      1.0000000      6.0000000
    IT9        13     4.3846154     1.7577666      1.0000000      6.0000000
    -------------------------------------------------------------------------
                          Correlation Analysis

      5 'VAR' Variables:  IT1RS    IT3RS    IT4S     IT6S     IT7S

                                 Simple Statistics
Variable       N     Mean    Std Dev     Sum      Minimum      Maximum
IT1RS         13        0   1.000000       0    -1.708456     1.067785
IT3RS         13        0   1.000000       0    -1.732051     1.154701
IT4S          12        0   1.000000       0    -1.157927     1.323346
IT6S          12        0   1.000000       0    -1.658312     1.356801
IT7S          13        0   1.000000       0    -1.538059     1.318336


                              Correlation Analysis
                           Cronbach Coefficient Alpha
                       for RAW variables          :  0.975822
                      for STANDARDIZED variables:  0.972620

                           Raw Variables                      Std. Variables
    Deleted         Correlation                         Correlation
    Variable         with Total             Alpha        with Total              Alpha
    ffffffffffffffffffffffffffffffffffffffffffffffffffffffffffffffffffffffffffffffff
      IT1RS            0.943833          0.967688          0.935001           0.963707
      IT3RS            0.939013          0.968428          0.932076           0.964164
      IT4S             0.888799          0.976050          0.876213           0.972786
      IT6S             0.929027          0.969955          0.915387           0.966759
      IT7S             0.944836          0.967534          0.943116           0.962438
                The SAS System                 13:32 Thursday, January 22, 1998   68

                                  Correlation Analysis

Pearson Correlation Coefficients / Prob > |R| under Ho: Rho=0 / Number of Observations

                   IT1RS        IT3RS          IT4S           IT6S          IT7S
       IT1RS     1.00000      0.98843       0.80100        0.85535       0.90687
                   0.0         0.0001        0.0017         0.0004        0.0001
                      13           13            12             12            13

       IT3RS     0.98843      1.00000       0.79341        0.85385       0.90703
                  0.0001         0.0         0.0021         0.0004        0.0001
                      13           13            12             12            13
```

```
IT4S      0.80100     0.79341     1.00000      0.89776     0.87782
           0.0017      0.0021         0.0       0.0001      0.0002
               12          12          12           12          12
IT6S      0.85535     0.85385     0.89776      1.00000     0.88462
           0.0004      0.0004      0.0001          0.0      0.0001
               12          12          12           12          12
IT7S      0.90687     0.90703     0.87782      0.88462     1.00000
           0.0001      0.0001      0.0002       0.0001         0.0
               13          13          12           12          13
            The SAS System             13:32 Thursday, January 22, 1998  69

                       Correlation Analysis
          4 'VAR' Variables:  IT2S      IT5S      IT8S      IT9S

                            Simple Statistics
Variable      N      Mean    Std Dev      Sum     Minimum     Maximum
IT2S         12         0   1.000000        0   -1.923968    1.087460
IT5S         11         0   1.000000        0   -1.312436    1.695230
IT8S         13         0   1.000000        0   -2.269994    1.243092
IT9S         13         0   1.000000        0   -1.925520    0.918998

                        Correlation Analysis
                     Cronbach Coefficient Alpha
               for RAW variables          :  0.897142
               for STANDARDIZED variables:  0.895873

                     Raw Variables                     Std. Variables
Deleted       Correlation                       Correlation
Variable       with Total            Alpha      with Total             Alpha
ƒƒƒƒƒƒƒƒƒƒƒƒƒƒƒƒƒƒƒƒƒƒƒƒƒƒƒƒƒƒƒƒƒƒƒƒƒƒƒƒƒƒƒƒƒƒƒƒƒƒƒƒƒƒƒƒƒƒƒƒƒƒƒƒƒƒƒƒƒƒƒƒƒƒƒƒƒ
 IT2S            0.803916         0.855245        0.830506          0.842650
 IT5S            0.763201         0.870324        0.711836          0.886557
 IT8S            0.903509         0.817014        0.916809          0.809002
 IT9S            0.626815         0.918565        0.631457          0.914788

Pearson Correlation Coefficients / Prob > |R| under Ho: Rho=0 / Number of Observations

                  IT2S              IT5S              IT8S              IT9S
IT2S           1.00000           0.73283           0.86405           0.57608
                   0.0            0.0159            0.0003            0.0500
                    12                10                12                12
IT5S           0.73283           1.00000           0.74788           0.44725
                0.0159               0.0            0.0081            0.1678
                    10                11                11                11
IT8S           0.86405           0.74788           1.00000           0.72770
                0.0003            0.0081           0.0                0.0048
                    12                11                13                13
IT9S           0.57608           0.44725           0.72770           1.00000
                0.0500            0.1678            0.0048               0.0
                    12                11                13                13
```

Fig. 3.11 SAS output example of reliability coefficient alpha (examp3-3.lst).

```
/*   examp3-4.sas
     Scales
*/
option ls=120;
data data1;
infile 'c:\SAMD\Chapter3\Examples\product.dat';
input prod rad it1 it2 it3 it4 it5 it6 it7 it8 it9;
if it1=9 then it1=.;
if it2=9 then it2=.;
if it3=9 then it3=.;
if it4=9 then it4=.;
if it5=9 then it5=.;
if it6=9 then it6=.;
if it7=9 then it7=.;
if it8=9 then it8=.;
if it9=9 then it9=.;
it1r=7-it1;
it3r=7-it3;
proc means;
     var it1r it2 it3r it4 it5 it6 it7 it8 it9;
     output out=results mean=m1r m2 m3r m4 m5 m6 m7 m8 m9
                   std=s1r s2 s3r s4 s5 s6 s7 s8 s9;
run;
data data2;
set data1;
if _n_=1 then set results;

it1rs=(it1r-m1r)/s1r;
it2s=(it2-m2)/s2;
it3rs=(it3r-m3r)/s3r;
it4s=(it4-m4)/s4;
it5s=(it5-m5)/s5;
it6s=(it6-m6)/s6;
it7s=(it7-m7)/s7;
it8s=(it8-m8)/s8;
it9s=(it9-m9)/s9;

tech=sum(it1rs,it3rs,it4s,it6s,it7s)/n(it1rs,it3rs,it4s,it6s,it7s);
mkt=sum(it2s,it5s,it8s,it9s)/n(it2s,it5s,it8s,it9s);
run;

proc anova;
  class rad;
  model tech mkt = rad;
  means rad;
run;
```

Fig. 3.12 SAS input file example for scale construction (examp3-4.sas).

```
Variable   N          Mean        Std Dev        Minimum        Maximum
-----------------------------------------------------------------------
IT1R      13     4.0769231      1.8009969      1.0000000      6.0000000
IT2       12     4.9166667      0.9962049      3.0000000      6.0000000
IT3R      13     4.0000000      1.7320508      1.0000000      6.0000000
IT4       12     3.3333333      2.0150946      1.0000000      6.0000000
IT5       11     3.1818182      1.6624188      1.0000000      6.0000000
IT6       12     3.7500000      1.6583124      1.0000000      6.0000000
IT7       13     3.6923077      1.7504578      1.0000000      6.0000000
IT8       13     4.2307692      1.4232502      1.0000000      6.0000000
IT9       13     4.3846154      1.7577666      1.0000000      6.0000000
-----------------------------------------------------------------------

                  Analysis of Variance Procedure
                     Class Level Information

                    Class     Levels     Values

                      RAD          2     0 1

               Number of observations in data set = 13

                                  Analysis of Variance Procedure
 Dependent Variable: TECH

Source               DF    Sum of Squares     Mean Square    F Value     Pr > F
Model                 1        4.20121164      4.20121164       7.21     0.0212
Error                11        6.40830330      0.58257303
Corrected Total      12       10.60951494
          R-Square               C.V.            Root MSE             TECH Mean
          0.395985           4051.201          0.76326472            0.01884045

Source         DF          Anova SS           Mean Square    F Value     Pr > F
RAD             1      4.20121164            4.20121164       7.21     0.0212

                      Analysis of Variance Procedure
Dependent Variable: MKT

Source               DF    Sum of Squares     Mean Square    F Value     Pr > F
Model                 1        5.18610513      5.18610513      14.41     0.0030
Error                11        3.95895360      0.35990487
Corrected Total      12        9.14505873
          R-Square               C.V.            Root MSE              MKT Mean
          0.567094           -9999.99          0.59992072           -0.00072912

Source               DF          Anova SS     Mean Square    F Value     Pr > F
RAD                   1        5.18610513      5.18610513      14.41     0.0030

                     Analysis of Variance Procedure
   Level of          ------------TECH-----------     -------------MKT-------------
   RAD         N        Mean            SD              Mean              SD
   0           6    -0.59518871     0.71757943      -0.68294587       0.80440030
   1           7     0.54515117     0.79934370       0.58402809       0.34728815
```

Fig. 3.13 SAS output example of scale construction and analysis of variance (examp3-4.lst).

```
/*      Assign3.sas       */
filename survey 'c:\SAMD\Chapter3\Assignments\survey.asc';
data new;
infile survey firstobs=19;
input   (Age Marital Income Educatn HHSize Occuptn Location
         TryHair LatStyle DrssSmrt BlndsFun LookDif
         LookAttr GrocShp LikeBkng ClthFrsh WashHnds Sportng LikeClrs
         FeelAttr TooMchSx Social LikeMaid ServDnrs SaveRcps LikeKtch) (3.)
        #2 (LoveEat SpirtVal Mother ClascMsc Children Applianc ClsFamly
         LovFamly TalkChld Exercise LikeSelf CareSkin MedChckp
         EvngHome TripWrld HomeBody LondnPrs Comfort Ballet Parties
         WmnNtSmk BrghtFun Seasonng ColorTV SlppyPpl Smoke) (3.)
        #3 (Gasoline Headache Whiskey Bourbon FastFood Restrnts OutFrDnr
         OutFrLnc RentVide Catsup KnowSont PercvDif BrndLylt
         CatgMotv BrndMotv OwnSonit NecssSon OthrInfl DecsnTim
         RdWomen RdHomSrv RdFashn RdMenMag RdBusMag RdNewsMg
         RdGlMag) (3.)
        #4 (RdYouthM RdNwsppr WtchDay WtchEve WtchPrm
         WTchLate WtchWknd WtchCsby WtchFmTs WtchChrs WtchMoon
         WtchBoss WtchGrwP WtchMiaV WtchDns WtchGold WtchBowl) (3.);
proc freq;
tables OwnSonit*(Age Marital Income Educatn HHSize Occuptn);
run;
```

Fig. 3.14 SAS file to Read SURVEY.ASC Data File (assign3.sas).

factors) are then calculated in Figure 3.10 when the variables are first standardized. Those variables with negative loadings are reversed so that each component has the same direction (positive correlations). The results are listed in Figure 3.11 which shows the reliability coefficient alpha for each scale and the improvements that could be obtained by deleting any single variable one at a time. Finally, Figure 3.12 shows how to create a scale composed of these standardized variables, scales that are used in a single analysis of variance example. The corresponding output in Figure 3.13 shows for example the means of the two scales (labeled Tech and MKT) for two levels of the variable RAD.

3.5 Assignment

The assignment consists in developing a composite scale, demonstrating its unidimensionality and computing its reliability. For that purpose, survey data are provided in the file SURVEY.ASC. These data concern items about psychographic variables which contain opinion, attitude and life style characteristics of individuals. The detailed description of the data is given in Appendix C. This type of data is useful for advertising and segmentation purposes.

In order to develop a scale, it may be useful to summarize the data using exploratory factor analysis on a wide range of variables. It is important, however, to make sure that only variables which possess the properties necessary for the analysis are included. For example, because factor analysis is based on correlations, categorical or ordinal scale variables should be excluded from the analysis, since correlations are not permissible statistics with such scales. The factors need to be interpreted and you can concentrate on a subset of these factors to derive a single or multiple composite scales.

An alternative would be to reflect on the questions which seem related and focus on those to develop a scale. This is in essence a mental factor analysis.

You need to demonstrate that each of the scales developed are unidimensional (through factor analysis) and that their reliability is sufficiently high.

Figure 3.14 lists the SAS file which can be used to read the data.

References

Basic Technical Readings

Bollen, K. and R. Lennox (1991), "Conventional Wisdom on Measurement: A Structural Equation Perspective," *Psychological Bulletin*, 110, 2, 305–314.

Cortina, J. M. (1993), "What is Coefficient Alpha? An Examination of Theory and Applications," *Journal of Applied Psychology*, 78, 1, 98–104.

Diamanopoulos, A. and H. M. Winklhofer (2001), "Index Construction with Formative Indicators: An Alternative to Scale Development," *Journal of Marketing Research*, 38, 2 (May), 269–277.

Green, P. E. (1978), *Mathematical Tools for Applied Multivariate Analysis*, New York, NY: Academic Press, [Chapter 5 and Chapter 6, section 6.4].

Lord, F. M. and M. R. Novick (1968), *Statistical Theories of Mental Test Scores*, Reading, MS: Addison-Wesley Publishing Company, Inc., [Chapter 4].

Nunnally, J. C. and I. H. Bernstein (1994), *Psychometric Theory*, Third Edition, New York: McGraw Hill.

Application Readings

Aaker, J. L. (1997), "Dimensions of Brand Personality", *Journal of Marketing Research*, 34, 3 (August), 347–356.

Anderson, E. (1985), "The Salesperson as Outside Agent or Employee: A Transaction Cost Analysis," *Marketing Science*, 4 (Summer), 234–254.

Anderson, R. and J. Engledow (1977), "A Factor Analytic Comparison of U.S. and German Information Seeker," *Journal of Consumer Research*, 3, 4, 185–196.

Blackman, A. W. (1973), "An Innovation Index Based on Factor Analysis," *Technological Forecasting and Social Change*, 4, 301–316.

Churchill, G. A., Jr. (1979), "A Paradigm for Developing Better Measures of Marketing Constructs," *Journal of Marketing Research*, 16 (February), 64–73.

Deshpande, R. (1982), "The Organizational Context of Market Research Use," *Journal of Marketing*, 46, 4 (Fall), 91–101.

Finn, A. and U. Kayandé (1997), "Reliability Assessment and Optimization of Marketing Measurement," *Journal of Marketing Research*, 34, 2 (May), 262–275.

Gilbert, F. W. and W. E. Warren (1995), "Psychographic Constructs and Demographic Segments," *Psychology & Marketing*, 12, 3 (May), 223–237.

Green, S. G., M. B. Gavin and L. Aiman-Smith (1995), "Assessing a Multidimensional Measure of Radical Technological Innovation", *IEEE Transactions on Engineering Management*, 42, 3, 203–214.

Murtha, T. P., S. A. Lenway and R. P. Bagozzi (1998), "Global Mind-sets and Cognitive Shift in a Complex Multinational Corporation," *Strategic Management Journal*, 19, 97–114.

Perreault, W. D., Jr. and L. E. Leigh (1989), "Reliability of Nominal Data Based on Qualitative Judgments," *Journal of Marketing Research*, 26 (May), 135–148.

Zaichowsky, J. L. (1985), "Measuring the Involvement Construct," *Journal of Consumer Research*, 12 (December), 341–352.

4. Multiple Regression with a Single Dependent Variable

In this chapter, are covered the principles which are basic to understanding properly the issues involved in the analysis of management data. This chapter cannot constitute the depth which goes into a specialized econometric book. It is, however, designed to provide the elements of econometric theory essential for a researcher to develop and evaluate regression models. Multiple regression is not a multivariate technique in a strict sense in that a single variable is the focus of the analysis: a single dependent variable. Nevertheless, the multivariate normal distribution is involved in the distribution of the error term which, combined with the fact that there are multiple independent or predictor variables, leads to considering simple multiple regression within the domain of multivariate data analysis techniques.

The first section of this chapter presents the basic linear model with inferences obtained through the estimation of the model parameters. The second section discusses an important aspect of data analysis, especially in the context of testing contingency theories – the issue of heterogeneity of coefficients. While many other econometric issues remain, such as autocorrelation or multicollinearity, the reader is referred to specialized books for these topics.

4.1 Statistical Inference: Least Squares and Maximum Likelihood

The linear model is first presented with its basic assumptions. Then, point estimates using the least squares criterion are derived, followed by the maximum likelihood estimation. Finally, the properties of these estimators are discussed.

4.1.1 The Linear Statistical Model

The dependent variable y_t is modeled as a linear function of K independent variables:

$$\underset{T\times 1}{\mathbf{y}} = \underset{T\times K}{\mathbf{X}}\,\underset{K\times 1}{\boldsymbol{\beta}} + \underset{T\times 1}{\mathbf{e}} \tag{4.1}$$

where T = number of observations (for example T periods), $\mathbf{X}$ = matrix of K independent variables, $\boldsymbol{\beta}$ = vector of K weights applied to each independent variable k, $\mathbf{y}$ = vector of the dependent variable for $t = 1$ to T, $\mathbf{e}$ = vector of residuals corresponding to a unique aspect of $\mathbf{y}$ which is not explained by $\mathbf{X}$.

It should be noted that **X** is given, fixed, observed data. **X** is, in fact, not only observable, but is also measured without error (the case of measurement error is discussed in Chapter 8). We assume that **X** is correctly specified. This means that **X** contains the proper variables explaining the dependent variable with the proper functional form (i.e., some of the variables expressed in **X** may have been transformed, for example by taking their logarithm). Finally, the first column of **X** is typically a vector where each element is 1. This means that the first element of the parameter vector $\boldsymbol{\beta}$ is a parameter which corresponds to a constant term which applies equally to each value of the dependent variable y_t from $t = 1$ to T.

4.1.1.1 Error structure

Some assumptions need to be made in order to be able to make some statistical inferences. Not all the assumptions below are used necessarily. In fact, in section 4.1.4.3, we identify which assumptions are necessary in order to be able to obtain the specific properties of the estimators. Because **y** and **X** are given data points and $\boldsymbol{\beta}$ is the parameter vector on which we want to make inferences, the assumptions can only be on the unobserved factor **e**.

Assumption 1: expected value of error term

$$E[\mathbf{e}] = 0 \tag{4.2}$$

Assumption 2: covariance matrix of error term

Homoscedasticity

Usually, each observation has an error term e_t independently and identically distributed with the same variance.

$$e_t \sim iid \Rightarrow E[\mathbf{e}\mathbf{e}'] = \sigma^2 \mathbf{I}_T \tag{4.3}$$

where $\mathbf{I}$ = identity matrix.

This means that the variances for each observation t are the same and that they are uncorrelated. The unknown parameters which need to be estimated are: $\boldsymbol{\beta}, \sigma^2$.

Heteroscedasticity

More generally

$$E[\mathbf{e}\mathbf{e}'] = \sigma^2 \boldsymbol{\Psi} = \boldsymbol{\Phi} \tag{4.4}$$

Note that $\boldsymbol{\Phi}$, a covariance matrix, is a symmetric matrix. Heteroscedasticity occurs, therefore when $\boldsymbol{\Psi} \neq \mathbf{I}$. This occurs if either the diagonal elements of the matrix $\boldsymbol{\Psi}$ are not identical (each error term e_t has a different variance), and/or if its off-diagonal elements are different from zero.

Assumption 3: normality of distribution

The probability density function of the error vector can be written formally as per Equation (4.5) for the case of homoscedasticity or Equation (4.6) for the case of heteroscedasticity:

$$\mathbf{e} \sim N(\mathbf{0}, \sigma^2\mathbf{I}) \tag{4.5}$$

or

$$\mathbf{e} \sim N(\mathbf{0}, \mathbf{\Phi}) \tag{4.6}$$

4.1.2 Point Estimation

Point estimates are inferences that can be made without the normality assumption of the distribution of the error term e. The problem can be defined as follows: to find a suitable function of the observed random variables y, given x, that will yield the "best" estimate of unknown parameters.

We will restrict $\boldsymbol{\beta}$ to the class that are linear functions of y.

$$\underset{K\times 1}{\hat{\boldsymbol{\beta}}} = \underset{K\times T}{\mathbf{A}}\,\underset{T\times 1}{\mathbf{y}} \tag{4.7}$$

The elements of the matrix $\mathbf{A}$, $\{a_{kt}\}$ are scalars that weight each observation; $\mathbf{A}$ is a summarizing operator.

In order to solve the problem defined above, we need (1) to select a criterion, (2) to determine the $\mathbf{A}$ matrix and consequently $\hat{\boldsymbol{\beta}}$, and (3) to evaluate the sampling performance of the estimator. These three issues are discussed in the following sections.

4.1.2.1 OLS estimator

We now consider the case of homoscedasticity where

$$\mathbf{\Psi} = \mathbf{I}_T \tag{4.8}$$

The criterion which is used to estimate the "best" parameter is to minimize the sum of squares residuals:

$$\text{Min } l_1 = \underset{1\times T}{\mathbf{e}'}\,\underset{T\times 1}{\mathbf{e}} = (\mathbf{y} - \mathbf{X}\boldsymbol{\beta})'(\mathbf{y} - \mathbf{X}\boldsymbol{\beta}) \tag{4.9}$$

$$= \mathbf{y}'\mathbf{y} - 2\mathbf{y}'\mathbf{X}\boldsymbol{\beta} + \boldsymbol{\beta}'\mathbf{X}'\mathbf{X}\boldsymbol{\beta}, \tag{4.10}$$

noting that $\mathbf{y}'\mathbf{X}\boldsymbol{\beta} = \boldsymbol{\beta}'\mathbf{X}'\mathbf{y}$ is a scalar.

This criterion is the least squares criterion and this problem is resolved by taking the derivative relative to the parameter vector $\boldsymbol{\beta}$, setting it to zero and solving that equation:

$$\frac{\partial l_1}{\partial \boldsymbol{\beta}} = 2\mathbf{X}'\mathbf{X}\boldsymbol{\beta} - 2\mathbf{X}'\mathbf{y} = 0 \tag{4.11}$$

Note that the derivative in Equation (4.11) is obtained by using the following matrix derivative rules also found in the appendix:

$$\frac{\partial \mathbf{a}'\mathbf{v}}{\partial \mathbf{v}} = \mathbf{a}, \quad \text{and}$$

$$\frac{\partial \mathbf{v}'\mathbf{A}\mathbf{v}}{\partial \mathbf{v}} = (\mathbf{A} + \mathbf{A}')\mathbf{v}$$

and especially:

$$\frac{\partial 2\mathbf{y}'\mathbf{X}\boldsymbol{\beta}}{\partial \boldsymbol{\beta}} = 2\mathbf{X}'\mathbf{y} \tag{4.12}$$

Therefore, applying these rules to Equation (4.10), one obtains:

$$\hat{\boldsymbol{\beta}} = \mathbf{b} = (\mathbf{X}'\mathbf{X})^{-1}\mathbf{X}'\mathbf{y} \tag{4.13}$$

This assumes that $\mathbf{X}'\mathbf{X}$ can be inverted. If collinearity in the data exists, i.e., if a variable $x_k$is a linear combination of a subset of the other x variables, the inverse does not exist (the determinant is zero). In a less strict case, multicollinearity can occur if the determinant of $\mathbf{X}'\mathbf{X}$ approches zero. The matrix may still be invertible and an estimate of $\boldsymbol{\beta}$ will exist. We will briefly discuss the problem in subsection "*computation of covariance matrix*" of section 4.1.4.2.

b is linear function of y:

$$\mathbf{b} = \mathbf{A}\mathbf{y} \tag{4.14}$$

where

$$\mathbf{A} = (\mathbf{X}'\mathbf{X})^{-1}\mathbf{X}' \tag{4.15}$$

4.1.2.2 GLS or Aitken estimator

In the general case of heteroscedasticity, the covariance matrix of the error term vector is positive definite symmetric:

$$\boldsymbol{\Psi} \neq \mathbf{I}_T \tag{4.16}$$

The criterion is the quadratic form of the error terms weighted by the inverse of the covariance matrix. The rationale for that criterion is best understood in the case where $\mathbf{\Psi}$ is diagonal. In such a case, it can be easily seen that the observations with the largest variances are given a smaller weight than the others.

The objective is then:

$$\text{Min } l_2 = \mathbf{e}'\mathbf{\Psi}^{-1}\mathbf{e} = (\mathbf{y} - \mathbf{X}\boldsymbol{\beta})'\mathbf{\Psi}^{-1}(\mathbf{y} - \mathbf{X}\boldsymbol{\beta}) \tag{4.17}$$

$$= (\mathbf{y}'\mathbf{\Psi}^{-1} - \boldsymbol{\beta}'\mathbf{X}'\mathbf{\Psi}^{-1})(\mathbf{y} - \mathbf{X}\boldsymbol{\beta}) \tag{4.18}$$

$$= \mathbf{y}'\mathbf{\Psi}^{-1}\mathbf{y} + \boldsymbol{\beta}'\mathbf{X}'\mathbf{\Psi}^{-1}\mathbf{X}\boldsymbol{\beta} - \underset{1\times k}{\boldsymbol{\beta}'}\ \underset{k\times T}{\mathbf{X}'}\ \underset{T\times T}{\mathbf{\Psi}^{-1}}\ \underset{T\times 1}{\mathbf{y}} - \underset{1\times 1}{\mathbf{y}'\mathbf{\Psi}^{-1}\mathbf{X}\boldsymbol{\beta}} \tag{4.19}$$

$$= \mathbf{y}'\mathbf{\Psi}^{-1}\mathbf{y} + \boldsymbol{\beta}'\mathbf{X}'\mathbf{\Psi}^{-1}\mathbf{X}\boldsymbol{\beta} - 2\mathbf{y}'\mathbf{\Psi}^{-1}\mathbf{X}\boldsymbol{\beta} \tag{4.20}$$

Minimizing the quadratic expression in Equation (4.20) is performed by solving the equation:

$$\frac{\partial l_2}{\partial \boldsymbol{\beta}} = 2(\mathbf{X}'\mathbf{\Psi}^{-1}\mathbf{X})\boldsymbol{\beta} - 2\mathbf{X}'\mathbf{\Psi}^{-1}\mathbf{y} = 0 \tag{4.21}$$

$$\Rightarrow \hat{\boldsymbol{\beta}} = \hat{\boldsymbol{\beta}}_{\text{GLS}} = (\mathbf{X}'\mathbf{\Psi}^{-1}\mathbf{X})^{-1}\mathbf{X}'\mathbf{\Psi}^{-1}\mathbf{y} \tag{4.22}$$

$\hat{\boldsymbol{\beta}}$ is still a linear function of y such as in Equation (4.14), but with the linear weights given by:

$$\mathbf{A} = (\mathbf{X}'\mathbf{\Psi}^{-1}\mathbf{X})^{-1}\mathbf{X}'\mathbf{\Psi}^{-1} \tag{4.23}$$

4.1.3 Maximum Likelihood Estimation

So far, the estimators which we have derived are point estimates. They do not allow the researcher to perform statistical tests of significance on the parameter vector $\boldsymbol{\beta}$. In this section, we will derive the maximum likelihood estimators, which lead to distributional properties of the parameters. The problem is to find the value of the parameter $\boldsymbol{\beta}$ which will maximize the probability of obtaining the observed sample.

The assumption which is needed to derive the maximum likelihood estimator is the normal distribution of the error term:

$$\mathbf{e} \sim N(\mathbf{0}, \sigma^2\mathbf{I}_T) \tag{4.24}$$

It is then possible to write the likelihood function which, for the homoscedastic case is:

$$l_1(\boldsymbol{\beta}, \sigma^2|\mathbf{y}) = (2\pi\sigma^2)^{-T/2}\exp\left\{-\frac{1}{2\sigma^2}(\mathbf{y} - \mathbf{X}\boldsymbol{\beta})'(\mathbf{y} - \mathbf{X}\boldsymbol{\beta})\right\} \tag{4.25}$$

or, for the case of heteroscedasticity:

$$l_2(\boldsymbol{\beta}, \sigma^2|\mathbf{y}) = (2\pi\sigma^2)^{-T/2}|\mathbf{\Psi}|^{-T/2}\exp\left\{-\frac{1}{2\sigma^2}(\mathbf{y} - \mathbf{X}\boldsymbol{\beta})'\mathbf{\Psi}^{-1}(\mathbf{y} - \mathbf{X}\boldsymbol{\beta})\right\} \tag{4.26}$$

We can then maximize the likelihood or, equivalently, its logarithm.

$$\text{Max } l_1 \Leftrightarrow \text{Max Ln } l_1 \Leftrightarrow \text{Max} \left[-\frac{T}{2}\text{Ln}(2\pi\sigma^2) - \frac{1}{2\sigma^2}(\mathbf{y} - \mathbf{X}\boldsymbol{\beta})'(\mathbf{y} - \mathbf{X}\boldsymbol{\beta}) \right] \tag{4.27}$$

which is equivalent to minimizing the negative of that expression, i.e.,

$$\text{Min} \left[\frac{T}{2}\text{Ln}(2\pi\sigma^2) + \frac{1}{2\sigma^2}(\mathbf{y} - \mathbf{X}\boldsymbol{\beta})'(\mathbf{y} - \mathbf{X}\boldsymbol{\beta}) \right] \tag{4.28}$$

This can be done by solving the derivative of Equation (4.28) relative to $\boldsymbol{\beta}$.

$$\frac{\delta[-\text{Ln}(l_1)]}{\delta\boldsymbol{\beta}} = 0 \Rightarrow \tilde{\boldsymbol{\beta}}_1 = (\mathbf{X}'\mathbf{X})^{-1}\mathbf{X}'\mathbf{y} \tag{4.29}$$

which is simply the least square estimator.

Similar computations lead to the maximum likelihood estimator in the case of heteroscedasticity which is identical to the generalized least squares estimator:

$$\tilde{\boldsymbol{\beta}}_2 = (\mathbf{X}'\boldsymbol{\Psi}^{-1}\mathbf{X})^{-1}\mathbf{X}'\boldsymbol{\Psi}^{-1}\mathbf{y} \tag{4.30}$$

We can now compute the maximum likelihood estimator of the variance by finding the value of σ that maximizes the likelihood or which minimizes the expression in Equation (4.28):

$$\underset{\sigma}{\text{Min}} \left[\frac{T}{2}\text{Ln}(2\pi) + T\text{Ln}(\sigma) + \frac{1}{2}\sigma^{-2}(\mathbf{y} - \mathbf{X}\boldsymbol{\beta})'(\mathbf{y} - \mathbf{X}\boldsymbol{\beta}) \right] \tag{4.31}$$

This is solved by setting the derivative relative to σ to zero:

$$\frac{\delta[-\text{Ln}(l_1)]}{\delta\sigma} = \frac{T}{\sigma} + \frac{1}{2}(-2\sigma^{-3})(\mathbf{y} - \mathbf{X}\boldsymbol{\beta})'(\mathbf{y} - \mathbf{X}\boldsymbol{\beta}) = 0 \tag{4.32}$$

This results in:

$$\frac{T}{\sigma} - \frac{1}{\sigma^3}(\mathbf{y} - \mathbf{X}\boldsymbol{\beta})'(\mathbf{y} - \mathbf{X}\boldsymbol{\beta}) = 0 \Rightarrow \frac{1}{\sigma^3}(\mathbf{y} - \mathbf{X}\boldsymbol{\beta})'(\mathbf{y} - \mathbf{X}\boldsymbol{\beta}) = \frac{T}{\sigma}$$

which leads to the maximum likelihood estimator:

$$\tilde{\sigma}^2 = \frac{1}{T}(\mathbf{y} - \mathbf{X}\tilde{\boldsymbol{\beta}}_1)'(\mathbf{y} - \mathbf{X}\tilde{\boldsymbol{\beta}}_1) = \frac{1}{T}\hat{\mathbf{e}}'\hat{\mathbf{e}} \tag{4.33}$$

where $\hat{\mathbf{e}}$ is the vector of residuals obtained when using the maximum likelihood estimator of $\boldsymbol{\beta}$ to predict $\mathbf{y}$.

The same computational approach can be done for the heteroscedastic case.

4.1.4 Properties of Estimator

We have obtained estimators for the parameters $\boldsymbol{\beta}$ and σ. The next question is to find out how good they are. Two criteria are important for evaluating these parameters. Unbiasedness refers to the fact that on the average they are correct, i.e., on the average we obtain the true parameter. The second criterion concerns the fact that it should have the smallest possible variance.

4.1.4.1 *Unbiasedness*

Definition:

$$E[\hat{\boldsymbol{\beta}}] = \boldsymbol{\beta} \tag{4.34}$$

$\mathbf{b}$ and $\hat{\boldsymbol{\beta}}$, and a fortiori the maximum likelihood estimators $\tilde{\boldsymbol{\beta}}_1$ and $\tilde{\boldsymbol{\beta}}_2$, are linear functions of random vector $\mathbf{y}$. Consequently they are also random vectors with the following mean:

$$E[\mathbf{b}] = E[(\mathbf{X}'\mathbf{X})^{-1}\mathbf{X}'\mathbf{y}] = E[(\mathbf{X}'\mathbf{X})^{-1}\mathbf{X}'(\mathbf{X}\boldsymbol{\beta} + \mathbf{e})] \tag{4.35}$$

$$= E\Big[\underbrace{(\mathbf{X}'\mathbf{X})^{-1}\mathbf{X}'\mathbf{X}}_{\mathbf{I}}\boldsymbol{\beta} + (\mathbf{X}'\mathbf{X})^{-1}\mathbf{X}'\mathbf{e}\Big] \tag{4.36}$$

$$= \boldsymbol{\beta} + (\mathbf{X}'\mathbf{X})^{-1}\mathbf{X}'\underbrace{\mathrm{E}[\mathbf{e}]}_{=\mathbf{0}} = \boldsymbol{\beta} \tag{4.37}$$

This proves the least square estimator is unbiased. Similarly for the generalized least squares estimator:

$$E[\hat{\boldsymbol{\beta}}] = E[(\mathbf{X}'\boldsymbol{\Psi}^{-1}\mathbf{X})^{-1}\mathbf{X}'\boldsymbol{\Psi}^{-1}\mathbf{y}] = \boldsymbol{\beta} + E[(\mathbf{X}'\boldsymbol{\Psi}^{-1}\mathbf{X})^{-1}\mathbf{X}'\boldsymbol{\Psi}^{-1}\mathbf{e}] = \boldsymbol{\beta} \tag{4.38}$$

This means that on the average it is the true parameter; it is unbiased.

4.1.4.2 *Best linear estimator*

How do the linear rules above compare with other linear unbiased rules in terms of the precision, i.e., in terms of the covariance matrix. We want an estimator which has the smallest variance possible. This means that we need to compute the covariance matrix of the estimator and then, we will need to show that it has minimum variance.

Computation of covariance matrix

The covariance of the least squares estimator $\mathbf{b}$ is:

$$\underset{K\times K}{\boldsymbol{\Sigma}_{\mathbf{b}}} = E[(\mathbf{b} - E[\mathbf{b}])(\mathbf{b} - E[\mathbf{b}])'] \tag{4.39}$$

$$= E[(\mathbf{b} - \boldsymbol{\beta})(\mathbf{b} - \boldsymbol{\beta})']$$

$$
\begin{aligned}
&= E[((\mathbf{X}'\mathbf{X})^{-1}\mathbf{X}'\mathbf{y} - \boldsymbol{\beta})((\mathbf{X}'\mathbf{X})^{-1}\mathbf{X}'\mathbf{y} - \boldsymbol{\beta})']\\
&= E[((\mathbf{X}'\mathbf{X})^{-1}\mathbf{X}'(\mathbf{X}\boldsymbol{\beta} + \mathbf{e}) - \boldsymbol{\beta})((\mathbf{X}'\mathbf{X})^{-1}\mathbf{X}'(\mathbf{X}\boldsymbol{\beta} + \mathbf{e}) - \boldsymbol{\beta})']\\
&= E[(\mathbf{X}'\mathbf{X})^{-1}\mathbf{X}'\mathbf{e}\mathbf{e}'\mathbf{X}(\mathbf{X}'\mathbf{X})^{-1}]\\
&= (\mathbf{X}'\mathbf{X})^{-1}\mathbf{X}'E[\mathbf{e}\mathbf{e}']\mathbf{X}(\mathbf{X}'\mathbf{X})^{-1}\\
&= (\mathbf{X}'\mathbf{X})^{-1}\mathbf{X}'(\sigma^2\mathbf{I})\mathbf{X}(\mathbf{X}'\mathbf{X})^{-1}\\
&= \sigma^2(\mathbf{X}'\mathbf{X})^{-1}\mathbf{X}'\mathbf{X}(\mathbf{X}'\mathbf{X})^{-1}\\
&= \sigma^2(\mathbf{X}'\mathbf{X})^{-1}
\end{aligned}
$$

Therefore,

$$
\underset{K\times K}{\boldsymbol{\Sigma}_{\mathbf{b}}} = \sigma^2(\mathbf{X}'\mathbf{X})^{-1} \tag{4.40}
$$

In the case of multicollinearity, $(\mathbf{X}'\mathbf{X})^{-1}$ is very large (because the determinants is close to zero). This means that the variance of the estimator will be very large. Consequently, multicollinearity results in parameter estimates which are unstable.

The variance covariance matrix of the generalized least squares estimator $\hat{\boldsymbol{\beta}}$ is, following similar calculations:

$$
\boldsymbol{\Sigma}_{\hat{\boldsymbol{\beta}}} = E[(\hat{\boldsymbol{\beta}} - \boldsymbol{\beta})(\hat{\boldsymbol{\beta}} - \boldsymbol{\beta})'] = E(\mathbf{X}'\boldsymbol{\Psi}^{-1}\mathbf{X})^{-1}\mathbf{X}'\boldsymbol{\Psi}^{-1}\mathbf{e}\mathbf{e}'\boldsymbol{\Psi}^{-1}\mathbf{X}(\mathbf{X}'\boldsymbol{\Psi}^{-1}\mathbf{X})^{-1} \tag{4.41}
$$

$$
\boldsymbol{\Sigma}_{\hat{\boldsymbol{\beta}}} = \sigma^2(\mathbf{X}'\boldsymbol{\Psi}^{-1}\mathbf{X})^{-1} \tag{4.42}
$$

BLUE (Best Linear Unbiased Estimator)

Out of the class of linear unbiased rules, the OLS (or the GLS depending on the error term covariance structure) estimator is the best, i.e., provides minimum variance. We will do the proof with the OLS estimator when $\boldsymbol{\Psi} = \mathbf{I}_T$; however, the proof is similar for the GLS estimator when $\boldsymbol{\Psi} \neq \mathbf{I}_T$.

The problem is equivalent to minimizing the variance of a linear combination of the k parameters for any linear combination.

Let $\underset{k\times 1}{\boldsymbol{\varphi}}$ be a vector of constants.

$$
\underset{1\times 1}{\boldsymbol{\theta}} = \underset{1\times k}{\boldsymbol{\varphi}'}\underset{k\times 1}{\boldsymbol{\beta}} \text{ is a scalar.}
$$

The least squares estimator of $\boldsymbol{\theta}$ is

$$
\hat{\boldsymbol{\theta}}_{\mathrm{LS}} = \boldsymbol{\varphi}'\mathbf{b} = \boldsymbol{\varphi}'(\mathbf{X}'\mathbf{X})^{-1}\mathbf{X}'\mathbf{y} \tag{4.43}
$$

The problem is therefore to find out if there exists another unbiased linear estimator which is better than the least squares estimator.

An alternative linear estimator is

$$\hat{\boldsymbol{\theta}} = \mathbf{A}'\mathbf{y} + \mathbf{a} \tag{4.44}$$

$\hat{\boldsymbol{\theta}}$ should be unbiased. This means that

$$\forall \boldsymbol{\beta}: \quad E[\hat{\boldsymbol{\theta}}] = \boldsymbol{\varphi}'\boldsymbol{\beta} \tag{4.45}$$

By substitution of the expression of the estimator $\hat{\theta}$:

$$E[\hat{\boldsymbol{\theta}}] = E[\mathbf{A}'\mathbf{y} + \mathbf{a}] = \mathbf{A}'E[\mathbf{y}] + \mathbf{a} \tag{4.46}$$

$$= \mathbf{A}'\mathbf{X}\boldsymbol{\beta} + \mathbf{a} \tag{4.47}$$

For $\hat{\boldsymbol{\theta}}$ to be unbiased, Equation (4.45) must be verified, i.e.,

$$\boldsymbol{\varphi}'\boldsymbol{\beta} = \mathbf{A}'\mathbf{X}\boldsymbol{\beta} + \mathbf{a} \tag{4.48}$$

This can only be true if

$$\mathbf{a} = 0 \tag{4.49}$$

and

$$\boldsymbol{\varphi}' = \mathbf{A}'\mathbf{X} \tag{4.50}$$

What is the value of A which will minimize the variance of the estimator? The variance is:

$$V[\hat{\boldsymbol{\theta}}] = \mathbf{A}'V[\mathbf{y}]\mathbf{A} \tag{4.51}$$

However,

$$\underset{T\times 1}{V[\mathbf{y}]} = V[\mathbf{X}\boldsymbol{\beta} + \mathbf{e}] = E\left[((\mathbf{X}\boldsymbol{\beta} + \mathbf{e}) - E(\mathbf{X}\boldsymbol{\beta} + \mathbf{e}))((\mathbf{X}\boldsymbol{\beta} + \mathbf{e})\right.$$

$$\left. -E(\mathbf{X}\boldsymbol{\beta} + \mathbf{e}))'\right] = E[\mathbf{e}\mathbf{e}'] = \sigma^2\mathbf{I} \tag{4.52}$$

Therefore,

$$V[\hat{\theta}] = \sigma^2\mathbf{A}'\mathbf{A} \tag{4.53}$$

The problem now is to minimize $V[\hat{\boldsymbol{\theta}}]$ subject to the unbiasedness restrictions stated in Equations (4.49) and (4.50), i.e.,

$$\text{Min } \sigma^2\mathbf{A}'\mathbf{A}$$

$$\text{s.t. } \boldsymbol{\varphi}' = \mathbf{A}'\mathbf{X}$$

This is a Lagrangian multiplier problem. The Lagrangian is

$$\mathbf{L} = \sigma^2 \underset{1\times T}{\mathbf{A}'} \underset{T\times 1}{\mathbf{A}} + 2 \underset{1\times k}{\boldsymbol{\lambda}'} \left(\underset{k\times 1}{\boldsymbol{\varphi}} - \underset{k\times T}{\mathbf{X}'} \underset{T\times 1}{\mathbf{A}} \right) \tag{4.54}$$

$$\frac{\delta \mathbf{L}}{\delta \mathbf{A}} = 2\sigma^2 \mathbf{A}' - 2\boldsymbol{\lambda}'\mathbf{X}' = \mathbf{0} \tag{4.55}$$

Therefore,

$$\sigma^2 \mathbf{A}' - \boldsymbol{\lambda}'\mathbf{X}' = \mathbf{0}$$

$$\sigma^2 \mathbf{A}'\mathbf{X} - \boldsymbol{\lambda}'\mathbf{X}'\mathbf{X} = \mathbf{0}$$

$$\boldsymbol{\lambda}' = \sigma^2 \mathbf{A}'\mathbf{X}(\mathbf{X}'\mathbf{X})^{-1}$$

$$\boldsymbol{\lambda}' = \sigma^2 \boldsymbol{\varphi}'(\mathbf{X}'\mathbf{X})^{-1} \tag{4.56}$$

In addition,

$$\frac{\delta \mathbf{L}}{\delta \boldsymbol{\lambda}} = \boldsymbol{\varphi}' - \mathbf{A}'\mathbf{X} = \mathbf{0} \tag{4.57}$$

Considering again the derivative relative to **A** given in Equation (4.55), i.e.,

$$\frac{\delta \mathbf{L}}{\delta \mathbf{A}} = 2\sigma^2 \mathbf{A}' - 2\boldsymbol{\lambda}'\mathbf{X}'$$

replacing $\boldsymbol{\lambda}$ by the expression obtained in Equation (4.56), we obtain

$$\frac{\delta \mathbf{L}}{\delta \mathbf{A}} = 2\sigma^2 \mathbf{A}' - 2\sigma^2 \boldsymbol{\varphi}'(\mathbf{X}'\mathbf{X})^{-1}\mathbf{X}' = \mathbf{0} \tag{4.58}$$

and, therefore,

$$\mathbf{A}' = \boldsymbol{\varphi}'(\mathbf{X}'\mathbf{X})^{-1}\mathbf{X}' \tag{4.59}$$

$$\boldsymbol{\theta} = \mathbf{A}'\mathbf{y}.$$

Thus, the minimum variance linear unbiased estimator of $\boldsymbol{\varphi}'\boldsymbol{\beta}$ is obtained by replacing $\mathbf{A}'$ with the expression in Equation (4.59)

$$\hat{\boldsymbol{\theta}} = \boldsymbol{\varphi}'(\mathbf{X}'\mathbf{X})^{-1}\mathbf{X}'\mathbf{y} \tag{4.60}$$

which is the one obtained from the ordinary least squares estimator:

$$\hat{\boldsymbol{\theta}} = \boldsymbol{\varphi}'\mathbf{b} \tag{4.61}$$

We have just shown that the OLS estimator has minimum variance.

Table 4.1 Properties of estimators

Property	Assumption(s) needed
$E[\mathbf{b}\vert\mathbf{X}] = \beta$	#1
$\mathbf{V}[\mathbf{b}\vert\mathbf{X}, \sigma^2] = \sigma^2(\mathbf{X}'\mathbf{X})^{-1}$	#1,2
$\mathbf{b}$ is BLUE	#1,2
$\mathbf{b}$ is the MLE	#3
$\mathbf{b} \sim N(\beta, \sigma^2(\mathbf{X}'\mathbf{X})^{-1})$	#3

4.1.4.3 Summary of properties

Not all three assumptions discussed in section 4.1.1 are needed for all the properties of the estimator. Unbiasedness only requires assumption #1. The computation of the variance and the BLUE property of the estimator only involve assumptions #1 and 2, and do not require the normal distributional assumption of the error term. Statistical tests about the significance of the parameters can only be performed with assumption #3 about the normal distribution of the error term. These properties are shown in Table 4.1.

4.2 Pooling Issues

The pooling issues refer to the ability to pool together subsets of data. Therefore, this concerns the extent to which datasets are homogeneous or are generated by the same data generating function. This question can be addressed by testing whether the parameters of different subsets of data are the same or not. If the parameters are different, the objective may become, in a second stage, to develop models which contain variables explaining why these parameters differ. This would lead to varying parameter models which are outside the scope of this book.

4.2.1 Linear Restrictions

Let us write a linear model for two sets of data with T_1 and T_2 observations respectively.

$$\text{Data set \#1:} \quad \underset{T_1\times 1}{\mathbf{y}_1} = \underset{T_1\times K}{\mathbf{X}_1}\,\beta_1 + \mathbf{u}_1 \tag{4.62}$$

$$\text{Data set \#2:} \quad \underset{T_2\times 1}{\mathbf{y}_2} = \underset{T_2\times k}{\mathbf{X}_2}\,\beta_2 + \mathbf{u}_2 \tag{4.63}$$

where the $\mathbf{y}$'s and the $\mathbf{X}$'s represent the same variables in each subset of data. The subscripts in Equations (4.62) and (4.63) represent the two subsets of observations. For example, the dependent variable may be sales of a product and **X** may contain a vector of 1's for an intercept and the price of the product. The subscript can represent the country (countries 1 and 2 in this case). There would be T_1 time periods of observations in country 1 and T_2 periods in country 2.

Assembling the two data sets together gives:

$$\begin{bmatrix} \mathbf{y}_1 \\ \mathbf{y}_2 \end{bmatrix} = \begin{bmatrix} \mathbf{X}_1 & \mathbf{0} \\ \mathbf{0} & \mathbf{X}_2 \end{bmatrix} \begin{bmatrix} \boldsymbol{\beta}_1 \\ \boldsymbol{\beta}_2 \end{bmatrix} + \begin{bmatrix} \mathbf{u}_1 \\ \mathbf{u}_2 \end{bmatrix} \tag{4.64}$$

or

$$\underset{T\times 1}{\mathbf{y}} = \underset{T\times 2K}{\tilde{\mathbf{X}}} \underset{2K\times 1}{\boldsymbol{\beta}} + \underset{T\times 1}{\mathbf{u}} \tag{4.65}$$

where $T = T_1 + T_2$. $\boldsymbol{\beta}_1 = \boldsymbol{\beta}_2$ can also be written as $\boldsymbol{\beta}_1 - \boldsymbol{\beta}_2 = 0$ or

$$[\mathbf{1} \quad -\mathbf{1}] \begin{bmatrix} \boldsymbol{\beta}_1 \\ \boldsymbol{\beta}_2 \end{bmatrix} = 0 \tag{4.66}$$

which can also be written as:

$$\mathbf{R}\boldsymbol{\beta} = \mathbf{0} \tag{4.67}$$

where $\mathbf{R} = [\mathbf{1} \quad -\mathbf{1}]$.

This can be generalized to more than two subsets of data. This linear restriction can also be represented by the model

$$\begin{bmatrix} \mathbf{Y}_1 \\ \mathbf{Y}_2 \end{bmatrix} = \begin{bmatrix} \mathbf{X}_1 \\ \mathbf{X}_2 \end{bmatrix} \boldsymbol{\beta} + \mathbf{u} \tag{4.68}$$

or

$$\underset{T\times 1}{\mathbf{y}} = \underset{T\times K}{\mathbf{X}} \underset{K\times 1}{\boldsymbol{\beta}} + \underset{T\times 1}{\mathbf{u}} \tag{4.69}$$

Let RRSS be the restricted residual sum of squares coming from Equation (4.68) and URSS be the unrestricted residual sum of squares coming from Equation (4.64) or obtained by summing up the residual sum of squares of each equation estimated separately. Each one is distributed as a chi-square:

$$\text{RRSS} \sim \chi^2_{\nu=T_1+T_2-K}$$

$$\text{URSS} \sim \chi^2_{\nu=T_1+T_2-2K}$$

The test involves checking if the fit is significantly worse by imposing the constraint on the parameters. Therefore, a test of the restriction that the coefficients from the two data sets are equal is given by the following F test, which compares the residual sum of squares after corrections for differences in degrees of freedom:

$$\frac{(\text{RRSS} - \text{URSS})/K}{\text{URSS}/(T_1 + T_2 - 2K)} \sim F^{\nu_1=K}_{\nu_2=T_1+T_2-2K} \tag{4.70}$$

This test necessitates that the number of observations in each set is greater than the number of parameters to have sufficient degrees of freedom. Otherwise, the unrestricted model cannot be estimated. If $T_2 < K$, it is still possible to test that the T_2 observations are generated by the same model as the one used for the T_1 observations.

The model is first estimated using only the T_1 observations from the first set of data, as in Equation (4.62). The residual sum of squares for these T_1 observations is RSS_1.

Then, the pooled model is estimated as in Equation (4.68) to obtain the residual sum of squares RRSS.

The two residual sums of squares RSS_1 and RRSS have independent chi squared distributions, each with respectively $T_1 - K$ and $T_1 + T_2 - K$ degrees of freedom. The test of homogeneity of coefficients is therefore obtained from the significance of the difference between the two residual sums of squares:

$$\frac{(\mathrm{RRSS} - \mathrm{RSS}_1)/(T_1 + T_2 - K - (T_1 - K))}{\mathrm{RSS}_1/(T_1 - K)}$$

Therefore, the test considers the F distribution:

$$\frac{(\mathrm{RRSS} - \mathrm{RSS}_1)/T_2}{\mathrm{RSS}_1/(T_1 - K)} = F^{\nu_1 = T_2}_{\nu_2 = T_1 - K} \tag{4.71}$$

4.2.2 Pooling Tests and Dummy Variable Models

In this section, we assume that there are multiple firms, individuals or territories. There are T observations for each of these N firms, individuals or territories. We can write the equation for a single observation y_{it}. The subscripts i and t indicates that the observations vary along two dimensions, for example individuals (i) and time (t). For example, y_{it} represents sales in a district in a given month. y_{it} can be expressed as a linear function of factors measured in this same territory at the same time period:

$$y_{it} = \beta_{1i} + \sum_{k=2}^{K} \boldsymbol{\beta}_k x_{kit} + e_{it} \tag{4.72}$$

β_{1i} represents the intercept for observation i. This can be expressed in terms of an individual difference from a mean value of the intercept across all observations:

$$\beta_{1i} = \bar{\boldsymbol{\beta}} + \mu_i \tag{4.73}$$

which, when inserted into Equation (4.72) gives:

$$y_{it} = \bar{\boldsymbol{\beta}}_1 + \mu_i + \sum_{k=2}^{K} \boldsymbol{\beta}_k x_{kit} + e_{it} \tag{4.74}$$

Depending on the nature of the variable μ, the model is a dummy variable model or an error component model.

If μ_i is fixed, then it is a dummy variable or covariance model. If μ_i is random, we would be facing an error component model. In this section, we consider the dummy variable model (i.e., μ_i is fixed).

Model with constant slope coefficients and an intercept that varies over individuals. The dummy variable model can be represented for all the T observations in a given territory i as:

$$\underset{T\times 1}{\mathbf{y}_i} = (\bar{\boldsymbol{\beta}}_1 + \mu_i)\underset{T\times 1}{\mathbf{j}_T} + \underset{T\times(K-1)}{\mathbf{X}_{si}}\underset{(K-1)\times 1}{\boldsymbol{\beta}_s} + \mathbf{e}_i \tag{4.75}$$

where

$$E[\mathbf{e}_i] = \mathbf{0}$$
$$E[\mathbf{e}_i\mathbf{e}_i'] = \sigma_e^2\mathbf{I}_T$$
$$E[\mathbf{e}_i\mathbf{e}_j'] = \mathbf{0} \quad \forall i \neq j$$

This is identical to creating a dummy variable for each observation d_{itk} where: $d_{itk} = 1$ if $i = k$ and 0 otherwise.

Equation (4.72) or (4.74) can be rewritten as:

$$y_{it} = \sum_{m=1}^{N} \beta_{1m} d_{itm} + \sum_{k=2}^{K} \boldsymbol{\beta}_k x_{kit} + e_{it} \tag{4.76}$$

We can then form a vector of dummy variables for each territory $(\mathbf{D}_1, \ldots, \mathbf{D}_i, \ldots, \mathbf{D}_N)$. Each of these dummy variables vector has T rows $(T \times 1)$ where each row is a 1. Then the full data can be expressed as:

$$\begin{bmatrix} \mathbf{y}_1 \\ \mathbf{y}_2 \\ \vdots \\ \mathbf{y}_i \\ \vdots \\ \mathbf{y}_N \end{bmatrix} = \begin{bmatrix} \mathbf{D}_1 & \mathbf{0} & \cdots & & \cdots & \mathbf{0} \\ \mathbf{0} & \mathbf{D}_2 & & & & \\ \vdots & & \ddots & & & \\ & & & \mathbf{D}_i & & \\ \vdots & & & & \ddots & \vdots \\ \mathbf{0} & \cdots & & & \cdots & \mathbf{D}_N \end{bmatrix} \begin{bmatrix} \beta_{11} \\ \beta_{12} \\ \vdots \\ \beta_{1i} \\ \vdots \\ \beta_{1N} \end{bmatrix} + \mathbf{X}_s\boldsymbol{\beta}_s + \mathbf{e} \tag{4.77}$$

Let us denote $\mathrm{PRSS}_{\mathrm{slopes}}$ the residual sum of squares obtained from least squares estimation of Equation (4.77). This indicates that the model is Partially Restricted (PR) on the slopes which are assumed to be equal.

The model with equal intercepts and different slopes is:

$$\begin{bmatrix} \mathbf{y}_1 \\ \mathbf{y}_2 \\ \vdots \\ \mathbf{y}_i \\ \vdots \\ \mathbf{y}_N \end{bmatrix} = \begin{bmatrix} \mathbf{D}_1 \\ \mathbf{D}_2 \\ \vdots \\ \mathbf{D}_i \\ \vdots \\ \mathbf{D}_N \end{bmatrix} b_1 + \begin{bmatrix} \mathbf{X}_{s1} & \mathbf{0} & \cdots & & \cdots & \mathbf{0} \\ \mathbf{0} & \mathbf{X}_{s2} & & & & \vdots \\ \vdots & & \ddots & & & \\ & & & \mathbf{X}_{si} & & \\ \vdots & & & & \ddots & \vdots \\ \mathbf{0} & \cdots & & & \cdots & \mathbf{X}_{sN} \end{bmatrix} \begin{bmatrix} \beta_s^1 \\ \beta_s^2 \\ \vdots \\ \beta_s^i \\ \vdots \\ \beta_s^N \end{bmatrix} + \mathbf{e} \tag{4.78}$$

Let us denote $\text{PPRSS}_{\text{intercept}}$ the residual sum of squares obtained form the least square estimation of Equation (4.78). This indicates a Partial Restriction on the intercepts which are assumed to be the same.

The model with complete restriction that the intercepts and slopes are equal is given by:

$$\begin{bmatrix} \mathbf{y}_1 \\ \mathbf{y}_2 \\ \vdots \\ \mathbf{y}_i \\ \vdots \\ \mathbf{y}_N \end{bmatrix} = \begin{bmatrix} \mathbf{X}_1 \\ \mathbf{X}_2 \\ \vdots \\ \mathbf{X}_i \\ \vdots \\ \mathbf{X}_N \end{bmatrix} \boldsymbol{\beta} + \mathbf{e} \tag{4.79}$$

This equation is the completely restricted case where intercepts and slopes are assumed to be equal. This results in the residual sum of squares CRSS.

Finally, the completely unrestricted model is one where slopes and intercepts are different. This model is estimated by running N separate regressions, for each individual or territory. The completely unrestricted residual sum of squares is CUSS.

Homogeneity of intercepts and/or slopes can be tested using F tests based on the comparison of restricted and unrestricted residual sum of squares. The next section discusses the strategies for such pooling tests. Note that in all cases, the homogeneity along the second dimension is assumed. For example, homogeneity across time periods is assumed and pooling tests are performed across sections (i.e., firms, territories or individuals for example).

4.2.3 Strategy for Pooling Tests

The strategies follow from decomposing the tests over intercept and slopes. The process follows the one depicted in Figure 4.1.

The first test consists of an overall test of homogeneity of intercept and slopes. For that purpose, the residual sum of squares from the completely unrestricted model (CUSS) is compared to the partially restricted model where intercept and slopes are restricted to be the same (CRSS). A failure to reject

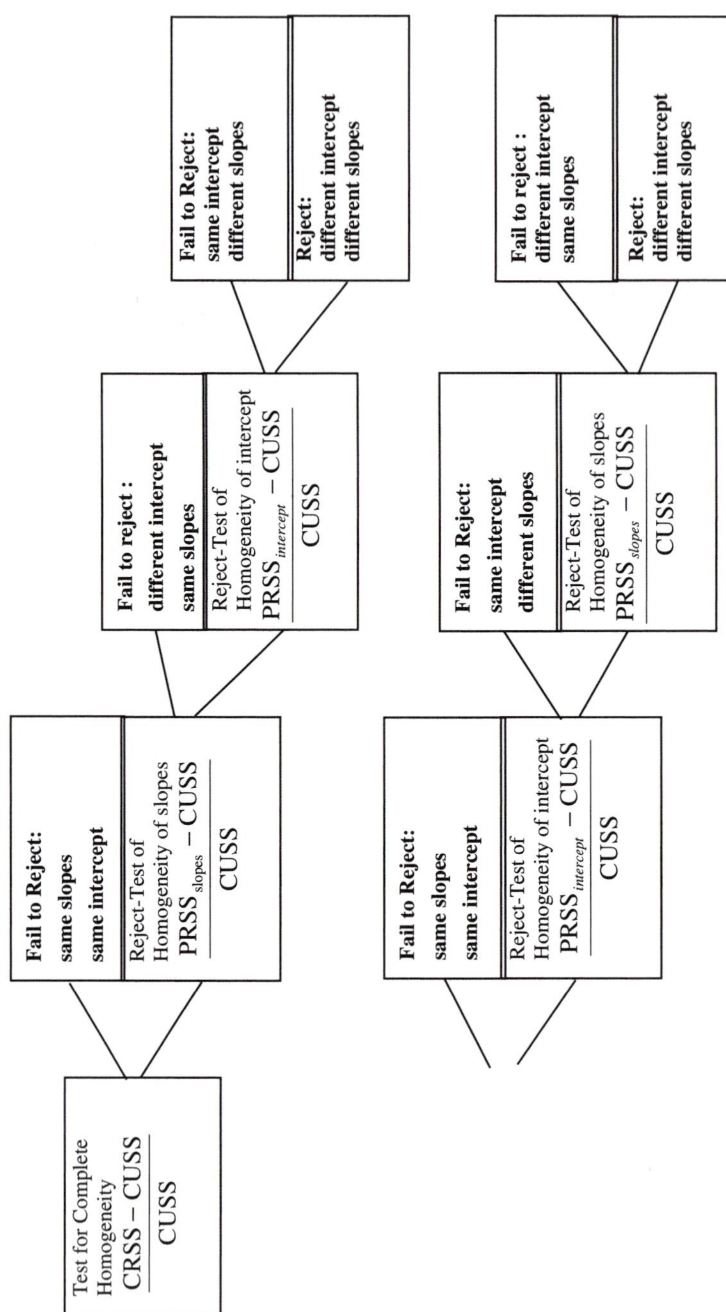

Fig. 4.1 Strategy for pooling tests.

this test indicates that the intercept and slopes are all the same across sections. No more test is needed. In the case of rejection of the equality of intercepts and slopes, we now must test whether the difference comes from the intercept only, the slope only or both. Then another test is now performed to check for the equality of the slopes.

For that purpose, we now compare the residual sum of squares from the completely unrestricted model (CUSS) with the residual sum of squares obtained from constraining the slopes to be equal ($PRSS_{slopes}$). A failure to reject the difference between these two models indicates that the slopes are equal. Because the slopes are equal but the full restriction leads to significant differences, one must conclude that the intercept is different across sections. If we reject the hypothesis of equal slopes, the slopes are different, in which case we must still find out if the intercept of the cross sections are the same or not.

Therefore, a third test is performed where we now compare the completely unrestricted residual sum of squares (CUSS) with the residual sum of squares of the model with the restriction that the intercept is the same across sections ($PRSS_{intercept}$). A failure to reject the hypothesis indicates that slopes are the only source of heterogeneity (the intercept is the same across sections). A rejection of the test indicates that both intercept and slopes are different across sections.

In this case, we started to check the source of heterogeneity by restricting the slopes and checking if the slopes were statistically different or not across sections. Instead, we could have first restricted the intercept, i.e., we could have tested for the homogeneity of the intercept first. If the hypothesis were rejected, we would then have tested for the homogeneity of slopes. This is the second line of tests shown in Figure 4.1.

4.3 Examples of Linear Model Estimation with SAS

Let us consider an example where the data set consists of the market share of four brands during seven periods. This market share is predicted by two variables, the percentage of distribution outlets carrying the brand during each period and the price charged for each brand during the period.

Figure 4.2 shows an example of a SAS file to run a regression with such data. The data are first read: period (period), brand number (brandno), market share (ms), distribution (dist) and price (price). The variables are then transformed to obtain their logarithms so that the coefficients correspond to sensitivity parameters. Dummy variables for each brand except the first one are created. These will be used for estimating a model with different intercept for each brand. They are also used to compute new variables created for distribution and price for each brand.

Three models are estimated as per the SAS file shown in Figure 4.2. The SAS procedure REG is first called. Then a model statement indicates the

```
OPTIONS LS=80;
DATA DATA1;
INFILE "c:\SAMD\Chapter4\Examples\Examp4.csv"  dlm = ',' ";
INPUT period brandno ms dist price;
if ms gt 0 then do;
  lms=log(ms);
  ldist=log(dist);
  lprice=log(price);
end;
else lms=.;
if brandno=2 then brand2=1; else brand2=0;
if brandno=3 then brand3=1; else brand3=0;
if brandno=4 then brand4=1; else brand4=0;
ldist2=ldist*brand2;
ldist3=ldist*brand3;
ldist4=ldist*brand4;
lprice2=lprice*brand2;
lprice3=lprice*brand3;
lprice4=lprice*brand4;

proc reg;
  model lms=brand2 brand3 brand4 ldist ldist2 ldist3 ldist4
            lprice lprice2 lprice3 lprice4;
  model lms=ldist lprice;
  model lms=brand2 brand3 brand4 ldist lprice;
run;
```

Fig. 4.2 Example of SAS input file for regression analysis (examp4.sas).

model specification with the dependent variable on the left side of the equal sign and the list of independent variables on the right side. The first model is the completely unrestricted model where each brand has different intercept and slopes. A second model statement is used for the completely restricted model (same intercept and slopes for all the brands). Finally, the third model statement corresponds to the partially restricted model where each brand has a different intercept but the same distribution and price parameters.

The output is shown in Figure 4.3. From the output, the residual sums of squares for the completely unrestricted model appears in the first model (i.e., CUSS = 0.14833). The degrees of freedom for this model is the number of observations (28 which follows from 4 brands with each 7 periods of data) minus the number of parameters (12), that is 16 degrees of freedom. The second model shows the completely restricted case where all intercepts are the same and the slopes are the same as well. There are 3 parameters estimated and the CRSS is 46.3733. The third model has a different intercept for each brand but the same slopes. Therefore, 6 parameters are estimated and the $PRSS_{slopes}$ is 0.19812.

```
Model: MODEL1
Dependent Variable: LMS
                              Analysis of Variance
                                 Sum of          Mean
        Source          DF      Squares        Square      F Value       Prob>F
        Model           11     47.19807       4.29073      462.832       0.0001
        Error           16      0.14833       0.00927
        C Total         27     47.34640

            Root MSE        0.09628      R-square         0.9969
            Dep Mean       -2.17730      Adj R-sq         0.9947
            C.V.           -4.42217

                              Parameter Estimates
                        Parameter       Standard     T for H0:
      Variable  DF       Estimate          Error    Parameter=0    Prob > |T|
      INTERCEP   1      -1.676908     0.03642376        -46.039        0.0001
      BRAND2     1      -2.231837     0.05161904        -43.237        0.0001
      BRAND3     1      -1.014442     0.05151212        -19.693        0.0001
      BRAND4     1       1.264971     0.05150013         24.562        0.0001
      LDIST      1       0.955385     0.51824563          1.843        0.0839
      LDIST2     1       0.106274     0.55309599          0.192        0.8500
      LDIST3     1      -0.034930     0.75256037         -0.046        0.9636
      LDIST4     1       0.704706     1.64183978          0.429        0.6735
      LPRICE     1       0.248777     0.80524111          0.309        0.7613
      LPRICE2    1      -1.855944     0.92552212         -2.005        0.0622
      LPRICE3    1      -0.905538     1.19626264         -0.757        0.4601
      LPRICE4    1      -1.104439     1.12309972         -0.983        0.3401


Model: MODEL2
Dependent Variable: LMS

                              Analysis of Variance
                                 Sum of          Mean
        Source          DF      Squares        Square      F Value       Prob>F
        Model            2      0.96907       0.48454        0.261       0.7722
        Error           25     46.37733       1.85509
        C Total         27     47.34640

            Root MSE        1.36202      R-square         0.0205
            Dep Mean       -2.17730      Adj R-sq        -0.0579
            C.V.          -62.55535

                              Parameter Estimates
                        Parameter       Standard     T for H0:
      Variable  DF       Estimate          Error    Parameter=0    Prob > |T|
      INTERCEP   1      -2.168119     0.25785160         -8.408        0.0001
      LDIST      1       1.724982     2.38741557          0.723        0.4767
      LPRICE     1      -1.191476     4.35217499         -0.274        0.7865
```

```
Model: MODEL3
Dependent Variable: LMS
                         Analysis of Variance
                            Sum of          Mean
        Source      DF     Squares        Square      F Value       Prob>F
        Model        5    47.14828       9.42966     1047.081       0.0001
        Error       22     0.19812       0.00901
        C Total     27    47.34640

            Root MSE       0.09490     R-square        0.9958
            Dep Mean      -2.17730     Adj R-sq        0.9949
            C.V.          -4.35852

                         Parameter Estimates
                    Parameter       Standard    T for H0:
      Variable  DF   Estimate          Error  Parameter=0   Prob > |T|
      INTERCEP   1  -1.678270     0.03587286      -46.784       0.0001
      BRAND2     1  -2.228246     0.05078652      -43.875       0.0001
      BRAND3     1  -1.012968     0.05072523      -19.970       0.0001
      BRAND4     1   1.265914     0.05072809       24.955       0.0001
      LDIST      1   1.057472     0.16668030        6.344       0.0001
      LPRICE     1  -0.939927     0.30325788       -3.099       0.0052
```

Fig. 4.3 SAS output for regression analysis (examp4.lst).

Tests of poolability can then be performed following the discussion in section 4.2. The test for complete homogeneity is given by the statistic:

$$\frac{(\text{CRSS} - \text{CUSS})/9}{\text{CUSS}/16} = \frac{(46.37733 - 0.14833)/9}{0.14833/16} = 554.07$$

Checking on the table for the F distribution with 9 and 16 degrees of freedom, the difference is clearly significant and the hypothesis of complete homogeneity is clearly rejected.

We then proceed with testing for the homogeneity of slopes. We therefore compare the completely unrestricted model with the model where the slopes are restricted to be equal, which corresponds to the specification of model 3. There are 6 parameters and the residual sum of squares is 0.19812. The test is, therefore,

$$\frac{(\text{PRSS}_{\text{slopes}} - \text{CUSS})/6}{\text{CUSS}/16} = \frac{(0.19812 - 0.14833)/6}{0.14833/16} = 0.895$$

Comparing this statistic with the critical value of F with 6 and 16 degrees of freedom, it is clear that the constraint does not imply a significantly worse fit. Consequently, we can conclude that the parameters of the distribution and price variables are homogeneous across the brands. However, each brand has a separate intercept.

4.4 Assignment

Two data sets are available which contain information about a market in which multiple brands compete in an industry composed of five market segments. The full description of the data is given in Appendix C.

The PANEL.CSV data set contains information at the segment level while the INDUP.CSV data set provides information at the industry level.

The file ASSIGN4.SAS in Figure 4.4 is a SAS file which reads both data sets (INDUP.CSV and PANEL.CSV) and merges the two files.

```
                    /* ---------------------------------*/
                    /*    Example of                    */
                    /*        (1)  Merging files for    */
                    /*        (2)  regression analysis  */
                    /*----------------------------------*/
option ls=80 ;
data panel;
  infile 'C:\SAMD\Chapter4\Assignments\panel.csv' firstobs=2   dlm = ',' ;

  input period  segment  segsize  ideal1-ideal3
         brand $  aware  intent shop1-shop3
         perc1-perc3 dev1-dev3 share ;

run;
proc sort data=panel;
        by period brand;
run;
/* proc print;
        title 'panel sorted';
run;
*/
data indup;
  infile 'C:\SAMD\Chapter4\Assignments\indup.csv' firstobs=2   dlm = ',' ;
  input period  firm  brand $ price  advert
         char1-char5 salmen1-salmen3
         cost dist1-dist3 usales  DSls1000  dsales  ushare dshare  adshare
         relprice ;
run;
proc sort data =indup;
        by period brand;
run;
/* proc print;
        title 'indup sorted';
run;
*/
data econ;
        merge panel indup;
        by period brand;
```

```
/* proc print;
        title 'merged data';
run;
*/
if segment<5 then delete;
run;
proc sort data=econ out=econ2;
        by brand period;
run;
data econ3;
set econ2;
lagaw =lag1(aware);
if period=0 then delete;
run;
/*proc print;
        var period segment brand aware lagaw;
run;*/
proc reg;
        model aware = lagaw adshare;
/*        by brand;*/
run;
```

Fig. 4.4 Example of SAS file for reading data sets INDUP.CSV and PANEL.CSV and for running regressions (assign4.sas).

The assignment consists in developing a model using cross sections and time series data. For example, it is possible to model sales for each brand as a function of the price and the advertising for the brand, sales force sizes, etc.

Regardless of the model, you need to test whether the intercepts and slopes are homogenous. As another example, lets say you decide to model the awareness of each brand as a function of the awareness in the prior period and of the brand advertising of the current period. You may want to test if the process of awareness development is the same across brands.

References

Basic Technical Readings

Chow, G. C. (1960), "Tests of Equality Between Subsets of Coefficients in Two Linear Regression," *Econometrica*, 591–605.

Fuller, W. A. and G. E. Battese (1973), "Transformation for Estimation of Linear Models with Nested Error Structure," *Journal of the American Statistical Association*, 68, 343 (September), 626–632.

Maddala, G. S. (1971), "The Use of Variance Component Models in Pooling Cross Section and Time Series Data," *Econometrica*, 39, 2 (March), 341–358.

Mundlack, Y. (1978), "On the Pooling of Time Series and Cross Section Data," *Econometrica*, 46, 69–85.

Nerlove, M. (1971), "Further Evidence on the Estimation of Dynamic Economic Relations from a Time Series of Cross Sections," *Econometrica*, 39, 2 (March), 359–382.

Application Readings

Bass, F. M. and R. P. Leone (1983), "Temporal Aggregation, the Data Interval Bias, and Empirical Estimation of Bimonthly Relations From Annual Data," *Management Science*, 29, 1 (January), 1–11.

Bass, F. M. and D. R. Wittink (1975), "Pooling Issues and Methods in Regression Analysis With Examples in Marketing Research," *Journal of Marketing Research*, 12, 4 (November), 414–425.

Bass, F. M., P. Cattin and D. R. Wittink (1978), "Firm Effects and Industry Effects in the Analysis of Market Structure and Profitability," *Journal of Marketing Research*, 15, 3–.

Bemmaor, A. C. (1984), "Testing Alternative Econometric Models on the Existence of Advertising Threshold Effect," *Journal of Marketing Research*, 21, 3 (August), 298–308.

Bowman, D. and H. Gatignon (1996), "Order of Entry as a Moderator of the Effect of the Marketing Mix on Market Share," *Marketing Science*, 15, 3, 222–242.

Gatignon, H. (1984), "Competition as a Moderator of the Effect of Advertising on Sales," *Journal of Marketing Research*, 21, 4 (November), 387–398.

Gatignon, H. and P. V. Abeele (1997), "Explaining Cross-Country Differences in Price and Distribution Effectiveness," Working Paper, INSEAD.

Gatignon, H. and D. M. Hanssens (1987), "Modeling Marketing Interactions with Application to Salesforce Effectiveness," *Journal of Marketing Research*, 24, 3 (August), 247–257.

Gatignon, H., J. Eliashberg and T. S. Robertson (1989), "Modeling Multinational Diffusion Patterns: An Efficient Methodology," *Marketing Science*, 8, 3 (Summer), 231–247.

Gatignon, H., T. S. Robertson and A. J. Fein (1997), "Incumbent Defense Strategies against New Product Entry," *International Journal of Research in Marketing*, 14, 163–176.

Gatignon, H., B. A. Weitz and P. Bansal (1989), "Brand Introduction Strategies and Competitive Environments," *Journal of Marketing Research*, 27, 4 (November), 390–401.

Hatten, K. J. and D. Schendel (1977), "Heterogeneity within an Industry: Firm Conduct in the U.S. Brewing Industry, 1952–71," *Strategic Management Journal*, 26, 2, 97–113.

Jacobson, R. and D. A. Aaker (1985), "Is Market Share All that it's Cracked Up to Be?," *Journal of Marketing*, 49 (Fall), 11–22.

Johar, G. V., K. Jedidi and J. Jacoby (1997), "A Varying-Parameter Averaging Model of On-line Brand Evaluations," *Journal of Consumer Research*, 24, September, 232–247.

Lambin, J.-J. (1970), "Optimal Allocation of Competitive Marketing Efforts: An Empirical Study," *Journal of Business*, 43, 4 (October), 468–484.

Miller, C. E., J. Reardon and D. E. McCorkle (1999), "The Effects of Competition on Retail Structure: An Examination of Intratype, Intertype, and Intercategory Competition," *Journal of Marketing*, 63, 4 (October), 107–120.

Montgomery, D. B. and A. J. Silk (1972), "Estimating Dynamic Effects of Market Communications Expenditures," *Management Science*, 18, 10 (June), B485–501.

Naert, P. and A. Bultez (1973), "Logically Consistent Market Share Models," *Journal of Marketing Research*, 10 (August), 334–340.

Parson, L. J. (1974), "An Econometric Analysis of Advertising, Retail Availability and Sales of a New Brand," *Management Science*, 20, 6 (February), 938–947.

Parson, L. J. (1975), "The Product Life Cycle and Time Varying Advertising Elasticities," *Journal of Marketing Research*, 12, 3 (November), 476–480.

Robinson, W. T. (1968), "Marketing Mix Reactions to Entry," *Marketing Science*, 7, 4 (Fall), 368–385.

Robinson, W. T. (1988), "Sources of Market Pioneer Advantages: The Case of Industrial Goods Industries," *Journal of Marketing Research*, 25, 1 (February), 87–94.

Robinson, W. T. and C. Fornell (1985), "Sources of Market Pioneer Advantages in Consumer Goods Industries," *Journal of Marketing Research*, 22, 3 (August), 305–317.

Steenkamp, J.-B. E.M., F. t. Hofstede, et al. (1999), "A Cross-National Investigation into the Individual and National Cultural Antecedents of Consumer Innovativeness," *Journal of Marketing* 63, April, 55–69.

Urban, G. L., T. Carter, S. Gaskin and Z. Mucha (1986), "Market Share Rewards to Pioneering Brands: An Empirical Analysis and Strategic Implications," *Management Science*, 32 (June), 645–659.

5. System of Equations

In this chapter we consider the case where several dependent variables are explained by linear relationships with other variables. Independent analysis of each relationship by Ordinary Least Squares could result in incorrect statistical inferences either because the estimation is not efficient (a simultaneous consideration of all the explained variables may lead to more efficient estimators for the parameters) or may be biased in cases where the dependent variables influence each other.

In the first section, a model of Seemingly Unrelated Regression is presented. In the second section, we discuss the estimation of simultaneous relationships between dependent or endogenous variables. Finally, in section three, we discuss the issue of identification when systems of equations are involved.

5.1 Seemingly Unrelated Regression (SUR)

The case of Seemingly Unrelated Regression occurs when several dependent variables are expressed as a linear function of explanatory variables, leading to multiple equations with error terms which may not be independent of each other. Therefore, each equation appears unrelated to the other. However, they are in fact linked by the error terms, which leads to a disturbance-related set of equations. We will first present the model. Then, we will derive the proper efficient estimator for the parameters and, finally, we will discuss the particular case when the predictor variables are the same in each equation.

5.1.1 Set of Equations with Contemporaneously Correlated Disturbances

Let us consider time series of M cross sections. Each cross section i presents T observations, usually over time, although t could represent individuals for which M characteristics are modeled. Therefore, for each cross section, the vector of dependent variables has T observations (the vector $\mathbf{y}_i$ is dimensioned $T \times 1$). In this equation for the i-th cross section, there are K_i predictor variables. A priori, the variables explaining a dependent variable y_{it} are different for each cross section or variable i. Consequently, the matrix $\mathbf{X}_i$ contains T rows and K_i columns. The linear equation for each cross section can, therefore, be represented by Equation (5.1):

$$\forall i = 1, \ldots, M: \quad \underset{T\times 1}{\mathbf{y}_i} = \underset{T\times K_i}{\mathbf{X}_i} \underset{K_i\times 1}{\boldsymbol{\beta}_i} + \underset{T\times 1}{\mathbf{e}_i} \tag{5.1}$$

Stacking all the cross sections together, the model for all cross sections can be expressed as:

$$\underset{MT\times 1}{\begin{bmatrix} \mathbf{y}_1 \\ \mathbf{y}_2 \\ \vdots \\ \mathbf{y}_i \\ \vdots \\ \mathbf{y}_M \end{bmatrix}} = \underset{MT\times K}{\begin{bmatrix} \mathbf{X}_1 & & & & & \\ & \mathbf{X}_2 & & & 0 & \\ & & \ddots & & & \\ & & & \mathbf{X}_i & & \\ & 0 & & & \ddots & \\ & & & & & \mathbf{X}_M \end{bmatrix}} \underset{K\times 1}{\begin{bmatrix} \boldsymbol{\beta}_1 \\ \boldsymbol{\beta}_2 \\ \vdots \\ \boldsymbol{\beta}_i \\ \vdots \\ \boldsymbol{\beta}_M \end{bmatrix}} + \underset{MT\times 1}{\begin{bmatrix} \mathbf{e}_1 \\ \mathbf{e}_2 \\ \vdots \\ \mathbf{e}_i \\ \vdots \\ \mathbf{e}_M \end{bmatrix}} \tag{5.2}$$

where $K = \sum_{i=1}^{M} K_i$.

This can be written more compactly as:

$$\mathbf{y} = \mathbf{Z}\boldsymbol{\beta} + \mathbf{e} \tag{5.3}$$

The error terms have zero mean, variances which vary for each equation, i.e., σ_{ii} and the covariance corresponding to the same time period t for each pair of cross section is σ_{ij}. All other covariances are zero. This can be expressed for each cross sectional vector of disturbances as

$$\forall i: \quad E[\mathbf{e}_i] = \mathbf{0} \tag{5.4}$$

and

$$\forall i, j: \quad E[\mathbf{e}_i \mathbf{e}'_j] = \sigma_{ij} \mathbf{I}_T \tag{5.5}$$

It may be useful to write the full expression for Equation (5.5) for two cross sections i and j:

$$E\left[\begin{pmatrix} e_{i1} \\ e_{i2} \\ \vdots \\ e_{it} \\ \vdots \\ e_{iT} \end{pmatrix} (e_{j1} \; e_{j2} \; \cdots \; e_{jt} \; \cdots \; e_{jT})\right] = \begin{bmatrix} \sigma_{ij} & & & & \\ & \sigma_{ij} & & & \\ & & \ddots & 0 & \\ & 0 & & \sigma_{ij} & \\ & & & & \ddots & \\ & & & & & \sigma_{ij} \end{bmatrix} \tag{5.6}$$

Let $\boldsymbol{\Sigma}$ be the contemporaneous covariance matrix, i.e., the matrix where each cell represents the covariance of the error term of two equations (cross sections) for the same t:

$$\boldsymbol{\Sigma} = \begin{bmatrix} \sigma_{11} & \sigma_{12} & \cdots & \sigma_{1M} \\ \sigma_{12} & \sigma_{22} & \cdots & \sigma_{2M} \\ \vdots & & \ddots & \vdots \\ \sigma_{1M} & \cdots & \cdots & \sigma_{MM} \end{bmatrix} \tag{5.7}$$

Consequently, using the Kronecker product, we can write the covariance matrix for the full set of cross sections and time series data:

$$E[\mathbf{ee}'] = \boldsymbol{\Omega} = \boldsymbol{\Sigma} \otimes \mathbf{I}_T \tag{5.8}$$

The matrix expressed in Equation (5.8) can be visualized below:

$$\boldsymbol{\Omega} = \left[\begin{array}{ccccccccccc}
\sigma_{11} & 0 & \cdots & 0 & \sigma_{12} & 0 & \cdots & 0 & & & \\
0 & \sigma_{11} & \cdots & 0 & 0 & \sigma_{12} & \cdots & 0 & & & \\
\vdots & \vdots & \ddots & \vdots & \vdots & \vdots & \ddots & \vdots & & & \\
0 & 0 & \cdots & \sigma_{11} & 0 & 0 & \cdots & \sigma_{12} & & & \\
\sigma_{12} & 0 & \cdots & 0 & \sigma_{22} & 0 & \cdots & 0 & & & \\
0 & \sigma_{12} & \cdots & 0 & 0 & \sigma_{22} & \cdots & 0 & & & \\
\vdots & \vdots & \ddots & \vdots & \vdots & \vdots & \ddots & \vdots & & & \\
0 & 0 & \cdots & \sigma_{12} & 0 & 0 & \cdots & \sigma_{22} & & & \\
\vdots & \vdots & & \vdots & & & & \vdots & \ddots & & \\
\vdots & \vdots & & \vdots & & & & \vdots & & \ddots & \\
\sigma_{1M} & 0 & \cdots & 0 & & & & & & & \ddots \\
0 & \sigma_{1M} & \cdots & 0 & & & & & & & \\
\vdots & \vdots & & \vdots & & & & & & & \\
0 & 0 & \cdots & \sigma_{1M} & \cdots & \cdots & & & & &
\end{array}\right] \tag{5.9}$$

5.1.2 Estimation

The structure of the covariance matrix of the error term is characteristic of heteroscedasticity. Consequently the Generalized Least Squares Estimator will be the Best Linear Unbiased Estimator:

$$\hat{\gamma}_{\text{GLS}} = (\mathbf{Z}'\boldsymbol{\Omega}^{-1}\mathbf{Z})^{-1}\mathbf{Z}'\boldsymbol{\Omega}^{-1}\mathbf{y} \tag{5.10}$$

However, from Equation (5.8) and using the property of the inverse of a Kronecker product of two matrices:

$$(\boldsymbol{\Sigma} \otimes \mathbf{I})^{-1} = \boldsymbol{\Sigma}^{-1} \otimes \mathbf{I} \tag{5.11}$$

and, therefore,

$$\hat{\gamma}_{\text{GLS}} = [\mathbf{Z}'(\boldsymbol{\Sigma}^{-1} \otimes \mathbf{I})\mathbf{Z}]^{-1}\mathbf{Z}'(\boldsymbol{\Sigma}^{-1} \otimes \mathbf{I})\mathbf{y} \tag{5.12}$$

This estimation only requires the inversion of an $M \times M$ matrix, the matrix of contemporaneous covariances.

The generalized Least Squares Estimator is unbiased:

$$E[\hat{\gamma}_{\text{GLS}}] = \gamma \tag{5.13}$$

Its variance-covariance matrix is:

$$V[\hat{\gamma}_{\text{GLS}}] = [\mathbf{Z}'(\mathbf{\Sigma}^{-1} \otimes \mathbf{I})\mathbf{Z}]^{-1} \tag{5.14}$$

In practice, the contemporaneous covariance matrix is, however, unknown. If it can be estimated by a consistent estimator, the Estimated Generalized Least Squares Estimator can be computed by replacing the contemporaneous covariance matrix in Equation (5.12) by its estimated value.

$\mathbf{\Sigma}$ is estimated by following the three steps below:

Step 1: Ordinary Least Squares are performed on each equation separately to obtain the parameters for each equation or cross section i:

$$b_i = (\mathbf{X}_i'\mathbf{X}_i)^{-1}\mathbf{X}_i'\mathbf{y}_i \tag{5.15}$$

These OLS estimators are unbiased.

Step 2: The residuals are computed:

$$\hat{\mathbf{e}}_i = \mathbf{y}_i - \mathbf{X}_i b_i \tag{5.16}$$

Step 3: The contemporaneous covariance matrix can then be computed:

$$\hat{\mathbf{\Sigma}} = \{\hat{\sigma}_{ij}\} = \left\{\frac{1}{T}\hat{\mathbf{e}}_i'\hat{\mathbf{e}}_j\right\} \tag{5.17}$$

alternatively, the cross-product residuals can be divided by $T - K_i$ instead of T.

The Estimated Generalized Least Squares Estimator is then found as:

$$\hat{\hat{\gamma}}_{\text{EGLS}} = [\mathbf{Z}'(\hat{\mathbf{\Sigma}}^{-1} \otimes \mathbf{I})\mathbf{Z}]^{-1}\mathbf{Z}'(\hat{\mathbf{\Sigma}}^{-1} \otimes \mathbf{I})\mathbf{y} \tag{5.18}$$

It is then possible to compute the new residuals obtained from the EGLS estimation and recalculate an updated covariance matrix to find a new EGLS estimate. This iterative procedure converges to the maximum likelihood estimator.

5.1.3 Special Cases

There are two special cases where it can be demonstrated that the Generalized Least Squares Estimator obtained from the Seemingly Unrelated Regression is identical to the Ordinary Least Squares estimator obtained one equation (cross section) over time. These two cases are when:

1. The independent variables in each equation are identical (i.e., same variables and same values):

$$\forall i, j: \quad \mathbf{X}_i = \mathbf{X}_j \tag{5.19}$$

2. The contemporaneous covariance matrix is diagonal, i.e., the errors across equations or cross sections are independent:

$$\boldsymbol{\Sigma} = \text{diag}\{\sigma_{ii}\} \tag{5.20}$$

Consequently in both of these cases, there is no need to compute the covariance matrix.

5.2 A System of Simultaneous Equations

5.2.1 The Problem

Again, the problem consists in estimating several equations, each corresponding to a variable to be explained by explanatory variables. The difference with the prior situation for Seemingly Unrelated Regression is that the variables which are explained by the model can be an explanatory variable of another one, thereby creating an endogenous system. These variables are then called endogenous variables and the variables which are not explained by the system are exogenous variables. Therefore, we need to estimate the parameters of a system of N linear equations, where there are T observations for each equation.

For one observation t:

$\underset{N\times 1}{\mathbf{y}_t}$ is a vector of endogenous variables

$\underset{K\times 1}{\mathbf{x}_t}$ is a vector of all the exogenous variables in the system.

The system of N equations for each t can therefore be expressed as:

$$\underset{1\times N}{\mathbf{y}_t'}\underset{N\times N}{\boldsymbol{\Gamma}} = \underset{1\times K}{\mathbf{x}_t'}\underset{K\times N}{\mathbf{B}} + \underset{1\times N}{\boldsymbol{\varepsilon}_t'} \tag{5.21}$$

where the matrices $\boldsymbol{\Gamma}$ and $\mathbf{B}$ are matrices containing the parameters of all equations. For example in the case of two equations (i.e., two endogenous variables) and two exogenous variables:

$$(y_{1t} \quad y_{2t})\begin{pmatrix}\gamma_{11} & \gamma_{21}\\ \gamma_{12} & \gamma_{22}\end{pmatrix} = (x_{1t} \quad x_{2t})\begin{pmatrix}\beta_{11} & \beta_{21}\\ \beta_{12} & \beta_{22}\end{pmatrix} + (\varepsilon_{1t} \quad \varepsilon_{2t}) \tag{5.22}$$

This corresponds to the two equations:

$$\begin{cases} \gamma_{11} y_{1t} + \gamma_{12} y_{2t} = \beta_{11} x_{1t} + \beta_{12} x_{2t} + \varepsilon_{1t} \\ \gamma_{21} y_{1t} + \gamma_{22} y_{2t} = \beta_{21} x_{1t} + \beta_{22} x_{2t} + \varepsilon_{2t} \end{cases} \tag{5.23}$$

In addition, the error terms have the following properties:

$$\forall t: \quad \underset{N \times N_t}{E\,[\boldsymbol{\varepsilon}]} = \underset{N \times 1}{\mathbf{0}} \tag{5.24}$$

and the contemporaneous covariance matrix is the symmetric matrix:

$$\forall t: \quad \underset{N \times N}{E[\boldsymbol{\varepsilon}_t \boldsymbol{\varepsilon}_t']} = \underset{N \times N}{\boldsymbol{\Sigma}} \tag{5.25}$$

while the non contemporaneous error terms are independent:

$$\forall t \neq j: \quad \underset{N \times N}{E[\boldsymbol{\varepsilon}_t \boldsymbol{\varepsilon}_j']} = \underset{N \times N}{\mathbf{0}} \tag{5.26}$$

The reduced form can be obtained by post-multiplying Equation (5.21) by $\boldsymbol{\Gamma}^{-1}$, assuming the inverse exists:

$$\mathbf{y}_t' = \mathbf{x}_t' \mathbf{B} \boldsymbol{\Gamma}^{-1} + \boldsymbol{\varepsilon}_t' \boldsymbol{\Gamma}^{-1} \tag{5.27}$$

or

$$\underset{1 \times N}{\mathbf{y}_t'} = \underset{1 \times K}{\mathbf{x}_t'} \underset{K \times N}{\boldsymbol{\Pi}} + \underset{1 \times N}{\mathbf{u}_t'} \tag{5.28}$$

where $\boldsymbol{\Pi} = \mathbf{B}\boldsymbol{\Gamma}^{-1}$

$$\mathbf{u}_t' = \boldsymbol{\varepsilon}_t' \boldsymbol{\Gamma}^{-1} \quad \text{or} \quad \mathbf{u}_t = (\boldsymbol{\Gamma}^{-1})' \boldsymbol{\varepsilon}_t$$

The elements of the matrix $\boldsymbol{\Pi}$ are the parameters of the reduced form of the system of equations.

The random term $\mathbf{u}_t$ is distributed with the following mean and covariance:

$$\forall_t: \quad \underset{N \times 1}{E[\mathbf{u}_t]} = 0 \tag{5.29}$$

$$\forall t: \quad E[\mathbf{u}_t \mathbf{u}_t'] = E[(\boldsymbol{\Gamma}^{-1})' \boldsymbol{\varepsilon}_t \boldsymbol{\varepsilon}_t' \boldsymbol{\Gamma}^{-1}] = (\boldsymbol{\Gamma}^{-1})' \boldsymbol{\Sigma} \boldsymbol{\Gamma}^{-1} \tag{5.30}$$

Equation (5.28) represents a straightforward set of equations similar to those discussed in Section 1 for Seemingly Unrelated Regressions. We can always get estimates $\hat{\boldsymbol{\Pi}}$. The issue is "can we go from $\hat{\boldsymbol{\Pi}}$ to $\hat{\boldsymbol{B}}$ and $\hat{\boldsymbol{\Gamma}}$, i.e., is the knowledge about $\hat{\boldsymbol{\Pi}}$ sufficient to enable us to make inferences about the individual coefficients of $\hat{\boldsymbol{B}}$ and $\hat{\boldsymbol{\Gamma}}$?"

Let us write the entire model represented by Equation (5.21) for the T observations ($t = 1, \ldots, T$).

Let

$$\underset{T\times N}{\mathbf{Y}} = \begin{bmatrix} \mathbf{y}_1' \\ \mathbf{y}_2' \\ \vdots \\ \mathbf{y}_t' \\ \vdots \\ \mathbf{y}_T' \end{bmatrix} = \begin{bmatrix} y_{11} & y_{21} & \cdots \\ y_{12} & y_{22} & \cdots \\ \vdots & \vdots & \\ y_{1t} & y_{2t} & \cdots \\ \vdots & \vdots & \\ y_{1T} & y_{2T} & \cdots \end{bmatrix}$$

and

$$\underset{T\times K}{\mathbf{X}} = \begin{bmatrix} \mathbf{x}_1' \\ \mathbf{x}_2' \\ \vdots \\ \mathbf{x}_t' \\ \vdots \\ \mathbf{x}_T' \end{bmatrix} = \begin{bmatrix} x_{11} & x_{21} & \cdots \\ x_{12} & x_{22} & \cdots \\ \vdots & \vdots & \\ x_{1t} & x_{2t} & \cdots \\ \vdots & \vdots & \\ x_{1T} & x_{2T} & \cdots \end{bmatrix}$$

Then, the system of equations is:

$$\underset{T\times N}{\mathbf{Y}}\underset{N\times N}{\mathbf{\Gamma}} = \underset{T\times K}{\mathbf{X}}\underset{K\times N}{\mathbf{B}} + \underset{T\times N}{\mathbf{E}} \tag{5.31}$$

Similarly to what was done above by post-multiplying by the inverse of $\mathbf{\Gamma}$:

$$\mathbf{Y} = \mathbf{XB\Gamma}^{-1} + \mathbf{E\Gamma}^{-1} \tag{5.32}$$

or

$$\underset{T\times N}{\mathbf{Y}} = \underset{T\times K}{\mathbf{X}}\underset{K\times N}{\mathbf{\Pi}} + \underset{T\times N}{\mathbf{U}} \tag{5.33}$$

Because $E[\mathbf{U}] = \mathbf{0}$, the Ordinary Least Squares Estimator of $\mathbf{\Pi}$ are unbiased:

$$\underset{K\times N}{\hat{\mathbf{\Pi}}} = \left(\underset{K\times T}{\mathbf{X}'}\underset{T\times K}{\mathbf{X}}\right)^{-1}\underset{K\times T}{\mathbf{X}'}\underset{T\times N}{\mathbf{Y}} \tag{5.34}$$

Therefore we can predict $\hat{\mathbf{Y}}$.

Why is this useful? Let us consider one equation ($i = 1$). Let $\mathbf{\Gamma} = [\mathbf{\Gamma}_1\mathbf{\Gamma}_2 \ldots \mathbf{\Gamma}_N]$ and $\mathbf{B} = [\mathbf{B}_1\mathbf{B}_2 \ldots \mathbf{B}_N]$

Then, the first equation can be represented by:

$$\underset{T\times N}{\mathbf{Y}}\underset{N\times 1}{\mathbf{\Gamma}_1} = \underset{T\times K}{\mathbf{X}}\underset{K\times 1}{\mathbf{B}_1} + \underset{T\times 1}{\mathbf{e}_1} \tag{5.35}$$

so that

$$\underset{T\times 1}{\mathbf{y}_1}\gamma_{11} + \mathbf{y}_2\gamma_{12} + \cdots + \mathbf{y}_N\gamma_{1N} = \underset{T\times 1}{\mathbf{x}_1}\beta_{11} + \underset{T\times 1}{\mathbf{x}_2}\beta_{12} + \cdots + \underset{T\times 1}{\mathbf{x}_K}\beta_{1K} + \mathbf{e}_1 \tag{5.36}$$

Let $\gamma_{11} = 1$

$$\mathbf{y}_1 = -\mathbf{y}_2\gamma_{12} - \cdots - \mathbf{y}_N\gamma_{1N} + \mathbf{x}_1\beta_{11} + \mathbf{x}_2\beta_{12} + \cdots + \mathbf{x}_K\beta_{1K} + \mathbf{e}_1 \quad (5.37)$$

or

$$\mathbf{y}_1 = \mathbf{Z}_1\boldsymbol{\alpha}_1 + \mathbf{e}_1 \quad (5.38)$$

Why can't we estimate the parameter vector $\boldsymbol{\alpha}$ using Ordinary Least Squares?

The reason is that the estimator would be biased due to the fact that $\mathbf{y}_n$ and $\mathbf{e}_1$ are correlated. This comes from the fact that $\mathbf{y}_n = \mathbf{Z}_n\boldsymbol{\alpha}_n + \mathbf{e}_n$ and $\mathbf{e}_1$ and $\mathbf{e}_n$ are correlated due to $\boldsymbol{\Sigma}$. Indeed, for example with two equations and one exogenous variable in each equation:

$$\begin{aligned} \mathbf{y}_1 &= -\mathbf{y}_2\gamma_{12} + \mathbf{x}_1\beta_{11} + \mathbf{e}_1 \\ \mathbf{y}_2 &= -\mathbf{y}_1\gamma_{21} + \mathbf{x}_2\beta_{22} + \mathbf{e}_2 \end{aligned} \quad (5.39)$$

The covariance matrix between $\mathbf{e}_1$ and $\mathbf{y}_2$ is:

$$\begin{aligned} &E[(\mathbf{e}_1 - E[\mathbf{e}_1])(\mathbf{y}_2 - E[\mathbf{y}_2])'] \\ &\quad = E[\mathbf{e}_1(-\mathbf{y}_1\gamma_{21} + \mathbf{x}_2\beta_{22} + \mathbf{e}_2 - E[-\mathbf{y}_1\gamma_{21} + \mathbf{x}_2\beta_{22} + \mathbf{e}_2])'] \\ &\quad = E[\mathbf{e}_1(-\mathbf{y}_1\gamma_{21} + \mathbf{x}_2\beta_{22} + \mathbf{e}_2 - \mathbf{x}_2\beta_{22} + \gamma_{21}E[\mathbf{y}_1])'] \\ &\quad = E[\mathbf{e}_1(-\mathbf{y}_1\gamma_{21} + \mathbf{e}_2 + \gamma_{21}E[\mathbf{y}_1])'] \\ &\quad = E[\mathbf{e}_1(\mathbf{e}_2 - \gamma_{21}(\mathbf{y}_1 - E[\mathbf{y}_1]))'] \\ &\quad = E[\mathbf{e}_1(\mathbf{e}_2 - \gamma_{21}\mathbf{e}_1)'] = E[\mathbf{e}_1\mathbf{e}_2' - \gamma_{21}\mathbf{e}_1\mathbf{e}_1'] \quad (5.40) \\ &\quad = \sigma_{12}\mathbf{I} - \gamma_{21}\sigma_{11}\mathbf{I} \neq \mathbf{0} \quad (5.41) \end{aligned}$$

Then, what can we do? We can predict $\hat{\mathbf{y}}_1$ from the reduced form which is:

$$\underset{T\times 1}{\mathbf{y}_1} = \underset{T\times K}{\mathbf{X}}\;\underset{K\times 1}{\boldsymbol{\Pi}_1} + \underset{T\times 1}{\mathbf{u}_1} \quad (5.42)$$

This estimation is based on the Ordinary Least Squares estimates of the $\boldsymbol{\Pi}$ parameters which are obtained by regressing $\mathbf{y}_1$ on the entire set of exogenous variables (not just the one in Equation 1, but in all the equations, as follows from Equation (5.42)). The OLS estimator is:

$$\hat{\boldsymbol{\Pi}}_1 = (\mathbf{X}'\mathbf{X})^{-1}\mathbf{X}'\mathbf{y} \quad (5.43)$$

Therefore, the predicted values of $\mathbf{y}_1$ are given by:

$$\hat{\mathbf{y}}_1 = \mathbf{X}\hat{\boldsymbol{\Pi}}_1 \quad (5.44)$$

Note that $\hat{\mathbf{y}}_1$ is not correlated with $\mathbf{e}_1$, because the $\mathbf{X}$'s are uncorrelated with $\mathbf{e}_1$ and that $\hat{\mathbf{y}}_2$ is not correlated with $\mathbf{e}_1$ because $\mathbf{e}_2$ has been removed. Therefore, one can replace $\mathbf{y}_2$ in Equation (5.38) by its predicted value $\hat{\mathbf{y}}_2$.

5.2.2 Two Stage Least Squares: 2SLS

This follows directly from the conclusion derived in the prior section. One can remove the bias introduced by the endogeneity of the dependent variables by first regressing separately each endogenous variable on the full set of exogenous variables and by using the estimated coefficients to predict each endogenous variable. In the second stage, each equation is estimated separately using the model as specified in each equation but replacing the actual values of the endogenous variables specified on the right hand side of the equation by its predicted values as computed from the first stage. More specifically:

Stage 1: Regress using Ordinary Least Squares each $\mathbf{y}$ on all exogenous variables $\mathbf{X}$

$$\mathbf{Y} = \mathbf{X\Pi} + \mathbf{U} \tag{5.45}$$

$$\Rightarrow \hat{\mathbf{\Pi}} = (\mathbf{X'X})^{-1}\mathbf{X'Y} \tag{5.46}$$

and compute the predicted endogenous variables $\mathbf{Y}$:

$$\hat{\mathbf{Y}} = \mathbf{X}\hat{\mathbf{\Pi}} \tag{5.47}$$

Stage 2: Regress using Ordinary Least Squares each $\mathbf{y}_n$ on the exogenous variables of that equation n and on the predicted endogenous as well as exogenous variables specified in that equation:

$$\mathbf{y}_n = \hat{\mathbf{Z}}_n \boldsymbol{\alpha}_n + \mathbf{e}_n \tag{5.48}$$

The parameters estimated $\hat{\mathbf{\Gamma}}_n$ and $\hat{\mathbf{B}}_n$ are unbiased.

However, because the non zero covariances ($\mathbf{\Sigma} \neq \text{diag}(\sigma_{nn})$), the estimation does not provide efficient estimators. The purpose of the third stage in the Three Stage Least Square estimation method is to get efficient estimates, at least asymptotically.

5.2.3 Three Stage Least Squares: 3SLS

The first two stages are identical to those described above for the Two Stage Least Squares estimation. We now add the third stage:

Stage 3: (i) Compute the residuals for each equation from the estimated coefficients obtained in the second stage:

$$\hat{\mathbf{e}}_n = \mathbf{y}_n - \hat{\mathbf{Z}}_n \hat{\boldsymbol{\alpha}}_n \tag{5.49}$$

(ii) Estimate the contemporaneous covariance matrix $\boldsymbol{\Sigma}$

$$\hat{\boldsymbol{\Sigma}} = \begin{bmatrix} \hat{\sigma}_{11} & \hat{\sigma}_{12} & \cdots & \hat{\sigma}_{1N} \\ \hat{\sigma}_{12} & \hat{\sigma}_{22} & \cdots & \vdots \\ \vdots & \vdots & \ddots & \\ \hat{\sigma}_{1\nu} & & & \\ \vdots & & & \\ \hat{\sigma}_{1N} & \cdots & \cdots & \hat{\sigma}_{NN} \end{bmatrix} \tag{5.50}$$

where

$$\hat{\sigma}_{in} = \frac{1}{T-K} \underset{1\times T}{\hat{\mathbf{e}}_i'} \underset{T\times 1}{\hat{\mathbf{e}}_n} \tag{5.51}$$

(iii) Compute the Estimated Generalized Least Squares estimate similarly to the Seemingly Unrelated Regression case with the system of equations

$$\begin{cases} \mathbf{y}_1 = \hat{\mathbf{Z}}_1 \boldsymbol{\alpha}_1 + \mathbf{e}_1 \\ \mathbf{y}_2 = \hat{\mathbf{Z}}_2 \boldsymbol{\alpha}_2 + \mathbf{e}_2 \\ \quad\vdots \\ \mathbf{y}_N = \hat{\mathbf{Z}}_N \boldsymbol{\alpha}_N + \mathbf{e}_N \end{cases}$$

5.3 Simultaneity and Identification

5.3.1 The Problem

The typical example used in economics to discuss the problem of identification concerns the supply and demand inter-relationships. While the curves of supply and demand in the Price–Quantity map can be represented as in Figure 5.1, we only observe P_t and Q_t.

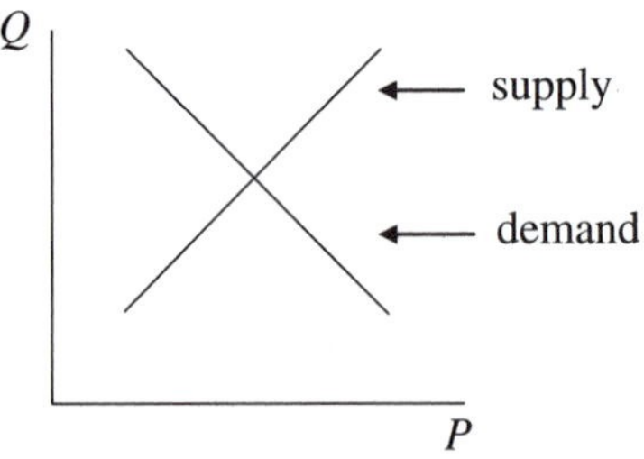

Fig. 5.1 Supply and demand curves.

The question consists, therefore, in determining how we can differentiate empirically between these two curves.

A similar marketing example can be used to illustrate the problem with Sales and Advertising expenditures. While Sales are a function of Advertising expenditures, very often, Advertising budgets reflect the level of sales. This is especially an issue with cross sectional data. Therefore, we are facing the two functions:

$$\text{Equation 1:} \quad S_t = f(A_t) \tag{5.52}$$

$$\text{Equation 2:} \quad A_t = g(S_t) \tag{5.53}$$

The first equation is the market response function. The second equation is the marketing decision function.

Fortunately, sales are not purely driven by advertising in most circumstances. Similarly, the decision regarding the advertising budget is a complex decision.

The solution to the identification problem resides in specifying additional variables that will help differentiate the two curves. It is important to note that these additional variables (exogenous) in each equation must be different across equations; otherwise, the problem remains.

5.3.2 Order and Rank Conditions

5.3.2.1 *Order condition*

If an equation n is identified, then the number of excluded variables in the equation n is at least equal to the number of equations minus 1 (i.e., $N - 1$). Therefore, checking for the order condition consists in making sure that each equation excludes on the right hand side at least $N - 1$ variables (exogenous or endogenous).

This condition is necessary but not sufficient for the system of equations to be identified.

5.3.2.2 *Rank condition*

The rank condition provides necessary and sufficient conditions for identification. Recall the system of equations for a time period or cross section t:

$$\underset{1\times N}{\mathbf{y}'_t}\ \underset{N\times N}{\boldsymbol{\Gamma}} = \underset{1\times K}{\mathbf{x}'_t}\ \underset{K\times N}{\mathbf{B}}\ \underset{1\times N}{\boldsymbol{\varepsilon}'_t} \tag{5.54}$$

We will use the example with two equations which, for a time period t can be written as:

$$(y_{1t} \quad y_{2t}) \begin{pmatrix} \gamma_{11} & \gamma_{21} \\ \gamma_{12} & \gamma_{22} \end{pmatrix} = (x_{1t} \quad x_{2t}) \begin{pmatrix} \beta_{11} & \beta_{21} \\ \beta_{12} & \beta_{22} \end{pmatrix} + (\varepsilon_{1t} \quad \varepsilon_{2t}) \tag{5.55}$$

or

$$\begin{aligned}\gamma_{11}y_{1t} + \gamma_{12}y_{2t} &= \beta_{11}x_{1t} + \beta_{12}x_{2t} + \varepsilon_{1t} \\ \gamma_{21}y_{1t} + \gamma_{22}y_{2t} &= \beta_{21}x_{1t} + \beta_{22}x_{2t} + \varepsilon_{2t}\end{aligned} \tag{5.56}$$

It should be clear from Equation (5.56) that the two equations are indistinguishable. More generally, from Equation (5.54)

$$\mathbf{y}_t'\boldsymbol{\Gamma} - \mathbf{x}_t'\mathbf{B} = \boldsymbol{\varepsilon}_t' \tag{5.57}$$

or

$$(\mathbf{y}_t' \ \mathbf{x}_t')\begin{pmatrix}\boldsymbol{\Gamma} \\ -\mathbf{B}\end{pmatrix} = \boldsymbol{\varepsilon}_t'$$

Let

$$\mathbf{A} = \begin{pmatrix}\boldsymbol{\Gamma} \\ -\mathbf{B}\end{pmatrix} = [\boldsymbol{\alpha}_1\boldsymbol{\alpha}_2 \ldots \boldsymbol{\alpha}_n \ldots \boldsymbol{\alpha}_N] \tag{5.58}$$

Using again the case of two equations expressed in Equation (5.56):

$$\mathbf{A} = \begin{bmatrix}\gamma_{11} & \gamma_{21} \\ \gamma_{12} & \gamma_{22} \\ -\beta_{11} & -\beta_{21} \\ -\beta_{12} & -\beta_{22}\end{bmatrix} = [\boldsymbol{\alpha}_1 \quad \boldsymbol{\alpha}_2] \tag{5.59}$$

Let $\mathbf{r}_n$ be the row vector of zeros and ones which applied to the corresponding column vector $\boldsymbol{\alpha}_n$ defines a restriction imposed on equation n.

For example, the restriction on equation 1 that $\beta_{11} = 0$ can be expressed in a general way as $\mathbf{r}_1\boldsymbol{\alpha}_1 = \mathbf{0}$.

It follows that $\beta_{11} = 0$ by defining $\mathbf{r}_1 = (0\ 0\ 1\ 0)$. Indeed, we have then

$$\mathbf{r}_1\boldsymbol{\alpha}_1 = (0\ 0\ 1\ 0)\begin{pmatrix}\gamma_{11} \\ \gamma_{12} \\ -\beta_{11} \\ -\beta_{12}\end{pmatrix} = \mathbf{0} \tag{5.60}$$

$$\Leftrightarrow \beta_{11} = 0$$

By post-multiplying the restriction vector $\mathbf{r}_n$ by the matrix $\mathbf{A}$, the rank condition for the equation n to be identified is that the rank of this matrix is at least equal to the number of equations minus one. The equation is just identified if $\rho(\mathbf{r}_n\mathbf{A}) = N - 1$. If the rank is less than $N - 1$, the equation is under-identified. If the rank is greater than $N - 1$, the equation is over-identified. The equation must be just or over-identified to be able to obtain parameter estimates. For example:

$$\mathbf{r}_1\mathbf{A} = (0\,0\,1\,0)\begin{bmatrix} \gamma_{11} & \gamma_{21} \\ \gamma_{12} & \gamma_{22} \\ -\beta_{11} & -\beta_{21} \\ -\beta_{12} & -\beta_{22} \end{bmatrix} \tag{5.61}$$

$$= (-\beta_{11} \quad -\beta_{21}) = (0 \quad -\beta_{21}) \tag{5.62}$$

if $\beta_{21} \neq 0$, then $\rho(\mathbf{r}_1\mathbf{A}) = 1$. Because $N - 1 = 1$ $(N = 2)$, the first equation is just identified.

5.4 Summary

In this chapter, we have presented the issue and estimation corresponding to multiple cases of simultaneity of variables. In fact, all the possible cases are embedded in the general case expressed in Equation (5.21).

5.4.1 Structure of Γ Matrix

If the matrix $\mathbf{\Gamma}$ is diagonal, the system of equations is not simultaneous, except as expressed by the correlation of the error terms. In such a case, the model corresponds to the case of Seemingly Unrelated Regressions. If the matrix $\mathbf{\Gamma}$ is not diagonal but triangular, this results in a system which is not truly simultaneous either. In such a case, a dependent variable may affect another one but not the other way around. The system is then recursive. The various estimations which are appropriate for each of these cases is summarized in Figure 5.2.

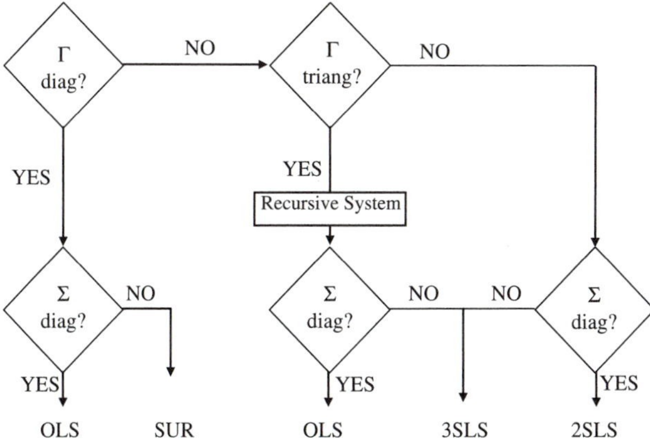

Fig. 5.2 Model specification and estimation methods (adapted from Parsons and Schultz 1976).

Following Figure 5.2, the estimation method depends on the model specification as reflected in the matrix $\mathbf{\Gamma}$ discussed above and in the covariance structure of the error term $\mathbf{\Sigma}$.

5.4.2 Structure of Σ Matrix

When $\mathbf{\Gamma}$ is diagonal, the EGLS estimator provides an efficient estimator if the covariance matrix $\mathbf{\Sigma}$ is not diagonal; otherwise, each equation can be estimated separately by OLS as the results are identical. If the covariance matrix $\mathbf{\Sigma}$ is not diagonal, Seemingly Unrelated Regression must be used.

If the $\mathbf{\Gamma}$ matrix is triangular, i.e., the case of a recursive system, OLS estimation of each equation separately provides unbiased parameter estimates. However, in the case where the covariance matrix $\mathbf{\Sigma}$ is not diagonal, the covariance structure must be taken into consideration and the EGLS obtained from the 3SLS procedure provides an efficient estimator. If $\mathbf{\Sigma}$ is diagonal, there is no need to proceed with multiple stage estimation.

Finally, if the system of equations is simultaneous, i.e., $\mathbf{\Gamma}$ is neither diagonal or triangular, the OLS estimators would be biased. Therefore, depending on whether $\mathbf{\Sigma}$ is diagonal or not, 2SLS or 3SLS should be used.

This points out the importance of knowing the structure of the covariance matrix $\mathbf{\Sigma}$. In most cases, it is an empirical question. Therefore, it is critical to estimate the covariance matrix, to report it and to use the estimator which is appropriate. This means that a test must be performed to check the structure of the error term covariance matrix $\mathbf{\Sigma}$.

5.4.3 Test of Covariance Matrix

The test concerns the hypothesis that the correlation matrix of the error terms is the identity matrix (Morrison 1976):

$$\begin{aligned} H_0&: \quad \mathbf{R} = \mathbf{I} \\ H_1&: \quad \mathbf{R} \neq \mathbf{I} \end{aligned} \tag{5.63}$$

where $\mathbf{R}$ is the correlation matrix computed from the covariance matrix $\mathbf{\Sigma}$.

Two statistical tests are possible.

5.4.3.1 Bartlett's test

The following function of the determinant of the correlation matrix follows a chi square distribution with ν degrees of freedom:

$$-\left(T - 1 - \frac{2N+5}{6}\right)\mathrm{Ln}|\mathbf{R}| = \chi^2_\nu \tag{5.64}$$

where T is the number of observations in each equation, N is the number of equations and $\nu = \frac{1}{2}N(N-1)$, i.e., the number of correlations in the correlation matrix.

5.4.3.2 *Lawley's approximation*

The test statistic as expressed in Equation (5.64) can be approximated by

$$\left(T - 1 - \frac{2N+5}{6}\right)\sum_{i}\sum_{j>i} r_{ij}^2 = \chi_\nu^2$$

where only the upper half of the correlations are considered in the summation.

5.4.4 3SLS versus 2SLS

The EGLS estimator is only asymptotically more efficient than the OLS estimator. Consequently, in small samples, it is not clear what the property of the EGLS estimator is. Therefore, sometimes, when the sample size is small, it may be appropriate to report the 2SLS estimates instead of the 3SLS ones.

5.5 Examples Using SAS

5.5.1 Seemingly Unrelated Regression Example

In the example below, three characteristics of innovations developed by firms are modeled as a function of firm factors and industry characteristics. The SAS file will be presented without going into the details of the substantive content of the model in order to focus on the technical aspects.

In Figure 5.3, it can be seen that after reading the file which contains the data, the variables are standardized and scales are built. The model is specified within the SAS **procedure SYSLIN** for systems of linear equations. The SUR statement following the PROC SYSLIN instruction indicates that the parameters will be estimated using Seemingly Unrelated Regression. The dependent variables concern the relative advantage of the innovation, the radicalness of the innovation and its relative cost. The **model** statements for each equation specifies the independent or predictor variables. Some variables are the same but others are different across equations.

The same model can also be estimated with Iterative Seemingly Related Regression. The only difference with the single iteration SUR in the SAS instructions is that SUR is replaced with ITSUR (see Figure 5.4).

The output of these two estimations is shown in Figures 5.5 and 5.6 respectively.

First, in both cases the OLS estimation is performed for each equation separately and the results are printed in the output.

```
/*    Examp5-1.sas     */
option ls=120;
data raw;
infile ' c:\SAMD\Chapter5\Examples\innov.asc ';
input #1 L1C1 L1C7 L1C10 L1C14 L1C19 L1C21 L1C23 L1C25 L1C27
         L1C29 L1C31 L1C33
      #2 L1C35 L1C37 L1C39 L1C41 L1C43 L1C45 L1C47 L1C49 L1C51
        . . .
/*----MISSING VALUES----*/
IF L1C7 =99 THEN L1C7=.;
IF L1C10=999 THEN L1C10=.;
IF L1C14=999 THEN L1C14=.;
        . . .
/*----reversal of items----*/
L1C21R=7-L1C21;
L1C23R=7-L1C23;
        . . .

/* Standardization of Variables*/
l1c41rs=l1c41r;
L1c45s=l1c45;
L1c53s=l1c53;
l1c55s=l1c55;
        . . .
proc standard mean=0 std=1 out=scale;
  var l1c41rs l1c45s l1c53s l1c55s l1c73s l1c61s l2c19s l1c69s
      l1c33rs l1c39s
        . . .
      L4C11s L4C67s L4C71s l1c59s l2c69s;

data data2;
set scale;
grow0=l1c14;
grow1=l2c7;

tech=sum(of L1C41Rs L1C45s L1C53s L1C55s L1C73s)/
     n(of L1C41Rs L1C45s L1C53s L1C55s L1C73s);

comp1=sum(of L1C59s L1C61s l2c19s)/
     n(of L1C59s L1C61s l2c19s);
        . . .
proc syslin sur;
     model dadvl =  dtol dresl;
     model dradicl = dcoll dtol dgrow0l ddemuncl dresl;
     model dcostl = dtol icl dgrow0l ddemuncl dresl;
run;
```

Fig. 5.3 Example of SAS input file for SUR estimation (examp5-1.sas).

```
proc syslin itsur;
     model dadvl =  dtol dresl;
     model dradicl = dcoll dtol dgrow01 ddemuncl dresl;
     model dcostl = dtol icl dgrow01 ddemuncl dresl;
run;
```

Fig. 5.4 Example of SAS input file for iterative SUR estimation (examp5-2.sas).

```
                          SYSLIN Procedure
                 Ordinary Least Squares Estimation


Model: DADVL
Dependent variable: DADVL

                     Analysis of Variance
                       Sum of        Mean
Source          DF     Squares       Square          F Value     Prob>F
Model            2     16.80451      8.40225         55.467      0.0001
Error          369     55.89682      0.15148
C Total        371     72.70133
          Root MSE      0.38921      R-Square        0.2311
          Dep Mean     -0.02430      Adj R-SQ        0.2270
          C.V.      -1601.97200


                     Parameter Estimates
                   Parameter     Standard    T for H0:
Variable  DF       Estimate         Error   Parameter=0    Prob > |T|
INTERCEP   1      -0.018943      0.020187        -0.938        0.3487
DTOL       1       0.272755      0.048234         5.655        0.0001
DRESL      1       0.223258      0.037982         5.878        0.0001



Model: DRADICL
Dependent variable: DRADICL

                    Analysis of Variance
                        Sum of        Mean
Source          DF     Squares        Square         F Value     Prob>F
Model            5     26.08201      5.21640         27.341      0.0001
Error          366     69.82941      0.19079
C Total        371     95.91142
          Root MSE      0.43680      R-Square        0.2719
          Dep Mean     -0.00971      Adj R-SQ        0.2620
          C.V.      -4500.00823
```

Parameter Estimates

Variable	DF	Parameter Estimate	Standard Error	T for H0: Parameter=0	Prob > |T|
INTERCEP	1	-0.103912	0.043629	-2.382	0.0177
DCO1L	1	-0.082012	0.044723	-1.834	0.0675
DTOL	1	0.611063	0.058287	10.484	0.0001
DGROW0L	1	0.024730	0.009733	2.541	0.0115
DDEMUNCL	1	-0.114126	0.048688	-2.344	0.0196
DRESL	1	-0.066688	0.042855	-1.556	0.1205

Model: DCOSTL
Dependent variable: DCOSTL

Analysis of Variance

Source	DF	Sum of Squares	Mean Square	F Value	Prob>F
Model	5	9.18586	1.83717	7.311	0.0001
Error	366	91.96704	0.25128		
C Total	371	101.15290			

Root MSE	0.50127	R-Square	0.0908
Dep Mean	-0.00616	Adj R-SQ	0.0784
C.V.	-8137.11204		

Parameter Estimates

Variable	DF	Parameter Estimate	Standard Error	T for H0: Parameter=0	Prob > |T|
INTERCEP	1	0.067374	0.049987	1.348	0.1785
DTOL	1	0.168913	0.066888	2.525	0.0120
IC1	1	-0.165205	0.039087	-4.227	0.0001
DGROW0L	1	-0.018627	0.011156	-1.670	0.0958
DDEMUNCL	1	-0.151016	0.055812	-2.706	0.0071
DRESL	1	0.129375	0.049100	2.635	0.0088

Seemingly Unrelated Regression Estimation

Cross Model Covariance

Sigma	DADVL	DRADICL	DCOSTL
DADVL	0.1514819026	0.0184780345	-0.022327822
DRADICL	0.0184780345	0.190790749	0.0047738768
DCOSTL	-0.022327822	0.0047738768	0.2512760723

Cross Model Correlation

Corr	DADVL	DRADICL	DCOSTL
DADVL	1	0.1086917903	-0.114443313
DRADICL	0.1086917903	1	0.0218030364
DCOSTL	-0.114443313	0.0218030364	1

Cross Model Inverse Correlation

Inv Corr	DADVL	DRADICL	DCOSTL
DADVL	1.026131149	-0.114146708	0.1199225933
DRADICL	-0.114146708	1.0131732649	-0.035153581
DCOSTL	0.1199225933	-0.035153581	1.0144907937

```
                   Cross Model Inverse Covariance
Inv Sigma                DADVL            DRADICL              DCOSTL
DADVL           6.7739520783       -0.671435594        0.6146743188
DRADICL         -0.671435594       5.3103898921        -0.160551863
DCOSTL          0.6146743188       -0.160551863        4.0373553464

   System Weighted MSE:  0.99999 with 1101 degrees of freedom.
   System Weighted R-Square:  0.2007


Model: DADVL
Dependent variable: DADVL

                    Parameter Estimates
                Parameter      Standard     T for H0:
Variable  DF     Estimate         Error   Parameter=0     Prob > |T|
INTERCEP   1    -0.018943      0.020187        -0.938         0.3487
DTOL       1     0.272755      0.048234         5.655         0.0001
DRESL      1     0.223258      0.037982         5.878         0.0001


Model: DRADICL
Dependent variable: DRADICL

                    Parameter Estimates
                Parameter      Standard     T for H0:
Variable  DF     Estimate         Error   Parameter=0     Prob > |T|
INTERCEP   1    -0.105821      0.043440        -2.436         0.0153
DCO1L      1    -0.084707      0.044444        -1.906         0.0574
DTOL       1     0.612306      0.058237        10.514         0.0001
DGROW0L    1     0.025224      0.009675         2.607         0.0095
DDEMUNCL   1    -0.112170      0.048400        -2.318         0.0210
DRESL      1    -0.066688      0.042852        -1.556         0.1205


Model: DCOSTL
Dependent variable: DCOSTL

                      Parameter Estimates
                Parameter      Standard     T for H0:
Variable  DF     Estimate         Error   Parameter=0     Prob > |T|
INTERCEP   1     0.069499      0.049748         1.397         0.1633
DTOL       1     0.169196      0.066825         2.532         0.0118
IC1        1    -0.165555      0.038818        -4.265         0.0001
DGROW0L    1    -0.019188      0.011083        -1.731         0.0842
DDEMUNCL   1    -0.153609      0.055445        -2.770         0.0059
DRESL      1     0.129626      0.049097         2.640         0.0086
```

Fig. 5.5 Example of SAS output file for SUR estimation (examp5-1.lst).

```
        Iterative Seemingly Unrelated Regression Estimation
                          Cross Model Covariance
Sigma                    DADVL             DRADICL              DCOSTL
DADVL             0.1514819026        0.0185171321        -0.022348653
DRADICL           0.0185171321        0.1907948382        0.0047481056
DCOSTL            -0.022348653        0.0047481056        0.2512793046

                         Cross Model Correlation
Corr                     DADVL             DRADICL              DCOSTL
DADVL                        1        0.1089206033        -0.114549349
DRADICL           0.1089206033                   1        0.0216849635
DCOSTL            -0.114549349        0.0216849635                   1

                     Cross Model Inverse Correlation
Inv Corr                  DADVL             DRADICL              DCOSTL
DADVL               1.026207679        -0.114378043         0.120031705
DRADICL            -0.114378043        1.0132186939        -0.035073541
DCOSTL              0.120031705        -0.035073541        1.0145101221

                      Cross Model Inverse Covariance
Inv Sigma                  DADVL             DRADICL              DCOSTL
DADVL               6.7744572875        -0.672789142        0.6152296236
DRADICL             -0.672789142        5.3105141817        -0.160183559
DCOSTL              0.6152296236        -0.160183559        4.0373803318

System Weighted MSE:  1 with 1101 degrees of freedom.
System Weighted R-Square:  0.2007


Model: DADVL
Dependent variable: DADVL

                         Parameter Estimates
                    Parameter      Standard    T for H0:
Variable  DF         Estimate         Error  Parameter=0     Prob > |T|
INTERCEP   1        -0.018943      0.020187       -0.938         0.3487
DTOL       1         0.272755      0.048234        5.655         0.0001
DRESL      1         0.223258      0.037982        5.878         0.0001


Model: DRADICL
Dependent variable: DRADICL

                         Parameter Estimates
                    Parameter      Standard    T for H0:
Variable  DF         Estimate         Error  Parameter=0     Prob > |T|
INTERCEP   1        -0.105825      0.043440       -2.436         0.0153
DCO1L      1        -0.084717      0.044443       -1.906         0.0574
DTOL       1         0.612311      0.058237       10.514         0.0001
DGROW0L    1         0.025226      0.009675        2.607         0.0095
DDEMUNCL   1        -0.112166      0.048399       -2.318         0.0210
DRESL      1        -0.066688      0.042852       -1.556         0.1205
```

```
Model: DCOSTL
Dependent variable: DCOSTL

                        Parameter Estimates
                  Parameter      Standard     T for H0:
Variable   DF      Estimate         Error   Parameter=0     Prob > |T|
INTERCEP    1      0.069501      0.049748         1.397         0.1632
DTOL        1      0.169194      0.066825         2.532         0.0118
IC1         1     -0.165553      0.038818        -4.265         0.0001
DGROWOL     1     -0.019189      0.011083        -1.731         0.0842
DDEMUNCL    1     -0.153611      0.055445        -2.771         0.0059
DRESL       1      0.129626      0.049098         2.640         0.0086
```

Fig. 5.6 Example of SAS output file for iterative SUR estimation (examp5-2.lst).

The correlations from the residuals estimated from the OLS estimates are then shown. A test should be performed to check that the correlation matrix is statistically significant from the identity matrix in order to detect whether it is useful to use the SUR estimator.

Finally, the SUR estimates (i.e., the EGLS estimator) are provided for each equation.

It can be seen from the output of the Iterative Seemingly Unrelated Regression that the steps are identical. The estimates reported are those obtained at the last step when convergence is achieved.

5.5.2 Two Stage Least Squares Example

In the example for two and three stage least squares, we now specify some endogeneity in the system in that some variables on the left hand side of an equation can also be found on the right hand side of another equation. In the example shown in Figure 5.7, the model definition shows that the variable "dadvl" is a predicted variable and is also found in the equation to predict "dcostl".

The endogenous variables are identified in a statement which lists the variable names after the identifier "ENDOGENOUS".

The statement "INSTRUMENTS" lists all the exogenous variables in the system. These variables will be used in stage 1 of the estimation procedure to calculate the predicted values of the endogenous variables which will be used for the estimation in the second stage.

The estimation method is simply indicated on the same procedure line by "2SLS".

The output shown in Figure 5.8 provides the estimates of the second stage for each equation.

```
/*    Examp5-3.sas */
          . . .

proc syslin 2SLS;
     endogenous dadvl dradicl dcostl;
     instruments dcoll dtol icl dresl dgrow01 ddemuncl;
     model dadvl =  dradicl dtol dresl;
     model dradicl = dcoll dtol dgrow01 ddemuncl dresl;
     model dcostl = dradicl dadvl dtol icl;
run;
```

Fig. 5.7 Example of SAS input file for two stage least squares estimation (examp5-3.sas).

```
                    SYSLIN Procedure
            Two-Stage Least Squares Estimation
Model: DADVL
Dependent variable: DADVL

                  Analysis of Variance
                     Sum of        Mean
Source        DF    Squares      Square      F Value      Prob>F
Model          3   16.84679     5.61560       35.317      0.0001
Error        368   58.51337     0.15900
C Total      371   72.70133
        Root MSE    0.39875    R-Square       0.2236
        Dep Mean   -0.02430    Adj R-SQ       0.2172
        C.V.    -1641.26304

                   Parameter Estimates
                Parameter      Standard    T for H0:
Variable  DF     Estimate         Error  Parameter=0    Prob > |T|
INTERCEP   1    -0.019782      0.020746       -0.954        0.3410
DRADICL    1    -0.120184      0.233060       -0.516        0.6064
DTOL       1     0.342387      0.143788        2.381        0.0178
DRESL      1     0.214282      0.042630        5.027        0.0001

Model: DRADICL
Dependent variable: DRADICL

                 Analysis of Variance
                     Sum of        Mean
Source        DF    Squares      Square      F Value      Prob>F
Model          5   26.08201     5.21640       27.341      0.0001
Error        366   69.82941     0.19079
C Total      371   95.91142
        Root MSE    0.43680    R-Square       0.2719
        Dep Mean   -0.00971    Adj R-SQ       0.2620
        C.V.    -4500.00823
```

```
                    Parameter Estimates
              Parameter      Standard    T for H0:
Variable  DF   Estimate         Error  Parameter=0   Prob > |T|
INTERCEP   1  -0.103912      0.043629       -2.382       0.0177
DCO1L      1  -0.082012      0.044723       -1.834       0.0675
DTOL       1   0.611063      0.058287       10.484       0.0001
DGROW0L    1   0.024730      0.009733        2.541       0.0115
DDEMUNCL   1  -0.114126      0.048688       -2.344       0.0196
DRESL      1  -0.066688      0.042855       -1.556       0.1205


Model: DCOSTL
Dependent variable: DCOSTL

                  Analysis of Variance
                      Sum of        Mean
Source          DF   Squares      Square      F Value       Prob>F
Model            4   7.24071     1.81018        4.530       0.0014
Error          367 146.66736     0.39964
C Total        371 101.15290
      Root MSE       0.63217    R-Square       0.0470
      Dep Mean      -0.00616    Adj R-SQ       0.0367
      C.V.      -10261.91552

                    Parameter Estimates
              Parameter      Standard    T for H0:
Variable  DF   Estimate         Error  Parameter=0   Prob > |T|
INTERCEP   1   0.013729      0.033768        0.407       0.6846
DRADICL    1   0.410360      0.387537        1.059       0.2903
DADVL      1   0.698638      0.309916        2.254       0.0248
DTOL       1  -0.268182      0.300295       -0.893       0.3724
IC1        1  -0.158223      0.049659       -3.186       0.0016
```

Fig. 5.8 Example of SAS output file for two stage least squares estimation (examp5-3.lst).

5.5.3 Three Stage Least Squares Example

Similarly to the case of two stage least squares, the estimation method is simply indicated on the SYSLIN procedure line by “3SLS”, as shown in Figure 5.9. All other statements are identical to those for two stage least squares.

The output for the 3SLS procedure provides first the estimates of the second stage for each equation (they are not shown in Figure 5.10 because they are identical to the SAS output shown in Figure 5.8. In Figure 5.10, however, the estimated correlation matrix of the error terms across equations are shown. A test of significance of the set of correlations can then be performed to know whether it can be useful to continue to the third stage. These third stage EGLS estimates are then provided in the SAS output.

```
/*     Examp5-4.sas    */
          . . .
proc syslin 3SLS;
     endogenous dadvl dradicl dcostl;
     instruments dcoll dtol icl dresl dgrow0l ddemuncl;
     model dadvl =  dradicl dtol dresl;
     model dradicl = dcoll dtol dgrow0l ddemuncl dresl;
     model dcostl = dradicl dadvl dtol icl;
run;
```

Fig. 5.9 Example of SAS input file for three stage least squares estimation (examp5-4.sas).

```
                         SYSLIN Procedure
               Three-Stage Least Squares Estimation

                     Cross Model Covariance
Sigma                  DADVL             DRADICL              DCOSTL

DADVL             0.1590037214      0.0413708009        -0.145342782
DRADICL           0.0413708009       0.190790749        -0.086434385
DCOSTL            -0.145342782      -0.086434385        0.3996385859

                      Cross Model Correlation
Corr                   DADVL             DRADICL              DCOSTL
DADVL                        1      0.2375262586        -0.576575413
DRADICL           0.2375262586                 1         -0.31302151
DCOSTL            -0.576575413       -0.31302151                   1

                  Cross Model Inverse Correlation
Inv Corr                DADVL             DRADICL              DCOSTL
DADVL              1.5061305177      -0.095251306        0.8385821181
DRADICL            -0.095251306        1.11464982        0.2939898081
DCOSTL             0.8385821181      0.2939898081        1.5755309649

                    Cross Model Inverse Covariance
Inv Sigma                DADVL             DRADICL              DCOSTL
DADVL                9.47229728      -0.546875716        3.3266586966
DRADICL            -0.546875716      5.8422634531        1.0646819995
DCOSTL             3.3266586966      1.0646819995        3.9423895005

System Weighted MSE:  1.136 with 1101 degrees of freedom.
System Weighted R-Square:  0.2316

Model: DADVL
Dependent variable: DADVL
```

```
                         Parameter Estimates
                   Parameter        Standard      T for H0:
Variable    DF      Estimate           Error    Parameter=0      Prob > |T|
INTERCEP     1     -0.020085        0.020745         -0.968          0.3336
DRADICL      1     -0.152241        0.232423         -0.655          0.5129
DTOL         1      0.364254        0.143318          2.542          0.0114
DRESL        1      0.205408        0.042269          4.860          0.0001


Model: DRADICL
Dependent variable: DRADICL

                          Parameter Estimates
                   Parameter        Standard      T for H0:
Variable    DF      Estimate           Error    Parameter=0      Prob > |T|
INTERCEP     1     -0.085557        0.042677         -2.005          0.0457
DCO1L        1     -0.090347        0.043264         -2.088          0.0375
DTOL         1      0.617819        0.058045         10.644          0.0001
DGROW0L      1      0.019859        0.009431          2.106          0.0359
DDEMUNCL     1     -0.126772        0.047199         -2.686          0.0076
DRESL        1     -0.068505        0.042754         -1.602          0.1099


Model: DCOSTL
Dependent variable: DCOSTL

                          Parameter Estimates
                   Parameter        Standard      T for H0:
Variable    DF      Estimate           Error    Parameter=0      Prob > |T|
INTERCEP     1      0.015590        0.033752          0.462          0.6444
DRADICL      1      0.485863        0.384568          1.263          0.2072
DADVL        1      0.767383        0.307292          2.497          0.0130
DTOL         1     -0.341931        0.296109         -1.155          0.2489
IC1          1     -0.148658        0.039986         -3.718          0.0002
```

Fig. 5.10 Example of SAS output file for three stage least squares estimation (examp5-4.lst).

5.6 Assignment

The data found in the files INDUP.CSV and PANEL.CSV which are described in the Appendix and for which Chapter 4 described how to read the data in SAS provide opportunities to apply the systems of equations discussed in this Chapter. The assignment consists simply in specifying a system of equations to be estimated via the proper estimation method, as presented in this chapter. The modeling exercise should include (1) a system of seemingly unrelated equations or a recursive system and (2) a model with simultaneous relationships.

Examples of such models can concern the following:

1. A model of the hierarchy of effects which consists in awareness, purchase intentions and sales.
2. A model of the sales or market share for multiple segments or for multiple brands.
3. A model of a market response function and marketing decision functions.

Proper justification of the estimation method used must be included (i.e., test of the covariance structure of the error terms).

References

Basic Technical Readings

Dhrymes, P. J. (1978), *Introductory Econometrics*, New York, NY: Spriner-Verlag New York Inc. [Chapter 6].

Judge, G. G., W. E. Griffiths, R. C. Hill, H. Lutkepohl and T.-C. Lee (1985), *The Theory and Practice of Econometrics*, New York, NY: John Wiley & Sons [Chapters 14 and 15].

Morrison, D. F. (1976), *Multivariate Statistical Methods*, New York, NY: McGraw-Hill Book Company.

Parsons, L. J. and R. L. Schultz (1976), *Marketing Models and Econometric Research*, New York, NY: North Holland.

Theil, H. (1971), *Principles of Econometrics*, John Wiley & Sons, Inc. [Chapters 9 and 10].

Application Readings

Bass, F. M. (1969), "A Simultaneous Equation Regression Study of Advertising and Sales of Cigarettes," *Journal of Marketing Research*, 6 (August), 291–300.

Bayus, B. L. and W. P. Putsis, Jr. (1999), "Product Proliferation: An Empirical Analysis of Product Line Determinants and Market Outcomes," *Marketing Science*, 18, 2, 137–153.

Beckwith, N. E. (1972), "Multivariate Analysis Sales Responses of Competing Brands to Advertising," *Journal of Marketing Research*, May, 168-.

Cool, K. and I. Dierickx (1993), "Rivalry, Strategic Groups and Firm Profitability," *Strategic Management Journal*, 14, 47–59.

Cool, K. and D. Schendel (1988), "Performance Differences Among Strategic Group Members," *Strategic Management Journal*, 9, 207–223.

Gatignon, H. and J.-M. Xuereb (1997), "Strategic Orientation of the Firm and New Product Performance," *Journal of Marketing Research*, 34, 1 (February), 77–90.

Lambin, J.-J., P. Naert and A. Bultez (1975), "Optimal Marketing Behavior in Oligopoly," *European Economic Review*, 6, 105–128.

Metwally, M. M. (1978), "Escalation Tendencies of Advertising," *Oxford Bulletin of Statistics*, 243–256.

Norton, J. A. and F. M. Bass (1986), "Diffusion and Theory Model of Adoption and Substitution for Successive Generations of High-Technology Products," *Management Science*, 33, 9 (September), 1069–1086.

Parker, P. M. and L.-H. Roller (1997), "Collusive Conduct in Duopolies: Multimarket Contact and Cross-Ownership in the Mobile Telephone Industry," *RAND Journal of Economics* 28, 2 (Summer), 304–322.

Reibstein, D. and H. Gatignon (1984), "Optimal Product Line Pricing: The Influence of Elasticities and Cross-Elasticities," *Journal of Marketing Research*, 21, 3 (August), 259–267.

Schultz, R. L. (1971), "Market Measurement and Planning With a Simultaneous Equation Model," *Journal of Marketing Research*, 8 (May), 153–164.

Wildt, A. (1974), "Multifirm analysis of Competitive Decision Variables," *Journal of Marketing Research*, 8 (May), 153–164.

6. Categorical Dependent Variables

In this chapter, we consider statistical models to analyze variables where the numbering does not have any meaning and, in particular, where there is no relationship between one level of the variable and another level. In these cases, we are typically trying to establish whether it is possible to explain with other variables the level observed of the criterion variable. The chapter is divided in two parts. The first part presents discriminant analysis, which is a traditional method in multivariate statistical analysis. The second part introduces quantal choice statistical models. The models are described, as well as their estimation. Their measures of fit are also discussed.

6.1 Discriminant Analysis

In presenting discriminant analysis, the discriminant criterion, which is at the basis of understanding of the methodology, is first introduced. Then the derivation and the explanation of the discriminant functions are provided. Finally, issues of classification and measures of fit are discussed.

6.1.1 The Discriminant Criterion

The objective in discriminant analysis is to determine a linear combination of a set of variables such that several group means will differ widely on this linear combination.

Let p = number of independent variables, N = number of observations, N_j = number of observations for group $j = 1, \ldots, K$, K = number of groups, $\underset{1\times p}{\mathbf{x}_i'}$ is the vector representing the values on p variables for one observation i, $\underset{p\times 1}{\mathbf{v}}$ is the vector of weights to be attributed to each of the p variables to form a linear combination. Therefore, this linear combination is given by Equation (6.1):

$$\underset{1\times 1}{\mathbf{y}_i} = \underset{1\times p}{\mathbf{x}_i'} \underset{p\times 1}{\mathbf{v}} = v_1 x_{i1} + v_2 x_{i2} + \cdots + v_p x_{ip} \tag{6.1}$$

We will assume that $\mathbf{x}_i$ follows a multivariate normal distribution. It follows that each $\mathbf{y}_i$ is normally distributed.

The problem consists in finding $\mathbf{v}$ which is going to maximize the F-ratio for testing the significance of the overall difference among several group means on a *single variable* y.

This value F is given by the ratio of the between group variance to the pooled within group variance of the variable y:

$$F = \frac{SS_b(\mathbf{y})/(K-1)}{SS_w(\mathbf{y})/(N-K)} \tag{6.2}$$

where N = number of observations or individuals, K = number of groups, $SS_b(\mathbf{y})$ = between group sum of squares, $SS_w(\mathbf{y})$ = pooled within group sum of squares.

In the case where there are only two groups and one single variable ($K = 2$, $p = 1$), it is the classic t test of a difference of two means. The problem, therefore, is to find the value of $\mathbf{v}$ which will maximize F.

The ratio $(K-1)/(N-K)$ is a constant; therefore,

$$\operatorname*{Max}_{\mathbf{v}} F \Leftrightarrow \operatorname*{Max}_{\mathbf{v}} \frac{SS_b(\mathbf{y})}{SS_w(\mathbf{y})} = \lambda.$$

The pooled within group sum of squares is the sum over the groups (j) of the squares of the deviations of variable y from their group mean.

$$SS_w(\mathbf{y}) = \sum_{j=1}^{K} SS_j(\mathbf{y}) \tag{6.3}$$

For each group j (where $j = 1, \ldots, K$), we can write the vector of the values obtained from the linear combination of the variables. This vector has N_j elements corresponding to the number of observations in group j.

Let

$$\forall j: \quad \underset{N_j \times 1}{\mathbf{y}_j^d} = \underset{N_j \times p}{(\mathbf{X}_j - \overline{\mathbf{X}}_j)} \underset{p \times 1}{\mathbf{v}} = \mathbf{X}_j^d \mathbf{v} \tag{6.4}$$

Then,

$$SS_j(\mathbf{y}) = \mathbf{y}_j^{d'} \mathbf{y}_j^d = \mathbf{v}' \underset{p \times p}{\mathbf{X}_j^{d'} \mathbf{X}_j^d} \mathbf{v} = \mathbf{v}' \mathbf{S}_j \mathbf{v} \tag{6.5}$$

where $\mathbf{S}_j = \mathbf{X}_j^{d'} \mathbf{X}_j^d$. Therefore,

$$\begin{aligned} SS_w(\mathbf{y}) &= \sum_{j=1}^{K} \mathbf{v}' \mathbf{S}_j \mathbf{v} \\ &= \mathbf{v}' \left(\sum_{j=1}^{K} \mathbf{S}_j \right) \mathbf{v} \end{aligned} \tag{6.6}$$

Let

$$\mathbf{W} = \sum_{j=1}^{K} \mathbf{S}_j \tag{6.7}$$

Then,

$$SS_w(\mathbf{y}) = \mathbf{v}'\mathbf{W}\mathbf{v} \tag{6.8}$$

Let

$\underset{N_j \times p}{\overline{\mathbf{X}}_j}$ = matrix composed of the vector of the means for group j of the p variables, repeated N_j times

and let

$$\underset{N \times p}{\overline{\mathbf{X}}} = \begin{bmatrix} \overline{\mathbf{X}}_1 \\ \overline{\mathbf{X}}_2 \\ \vdots \\ \overline{\mathbf{X}}_K \end{bmatrix}$$

$\underset{N \times p}{\overline{\overline{\mathbf{X}}}}$ = matrix composed of the vector of grand means (across all groups) repeated N times.

$$\mathbf{B} = (\overline{\mathbf{X}} - \overline{\overline{\mathbf{X}}})'(\overline{\mathbf{X}} - \overline{\overline{\mathbf{X}}}) \tag{6.9}$$

Therefore,

$$SS_b(\mathbf{y}) = \mathbf{v}'\mathbf{B}\mathbf{v} \tag{6.10}$$

and consequently,

$$\boldsymbol{\lambda} = \frac{\mathbf{v}'\mathbf{B}\mathbf{v}}{\mathbf{v}'\mathbf{W}\mathbf{v}} \tag{6.11}$$

We can maximize $\boldsymbol{\lambda}$ (the discriminant criterion) by taking the first derivative relative to $\mathbf{v}$ and setting it equal to 0 (we use the matrix derivation rule A.2 in Appendix A: $(\partial \mathbf{v}'\mathbf{A}\mathbf{v}/\partial \mathbf{v}) = 2\mathbf{A}\mathbf{v}$:

$$\frac{\partial \boldsymbol{\lambda}}{\underset{p\times 1}{\partial \mathbf{v}}} = \frac{\underset{1\times 1}{(\mathbf{v}'\mathbf{W}\mathbf{v})}(2\underset{p\times p}{\mathbf{B}}\underset{p\times 1}{\mathbf{v}}) - \underset{1\times 1}{(\mathbf{v}'\mathbf{B}\mathbf{v})}(2\underset{p\times p}{\mathbf{W}}\underset{p\times 1}{\mathbf{v}})}{\underset{1\times 1}{(\mathbf{v}'\mathbf{W}\mathbf{v})^2}} = \mathbf{0} \tag{6.12}$$

After replacing $\mathbf{v}'\mathbf{B}\mathbf{v}$ by $\boldsymbol{\lambda}\mathbf{v}'\mathbf{W}\mathbf{v}$, which follows from Equation (6.11), in Equation (6.12), it becomes:

$$\underset{p\times 1}{\frac{\partial \boldsymbol{\lambda}}{\partial \mathbf{v}}} = 2\left[\frac{\mathbf{B}\mathbf{v}}{\mathbf{v}'\mathbf{W}\mathbf{v}} - \frac{\boldsymbol{\lambda}\mathbf{W}\mathbf{v}}{\mathbf{v}'\mathbf{W}\mathbf{v}}\right] = 0 \tag{6.13}$$

$$\frac{\mathbf{B}\mathbf{v} - \boldsymbol{\lambda}\mathbf{W}\mathbf{v}}{\mathbf{v}'\mathbf{W}\mathbf{v}} = 0 \tag{6.14}$$

$$\mathbf{B}\mathbf{v} - \boldsymbol{\lambda}\mathbf{W}\mathbf{v} = \mathbf{0} \tag{6.15}$$

$$(\mathbf{B} - \boldsymbol{\lambda}\mathbf{W})\mathbf{v} = \mathbf{0} \tag{6.16}$$

which premultiplying by $\mathbf{W}^{-1}$ gives:

$$(\mathbf{W}^{-1}\mathbf{B} - \boldsymbol{\lambda}\mathbf{I})\mathbf{v} = \mathbf{0} \tag{6.17}$$

Therefore, the solution for $\boldsymbol{\lambda}$ is given by the eigenvalues of $\mathbf{W}^{-1}\mathbf{B}$, and the solution for $\mathbf{v}$ is given by the corresponding eigenvectors of $\mathbf{W}^{-1}\mathbf{B}$.

6.1.2 Discriminant Function

The matrix $\mathbf{W}^{-1}\mathbf{B}$ is not symmetric. In fact, there are $K-1$ linearly independent rows in $\bar{\mathbf{X}} - \bar{\bar{\mathbf{X}}}$.

Consequently, the rank of $\mathbf{B}$ is $K-1$. $\mathbf{W}^{-1}$ is of full rank (p); if it were singular, it could not be inverted.

Therefore, the number of non-zero eigenvalues is the smaller of the rank of $\mathbf{W}^{-1}$ and of $\mathbf{B}$, which is usually $K-1$ (following from the fact that typically there are more variables than groups, i.e., $K-1 < p$).

This means that discriminant analysis provides $K-1$ non-zero eigenvalues and $K-1$ discriminant functions.

The first discriminant function $\mathbf{v}_1$ has the largest discriminant criterion value λ_1 (eigenvalue), and each of the others has a *conditionally* maximal discriminant criterion value.

The centroids for each group j consist of the mean value of y for the group for each of the $K-1$ eigenvectors or discriminating functions:

$$\bar{y}_{1j}, \bar{y}_{2j}, \ldots, \bar{y}_{rj}, \ldots, \bar{y}_{K-1,j} \tag{6.18}$$

where r represents the index for the rth eigenvalue and eigenvector:

$$\bar{y}_{rj} = \bar{\mathbf{x}}_j'\mathbf{v}_r \tag{6.19}$$

These are the dimensions along which one can find the largest differences across groups.

6.1.2.1 Special case of $K = 2$

It is possible to estimate a multiple regression equation where the dependent variable is a dummy variable (0 for alternative 1 and 1 for the other alternative). Such a regression would yield weights for the independent variables which would be proportional to the discriminant weights. However, it is important to note that the t statistics should not be used. Indeed, the errors are not normally distributed with mean 0 and variance $\sigma^2\mathbf{I}$, as will be demonstrated in the sections below.

6.1.3 Classification and Fit

6.1.3.1 Classification

The issue we need to address now concerns how to classify the observations.

A group prediction can be made, based on the value of the linear combination obtained from the first discriminant function:

$$\hat{y}_{1i} = \mathbf{x}_i'\hat{\mathbf{v}}_1 \tag{6.20}$$

The group prediction then depends on the value obtained in Equation (6.20), relative to a critical value $y_{1\text{crit}}$, i.e., based on the sign of

$$\hat{y}_{1i} - y_{1\text{crit}} \tag{6.21}$$

The rule can then be based on the distance from group means: assign observation i to the group to which it is closest (corrected for covariance). The mid points are then used as the critical values.

For example in the two-group case, there is a single eigenvector:

$$\mathbf{v} = \mathbf{W}^{-1}(\bar{\mathbf{x}}_1 - \bar{\mathbf{x}}_2) \tag{6.22}$$

$$y = \mathbf{x}'\mathbf{W}^{-1}(\bar{\mathbf{x}}_1 - \bar{\mathbf{x}}_2) \tag{6.23}$$

$$\text{Group 1} \quad \bar{y}_1 = \bar{\mathbf{x}}_1'\mathbf{W}^{-1}(\bar{\mathbf{x}}_1 - \bar{\mathbf{x}}_2) \tag{6.24}$$

$$\text{Group 2} \quad \bar{y}_2 = \bar{\mathbf{x}}_2'\mathbf{W}^{-1}(\bar{\mathbf{x}}_1 - \bar{\mathbf{x}}_2) \tag{6.25}$$

The classification is based on the mid point:

$$y_{\text{crit}} = \tfrac{1}{2}(\bar{y}_1 + \bar{y}_2) \Rightarrow y_{\text{crit}} = \tfrac{1}{2}(\bar{\mathbf{x}}_1 + \bar{\mathbf{x}}_2)'\mathbf{W}^{-1}(\bar{\mathbf{x}}_1 + \bar{\mathbf{x}}_2) \tag{6.26}$$

Then the classification rule is:

$$\text{if } y_{1i} < y_{\text{crit}} \Rightarrow i \in \text{ Group 1 else } i \in \text{ Group 2},$$

which is equivalent to defining w as:

$$w = y_i - y_{\text{crit}}$$

Then, if $w < 0$ then $i \in$ Group 1 else $i \in$ Group 2. Graphically, this is represented on Figure 6.1 below, where the dotted vertical line represents the

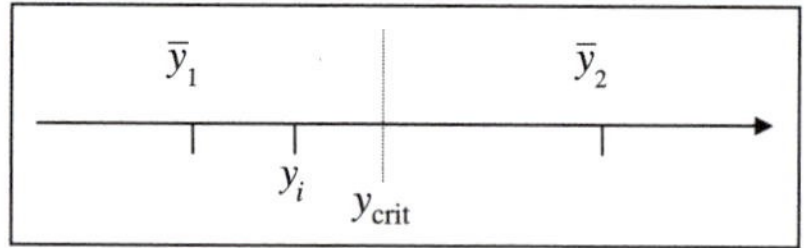

Fig. 6.1 Classification of observations.

critical value appearing at the mid point between the mean of each of the two groups $\bar{y}_1$ and $\bar{y}_2$.

As discussed above:

$$y_i < y_{\text{crit}} \Rightarrow i \in \text{ Group 1}$$

or equivalently:

$$w = y_i - y_{\text{crit}} < 0 \Rightarrow i \in \text{ Group 1}$$

For more than two groups (i.e., $K > 2$), similar concepts apply.

Let

$$w_{jk}(i) = \underbrace{\mathbf{x}_i'\mathbf{W}^{-1}(\bar{\mathbf{x}}_j - \bar{\mathbf{x}}_k)}_{y_i} - \underbrace{\tfrac{1}{2}(\bar{\mathbf{x}}_j + \bar{\mathbf{x}}_k)'\mathbf{W}^{-1}(\bar{\mathbf{x}}_j - \bar{\mathbf{x}}_k)}_{y_{\text{crit}}} \tag{6.27}$$

The rule consists of assigning i to group j if $w_{jk}(i) > 0$ for all $k \neq j$, which means that y_i is closer to k than to j. For example, for three groups: $K = 3$. We can compute w_{12}, w_{13}, w_{23} (note that $w_{21} = -w_{12}$). But because $w_{23} = w_{13} - w_{12}$, we do not need w_{23}.

Then we can classify i as belonging to

$$\begin{array}{ll} \text{Group 1} & \text{if } w_{12} > 0 \text{ and } w_{13} > 0 \\ \text{Group 2} & \text{if } w_{12} < 0 \text{ and } w_{13} > w_{12} \\ \text{Group 3} & \text{if } w_{13} < 0 \text{ and } w_{12} > w_{13} \end{array}$$

For more than two groups, a plot of the centroids $\bar{y}_j$ on the discriminant functions as axes can help to interpret them.

6.1.3.2 Measures of fit

Fit measures are based on the ability of the discriminant functions to classify observations correctly. This information is contained in the classification table, as shown in Figure 6.2.

Percent correctly classified

The classification table is a $K \times K$ matrix which indicates the number or percentage of observations which are part of each group and which have been classified into that group (correctly classified) or into another group.

It can be seen in Figure 6.2 that the diagonal cells represent the observations which are correctly classified. The percentage of correctly classified

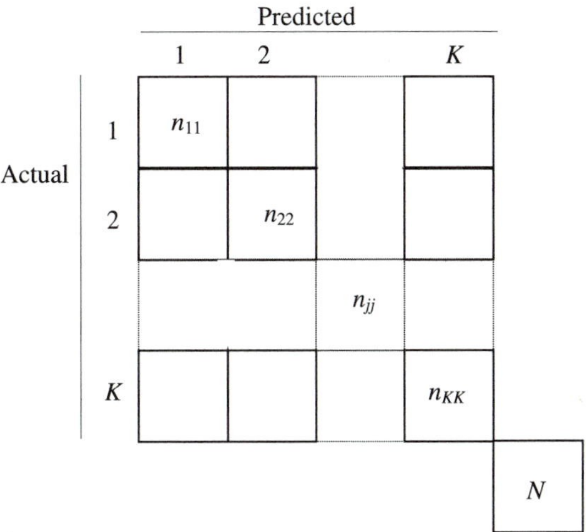

Fig. 6.2 Classification table.

observations can easily be computed as:

$$\frac{\sum_j n_{jj}}{N} \tag{6.28}$$

where n_{ij} = number of observations actually in category i and predicted to be in category j, N = total number of observations.

This measure of fit presents two problems:

- it uses the same N individuals for discrimination and prediction. This leads to an upward bias in the probability of classifying the observations correctly. A solution is to use a split sample for prediction.
- if the sample is not distributed evenly across the groups, i.e., the observed proportions are different across groups. Then by merely classifying all observations arbitrarily into the group with the highest proportion, one can get at least max $\{p_j\}$ classified correctly, where p_j is the actual proportion of observations in Group j.

Maximum chance criterion

This last value, i.e., max $\{p_j\}$, is defined as the maximum chance criterion. Because it does not require any model to be able to arrive at such a rate of correct assignment to groups, this can be used as a minimum standard, and any model should be able to improve on this rate.

Percent correctly classified by chance: the proportional chance criterion

Assume 2 groups:

$$P(\text{correct}) = P(\text{correct}|j = 1) \cdot P(j = 1) \\ + P(\text{correct}|j = 2) \cdot P(j = 2)$$

Let p_j be the observed proportion of observations actually in group j, as defined earlier, and α_j the proportion of observations classified in group j.

$$P\begin{pmatrix}\text{correct}\\ \text{by chance}\end{pmatrix} = \sum_j p_j \alpha_j \tag{6.29}$$

Let us assume that the discriminant function is meaningful. Then we want to classify in the same proportion as the actual groups. Under our decision rule, $\alpha_j = p_j$. Therefore,

$$P\begin{pmatrix}\text{correct}\\ \text{by chance}\end{pmatrix} = \sum_j p_j \alpha_j = \sum_j p_j^2 \tag{6.30}$$

Equation (6.30) provides the formula for the proportional chance criterion.

Tau statistic

The tau statistic involves the same rationale but standardizes the information:

$$\tau = \frac{n_c - \sum_j p_j n_j}{N - \sum_j p_j n_j} = \frac{(n_c/N) - \sum_j p_j \alpha_j}{1 - \sum_j p_j \alpha_j} \tag{6.31}$$

where n_j = number of observations classified in group j, n_c = number of correctly classified observations.

6.2 Quantal Choice Models

In this section, we will introduce logit models of choice. Although probit models could also be discussed in this section, they will not be discussed because they follow the same rationale as for the logit model. We start by discussing the difficulties inherent in using the standard regression model with a categorical dependent variable, even a binomial one. Then we discuss methodologies which can be used to resolve some of those problems. We then present the logit model with two variants and explain the estimation of the logit model parameters. Finally, we present the various measures of fit.

6.2.1 The Difficulties of the Standard Regression Model with Categorical Dependent Variables

Let us assume the case of two groups. The variable representing the group assigment can take two values, 0 and 1:

$$y_i = \begin{cases} 0 \\ 1 \end{cases} \tag{6.32}$$

This group assignment is made on the basis of a linear model:

$$\forall i = 1, \ldots, N: \quad \underset{1\times 1}{\mathbf{y}_i} = \underset{1\times p}{\mathbf{x}_i'} \underset{p\times 1}{\boldsymbol{\beta}} + \underset{1\times 1}{\mathbf{e}_i} \tag{6.33}$$

Are the usual assumptions verified?

1. is $E[e_i] = 0$?

   This would imply in this case that the error terms for each observation follow a specific random process. Indeed, from Equation (6.33) it follows that:

   $$\mathbf{e}_i = \mathbf{y}_i - \mathbf{x}_j' \boldsymbol{\beta} \tag{6.34}$$

   Consequently, the following distribution for $\mathbf{y}_i$ would be required so that the equality $E[e_i] = 0$ be verified:

   $$P(\mathbf{y}_i = 0) = 1 - \mathbf{x}_i' \boldsymbol{\beta} \tag{6.35}$$

   $$P(\mathbf{y}_i = 1) = \mathbf{x}_i' \boldsymbol{\beta} \tag{6.36}$$

   However, this is not generally the case, in part because

   $$\mathbf{x}_i' \boldsymbol{\beta} \notin [0, 1]$$

   Therefore, the distribution is impossible. Hence, $\hat{\boldsymbol{\beta}}_{\text{OLS}}$ is biased.
2. is $E[e_i^2] = \sigma^2$? The second assumption is the homoscedasticity of the error terms.

   $\mathbf{e}_i$ is distributed as a Bernoulli process.

   $$V[\mathbf{e}_i] = (\mathbf{x}_i' \boldsymbol{\beta})(1 - \mathbf{x}_i' \boldsymbol{\beta}) \tag{6.37}$$

   This implies heteroscedasticity, and consequently Ordinary Least Squares are inefficient.
3. The range constraint problem: $\hat{\mathbf{y}}_i \notin [0, 1]$

   A third problem occurs due to the fact that the predicted values of the predicted variable can be outside the range of the theoretical values, which are either 0 or 1.

6.2.2 Transformational Logit

6.2.2.1 Resolving the Efficiency Problem

We may be able to solve the efficiency problem.

Let us assume that the data can be grouped into K groups.

$$j = 1, \ldots, K$$

$$n_j = \text{size of group } j$$

where the K groups correspond to "settings" of independent variables.

Let

$$z_j = \sum_{i|j} y_{ij} \tag{6.38}$$

where

$$y_{ij} = \begin{cases} 0 \\ 1 \end{cases}$$

z_j is the number of 1's in group j.

$$p_j = \frac{z_j}{n_j} \tag{6.39}$$

The model for a given group is:

$$p_j = \mathbf{X}_j \boldsymbol{\beta} + e_j \tag{6.40}$$

For the entire K groups, the proportions are represented by

$$\underset{K\times 1}{\mathbf{p}} = \underset{K\times p}{\mathbf{X}} \underset{p\times 1}{\boldsymbol{\beta}} + \underset{K\times 1}{\mathbf{e}} \tag{6.41}$$

In Equation (6.40), the true proportion for group j is given by

$$P_j = \mathbf{X}_j \boldsymbol{\beta} \tag{6.42}$$

Therefore,

$$p_j = P_j + e_j \tag{6.43}$$

e_j follows a binomial distribution:

$$e_j \sim B\left(0, \frac{P_j(1-P_j)}{n_j}\right) \tag{6.44}$$

The variance is obtained because z_j is such that:

$$E[z_j] = n_j P_j \tag{6.45}$$

$$V[z_j] = n_j P_j (1 - P_j) \tag{6.46}$$

Therefore, dividing by n_j:

$$E[p_j] = E\left[\frac{z_j}{n_j}\right] = P_j \tag{6.47}$$

$$V[p_j] = V\left[\frac{z_j}{n_j}\right] = \frac{1}{n_j^2} V[z_j] = \frac{P_j(1-P_j)}{n_j} \tag{6.48}$$

Consequently, the covariance of the error term in Equation (6.41) is:

$$E[\boldsymbol{ee}'] = \boldsymbol{\Phi} = \text{diag}\left\{\frac{P_j(1-P_j)}{n_j}\right\} \tag{6.49}$$

The generalized least squares estimator would be:

$$\hat{\boldsymbol{\beta}}_{\text{GLS}} = (\mathbf{X}'\boldsymbol{\Phi}^{-1}\mathbf{X})^{-1}\mathbf{X}'\boldsymbol{\Phi}^{-1}\mathbf{p} \tag{6.50}$$

But $\boldsymbol{\Phi}$ is unknown. It can be replaced by a consistent estimator to obtain the Estimated Generalized Least Squares Estimator. Such an estimator of $\boldsymbol{\Phi}$ is:

$$\hat{\boldsymbol{\Phi}} = \text{diag}\left\{\frac{\hat{\boldsymbol{p}}_j(1-\hat{\boldsymbol{p}}_j)}{n_j}\right\} \tag{6.51}$$

where

$$\hat{\mathbf{p}} = \mathbf{Xb} = \mathbf{X}(\mathbf{X}'\mathbf{X})^{-1}\mathbf{X}'\mathbf{p} \tag{6.52}$$

The ordinary Least Squares estimator $\mathbf{b}$ provides estimates for p which are consistent with the theoretical model specification. The Estimated Generalized Least Squares Estimator is:

$$\hat{\boldsymbol{\beta}}_{\text{EGLS}} = (\mathbf{X}'\hat{\boldsymbol{\Phi}}^{-1}\mathbf{X})^{-1}\mathbf{X}'\hat{\boldsymbol{\Phi}}^{-1}\mathbf{p} \tag{6.53}$$

Several problems remain:

(i) There is no guarantee that the predicted probabilities $\hat{\boldsymbol{p}}_j = \mathbf{X}_j\mathbf{b}$ are between 0 and 1: an empirical solution which has been recommended is to restrict the variance so that if $\hat{\boldsymbol{p}}_i(1-\hat{\boldsymbol{p}}_i) \leq 0$, set $\hat{\boldsymbol{p}}_j = 0.05$ or $\hat{\boldsymbol{p}}_j = 0.98$.

(ii) Even then, there is no guarantee that $\hat{\hat{\boldsymbol{p}}}$ based on $\hat{\boldsymbol{\beta}}_{\text{EGLS}}$ is between 0 and 1. This points out the need to constrain the range of p to the interval [0,1].

6.2.2.2 Resolving the Range Constraint Problem

We can solve the range constraint problem: Transformational logit.
Let

$$\mathbf{I}_j = \mathbf{x}_j'\boldsymbol{\beta} \tag{6.54}$$

$$P_j = \frac{1}{1+e^{-\mathbf{I}_j}} \tag{6.55}$$

$$p_j = P_j + e_j = \frac{1}{1+e^{-\mathbf{I}_j}} + e_j \tag{6.56}$$

It can be shown that:

$$\text{Ln}\left(\frac{p_j}{1-p_j}\right) = \mathbf{x}_j'\boldsymbol{\beta} + \frac{e_j}{P_j(1-P_j)} \tag{6.57}$$

Let

$$\mathrm{Ln}\left(\frac{p_j}{1-p_j}\right) = v_j \quad \text{and} \quad \frac{e_j}{P_j(1-P_j)} = u_j$$

Then

$$v_j = \mathbf{x}'_j\boldsymbol{\beta} + u_j \tag{6.58}$$

or, for the full sample:

$$\underset{K\times 1}{\mathbf{v}} = \underset{K\times p}{\mathbf{X}}\ \underset{p\times 1}{\boldsymbol{\beta}} + \underset{K\times 1}{\mathbf{u}} \tag{6.59}$$

$$\boldsymbol{\Phi} = \underset{K\times K}{E[\boldsymbol{uu}']} = \mathrm{diag}\{E[u_j^2]\} \tag{6.60}$$

$$E[u_j^2] = E\left[\left(\frac{e_j}{P_j(1-P_j)}\right)^2\right] = \frac{1}{P_j^2(1-P_j)^2}V[e_j] \tag{6.61}$$

$$= \frac{1}{P_j^2(1-P_j)^2}\left[\frac{P_j(1-P_j)}{n_j}\right] \tag{6.62}$$

$$= \frac{1}{n_jP_j(1-P_j)} \tag{6.63}$$

Therefore, the Generalized Least Squares Estimator provides the minimum variance estimator:

$$\hat{\boldsymbol{\beta}}_{\mathrm{GLS}} = (\mathbf{X}'\boldsymbol{\Phi}^{-1}\mathbf{X})^{-1}\mathbf{X}'\boldsymbol{\Phi}^{-1}\mathbf{v} \tag{6.64}$$

where

$$\boldsymbol{\Phi} = \mathrm{diag}\left\{\frac{1}{n_jP_j(1-P_j)}\right\} \tag{6.65}$$

But P_j is unknown. We can replace P_j by p_j in Equation (6.65) and obtain the Estimated Generalized Least Squares Estimator:

$$\hat{\boldsymbol{\beta}}_{\mathrm{EGLS}} = (\mathbf{X}'\hat{\boldsymbol{\Phi}}^{-1}\mathbf{X})^{-1}\mathbf{X}'\hat{\boldsymbol{\Phi}}^{-1}\mathbf{v} \tag{6.66}$$

In practice, let us define

$$\hat{\boldsymbol{\Phi}}^{-1/2} = \mathrm{diag}\{[n_ip_i(1-p_i)]^{1/2}\} \tag{6.67}$$

$$\hat{\boldsymbol{\beta}}_{\mathrm{EGLS}} = (\mathbf{X}'\hat{\boldsymbol{\Phi}}^{-1/2}\hat{\boldsymbol{\Phi}}^{-1/2}\mathbf{X})^{-1}\mathbf{X}'\hat{\boldsymbol{\Phi}}^{-1/2}\hat{\boldsymbol{\Phi}}^{-1/2}\mathbf{v} \tag{6.68}$$

Therefore, we can perform a transformation of the right and of the left hand sides of the equation and obtain the Ordinary Least Squares of the transformed variables.

Let

$$\mathbf{v}^* = \hat{\boldsymbol{\Phi}}^{-1/2}\mathbf{v} \tag{6.69}$$

$$\mathbf{X}^* = \hat{\boldsymbol{\Phi}}^{-1/2}\mathbf{X} \tag{6.70}$$

and consequently,

$$\hat{\beta}_{\text{EGLS}} = (\mathbf{X}^{*\prime}\mathbf{X}^{*})^{-1}\mathbf{X}^{*\prime}\mathbf{v}^{*} \tag{6.71}$$

6.2.3 Conditional Logit Model

Let us consider an individual i considering a choice among K alternatives. Let us define the variable y_{ij}:

$$\forall j = 1, \ldots, K: \quad y_{ij} = \begin{cases} 1 & \text{if alternative } j \text{ is chosen} \\ 0 & \text{otherwise} \end{cases} \tag{6.72}$$

$$P_{ij} = P[y_{ij} = 1] \tag{6.73}$$

Only one alternative can be chosen so that:

$$\sum_{j=1}^{K} y_{ij} = 1 \tag{6.74}$$

$$\sum_{j=1}^{K} P_{ij} = 1 \tag{6.75}$$

The likelihood function for all individuals is:

$$\ell = \prod_{i=1}^{N} \prod_{j=1}^{K} P_{ij}^{y_{ij}} \tag{6.76}$$

For the Multinomial logit model, if the unobserved utilities are a function of attributes and an error term that is distributed iid with the extreme value distribution (i.e., the cumulative distribution function is $F(\varepsilon_i < \varepsilon) = \exp(-e^{-\varepsilon})$), then the probability P_{ij} is defined as:

$$P_{ij} = \frac{e^{u_{ij}}}{\sum_{k=1}^{K} e^{u_{ik}}} \tag{6.77}$$

where u_{ij} represents the utility associated with alternative j for individual i.

Two cases can be found depending on whether the explanatory variables determining the utility of the alternatives vary across alternatives or not. The first case of Conditional Logit – Case 1 (or discrete choice in LIMDEP) concerns the case where the variation in utilities of the alternatives comes from the differences in the explanatory variables but the marginal utilities are invariant. The second case of the Conditional Logit model – Case 2 is when the source of variation in the utilities of the alternatives come from the marginal utilities only.

6.2.3.1 Conditional logit – case 1 (or discrete choice in LIMDEP)

The utility of an option varies because of different values of X's (e.g., attribute values of a brand).

$$P_{ij} = \frac{e^{\mathbf{x}'_{ij}\boldsymbol{\beta}}}{\sum_{k=1}^{K} e^{\mathbf{x}'_{ik}\boldsymbol{\beta}}} \tag{6.78}$$

For identification, we set $\mathbf{x}'_{i1} = \mathbf{0}$ or let us define

$$\mathbf{x}^{*\prime}_{ij} = \mathbf{x}'_{ij} - \mathbf{x}'_{i1} \tag{6.79}$$

This demonstrates that no constant term can be estimated in this model; a constant term would be indeterminate because the intercept disappears in Equation (6.79).

The model parameters are estimated by maximum likelihood. The likelihood for individual i is:

$$\ell_i = \prod_{j=1}^{K} P_{ij}^{y_{ij}} \tag{6.80}$$

$$= \prod_{j=1}^{K} \left(\frac{e^{\mathbf{x}'_{ij}\boldsymbol{\beta}}}{\sum_{k=1}^{K} e^{\mathbf{x}'_{ij}\boldsymbol{\beta}}} \right)^{y_{ij}} \tag{6.81}$$

For the N observations, the likelihood is:

$$\ell = \prod_{i=1}^{N} \ell_i = \prod_{i=1}^{N} \prod_{j=1}^{K} \left(\frac{e^{\mathbf{x}'_{ij}\boldsymbol{\beta}}}{\sum_{k=1}^{K} e^{\mathbf{x}'_{ik}\boldsymbol{\beta}}} \right)^{y_{ij}} \tag{6.82}$$

$$\mathbf{L} = \mathrm{Ln}(\ell) = \sum_{i=1}^{N} \sum_{j=1}^{K} \mathrm{Ln} \left(\frac{e^{\mathbf{x}'_{ij}\boldsymbol{\beta}}}{\sum_{k=1}^{K} e^{\mathbf{x}'_{ik}\boldsymbol{\beta}}} \right)^{y_{ij}} \tag{6.83}$$

$$= \sum_{i=1}^{N} \sum_{j=1}^{K} y_{ij} \mathrm{Ln} \left(\frac{e^{\mathbf{x}'_{ij}\boldsymbol{\beta}}}{\sum_{k=1}^{K} e^{\mathbf{x}'_{ik}\boldsymbol{\beta}}} \right) \tag{6.84}$$

$$\mathbf{L} = \sum_{i=1}^{N} \sum_{j=1}^{K} y_{ij} \left(\mathbf{x}'_{ij}\boldsymbol{\beta} - \mathrm{Ln} \sum_{k=1}^{K} e^{\mathbf{x}'_{ik}\boldsymbol{\beta}} \right) \tag{6.85}$$

The optimization follows the iterative procedure described below:
Let t = iteration number. The gradient at iteration t is

$$\underset{p\times 1}{S}[\boldsymbol{\beta}(t)] = \left\{\frac{\partial L}{\partial \beta_p(t)}\right\} \tag{6.86}$$

Let us further define:

$$\underset{p\times p}{Q}[\boldsymbol{\beta}(t)] = \sum_{i=1}^{N}\{S_i[\boldsymbol{\beta}(t)]\, S_i[\boldsymbol{\beta}(t)]'\}$$

The value of the parameters at the next iteration is given by Equation (6.87):

$$\underset{p\times 1}{\boldsymbol{\beta}(t+1)} = \boldsymbol{\beta}(t) + \{Q[\boldsymbol{\beta}(t)]^{-1} S[\boldsymbol{\beta}(t)]\} \tag{6.87}$$

The parameter estimates are obtained by convergence when the gradient vector approaches zero.

6.2.3.2 Conditional logit – case 2

In this case, the utility of an option varies because of different values of the marginal utilities $\boldsymbol{\beta}$'s and the factors predicting the utilities are the same across options.

$$P_{ij} = \frac{e^{\mathbf{x}_i'\boldsymbol{\beta}_j}}{\sum_{k=1}^{K} e^{\mathbf{x}_i'\boldsymbol{\beta}_k}} \tag{6.88}$$

For identification, it is necessary to set $\boldsymbol{\beta}_1 = \mathbf{0}$.

The estimation of the model follows the procedure as in the prior case.

$$\ell = \prod_{i=1}^{N}\prod_{j=1}^{K}\left(\frac{e^{\mathbf{x}_i'\boldsymbol{\beta}_j}}{\sum_{k=1}^{K} e^{\mathbf{x}_i'\boldsymbol{\beta}_k}}\right)^{y_{ij}} \tag{6.89}$$

Taking the logarithms,

$$L = \sum_{i=1}^{N}\sum_{j=1}^{K} y_{ij}\mathbf{x}_i'\boldsymbol{\beta}_j - \sum_{i=1}^{N}\mathrm{Ln}\sum_{j=1}^{K} e^{\mathbf{x}_i'\boldsymbol{\beta}_j} \tag{6.90}$$

An iterative procedure similar to case 1 above is used to obtain the maximum likelihood estimates. The only difference compared with case 1 comes from the larger size of the vector of parameters. The vector of all coefficients at iteration t is the vector with $(K-1)p$ elements $\underset{(K-1)p\times 1}{\boldsymbol{\beta}(t)}$.

The interpretation is, therefore, somewhat more complex in the case 2 model. The marginal utilities due to the increase of a unit of an explanatory variable are different across alternatives. Therefore, for example, marginally, variable x_1 may contribute to the utility of alternative j but not significantly to the utility of alternative k.

6.2.4 Fit Measures

The fit measures follow for the most part those used in discriminant analysis, which are based on the classification table. However, some additional measures are available because of the maximum likelihood estimation and its properties.

6.2.4.1 Classification table

These measures are the same as in discriminant analysis:

- Percentage of observations correctly classified
- Maximum chance criterion
- Proportional chance criterion
- Tau statistic

6.2.4.2 Statistics of fit

Because of the properties of the likelihood function, two statistics can be used to test the model.

Log likelihood chi-square test

The null model is that the marginal utilities, apart from the constant term, are zero:

$$H_0: \quad \beta_{\text{slopes}} = 0$$

if n is the number of successes ($y_i = 1$) observed in T observations, e.g., in the binary case:

$$\text{under } H_0: \quad \ell(\hat{\boldsymbol{\beta}}_0) = \left(\frac{n}{T}\right)^n \left(\frac{T-n}{T}\right)^{T-n} \tag{6.91}$$

where $\hat{\boldsymbol{\beta}}_0$ represents the maximum likelihood estimates of the parameters of the reduced model with no slopes and $\ell(\hat{\beta}_0)$ is the value of the likelihood function obtained with these parameter estimates.

Taking the logarithm:

$$\text{Ln}\,\ell(\hat{\boldsymbol{\beta}}_0) = n\,\text{Ln}\frac{n}{T} + (T-n)\,\text{Ln}\left(\frac{T-n}{T}\right) \tag{6.92}$$

If $\hat{\boldsymbol{\beta}}_1$ is the value of the likelihood function estimated at the maximum likelihood estimate $\hat{\boldsymbol{\beta}}_1$, then,

$$-2[\text{Ln}\,\ell(\hat{\boldsymbol{\beta}}_0) - \text{Ln}\,\ell(\hat{\boldsymbol{\beta}}_1)] \sim \chi^2_{(p-1)} \tag{6.93}$$

Therefore, an obvious advantage of the logit model vis a vis discriminant analysis is that it offers the possibility of testing the significance of the model.

Likelihood ratio index or pseudo-R^2

Based on the same properties, the following index can be used.

$$\rho^2 = 1 - \frac{\operatorname{Ln} \ell(\hat{\boldsymbol{\beta}}_1)}{\operatorname{Ln} \ell(\hat{\boldsymbol{\beta}}_0)} \tag{6.94}$$

If the model is a perfect predictor in the sense that $\hat{\boldsymbol{P}}_i = 1$ when $y_i = 1$ and $\hat{\boldsymbol{P}}_i = 0$ when $y_i = 0$, then,

$$\ell(\hat{\boldsymbol{\beta}}_1) = 1 \Rightarrow \operatorname{Ln} \ell(\hat{\boldsymbol{\beta}}_1) = 0 \Rightarrow \rho^2 = 1 \tag{6.95}$$

When there is no improvement in fit due to the predictor variables, then,

$$\operatorname{Ln} \ell(\hat{\boldsymbol{\beta}}_1) = \operatorname{Ln} \ell(\hat{\boldsymbol{\beta}}_0) \Rightarrow \rho^2 = 0 \tag{6.96}$$

6.3 Examples

6.3.1 Example of Discriminant Analysis Using SAS

In Figure 6.3, the SAS procedure "discrim" is used. The variables used to discriminate are listed after the "var" term and then the variable which contains the group numbering follows the term "class" to indicate that it is a categorical variable. The key sections of the SAS output are shown in Figure 6.4.

The output of discriminant analysis clearly shows (Figure 6.4) the within group SSCP matrices (separately for each group), the pooled within SSCP matrix **W**, the Between group SSCP matrix **B** and the total sample SSCP matrix **T**. The raw (unstandardized) and standardized (correcting for the different units and variances of each of the variables) canonical coefficients,

```
OPTIONS LS=80;
DATA ALLIANCE;
INFILE "c:\SAMD\Chapter6\Examples\al8.dat";
INPUT   #1 choice dunc techu grow
        #2 firmsiz x1 7.4 x2 x3 asc
        #3 nccc;

proc discrim bsscp psscp wsscp tsscp canonical ;
        var dunc techu grow firmsiz asc nccc;
        class choice;
run;
```

Fig. 6.3 Example of SAS file for discriminant analysis (examp6-1.sas).

The DISCRIM Procedure

Observations	200	DF Total	199
Variables	6	DF Within Classes	198
Classes	2	DF Between Classes	1

Class Level Information

choice	Variable Name	Frequency	Weight	Proportion	Prior Probability
1	_1	155	155.0000	0.775000	0.500000
2	_2	45	45.0000	0.225000	0.500000

The SAS System 2

The DISCRIM Procedure
Within-Class SSCP Matrices

choice = 1

Variable	dunc	techu	grow
dunc	113.3	39.3	9.5
techu	39.3	79.4	48.0
grow	9.5	48.0	99.8
firmsiz	-9339.1	-9615.8	-7354.2
asc	-27.4	1.7	6.4
nccc	-23.0	0.3	1.8

choice = 1

Variable	firmsiz	asc	nccc
dunc	-9339.1	-27.4	-23.0
techu	-9615.8	1.7	0.3
grow	-7354.2	6.4	1.8
firmsiz	184070705.5	24104.1	9078.2
asc	24104.1	132.8	21.5
nccc	9078.2	21.5	83.9

---

choice = 2

Variable	dunc	techu	grow
dunc	30.27	14.71	11.68
techu	14.71	26.14	14.97
grow	11.68	14.97	31.81
firmsiz	981.28	4710.89	12027.31
asc	-4.70	1.40	6.08
nccc	0.10	6.50	0.38

choice = 2

Variable	firmsiz	asc	nccc
dunc	981.28	-4.70	0.10
techu	4710.89	1.40	6.50
grow	12027.31	6.08	0.38
firmsiz	64024111.11	2718.02	-418.20
asc	2718.02	22.14	8.67
nccc	-418.20	8.67	22.90

Pooled Within-Class SSCP Matrix

Variable	dunc	techu	grow
dunc	143.6	54.0	21.2
techu	54.0	105.5	62.9
grow	21.2	62.9	131.6
firmsiz	-8357.8	-4904.9	4673.2
asc	-32.1	3.1	12.5
nccc	-22.9	6.8	2.2

Pooled Within-Class SSCP Matrix

Variable	firmsiz	asc	nccc
dunc	-8357.8	-32.1	-22.9
techu	-4904.9	3.1	6.8
grow	4673.2	12.5	2.2
firmsiz	248094816.6	26822.2	8660.0
asc	26822.2	154.9	30.2
nccc	8660.0	30.2	106.8

Between-Class SSCP Matrix

Variable	dunc	techu	grow
dunc	0.6129	-0.4180	0.7117
techu	-0.4180	0.2851	-0.4854
grow	0.7117	-0.4854	0.8264
firmsiz	-467.3848	318.7464	-542.7074
asc	-1.7287	1.1790	-2.0074
nccc	0.2759	-0.1881	0.3203

Between-Class SSCP Matrix

Variable	firmsiz	asc	nccc
dunc	-467.3848	-1.7287	0.2759
techu	318.7464	1.1790	-0.1881
grow	-542.7074	-2.0074	0.3203
firmsiz	356391.4050	1318.2102	-210.3682
asc	1318.2102	4.8758	-0.7781
nccc	-210.3682	-0.7781	0.1242

Total-Sample SSCP Matrix

Variable	dunc	techu	grow
dunc	144.2	53.6	21.9
techu	53.6	105.8	62.5
grow	21.9	62.5	132.4
firmsiz	-8825.2	-4586.1	4130.4
asc	-33.9	4.3	10.5
nccc	-22.6	6.7	2.5

Total-Sample SSCP Matrix

Variable	firmsiz	asc	nccc
dunc	-8825.2	-33.9	-22.6
techu	-4586.1	4.3	6.7
grow	4130.4	10.5	2.5
firmsiz	248451208.0	28140.4	8449.6
asc	28140.4	159.8	29.4
nccc	8449.6	29.4	106.9

Pooled Covariance Matrix Information

Covariance Matrix Rank	Natural Log of the Determinant of the Covariance Matrix
6	11.06578

Pairwise Generalized Squared Distances Between Groups

$$D^2(i|j) = (\bar{X}_i - \bar{X}_j)' \, COV^{-1} \, (\bar{X}_i - \bar{X}_j)$$

Generalized Squared Distance to choice

From choice	1	2
1	0	0.39588
2	0.39588	0

Canonical Discriminant Analysis

	Canonical Correlation	Adjusted Canonical Correlation	Approximate Standard Error	Squared Canonical Correlation
1	0.255312	0.209914	0.066267	0.065184

Eigenvalues of Inv(E)*H
= CanRsq/(1-CanRsq)

```
        Eigenvalue    Difference    Proportion    Cumulative

  1        0.0697                       1.0000        1.0000

      Test of H0: The canonical correlations in the
        current row and all that follow are zero

      Likelihood    Approximate
           Ratio        F Value     Num DF     Den DF      Pr > F

1     0.93481561           2.24          6        193      0.0408

            NOTE: The F statistic is exact.

            Canonical Discriminant Analysis
               Total Canonical Structure

               Variable              Can1

               dunc              0.255331
               techu            -0.203296
               grow              0.309396
               firmsiz          -0.148344
               asc              -0.684158
               nccc              0.133471

               Between Canonical Structure
               Variable              Can1

               dunc              1.000000
               techu            -1.000000
               grow              1.000000
               firmsiz          -1.000000
               asc              -1.000000
               nccc              1.000000

            Pooled Within Canonical Structure
               Variable              Can1

               dunc              0.247396
               techu            -0.196824
               grow              0.300080
               firmsiz          -0.143531
               asc              -0.671812
               nccc              0.129123

            Canonical Discriminant Analysis
    Total-Sample Standardized Canonical Coefficients

               Variable              Can1

               dunc          0.3875344511
               techu         -.7516524862
```

```
              grow            0.7000312218
              firmsiz         -.0910945522
              asc             -.7239897268
              nccc            0.4082828732

       Pooled Within-Class Standardized Canonical Coefficients
              Variable                Can1

              dunc            0.3876854449
              techu           -.7525324874
              grow            0.6996037720
              firmsiz         -.0912587756
              asc             -.7146572217
              nccc            0.4090748704

              Raw Canonical Coefficients
              Variable                Can1

              dunc             0.455199542
              techu           -1.030770927
              grow             0.858082117
              firmsiz         -0.000081526
              asc             -0.807915970
              nccc             0.556967570

          Class Means on Canonical Variables
               choice               Can1

                    1       0.1415685600
                    2       -.4876250399

              Linear Discriminant Function


                 _      -1 _                                 -1 _
Constant = -.5 X' COV    X       Coefficient Vector = COV    X
                 j         j                                    j


          Linear Discriminant Function for choice

           Variable              1              2

           Constant       -0.49854       -1.04596
           dunc            0.28366       -0.00275
           techu          -0.21886        0.42970
           grow            0.03893       -0.50097
           firmsiz       0.0004568      0.0005081
           asc             0.94089        1.44923
           nccc           -0.24923       -0.59967
```

```
Classification Summary for Calibration Data: WORK.ALLIANCE
Resubstitution Summary using Linear Discriminant Function

          Generalized Squared Distance Function

                    2          _      -1    _
                   D (X)  = (X-X )' COV   (X-X )
                   j            j              j

      Posterior Probability of Membership in Each choice

                          2                    2
      Pr(j|X)  = exp(-.5 D (X)) / SUM exp(-.5 D (X))
                          j         k           k

Number of Observations and Percent Classified into choice
 From choice              1             2          Total

           1             97            58            155
                      62.58         37.42         100.00

           2             12            33             45
                      26.67         73.33         100.00

       Total            109            91            200
                      54.50         45.50         100.00

      Priors            0.5           0.5

             Error Count Estimates for choice
                              1             2          Total

     Rate                0.3742        0.2667         0.3204
     Priors              0.5000        0.5000
```

Fig. 6.4 SAS output for discriminant analysis (examp6-1.lst).

that is the discriminant coefficients, are then listed. The raw coefficients indicate the weights to apply to the p variates in order to form the most discriminating linear function. In the example, $y_i = 0.455*\mathrm{DUNC}_i - 1.031*\mathrm{TECHU}_i + 0.858*\mathrm{GROW}_i - 0.00008*\mathrm{FIRMSIZ}_i - 0.808*\mathrm{ASC}_i + 0.557*\mathrm{NCCC}_i$. In the particular case where only two groups are analyzed, a single discriminant function exists; there is only one eigen vector. The eigen vectors or discriminant functions discussed earlier are interpretable in a way such that a positive (negative) sign of the discriminant function coefficients (weights) indicates that the corresponding variable contributes positively (negatively) to the discriminant function. A comparison with the group means on the discriminant function indicates in what way the variates discriminate among the groups. For example, in Figure 6.4, Choice 1 has a higher (positive) mean value (0.142) on the discriminant function y (the mean for Choice 2 is negative, i.e., −0.488).

Therefore, the positive coefficient of DUNC means that the higher the demand uncertainty (the higher the value on DUNC), the higher the discriminant function and, consequently, the more likely choice 1 (internal development mode). On the opposite, because of the negative coefficient of TECHU, the higher the technological uncertainty, the more likely choice 2 of using an alliance.

In addition, the absolute value of the standardized discriminant function coefficients (where the raw coefficients are multiplied by the standard deviation of the corresponding variables) reflect the contribution of the variables to that discriminant function so that a larger standardized weight indicates a bigger role of that variable in discriminating between the options. For example, the variable technology uncertainty ("techu") appears the most discriminant variable (−0.75), followed closely by the variables "asc" (−0.71) and "grow" (0.69) although observations with higher values of growth ("grow") are likely to belong to different groups from those with high ratings on "asc" and "techu" because of the opposite signs of these coefficients. Therefore, these standardized coefficients explain the contribution (extent and direction) of each variable for discriminating between the two groups.

For two-group discriminant analysis, the interpretation of the discriminant function weights is relatively clear, as presented above. When there are more than two groups, each discriminant function represents different dimensions on which the discrimination between groups would occur. For example, the first discriminant function could discriminate between groups 1 and 3 versus group 2, and the second discriminant function could discriminate between groups 1 and 2 on the one hand and group 3 on the other hand. The interpretation in such cases requires the comparison of the group means on the discriminant function values (y). A plot of the group means or centroids on the discriminant functions as axes helps the interpretation of these discriminant functions which can be difficult. It is also very useful to analyze the profiles of each group in terms of the means of the predictor variables for each group.

In Figure 6.4, a vector of coefficients for each group is printed under the heading of "linear discriminant function". These are not, however, the discriminant functions discussed earlier; they are the classification functions. Indeed, in that particular example with two choices only, there could not be two discriminant functions. What the SAS output shows are the classification functions, which are the two components of equation (6.22) above, i.e., $\mathbf{W}^{-1}\bar{\mathbf{x}}_1$ and $\mathbf{W}^{-1}\bar{\mathbf{x}}_2$.

The classification table is also shown in Figure 6.4. In this example, 62.58% of the observations in Group 1 were classified in the correct group and 73.3% for Group 2.

6.3.2 Example of Multinomial Logit – Case 1 Analysis Using LIMDEP

Figure 6.5 presents a typical input file using LIMDEP to estimate a logit model of the case 1 type. The data set used for this example, scanner.dat, has

```
read; nrec = 4648; nvar=14; file = scanner.dat;
format = (f8.0,f4.0,2f2.0,f3.0,2f5.2,f2.0,f9.6,5f2.0);
names(x1  = panelid,
      x2  = week,
      x3  = purchase,
      x4  = count,
      x5  = brand,
      x6  = price,
      x7  = prcut,
      x8  = feature,
      x9  = loy,
      x10 = dum1,
      x11 = dum2,
      x12 = dum3,
      x13 = dum4,
      x14 = dum5,
$
open; output=c:\SAMD\Chapter6\Examples\Examp6-2.out$
discrete choice; lhs=purchase, count;
         rhs=price, prcut, feature, loy, dum1, dum2, dum3, dum4, dum5$
close$
```

Fig. 6.5 Example of LIMDEP file for logit model – Case 1 (examp6-2.lim).

the same structure as the data scan.dat described in Appendix C. The first part of the file defines the data variables and reads them from the data file. The specification of the analysis follows in the second part with the procedure "discrete choice". The variables in the left hand side of the equation are then specified (purchase) following the code "lhs=". Finally, the explanatory variables are listed after the code "rhs=" for the right hand side of the equation. It is important to note that in LIMDEP, the options must be coded from 0 to $K - 1$. The predicted variables in the example of Figure 6.5 consist of the price of each brand, any price cut applied to each transaction and whether the brand was on display on not. Each brand is also specified as having a different intrinsic preference or utility which is modeled as a different constant term with dummy variables (the reference where all brand dummies are zero correspond to private labels). Some heterogeneity in preferences across consumers is also captured by a loyalty measure representing past purchases of the brand. The LIMDEP output is shown in Figure 6.6.

The output shown in Figure 6.6 should be self explanatory. The gradient is printed at each iteration until convergence is achieved. Then, the estimated parameters are listed with the usual statistics which enable the test of hypotheses and the computation of the fit statistics based on the likelihood function. The coefficients represent the marginal utility of each choice option (brand) of one additional unit of the corresponding variable. In the example in Figure 6.6, price has a significant negative impact while price cuts and being on display add to the brand utility.

```
Normal exit from iterations. Exit status=0.
 : LIMDEP Estimation Results                          Run log line     3  Page    1 :
 : Current sample contains    4648 observations.                                  :


                +--------------------------------------------+
                | Discrete choice (multinomial logit) model   |
                | Maximum Likelihood Estimates                |
                | Dependent variable                 Choice   |
                | Weighting variable                    ONE   |
                | Number of observations                949   |
                | Iterations completed                    6   |
                | Log likelihood function         -814.1519   |
                | Log-L for Choice     model =    -814.1519   |
                | R2=1-LogL/LogL*  Log-L fncn  R-sqrd  RsqAdj |
                | No coefficients  -1700.3797  .52119  .52003 |
                | Constants only.  Must be computed directly. |
                |                  Use NLOGIT ;...; RHS=ONE $ |
                | Response data are given as ind. choice.     |
                | Number of obs.=   949, skipped   0 bad obs. |
                +--------------------------------------------+

 +---------+--------------+----------------+--------+---------+----------+
 |Variable | Coefficient  | Standard Error |b/St.Er.|P[|Z|>z] | Mean of X|
 +---------+--------------+----------------+--------+---------+----------+
  PRICE    -2.372695061       .33603584       -7.061   .0000
  PRCUT     1.973968500       .35129043        5.619   .0000
  FEATURE   .7023317528       .13901356        5.052   .0000
  LOY       3.791733215       .15780806       24.028   .0000
  DUM1      .9717318976E-01   .24160340         .402   .6875
  DUM2      .9067318292       .25947016        3.495   .0005
  DUM3      .9511561911       .31347219        3.034   .0024
  DUM4      .4835120963       .25106381        1.926   .0541
  DUM5      .9019121730       .38997209        2.313   .0207
```

Fig. 6.6 LIMDEP output for logit model – Case 1 (examp6-2.out).

6.3.3 Example of Multinomial Logit – Case 2 Analysis Using LOGIT.EXE

This program was written to estimate the parameters of a multinomial logit model. The model and the likelihood function are described in Gatignon, H. and E. Anderson (1988), "The Multinational Corporation's Degree of Control Over Foreign Subsidiaries: An Empirical Test of a Transaction Cost Explanation," *Journal of Law, Economics and Organization*, 4, 2 (Fall), 89–120. The program can be used for the binomial logit model specification as well.

The multivariate logit program LOGIT.EXE runs on a personal computer under Windows. There are three files, in addition to the data file. These files, including the data files, must be located in the same directory or folder. The three files are:

LOGIT.EXE: the main source program in its compiled form which needs to be executed.
LOGIT.PRM: the file containing the run parameters (see description below).
LOGIT.RES: the file containing the output.

Executing the program

Once the parameter file LOGIT.PRM has been created (using Notepad or a word processor and saved as text), the program can be executed by using Microsoft Explorer and clicking on the LOGIT.EXE file name. Again, this assumes that all the relevant files are in the same directory.

The output is saved in the file LOGIT.RES and can be printed using Notepad or a word processor.

Description of parameter file

Each line of the parameter file LOGIT.PRM is described in Figure 6.7 below on the right side of each line in italic characters. It should be noted that, contrary to LIMDEP, the options must be coded from 1 to K.

The results are shown in the output file LOGIT.RES, as in Figure 6.8. The information provided is similar to the information provided in the LIMDEP output of the logit model – case 1. It should be pointed out that this example is a binomial logit case where the coefficients for option 1 are not shown since they are all zeros. Only the coefficients for option 2 and the corresponding statistics are shown. Finally, the output provides the classification table with the proportion of correctly classified observations (0.815 in Figure 6.8) and the value of the pseudo R-squared.

`Alliance Decision model`	*Title*
`2 8`	*Nbr of options, Nbr of variables (including constant)*
`al8.dat`	*Name of file containing data*
`(i1,3f8.4,/,f17.4,8x,8x,`	*Format of input (Fortran style)*
`8x,f8.4/f17.4,8x,16x,f8.4)`	
`dunc`	*Variable label*
`techu`	*Variable label*
`grow`	*Variable label*
`firmsiz`	*Variable label*
`as2`	*Variable label*
`nccc`	*Variable label*
`ads`	*Variable label*
`0`	*Code for printing predicted probabilities (0=No; 1=Yes)*

Fig. 6.7 Example of a parameter file LOGIT.PRM.

```
   MULTINOMIAL LOGIT ESTIMATION PROGRAM
   VERSION 1.0 -  SEPTEMBER 27, 1986
   Hubert Gatignon

   ************************************

          TITLE: Alliance Decision model - al8.DAT
          FILE CONTAINING DATA: al8.dat

          NUMBER OF CHOICE OPTIONS:  2
          NUMBER OF PREDICTOR VARIABLES:   8

     MULTINOMIAL LOGIT
     MAXIMUM LIKELIHOOD ESTIMATION
...

GRADIANT VECTOR
 -1.423115900252014D-004 -6.222515634091152D-006  1.630499013005604D-005
4.129291539478608D-006      -0.109796197211836 -9.564753681789994D-005
-2.026881757305476D-005  8.849901539398353D-005
        LOG LIKELIHOOD =       -73.5768127


     CONVERGENCE ACHIEVED AFTER     5 ITERATIONS.

 CHOICE VARIABLE              COEFFICIENT     STD ERR.    T-STAT
    2       1      CST           -2.24760     0.40471   -5.55366
    2       2      dunc          -0.13411     0.30167   -0.44456
    2       3      techu          0.52176     0.38423    1.35793
    2       4      grow          -0.77679     0.32770   -2.37046
    2       5      firmsiz        0.00012     0.00017    0.71302
    2       6      as2            0.18251     0.27623    0.66074
    2       7      nccc          -0.67369     0.31454   -2.14178
    2       8      ads            2.03888     0.36284    5.61922
 ESTIMATED CHOICE PROBABILITIES
...

 CHOICE PREDICTED FREQUENCY  OBSERVED FREQUENCY  %      CORREC CLASS
 ------ ------------------  ------------------             --------------
   1           168    0.8400          155    0.7750     143  0.9226
   2            32    0.1600           45    0.2250      20  0.4444

               200                   200                  163.   0.8150

     Pseudo-R2 =  0.20567
```

Fig. 6.8 Example of output file LOGIT.RES using LOGIT.EXE.

6.3.4 Example of Multinomial Logit – Case 2 Analysis Using LIMDEP

Figure 6.9 shows the LIMDEP file which estimates the same model as above. There are two aspects to pay particular attention to:

1. The choice variables should have a value of zero for the base case, up to the number of choice options minus one. In the example, the choice variable, which is the R&D mode is re-coded to take the value 0 or 1 dependent on whether the original variable read from the data file is 1 or 2.
2. The second point is that LIMDEP does not automatically estimate a constant term. Therefore, if one expects different proportions to be chosen for the same values of the independent variables, then the variable called "one" in LIMDEP serves to add the constant term.

It can be seen from the LIMDEP output, shown in Figure 6.10, that the results are the same as described previously, in terms of the parameter estimates and of the classification table. The information necessary to compute the likelihood ratio test are also given with the log-likelihood functions for the full model and for the restricted version (no slopes). The chi squared statistic is also provided. The pseudo R squared can be computed with this information as well.

```
read; nrec = 200; nvar=8; file = al8.dat;
format = (f1.0,3f8.4/f17.4,24x,f8.4/f17.4,24x,f8.4);
names(x1 = rdmode,
        x2 = dunc,
        x3 = techu,
        x4 = grow,
        x5 = firmsiz,
        x6 = as2,
        x7 = nccc,
        x8 = ads,
$
create; rdmode= rdmode-1$
open; output=c:\SAMD\chapter6\examples\examp6-3.out$
        logit; lhs=rdmode;
                 rhs=one, dunc, techu, grow, firmsiz, as2, nccc, ads$
close$
```

Fig. 6.9 Example of input for logit model using LIMDEP (examp6-3.lim).

```
: LIMDEP Estimation Results                       Run log line    4  Page    1 :
: Current sample contains     200 observations.                                :

             +-----------------------------------------------+
             | Multinomial logit model                        |
             | There are  2 outcomes for LH variable RDMODE   |
             | These are the OLS start values based on the    |
             | binary variables for each outcome Y(i) = j.    |
             | Coefficients for LHS=0 outcome are set to 0.0  |
             +-----------------------------------------------+

+---------+-------------+---------------+--------+---------+----------+
|Variable | Coefficient  | Standard Error |b/St.Er.|P[|Z|>z] | Mean of X|
+---------+-------------+---------------+--------+---------+----------+
         Characteristics in numerator of Prob[Y = 1]
 Constant  .2071964751      .38692314E-01    5.355   .0000
 DUNC     -.1371394030E-01  .36081756E-01    -.380   .7039 -.22794000E-01
 TECHU     .5819511367E-01  .47307026E-01    1.230   .2186 -.11773500E-01
 GROW     -.8250070805E-01  .37666224E-01   -2.190   .0285  .19359500E-01
 FIRMSIZ   .1275473374E-04  .23474470E-04     .543   .5869  706.10000
 AS2       .1665741370E-01  .32130499E-01     .518   .6042  .79726850
 NCCC     -.4558722443E-01  .37072263E-01   -1.230   .2188 -.24566500E-01
 ADS       .2261545326      .31404416E-01    7.201   .0000 -.16065145E-01

Normal exit from iterations. Exit status=0.

: LIMDEP Estimation Results                       Run log line    4  Page    2 :
: Current sample contains     200 observations.                                :

               +----------------------------------------------+
               | Multinomial Logit Model                       |
               | Maximum Likelihood Estimates                  |
               | Dependent variable                 RDMODE     |
               | Weighting variable                    ONE     |
               | Number of observations                200     |
               | Iterations completed                    7     |
               | Log likelihood function         -73.57682     |
               | Restricted log likelihood       -106.6328     |
               | Chi-squared                      66.11190     |
               | Degrees of freedom                      7     |
               | Significance level               .0000000     |
               +----------------------------------------------+

+---------+-------------+---------------+--------+---------+----------+
|Variable | Coefficient  | Standard Error |b/St.Er.|P[|Z|>z] | Mean of X|
+---------+-------------+---------------+--------+---------+----------+
         Characteristics in numerator of Prob[Y = 1]
 Constant -2.247599465      .40470933       -5.554   .0000
 DUNC     -.1341133808      .30167521        -.445   .6566 -.22794000E-01
 TECHU     .5217618767      .38423330        1.358   .1745 -.11773500E-01
 GROW     -.7767888885      .32769650       -2.370   .0178  .19359500E-01
 FIRMSIZ   .1237468921E-03  .17355371E-03     .713   .4758  706.10000
```

```
  AS2        .1825140247       .27622638          .661    .5088   .79726850
  NCCC      -.6736865330       .31454643        -2.142    .0322 -.24566500E-01
  ADS       2.038879995        .36284355         5.619    .0000 -.16065145E-01


Frequencies of actual & predicted outcomes
Predicted outcome has maximum probability.

             Predicted
------   ----------   +   -----
Actual      0     1   |   Total
------   ----------   +   -----
  0       143    12   |    155
  1        25    20   |     45
------   ----------   +   -----
Total     168    32   |    200
```

Fig. 6.10 Example of LIMDEP output for logit model (examp6-3.out).

6.4 Assignment

Use SURVEY.ASC data to run a model where the dependent variable is a categorical scale (choose especially a variable with more than two categories). For example, you may want to address the following questions:

Can purchase process variables be explained by psychographics?
Are demographics and/or psychographics determinants of media habits?

Note that for these analyses, you can use Discriminant Analysis with SAS or the Multinomial logit – case 2 – model estimated using LOGIT.EXE or LIMDEP. In both cases (discriminant analysis and logit model), provide fit statistics in addition to the explanation of the coefficients. Compare the results of both analyses. Pay particular attention to the format for reading the variables in LIMDEP, as the windows version does not recognize format "i" for integers.

Model the brand choice of orange juice using scanner data in the file SCAN.DAT (the description of the file can be found in Appendix C). Use LIMDEP to estimate the Multinomial logit – case 1 – models.

You may want to consider the following ideas for possible analysis:

- What does the inclusion of the "loyalty" variable (i.e., a measure of cross-sectional heterogeneity and nonstationarity) do to the brand choice model?
- What is the optimal value of the smoothing constant? Is it significantly different from 0.8?
- What do we gain, if anything, by separating price paid into its two components?
- Are there brand-specific price effects?

References

Basic Technical Readings

Maddala, G. S. (1983), *Limited-dependent and Qualitative Variables in Econometrics*, Cambridge: Cambridge University Press, [Chapters 3 and 4].

McFadden, D. (1974), "Conditional Logit Analysis of Qualitative Choice Behavior," in P. Zarembka, ed., *Frontiers in Econometrics*, New York, NY: Academic Press.

McFadden, D. (1980), "Econometric Models of Probabilistic Choice Among Products," *Journal of Business*, 53, S13–.

Morrison, D. G. (1969), "On the Interpretation of Discriminant Analysis," *Journal of Marketing Research*, 6 (May), 156–163.

Schmidt, P. and R. P. Strauss (1975), "The Prediction of Occupation Using Multiple Logit Models," *International Economic Review*, 16, 2 (June), 471–486.

Application Readings

Bruderl, J. and R. Schussler (1990), "Organizational Mortality: The Liabilities of Newness and Adolescence," *Administrative Science Quarterly*, 35, 530–547.

Corstjens, M. L. and D. A. Gautschi (1983), "Formal Choice Models in Marketing," *Marketing Science*, 2, 1, 19.

Fader, P. S. and J. M. Lattin (1993), "Accounting for Heterogeneity and Nonstationarity in a Cross-Sectional Model of Consumer Purchase Behavior," *Marketing Science*, 12, 3, 304.

Fader, P. S., J. M. Lattin and J. D. C. Little (1992), "Estimating Nonlinear Parameters in the Multinomial Logit Model," *Marketing Science*, 11, 4, 372.

Foekens, E. W., P. S. H. Leeflang and D. Wittink (1997), "Hierarchical versus Other Market Share Models for Markets with Many Items," *International Journal of Research in Marketing*, 14, 359–378.

Fotheringham, A. S. (1988), "Consumer Store Choice and Choice Set Definition," *Marketing Science*, 7, 3 (Summer), 299–310.

Gatignon, H. and E. Anderson (1988), "The Multinational Corporation's Degree of Control Over Foreign Subsidiaries: An Empirical Test of a Transaction Cost Explanation," *Journal of Law, Economics and Organization*, 4, 2 (Fall), 89–120.

Gatignon, H. and D. J. Reibstein (1986), "Pooling Logit Models," *Journal of Marketing Research*, 23, 3 (August), 281–285.

Guadagni, P. M. and J. D. C. Little (1983), "A Logit Model Brand Choice Calibrated on Scanner Data," *Marketing Science*, 2 (Summer), 203–238.

Gupta, S. (1988), "Impact of Sales Promotions on When, What, and How Much to Buy," *Journal of Marketing Research*, 25 (November), 342–355.

Gupta, S., P. K. Chintagunta and D. R. Wittink (1997), "Household Heterogeneity and State Dependence in a Model of Purchase Strings: Empirical Results and Managerial Implications," *International Journal of Research in Marketing*, 14, 341–357.

Hardie, B. G. S., E. J. Johnson, and P. S. Fader (1992), "Modeling Loss Aversion and Reference Dependence Effects on Brand Choice," *Marketing Science*, 12, 4, 378.

Robertson, T. S. and H. Gatignon (1998), "Technology Development Mode: A Transaction Cost Conceptualization," *Strategic Management Journal*, 19, 6, 515–532.

Sinha, A. (2000), "Understanding Supermarket Competition Using Choice Maps," *Marketing Letters*, 11, 1, 21–35.

Tallman, S. B. (1991), "Strategic Management Models and Resource-Based Strategies Among MNEs in a Host Market," *Strategic Management Journal*, 12, 69–82.

Wiggins, R. R. and T. W. Ruefli (1995), "Necessary Conditions for the Predictive Validity of Strategic Groups: Analysis Without Reliance on Clustering Techniques," *Academy of Management Journal*, 38, 6, 1635–1656.

Yapa, L. S. and R. C. Mayfield (1978), "Non-Adoption of Innovations: Evidence from Discriminant Analysis," *Economic Geography*, 54, 2, 145–156.

7. Rank Ordered Data

When the criterion variable is defined on an ordinal scale, the typical analyses based on correlations or covariances are not appropriate. The methods described in Chapter 6 do not use the ordered nature of the data and, consequently, do not use all the information available. In this chapter, we present methodologies that take the ordinal property of the dependent variable into account.

A particular methodology which typically uses ordinal dependent variable is based on experimental designs to obtain preferences of respondents to different stimuli: conjoint analysis. We first discuss the methodology involved in conjoint analysis and the methods used to estimate the parameters of the conjoint models, i.e., monotone analysis of variance (MONANOVA). Then, we discuss a choice probability model which takes the ordinal property of the dependent variable into consideration, the ordered probit model.

7.1 Conjoint Analysis – MONANOVA

In the conjoint problem, preference responses to stimuli are obtained. These stimuli are designed to represent a combination of characteristics or attributes. Therefore, we start discussing the design itself which defines the independent or predictor variables and the manners in which the combination of attributes can be coded for analysis.

7.1.1 Effect Coding Versus Dummy Variable Coding

In a typical experimental setting, the independent variables which characterize the conditions of a cell or a stimulus are discrete categories or levels of attributes. For example the color of the packaging of a product is red or yellow. It can be ordered (for example a "low", "medium" or "high" value) or not (e.g., colors). Each combination of level of all the attributes can correspond in principle to a stimulus, although responses to all the combinations may not be necessary. Two methods can be used to code these combinations of levels of attributes. Effect coding is the traditional method in experimental research using analyses of variance models. Dummy variables are typically used in regression analysis. We present each coding scheme and discuss the differences.

The coding principle is best described by taking an example of a two by two factorial design. This means that there are two factors in the experiment, each with two levels. For example, the stimulus may or may not have property A and may or may not have property B. This is illustrated in Table 7.1.

Table 7.1 A 2 × 2 factorial design

		A		
		$\bar{a}$	a	
B	$\bar{b}$	40.9 (1)	47.8 (a)	44.4
	b	42.4 (b)	50.2 (ab)	46.3
		41.6	49.0	45.3

This 2^2 factorial design can easily be generalized to the 2^n design or any design $m \times n \times \cdots \times k$.

In Table 7.1, the stimulus possesses the attribute A or not. If it does, the condition is noted as a, and if it does not, it is noted as $\bar{a}$. The same two cases for attribute B are noted as b and $\bar{b}$. The combinations of levels of the two attributes lead to the following cases:

(1) = Treatment combination which consists of the 1st level of all factors,
(a) = Treatment combination which consists of the 2nd level of the first factor and the 1st level of the second factor,
(b) = Treatment combination which consists of the 1st level of the first factor and the 2nd level of the second factor,
(ab) = Treatment combination which consists of the 2nd level of the two factors.

These labels of each treatment condition are shown in each cell of the table describing the design in Table 7.1. Assuming that the various stimuli are evaluated on an intervally scaled response measure, the values also shown in each cell of Table 7.1 are the average ratings provided by respondents in each of these conditions. Assuming that the number of respondents in each cell are the same, one can derive the grand mean rating, the main effects of each attribute or factor and the specific incremental effect of the combination of A and B.

The grand mean is the average value across the four cells:

$$M = \text{Grand Mean} = \tfrac{1}{4}[(ab) + (a) + (b) + (1)] \tag{7.1}$$

The main effect of A is the average of the effect of the presence of A (i.e., the difference in the ratings whether A is present or not) across the two conditions determined by whether B is present or not. If B is present, the effect of A is $(ab) - (b)$; if B is not present, it is $(a) - (1)$, or:

$$A\ (\text{Main Effect of } A) = \tfrac{1}{2}[\{(a) - (b)\} + \{(a) - (1)\}] \tag{7.2}$$

Similarly, the main effect of B is the average of the effect of the presence of B (i.e., the difference in the ratings whether B is present or not) across the two conditions determined by whether A is present or not. If A is present, the effect of B is $(ab) - (a)$; if B is not present, it is $(b) - (1)$, or:

$$B \text{ (Main Effect of } B) = \tfrac{1}{2}[\{(ab) - (a)\} + \{(b) - (1)\}] \tag{7.3}$$

The joint effect of A and B beyond the main effects of A and B is given by the difference between the value of the criterion variable when both effects are present and its value when none are present (i.e., $(ab) - (1)$), after removing the main effect of A (i.e., $(a) - (1)$) and the main effect of B (i.e., $(b) - (1)$):

$$\begin{aligned} AB &= [\{(ab) - (1)\} - \{(b) - (1)\} - \{(a) - (1)\}] \\ &= [(ab) - (b) - (a) + (1)] \end{aligned} \tag{7.4}$$

Using the data in Table 7.1, $(1) = 40.9$, $(ab) = 50.2$, $(a) = 47.8$, $(b) = 42.4$. Therefore, using Equations (7.2) to (7.4):

$$\begin{aligned} A &= \tfrac{1}{2}[50.2 - 42.4 + 47.8 - 40.9] = \tfrac{1}{2}(7.8 + 6.9) = 7.4 \\ B &= \tfrac{1}{2}[50.2 - 47.8 + 42.4 - 40.9] = \tfrac{1}{2}(2.4 + 1.5) = 1.9 \\ AB &= [50.2 - 42.4 - 47.8 + 40.9] = 0.9 \end{aligned}$$

These effects can simply be computed using a linear model where the independent variables are coded using a specific scheme. The coding scheme is different depending on whether the effects are coded directly (effect coding) or whether the levels are coded (dummy coding).

7.1.1.1 Effect coding

A variable will be created for each factor, for example x_1 for factor A and x_2 for factor B. We will first present the coding scheme with two levels and then when more than two levels are involved.

Effect coding with two levels

Let us assume a factor with two levels. The upper level will be coded "+1" and the lower level "−1".

Therefore, a stimulus (a cell) will be represented by the vector $(x_1, x_2)'$, which for the four cells in Table 7.1 gives the following combinations:

$$1\begin{pmatrix}-1\\-1\end{pmatrix} \quad a\begin{pmatrix}1\\-1\end{pmatrix}$$

$$b\begin{pmatrix}-1\\1\end{pmatrix} \quad ab\begin{pmatrix}1\\1\end{pmatrix}$$

A main effect model can be represented by the linear model:

$$y = \beta_0 + \beta_1 x_1 + \beta_2 x_2 \tag{7.5}$$

The individual cells' ratings can then be obtained by the combination of the values of x_1 and x_2 as indicated below:

	x_1	x_2
(1)	−1	−1
(*a*)	1	−1
(*b*)	−1	1
(*ab*)	1	1

For each cell, this leads to the equations:

$$\begin{array}{ll} (1) & y = \beta_0 - \beta_1 - \beta_2 \\ (a) & y = \beta_0 + \beta_1 - \beta_2 \\ (b) & y = \beta_0 - \beta_1 + \beta_2 \\ (ab) & y = \beta_0 + \beta_1 + \beta_2 \end{array}$$

The effects of each factor are therefore represented by the values of the βs.

$$\begin{aligned} A &= \tfrac{1}{2}(\beta_0 + \beta_1 - \beta_2) - (\beta_0 - \beta_1 - \beta_2) \\ &\quad + (\beta_0 + \beta_1 + \beta_2) - (\beta_0 - \beta_1 + \beta_2) \\ &= \beta_1 - \beta_2 + \beta_1 + \beta_2 + \beta_1 + \beta_2 + \beta_1 - \beta_2 \\ &= \beta_1 + \beta_1 = 2\beta_1 \\ B &= \beta_1 + \beta_2 - (\beta_1 - \beta_2) = \beta_1 + \beta_2 - \beta_1 + \beta_2 \\ &\quad - \beta_1 + \beta_2 - (-\beta_1 - \beta_2) = -\beta_1 + \beta_2 + \beta_1 + \beta_2 \\ &= \beta_2 + \beta_2 = 2\beta_2 \end{aligned}$$

Effect coding with more than two levels

When more than two levels are involved, the coding scheme depends on the assumptions made about the functional form of the relationship between the variable (factor) and the dependent variable. This issue obviously does not arise in the case of only two levels.

We present below the case of three levels of a variable. The effects can be coded to reflect a linear relationship or a non-linear one.

Linear effect coding

Let us consider first the coding scheme for a linear effect. Such a coding is represented in Table 7.2.

It can be seen that the difference between level one and level two is the same as the difference between level two and level three, that is one unit. The difference between level one and level three is twice the difference between level one an level two. Therefore, the effect is linear.

Table 7.2 Linear effect coding for 3 level variable

Level	Coding
1	−1
2	0
3	+1

Table 7.3 Quadratic effect coding for 3 level variable

Level	Coding
1	+1
2	−2
3	+1

Non-linear effect coding

The coding of non-linear effects varies depending on the functional form which the researcher wants to represent and test. Table 7.3 shows the coding scheme for a quadratic form.

The shape of the function shows symmetry around level two and the values depend on the coefficient which multiplies this variable. Furthermore, a positive value of the coefficient would imply a decreasing and then increasing function and vice-versa for a negative coefficient.

The coding scheme can become quite complex. For more than 3 levels, Table 7.4 provides the appropriate schemes.

7.1.1.2 Dummy variable

Dummy Coding corresponds to creating a variable (dummy variable) for each level of each factor minus one. Therefore, for a design where a factor has three levels, two variables are created: variable x_1 takes the value 0 for level one and level three, and 1 for level two and x_2 takes the value 0 for level one and level two, and 1 for level three. This implies that a separate coefficient will be estimated for each level, relative to the reference cell where all the dummy variables are 0.

7.1.1.3 Comparing effect coding and dummy coding

The two coding schemes do not give identical results because, from the presentation above, it is clear that effect coding places a restriction on the relationship which does not apply to dummy variable coding. Consequently, like any restricted form of a relationship compared to its unrestricted form, a test of the appropriateness of the restriction can be performed. The two approaches can consequently be combined to perform tests about the functional forms.

Table 7.4 Coefficient of orthogonal polynomials

Number of levels	Polynomial	Coefficients (di)										$\sum d_i^2$
3	Linear	−1	0	1								2
	Quadratic	1	−2	1								6
4	Linear	−3	−1	1	3							20
	Quadratic	1	−1	−1	1							4
	Cubic	−1	3	−3	1							20
5	Linear	−2	−1	0	1	2						10
	Quadratic	2	−1	−2	−1	2						14
	Cubic	−1	2	0	−2	1						10
	Quartic	1	−4	6	−4	1						70
6	Linear	−5	−3	−1	1	3	5					70
	Quadratic	5	−1	−4	−4	−1	5					84
	Cubic	−5	7	4	−4	−7	5					180
	Quartic	1	−3	2	2	−3	1					28
7	Linear	−3	−2	−1	0	1	2	3				28
	Quadratic	5	0	−3	−4	−3	0	5				84
	Cubic	−1	1	1	0	−1	−1	1				6
	Quartic	3	−7	1	6	1	−7	3				154
8	Linear	−7	−5	−3	−1	1	3	5	7			168
	Quadratic	7	1	−3	−5	−5	−3	1	7			168
	Cubic	−7	5	7	3	−3	−7	−5	7			264
	Quartic	7	−13	−3	9	9	−3	−13	7			616
	Quintic	−7	23	−17	−15	15	17	−23	7			2184
9	Linear	−4	−3	−2	−1	0	1	2	3	4		60
	Quadratic	28	7	−8	−17	−20	−17	−8	7	28		2772
	Cubic	−14	7	13	9	0	−9	−13	−7	14		990
	Quartic	14	−21	−11	9	18	9	−11	−21	14		2002
	Quintic	−4	11	−4	−9	0	9	4	−11	4		468
10	Linear	−9	−7	−5	−3	−1	1	3	5	7	9	330
	Quadratic	6	2	−1	−3	−4	−4	−3	−1	2	6	132
	Cubic	−42	14	35	31	12	−12	−31	−35	−14	42	8580
	Quartic	18	−22	−17	3	18	18	3	−17	−22	18	2860
	Quintic	−6	14	−1	−11	−6	6	11	1	−14	6	780

Adapted from: Fisher and Yates, *Statistical Tables for Biological, Agricultural and Medical Research*, published by Oliver and Boyd Ltd., Edinburgh (Table 23).

In summary, effect coding is appropriate when testing for the significance of the effect of a variable (conditionally on assuming a specific form of the relationship). Dummy coding is used to estimate and to test the effects of each level of a variable, independently of the other levels.

7.1.2 Design Programs

A particularity of conjoint analysis concerns the generation of the experimental design itself. Recently, several companies have developed PC based software for generating stimuli reflecting the combination of the levels of attributes. Two such software packages are Conjoint Designer, by Bretton-Clark and Consurv, by IMS Inc. Each of these packages offer similar services where, once the attributes and their levels are determined, generate the combination of the attributes in the form of the description of the stimuli, enable the entry of the data by respondents and analyze the data.

7.1.3 Estimation of Part-worth Coefficients

In section 7.1.1, we have discussed one of the characteristics of conjoint analysis: the specific nature of the independent variables. The other characteristic of conjoint analysis concerns the rank ordered nature of the dependent variable. Although the term "conjoint" has recently been used in more broadly contexts, these two aspects were initially what distinguished conjoint analysis from other methodologies. MONANOVA was developed as an appropriate methodology for estimating the effects of variables using the rank ordered nature of the dependent variable. More recently, as conjoint studies developed successfully in industry, the simpler Ordinary Least Squares estimation has replaced the use of MONANOVA. This is due not only to the simplicity but also to two other factors: (1) the robustness of OLS which gives generally similar results to those obtained from MONANOVA and (2) the increased usage of ratings instead of rankings for the dependent variables.

We first present MONANOVA and the estimation using PC-MDS. We then show how to perform OLS estimations using the SAS GLM procedure.

7.1.3.1 MONANOVA

Monotone Analysis of Variance is an estimation procedure based on an algorithm which transforms the dependent variable using a monotonic transformation so that the data can best be explained by a linear model of main effects of the independent variables or factors. More formally, let the data be represented by the set of values $\{\delta_{ij}\}$, each corresponding to the evaluation of alternative j by individual i ($i = 1, \ldots, I$; $j = 1, \ldots, J$). The data consists, therefore, for each individual of a table such as the one represented in Table 7.5.

Table 7.5 Example of input data for a 2 × 3 design

		2nd Factor		
	Levels	1	2	3
1st Factor	1	δ_{11}	δ_{12}	δ_{13}
	2	δ_{21}	δ_{22}	δ_{23}

The objective is, therefore, to estimate the main effects of each factor to fit best the relationship:

$$f(\delta_{ij}) = \beta_0 + \beta_1 x_{1ij} + \beta_2 x_{2ij} + \varepsilon_{ij} \tag{7.6}$$

where $f(\cdot)$ is a monotonic transformation of the rank ordered dependent variable and x_1 and x_2 are the variables representing the main effects of the two factors using effects coding.

The monotone transformations are performed using an algorithm to improve the fit.

7.1.3.2 OLS estimation

The GLM procedure found in SAS creates automatically the dummy variables which correspond to the design. By defining a variable as a discrete variable using the CLASS function, the levels of the variable are automatically generated with the proper dummy variables. The model is linear and the estimation follows the OLS estimation described in Chapter 4.

It remains that MONANOVA is technically more appropriate when rank data is obtained and used as a dependent variable. This is particularly important for academic research where inappropriate methods should not be used, even if technically inappropriate methods provide generally robust results. Obviously, the use of ratings makes OLS a perfectly appropriate methodology.

7.2 Ordered Probit

Ordered probit modeling is a relatively recent approach to analysing rank-ordered dependent variables (McKelvey and Zavoina 1975). Let us assume that there exists an unobserved variable Y, which can be expressed as a linear function of a single predictor variable X. Furthermore, while the variable Y is not observed, only discrete levels of that variable can be observed (levels one, two and three).

Figure 7.1 illustrates the case of a trichotomous dependent variable (observed variable) with a single independent variable.

It is important to make the distinction between the theoretical dependent variable Y and the observed dependent variable Z, which, in the example of Figure 7.1 takes three possible values.

The variable Y is an interval scale variable and, if we could observe it, it would fit a linear model $Y = X\beta + u$.

The variable Z is ordinal, and generally presents M observed response categories $R_1, \ldots, R_M$.

The model of the unobserved dependent variable Y follows the usual linear model assumptions:

$$Y = X\beta + u \tag{7.7}$$

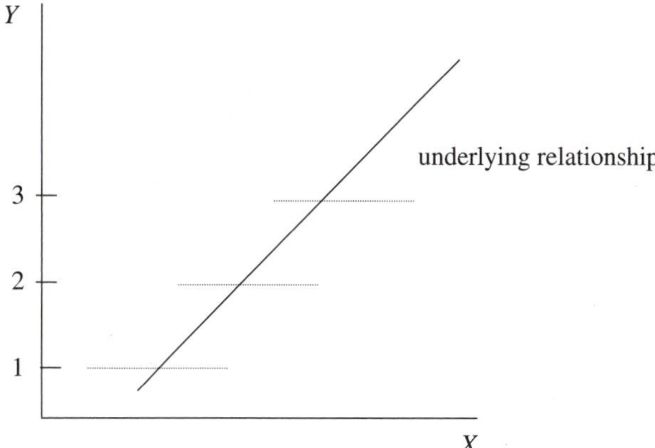

Fig. 7.1 The underlying linear relationship of the ordered probit model.

with

$$u \sim N(0, \sigma^2 I) \tag{7.8}$$

We define $M + 1$ real numbers $\mu_0, \ldots, \mu_M$ with the following prespecified values:

$$\mu_0 = -\infty$$
$$\mu_M = +\infty$$

These values are rank ordered such that $\mu_0 \leq \mu_1 \leq \cdots \leq \mu_M$.

Let us consider an individual observation i. The value of the dependent variable Z_{ij} will be one if the underlying unobserved variable falls within the values of Y_i in the range of $[\mu_{j-1}, \mu_j]$. This can be expressed as:

$$\mu_{j-1} < Y_i \leq \mu_j \Leftrightarrow Z_{ij} = 1; \quad \forall k \neq j; \;\; Z_{ik} = 0 \tag{7.9}$$

Let us focus our attention on the interval in which the value of Y_i falls.

$$\mu_{j-1} < Y_i \leq \mu_j \tag{7.10}$$

We can replace the unobserved variable by the linear function of observed variables which determines it.

$$\mu_{j-1} < X_i\beta + u_i \leq \mu_j \tag{7.11}$$

Subtracting the deterministic component from the boundaries, we obtain:

$$\mu_{j-1} - X_i\beta < u_i \leq \mu_j - X_i\beta \tag{7.12}$$

We can now standardize the values by dividing each element of the inequality by the standard deviation of the error term:

$$\frac{\mu_{j-1} - X_i\beta}{\sigma} < \frac{u_i}{\sigma} \leq \frac{\mu_j - X_i\beta}{\sigma} \tag{7.13}$$

The central element is a random variable with the normal distribution:

$$\frac{u_i}{\sigma} \sim N(0, 1) \tag{7.14}$$

We can therefore write the probability that this variable is within the range given by Equation (7.13) by subtracting the cumulative density functions at the upper and lower levels:

$$P[Z_{ij} = 1] = \phi\left[\frac{\mu_j - X_i\beta}{\sigma}\right] - \phi\left[\frac{\mu_{j-1} - X_i\beta}{\sigma}\right] \tag{7.15}$$

where ϕ is the cumulative density function:

$$\phi(t) = \int_{-\infty}^{t} \frac{1}{\sqrt{2\Pi}} e^{-x^2/2}\, dx \tag{7.16}$$

In order to identify the model, we need to impose the restrictions:

$$\mu_1 = 0$$
$$\sigma = 1$$

The first restriction has no consequence and the unit variance of the unobserved variable simply standardizes that variable. Consequently, Equation (7.15) reduces to:

$$P[Z_{ij} = 1] = \phi[\mu_j - X_i\beta] - \phi[\mu_{j-1} - X_i\beta] \tag{7.17}$$

The parameters which need to be estimated are:

$$\underset{k\times 1}{\beta}\,; \quad \mu_2, \ldots, \mu_{M-1}$$

This means that there are $(K + M - 2)$ parameters to be estimated.
The estimation is obtained by maximum likelihood.
Let

$$Y_{ij} = \mu_j - X_i\beta \tag{7.18}$$

and, for simplification of the notation:

$$\phi_{i,j} = \phi(Y_{ij}) \tag{7.19}$$

Then, the probability of Z_{ij} being in the interval $[\mu_{j-1}, \mu_j]$ is

$$P[Z_{ij} = 1] = \phi_{i,j} - \phi_{i,j-1} \tag{7.20}$$

Consequently, the likelihood of observing all the values of Z for all the observations in the data set is:

$$\mathbf{L} = \mathbf{L}(Z|\beta; \mu_2, \ldots, \mu_{M-1}) \tag{7.21}$$

$$= \prod_{i=1}^{N} \prod_{j=1}^{M} (\phi_{i,j} - \phi_{i,j-1})^{Z_{ij}} \tag{7.22}$$

The logarithm of the likelihood is:

$$\ell = \mathrm{Ln}\,\mathbf{L} = \sum_{i=1}^{N} \sum_{j=1}^{M} Z_{ij} \mathrm{Ln}(\phi_{i,j} - \phi_{i,j-1}) \tag{7.23}$$

The estimation problem consists in finding the values of the parameters which maximize the logarithm of the likelihood function ℓ, subject to the inequality constraints about the values of μs, i.e.,

$$\mu_1 \leq \mu_2 \leq \cdots \leq \mu_{M-1}$$

One issue can be raised as, sometimes, it is not always clear whether the dependent variable is ordered or not. The question is then to know whether one is better off using ordered versus an unordered model.

On the one hand, using an ordered model assumption when the true model is unordered creates a bias of the parameter estimates. On the other hand, using an unordered model when the true model is ordered does not create a bias but a loss of efficiency rather than consistency (Amemiya 1985, p. 293). Consequently, if the data is indeed ordered, the efficient and unbiased estimator will be provided by the Ordered model. Using an Unordered model may lead to parameters which are not significant but which would have been significant, had the most efficient model been used. Of course, this may not be an issue if all the parameters are significant. Using an ordered model if the data is not ordered is more dangerous because the parameter estimates are biased. Consequently, unless there is a strong theoretical reason for using an Ordered model, it is recommended to use a non-ordered model when the order property of the dependent variable is not clearly proven.

7.3 Examples

7.3.1 Example of MONANOVA Using PC-MDS

We will take the example of a $2 \times 2 \times 2$ design where the data is as given in Table 7.6.

Table 7.6 Example of data for data entry using PC-MDS MONANOVA (A 2^3 design)

		3rd Factor			
		2nd Factor		2nd Factor	
	Level	1	2	1	2
1st Factor	1	x_{111}	x_{121}	x_{112}	x_{122}
	2	x_{211}	x_{221}	x_{212}	x_{222}

Table 7.7 Parameter line for reading data shown in Table 7.6

Parameter line	3	2	2	2	1
	# of factors	# of levels of 1st Factor	# of levels of 2nd Factor	# of levels of 3rd Factor	# of replications

```
3  2  2  2  1
(8F10.2)
98.18     65.62     39.97     7.41      87.08     54.52     28.86     .0
```

Fig. 7.2 Example of input file for MONANOVA using PC-MDS (examp7-1.dat).

The MONANOVA program is ran by clicking on the monanova.exe file from Windows' Exporer. The data as well as the information about the run are contained in an input file. An example is given in Figure 7.2. The first line shows the parameters of the problem, as shown in Table 7.7.

The second line corresponds to the format in which the data can be read using FORTRAN conventions.

The third line (and subsequent lines if there are more than one replication) corresponds to the data line(s). The data must be entered in a specific sequence. This sequence is best described through an example. In our $2 \times 2 \times 2$ example, the indices of the x variable are such that the first index represents the level on the first factor, the second represents the level on the second factor and the third the level on the third factor. The sequence should then be as shown below:

$$\begin{array}{cccc} 111 & 112 & 121 & 122 \\ 211 & 212 & 221 & 222 \end{array}$$

The full input file is shown in Figure 7.2.

The results of the MONANOVA analysis are shown in Figure 7.3.

```
                        M O N A N O V A
               MONOTONE  ANALYSIS  OF  VARIANCE
                 WRITTEN BY DR. J. B. KRUSKAL
                        PC-MDS VERSION


ANALYSIS TITLE:              Monanova
DATA IS READ FROM FILE:      examp7-1.dat
OUTPUT FILE IS:              examp7-1.out

ANALYSIS START:  DATE  03/18/1999,  TIME  15:09:49

INPUT DATA FILE PARAMETERS:  3  2  2  2  1
INPUT FORMAT:          (8F10.2)


SEQ. NO.    DATA     SUBSCRIPTS

    1       98.18000    1    1    1
    2       65.62000    1    1    2
    3       39.97000    1    2    1
    4        7.41000    1    2    2
    5       87.08000    2    1    1
    6       54.52000    2    1    2
    7       28.86000    2    2    1
    8         .00000    2    2    2

HISTORY OF COMPUTATION.

ITERAT STRESS  SRAT  SRTAVG CAGRGL  COSAV  ACSAV   GRMAG   GRMULT   STEP
   0   .000   .0000 1.2000   .000   .000   .200  .00000  .00000 .00000

ZERO STRESS WAS REACHED
MINIMUM WAS ACHIEVED
SATISFACTORY STRESS WAS REACHED
FINAL CONFIGURATION HAS STRESS OF     .0 PERCENT.

Monanova

UTILITIES OUTPUT FOR LEVELS WITHIN FACTORS


  2   .266  -.266
  2  1.498 -1.498
  2   .827  -.827



              .    5.8908.  27.4904.  49.0900.  70.6896.  92.2892.
            -4.9090    16.6906    38.2902    59.8898    81.4894  103.0890
             *.****.****.****.****.****.****.****.****.****.****.*
        2.85 ..                                                .. 2.85
 T      2.64 ..                                            0   .. 2.64
```

```
H      2.43 ..                                                      ..   2.43
E      2.22 ..                                                      ..   2.22
       2.01 ..                                           0          ..   2.01
X      1.80 ..                                                      ..   1.80
       1.58 ..                                                      ..   1.58
A      1.37 ..                                                      ..   1.37
R      1.16 ..                                                      ..   1.16
E       .95 ..                                   0                  ..    .95
        .74 ..                                                      ..    .74
T       .53 ..                                                      ..    .53
H       .32 ..                               0                      ..    .32
E       .11 ..                                                      ..    .11
       -.11 ..                                                      ..   -.11
L      -.32 ..                        0                             ..   -.32
I      -.53 ..                                                      ..   -.53
N      -.74 ..                                                      ..   -.74
E      -.95 ..                   0                                  ..   -.95
A     -1.16 ..                                                      ..  -1.16
R     -1.37 ..                                                      ..  -1.37
      -1.58 ..                                                      ..  -1.58
M     -1.80 ..                                                      ..  -1.80
O     -2.01 ..       0                                              ..  -2.01
D     -2.22 ..                                                      ..  -2.22
E     -2.43 ..                                                      ..  -2.43
L     -2.64 ..  0                                                   ..  -2.64
      -2.85 ..                                                      ..  -2.85
              *.****.****.****.****.****.****.****.****.****.****.*
               .   5.8908.  27.4904.  49.0900.  70.6896.  92.2892.
             -4.9090   16.6906   38.2902   59.8898   81.4894  103.0890


SEQ NO  DATA      LINEAR   MONOTONE MODELS
   1    98.180     2.592     2.592
   2    65.620      .937      .937
   3    39.970     -.405     -.405
   4     7.410    -2.059    -2.059
   5    87.080     2.059     2.059
   6    54.520      .405      .405
   7    28.860     -.937     -.937
   8      .000    -2.592    -2.592

                               ************

          SPEARMAN-S RANK DIFFERENCE CORRELATION COEFFICIENT (RD)
                               RD           =  1.000000

                               RD - SQUARED =  1.000000

END MONANOVA RUN: Monanova
```

Fig. 7.3 Output File for MONANOVA example (examp7-1.out).

The utilities for the levels within each factor are shown under the heading "UTILITIES OUTPUT FOR LEVELS WITHIN FACTORS."

7.3.2 Example of Conjoint Analysis Using SAS

In the example below, data representing the ratings of different hypothetical schools are being used. The hypothetical schools were described in terms of (1) being either (a) not very or (b) very quantitative, (2) using methods of instructions characterized by (a) the case method, (b) half case and half lectures or (c) using only lectures, (3) the research reputation of the Faculty which can be (a) low, (b) moderate or (c) high, (4) the teaching reputation of the Faculty which can be also (a) low, (b) moderate or (c) high, and the overall prestige of the school as (a) one of the ivy league colleges, (b) a private school but not part of the ivy league and (c) a state school. The sample input file used with SAS is given in Figure 7.4.

Figure 7.5 gives the output of such analysis. The tests of significance of each factor are performed and then the marginal means of the dependent variable is shown for each level of each factor, one at a time. The example also illustrates the test of some restrictions on the parameters such as for linear effects.

7.3.3 Example of Ordered Probit Analysis Using LIMDEP

The input file for LIMDEP which enables the estimation of an ordered probit model is straightforward (Figure 7.6). The only difference with the statements for a logit type model specification is the use of the command

```
options ls=80;
DATA DATA1;
INFILE "C:\SAMD\Chapter7\Examples\Examp7-2.dat";
INPUT rating xid quant instruct resrep tearep
prestige;
PROC glm;
CLASS xid quant instruct resrep tearep prestige;
MODEL rating = quant instruct resrep tearep prestige;
MEANS QUANT INSTRUCT RESREP TEAREP PRESTIGE;
estimate 'quant' quant 1 -1;
estimate 'instr2 vs 1' instruct 1 -1 0;
estimate 'instr3 vs 1' instruct 1 0 -1;
run;
quit;
```

Fig. 7.4 Example of input file for conjoint analysis using SAS (examp7-2.sas).

```
The SAS System
                         General Linear Models Procedure
                            Class Level Information

                       Class      Levels     Values

                       XID             9     1 2 3 4 5 6 7 8 9

                       QUANT           2     1 2

                       INSTRUCT        3     1 2 3

                       RESREP          3     1 2 3

                       TEAREP          3     1 2 3

                       PRESTIGE        3     1 2 3

                     Number of observations in data set = 162

                         General Linear Models Procedure

Dependent Variable: RATING
                                         Sum of            Mean
Source                      DF          Squares          Square    F Value      Pr > F

Model                        9     465.30941469     51.70104608      24.01      0.0001

Error                      152     327.33256062      2.15350369

Corrected Total            161     792.64197531

                      R-Square             C.V.        Root MSE           RATING Mean

                      0.587036         33.76876       1.4674821             4.3456790

Source                      DF        Type I SS     Mean Square    F Value      Pr > F

QUANT                        1       0.00308642      0.00308642       0.00      0.9699
INSTRUCT                     2      21.48504274     10.74252137       4.99      0.0080
RESREP                       2      75.94088319     37.97044160      17.63      0.0001
TEAREP                       2     332.45486111    166.22743056      77.19      0.0001
PRESTIGE                     2      35.42554123     17.71277062       8.23      0.0004

Source                      DF      Type III SS     Mean Square    F Value      Pr > F

QUANT                        1       0.02816755      0.02816755       0.01      0.9091
INSTRUCT                     2      14.50887457      7.25443728       3.37      0.0370
RESREP                       2      64.20418593     32.10209297      14.91      0.0001
TEAREP                       2     302.01431665    151.00715833      70.12      0.0001
PRESTIGE                     2      35.42554123     17.71277062       8.23      0.0004
```

```
                 General Linear Models Procedure

             Level of          ------------RATING-----------
             QUANT        N        Mean                 SD

             1          108      4.34259259        2.27609289
             2           54      4.35185185        2.12049663

             Level of          ------------RATING-----------
             INSTRUCT     N        Mean                 SD

             1           63      4.30158730        2.35300029
             2           45      3.86666667        1.64593162
             3           54      4.79629630        2.41363759

             Level of          ------------RATING-----------
             RESREP       N        Mean                 SD

             1           54      3.37037037        1.85610971
             2           54      4.72222222        1.99448926
             3           54      4.94444444        2.46037784

             Level of          ------------RATING-----------
             TEAREP       N        Mean                 SD

             1           54      2.46296296        1.29895405
             2           54      4.62962963        1.61708212
             3           54      5.94444444        2.08694655

             Level of          ------------RATING-----------
             PRESTIGE     N        Mean                 SD

             1           54      4.94444444        2.34252457
             2           45      4.95555556        2.22542698
             3           63      3.39682540        1.75554130

                 General Linear Models Procedure

Dependent Variable: RATING

                                        T for H0:    Pr > |T|   Std Error of
Parameter                 Estimate   Parameter=0                  Estimate

quant                   0.02821743          0.11      0.9091      0.24672641
instr2 vs 1             0.13109512          0.42      0.6762      0.31324315
instr3 vs 1            -0.57290168         -2.04      0.0432      0.28097845
```

Fig. 7.5 Output for GLM procedure using SAS example (examp7-2.lst).

```
read; file = Examp7-3.wks;
format = WKS ;
names
$

open; output = c:\SAMD\Chapter7\Examples\Examp7-3.out$
ORDERED; lhs = Rnk;
         rhs = ONE, MBA_rate, Div_rate, R_Drate $
close$
```

Fig. 7.6 Example of ordered probit estimation using LIMDEP (examp7-3.lim).

"ORDERED". It should be noted that the right hand side list of variables must include one. This particular example concerns the ranking of business schools as a function of ratings on the MBA program, the diversity of populations represented in the schools and the rating of research activities of the schools. Figure 7.7 shows the results of the analysis.

Diversity appears insignificant but the rating of the MBA program as well as the rating of the school on R&D appear to strongly predict the overall ranking of the school.

7.4 Assignment

1. Decide on an issue to be analyzed with a conjoint study and gather data yourself on a few (10 to 20) individuals. Make sure that at least one of the factors has more than two levels.

   Investigate issues concerned with level of analysis and estimation procedures:

   Types of analysis:
   Aggregate analysis
   Individual level analysis

   Estimation:
   SAS GLM
   SAS with dummy variables
   SAS with effect coding
   MONANOVA

2. Using data from the SURVEY data, choose a rank ordered variable and develop a model to explain and predict this variable. Compare the multinomial logit model with the ordered logit or probit model. Use also a variable which is categorical and illustrate the problem of using an ordered logit or probit model when it is not appropriate.

```
: LIMDEP Estimation Results                        Run log line    3  Page    1 :
: Current sample contains      50 observations.                                 :
+==============================================================================+


+-----------------------------------------------------------------------+
| Dependent variable is binary, y=0 or y not equal 0                    |
| Ordinary    least squares regression    Weighting variable = none     |
| Dep. var. = Y=0/Not0 Mean=   .9000000000    , S.D.=    .3030457634    |
| Model size: Observations =       50, Parameters =   4, Deg.Fr.=    46 |
| Residuals:  Sum of squares= 1023.254148    , Std.Dev.=        4.71642 |
| Fit:        R-squared=*********, Adjusted R-squared =      -241.21958 |
| Diagnostic: Log-L =    -146.4149, Restricted(b=0) Log-L =    -10.7483 |
|             LogAmemiyaPrCrt.=    3.179, Akaike Info. Crt.=      6.017 |
+-----------------------------------------------------------------------+
+---------+--------------+----------------+--------+---------+----------+
|Variable | Coefficient  | Standard Error |b/St.Er.|P[|Z|>z] | Mean of X|
+---------+--------------+----------------+--------+---------+----------+
 Constant  1.299653062      2.8185737          .461   .6447
 MBA_RATE -.1151966230E-02  .51232691E-01    -.022   .9821  52.493633
 DIV_RATE -.4042208781E-02  .12218127        -.033   .9736  9.5247202
 R_DRATE  -.8542081297E-02  .34109580E-01    -.250   .8023  35.200000

Normal exit from iterations. Exit status=0.
+==============================================================================+
: LIMDEP Estimation Results                        Run log line    3  Page    2 :
: Current sample contains      50 observations.                                 :
+==============================================================================+

              +---------------------------------------------+
              | Ordered Probit Model                        |
              | Maximum Likelihood Estimates                |
              | Dependent variable                  RNK     |
              | Weighting variable                  ONE     |
              | Number of observations               50     |
              | Iterations completed                 27     |
              | Log likelihood function       -76.87438     |
              | Restricted log likelihood     -115.1293     |
              | Chi-squared                    76.50975     |
              | Degrees of freedom                    3     |
              | Significance level             .0000000     |
              |    Cell frequencies for outcomes            |
              |  Y Count Freq  Y Count Freq  Y Count Freq   |
              |  0      5 .100  1      5 .100  2      5 .100 |
              |  3      5 .100  4      5 .100  5      5 .100 |
              |  6      5 .100  7      5 .100  8      5 .100 |
              |  9      5 .100                              |
              +---------------------------------------------+

+---------+--------------+----------------+--------+---------+----------+
|Variable | Coefficient  | Standard Error |b/St.Er.|P[|Z|>z] | Mean of X|
+---------+--------------+----------------+--------+---------+----------+
```

```
         Index function for probability
Constant  11.27611554       1.9470225        5.791   .0000
MBA_RATE -.9184333969E-01  .14200317E-01   -6.468   .0000  52.493633
DIV_RATE  .6944545143E-02  .33367796E-01     .208   .8351  9.5247202
R_DRATE  -.8690702844E-01  .17888303E-01   -4.858   .0000  35.200000
         Threshold parameters for index
Mu( 1)    1.132867414       .41874468        2.705   .0068
Mu( 2)    2.318480730       .70743429        3.277   .0010
Mu( 3)    3.227069878       .78748983        4.098   .0000
Mu( 4)    3.929271873       .82592852        4.757   .0000
Mu( 5)    4.474735177       .84409675        5.301   .0000
Mu( 6)    5.000183482       .88623007        5.642   .0000
Mu( 7)    5.573052169       .95533576        5.834   .0000
Mu( 8)    6.311310116      1.0282479         6.138   .0000
```

Fig. 7.7 Output of ordered probit model using LIMPEP (examp7-3.out).

References

Basic Technical Readings

Amemiya, T. (1985), *Advanced Econometrics*, Cambridge, MS: Harvard University Press, [Chapter 9].

Cattin, P., A. E. Gelfand and J. Danes (1983), "A Simple Bayesian Procedure for Estimation in a Conjoint Model," *Journal of Marketing Research*, 20 (February), 29–35.

Green, P. E. and V. R. Rao (1971), "Conjoint Measurement for Quantifying Judgmental Data," *Journal of Marketing Research*, 8 (August), 355–363.

Louviere, J. J. (1988), "Conjoint Analysis Modeling of Stated Preferences," *Journal of Transport Economics and Policy*, 22, 1 (January), 93–119.

McKelvey, R. D. and W. Zavoina (1975), "A Statistical Model for the Analysis of Ordinal Level Dependent Variables," *Journal of Mathematical Sociology*, 4, 103–120.

Application Readings

Beggs, S., S. Cardell and J. Hausman (1981), "Assessing The Potential Demand for Electric Cars," *Journal of Econometrics*, 16, 1–19.

Bowman, D. and H. Gatignon (1995), "Determinants of Competitor Response Time to a New Product Introduction," *Journal of Marketing Research*, 32, 1 (February), 42–53.

Bunch, D. S. and R. Smiley (1992), "Who Deters Entry? Evidence on the Use of Strategic Entry Deterrents," *The Review of Economics and Statistics*, 74, 3 (August), 509–521.

Chu, W. and E. Anderson (1992), "Capturing Ordinal Properties of Categorical Dependent Variables: A Review with Applications to Modes of Foreign Entry and Choice of Industrial Sales Force," *International Journal of Research in Marketing*, 9, 149–160.

Green, P. E. (1984), "Hybrid Models for Conjoint Analysis: An Expository Review," *Journal of Marketing Research*, 21 (May), 155–169.

Green, P. E. and V. Srinivasan (1978), "Conjoint Analysis in Consumer Research: Issues and Outlook," *Journal of Consumer Research*, 5 (September), 103–123.

Green, P. E. and V. Srinivasan (1990), "Conjoint Analysis in Marketing: New Developments With Applications for Research and Practice," *Journal of Marketing*, October, 3–19.

Green, P. E. and Y. Wind (1975), "A New Way to Measure Consumers' Judgements," *Harvard Business Review*, July–August, 107–117.

Green, P. E., A. M. Krieger and M. K. Agarwal (1991), "Adaptive Conjoint Analysis: Some Caveats and Suggestions," *Journal of Marketing Research*, 28, May, 215–222.

Jain, D. C., E. Muller, et al. (1999), "Pricing Patterns of Cellular Phones and Phonecalls: A Segment-Level Analysis," *Management Science* 45, 2 (February), 131–141.

Mahajan, V., P. E. Green and S. M. Goldberg (1982), "A Conjoint Model for Measuring Self- and Cross-Price/Demand Relationships," *Journal of Marketing Research*, 19 (August), 334–342.

Page, A. L. and H. F. Rosenbaum (1987), "Redesigning Product Lines with Conjoint Analysis: How Sunbeam Does it," *Journal of Product Innovation Management*, 4, 120–137.

Priem, R. L. (1992), "An Application of Metric Conjoint Analysis for the Evaluation of Top Managers' Individual Strategic Decision Making Processes: A Research Note," *Strategic Management Journal*, 13, 143–151.

Rangaswami, A. and G. R. Shell (1997), "Using Computers to Realize Joint Gains in Negociations: Toward an "Electronic Bargaining Table"," *Management Science* 43, 8 (August), 1147–1163.

Srinivasan, V. and C. S. Park (1997), "Surprising Robustness of the Self-Explicated Approach to Customer Preference Structure Measurement", *Journal of Marketing Research*, 34, 2 (May), 286–291.

Wind, J., P. E. Green, D. Shifflet and M. Scarbrough (1989), "Courtyard by Marriott: Designing a Hotel Facility with Consumer-Based Marketing Models" *Interfaces*, 19 (January–February), 25–47.

8. Error in Variables – Analysis of Covariance Structure

We will demonstrate that a bias is introduced when estimating the relationship between two variables measured with error. We will then present a methodology for estimating the parameters of structural relationships between variables which are not observed directly: the analysis of covariance structures. We will discuss especially the confirmatory factor analytic model, as presented in Chapter 3 and we will elaborate on the estimation of the measurement model parameters.

8.1 The Impact of Imperfect Measures

In this section, we discuss the bias introduced by estimating a regression model with variables which are measured with error.

8.1.1 Effect of Errors-in-variables

Let us assume two variables, a dependent variable and an independent variable, y_t and x_t respectively, which are observed. However, these variables are imperfect measures of the true unobserved variables y_t^* and x_t^*. The measurement models for both variables are expressed by the equations:

$$x_t = x_t^* + u_t \tag{8.1}$$

$$y_t = y_t^* + v_t \tag{8.2}$$

There exist a relationship, a structural relationship, between these two unobserved variables, as indicated by the equation below:

$$y_t^* = x_t^* \beta \tag{8.3}$$

This equation can be expressed in terms of the observed variables by replacing the unobserved variables by their expression as a function of the observed variables obtained from Equations (8.1) and (8.2):

$$y_t = (x_t - u_t)\beta + v_t \tag{8.4}$$

or, placing the random error terms at the end:

$$y_t = x_t\beta + v_t - u_t\beta \tag{8.5}$$

It should be noted that the error on the dependent variable y is similar to the error on the structural relationship. Indeed, if we had added an error term to Equation (8.3), it would have been confounded with the measurement error of the dependent variable v_t.

Because the variables are not observed, only the relationship between the observed variables can be estimated. This can be done by using the Ordinary Least Square estimator of the regression of y_t on x_t:

$$\hat{\boldsymbol{\beta}}_{\text{OLS}} = (\mathbf{x}'\mathbf{x})^{-1}\mathbf{x}'\mathbf{y} \tag{8.6}$$

The bias can be evaluated by taking the expectation of the OLS estimator:

$$\begin{aligned} E[\hat{\boldsymbol{\beta}}_{\text{OLS}}] &= E[(\mathbf{x}'\mathbf{x})^{-1}\mathbf{x}'\mathbf{y}] \\ &= E[(\mathbf{x}'\mathbf{x})^{-1}\mathbf{x}'(\mathbf{x}\beta + v - u\beta)] \\ &= \beta + (\mathbf{x}'\mathbf{x})^{-1}E[\mathbf{x}'(v - u\beta)] \\ &= \beta + (\mathbf{x}'\mathbf{x})^{-1}E[(\mathbf{x}^* + u)'(v - u\beta)] \\ E[\hat{\boldsymbol{\beta}}_{\text{OLS}}] &= \beta + E\left[(\mathbf{x}'\mathbf{x})^{-1}(-\beta\sigma_u^2)\right] \end{aligned} \tag{8.7}$$

where $E[u'u] = \sigma_u^2$. Therefore, the bias is:

$$E[\hat{\boldsymbol{\beta}}_{\text{OLS}}] - \beta = E[(\mathbf{x}'\mathbf{x})^{-1}(-\beta\sigma_u^2)] \tag{8.8}$$

if x has mean of 0, the bias is

$$-\beta\frac{\sigma_u^2}{\sigma_x^2} \tag{8.9}$$

since $\sigma_x^2 = \sigma_{x^*}^2 + \sigma_u^2$, the bias can be expressed as

$$-\beta\frac{\sigma_u^2}{\sigma_{x^*}^2 + \sigma_u^2} = -\beta\frac{1}{1+\rho} \tag{8.10}$$

where $\rho = \sigma_{x^*}^2/\sigma_u^2$ is the signal to noise ratio.

From Equation (8.10), we can not only assert that there is a bias but we can also indicate properties about this bias. Because the variances in the signal to noise ratio are positive ($\sigma_u^2, \sigma_{x^*}^2 > 0$), this means that the bias is always negative (Equation (8.10) is always negative), i.e., the OLS estimates are under-estimated when using a predictor variable with error. This may lead to failing to reject the null hypothesis that the effect of the independent variable on the dependent variable is insignificant.

As the signal to noise ratio ρ increases, the bias decreases [$1/(1+\rho)$ becomes smaller]. Therefore, we can summarize the results as follows:

1. We have found a lower bound for b. Indeed, we have shown that the OLS estimator $\hat{\boldsymbol{\beta}}_{\text{OLS}}$ is smaller than the true β.

2. Error in measurement of x attenuates the effect of x.
3. Error in measurement of y does not bias the effect of x (the measurement error is then confounded with the noise in the relationship between the independent and dependent variables).

8.1.2 Reversed Regression

Let us write the equation which expresses the independent variable x_t as a function of the dependent variable y_t:

$$x_t = \gamma y_t + \varepsilon_t \tag{8.11}$$

Or, for all the observations:

$$\mathbf{x} = \gamma \mathbf{y} + \boldsymbol{\varepsilon} \tag{8.12}$$

The OLS estimator of the parameter γ is:

$$\hat{\gamma}_{\text{OLS}} = (\mathbf{y}'\mathbf{y})^{-1}\mathbf{y}'\mathbf{x} \tag{8.13}$$

Let

$$\hat{\boldsymbol{\beta}}^R = \frac{1}{\hat{\gamma}_{\text{OLS}}} = \frac{\mathbf{y}'\mathbf{y}}{\mathbf{y}'\mathbf{x}} \tag{8.14}$$

If the variables are centered to zero mean:

$$\hat{\boldsymbol{\beta}}^R = \frac{V[y]}{\text{Cov}[x, y]} \tag{8.15}$$

However, from Equations (8.2) and (8.3):

$$y = x^*\beta + v \tag{8.16}$$

Consequently,

$$V[y] = \beta^2\sigma_{x^*}^2 + \sigma_v^2 \tag{8.17}$$

and

$$\text{Cov}[x, y] = \beta\sigma_{x^*}^2 \tag{8.18}$$

Therefore, Equation (8.15) can be expressed as

$$\begin{aligned} \hat{\boldsymbol{\beta}}^R &= \frac{\beta^2\sigma_{x^*}^2 + \sigma_v^2}{\beta\sigma_{x^*}^2} = \beta\left(\frac{\beta^2\sigma_{x^*}^2 + \sigma_v^2}{\beta^2\sigma_{x^*}^2}\right) \\ &= \beta\left(1 + \frac{\sigma_v^2}{\beta^2\sigma_{x^*}^2}\right) = \beta(1 + \omega) \end{aligned} \tag{8.19}$$

where $\omega = \sigma_v^2/(\beta^2\sigma_{x^*}^2)$, which is always positive.

Because ω is positive, it follows that $\hat{\boldsymbol{\beta}}^R$ overestimates β. If we recall that the coefficient obtained from a direct regression (Equation (8.6)), which we may call $\hat{\boldsymbol{\beta}}^D$, always under-estimates the true value of β, we then have shown that $\hat{\boldsymbol{\beta}}^D$ and $\hat{\boldsymbol{\beta}}^R$ provide bounds in the range where the true β falls.

Consequently, the choice of the dependent variable in a simple regression has nothing to do with causality. It follows from the analysis presented above that if σ_v^2 is small, one should use reversed regression (ω in Equation (8.19) is then close to 0 and the bias is small). If, however, σ_u^2 is small, direct regression should be used because the bias in Equation (8.6) is then small. From this discussion, it follows that the researcher should select for the dependent variable, the variable with the largest measurement error.

8.1.3 Case with Multiple Independent Variables

The case where there are several independent variables is more complex. Let us consider Equation (8.20) where some variables ($\mathbf{z}_t$) are estimated without error, and others ($\mathbf{x}_t^*$) are estimated with measurement error:

$$y_t^* = \mathbf{z}_t\gamma + \mathbf{x}_t^*\beta \tag{8.20}$$

In such cases, the direction of the bias is not easy to analyze. Some conclusions are possible, however, in the special case when only one of the independent variables is measured with error, i.e., $\mathbf{x}_t$ is a single variable. Then, it can be shown that the bias can be expressed as follows:

$$-\beta\frac{\sigma_u^2}{\sigma_x^2(1 - R_{x\mathbf{z}}^2)} \tag{8.21}$$

where $R_{x\mathbf{z}}^2$ is the R-squared of the regression of the variable measured with error (x_t) on those measured without error ($\mathbf{z}_t$).

Because the ratio which multiplies $-\beta$ in Equation (8.21) is always positive, the coefficient is, therefore, always under-estimated.

It should be noted that having one of the independent variable measured with error does not affect only the estimation of the impact of that variable. It also affects the coefficients of the variables measured without error. Furthermore, both the overall F statistics and the individual coefficient variances are affected. The F Statistic is always understated. Therefore, we would expect to reject the models more often than we should. The impact on individual statistics is not as clear, however, as there is no unambiguous bias.

This case of a single variable measured with error is, however, unusal. Most of the research in the social sciences involves the formation of scales that cannot be considered to be without measurement error. In such cases, the analysis shown in the first section of this chapter does not provide any guidance. The second section presents a methodology, the analysis of covariance structure, which takes care of the problems associated with measurement errors.

8.2 Analysis of Covariance Structures

In the analysis of covariance structure, both the measurement errors and the structural relationships between the variables of interest are modeled.

8.2.1 Description of Model

We start with a system of simultaneous equations identical to the ones analyzed in Chapter 5:

$$\underset{m\times m}{\mathbf{B}}\;\underset{m\times 1}{\eta} = \underset{m\times n}{\mathbf{\Gamma}}\;\underset{m\times 1}{\xi} + \underset{m\times 1}{\zeta} \tag{8.22}$$

where m = number of endogenous constructs, n = number of exogenous constructs, η = column vector of m endogenous constructs, ξ = column vector of n exogenous constructs, ζ = column vector of m disturbance terms, $\mathbf{B}$ = matrix of structural parameters of endogenous variables, $\mathbf{\Gamma}$ = matrix of structural parameters of exogenous variables.

The endogenous constructs are represented by the vector η and the exogenous ones by ξ. Equation (8.22) represents the structural relationships that exist among the constructs η and ξ with a random disturbance ζ. The diagonal elements of the matrix $\mathbf{B}$ are specified as being equal to one without affecting the generality of the model. The endogenous and exogenous constructs η and ξ are not observed but are, instead, measured with error using multiple items. Before defining the measurement models, we should note that these unobserved constructs are defined as centered with zero mean without any loss of generality.

$$E[\eta] = E[\xi] = 0 \tag{8.23}$$

Like for the regression model, the error term is assumed to have zero mean:

$$E[\zeta] = 0 \tag{8.24}$$

In addition, the matrix of parameters $\mathbf{B}$ should be nonsingular.

Let us now define the factor analytic measurement models. These are represented by Equations (8.25) and (8.26). There are p items or observable variables reflecting the m endogenous constructs and there are q items or observable variables reflecting the n exogenous constructs

$$\underset{p\times 1}{\mathbf{y}} = \underset{p\times m}{\mathbf{\Lambda}_y}\;\underset{m\times 1}{\eta} + \underset{p\times 1}{\boldsymbol{\varepsilon}} \tag{8.25}$$

where p = number of items measuring the m endogenous constructs, $\mathbf{y}$ = column vector of the p items or observable variables reflecting the endogenous constructs, $\mathbf{\Lambda}_y$ = matrix of factor loadings, $\boldsymbol{\varepsilon}$ = column vector of measurement errors.

The elements of the matrix $\mathbf{\Lambda}_y$ represent the factor loadings. Similarly for the measurement model of the exogenous constructs:

$$\underset{q\times 1}{\mathbf{x}} = \underset{q\times n}{\mathbf{\Lambda}_x}\ \underset{n\times 1}{\boldsymbol{\xi}} + \underset{q\times 1}{\boldsymbol{\delta}} \tag{8.26}$$

where q = number of items measuring the n exogenous constructs, $\mathbf{x}$ = column vector of the q items or observable variables reflecting the exogenous constructs, $\mathbf{\Lambda}_x$ = matrix of factor loadings, $\boldsymbol{\delta}$ = column vector of measurement errors.

Furthermore, we can express the covariances of the latent variables and of the error terms according to Equations (8.27) through (8.30).

$$E[\boldsymbol{\xi}\boldsymbol{\xi}'] = \underset{n\times n}{\mathbf{\Phi}} \tag{8.27}$$

$$E[\boldsymbol{\zeta}\boldsymbol{\zeta}'] = \underset{m\times m}{\mathbf{\Psi}} \tag{8.28}$$

$$E[\boldsymbol{\varepsilon}\boldsymbol{\varepsilon}'] = \underset{p\times p}{\mathbf{\Theta}_{\varepsilon}} \tag{8.29}$$

$$E[\boldsymbol{\delta}\boldsymbol{\delta}'] = \underset{q\times q}{\mathbf{\Theta}_{\delta}} \tag{8.30}$$

We can now write the expression of what would theoretically be the covariance matrix of all the observed variables ($\mathbf{x}$ and $\mathbf{y}$), assuming the model expressed in the equations above. Let

$$\underset{(p+q)\times 1}{\mathbf{z}} = \begin{pmatrix} \mathbf{y} \\ \mathbf{x} \end{pmatrix} \tag{8.31}$$

The theoretical covariance matrix of $\mathbf{z}$ is

$$\mathbf{\Sigma} = E[\mathbf{z}\mathbf{z}'] = E\left[\begin{pmatrix} \mathbf{y} \\ \mathbf{x} \end{pmatrix} (\mathbf{y}' \quad \mathbf{x}')\right] = E\begin{bmatrix} \mathbf{y}\mathbf{y}' & \mathbf{y}\mathbf{x}' \\ \mathbf{x}\mathbf{y}' & \mathbf{x}\mathbf{x}' \end{bmatrix} \tag{8.32}$$

We will derive the expression of each of the four submatrices in Equation (8.32) with the following three blocks (the off-diagonal blocks are symmetric):

$$\begin{aligned} E[\mathbf{x}\mathbf{x}'] &= E[(\mathbf{\Lambda}_x\boldsymbol{\xi} + \boldsymbol{\delta})(\mathbf{\Lambda}_x\boldsymbol{\xi} + \boldsymbol{\delta})'] \\ &= E[\mathbf{\Lambda}_x\boldsymbol{\xi}\boldsymbol{\xi}'\mathbf{\Lambda}_x'] + E[\boldsymbol{\delta}\boldsymbol{\delta}'] \\ &= \mathbf{\Lambda}_x\mathbf{\Phi}\mathbf{\Lambda}_x' + \mathbf{\Theta}_{\delta} \end{aligned} \tag{8.33}$$

$$
\begin{aligned}
E[\mathbf{y}\mathbf{y}'] &= E\left[(\boldsymbol{\Lambda}_y\boldsymbol{\eta}+\boldsymbol{\varepsilon})(\boldsymbol{\Lambda}_y\boldsymbol{\eta}+\boldsymbol{\varepsilon})'\right]\\
&= \boldsymbol{\Lambda}_y E[\boldsymbol{\eta}\boldsymbol{\eta}']\boldsymbol{\Lambda}_y' + \boldsymbol{\Theta}_\varepsilon\\
&= \boldsymbol{\Lambda}_y E[\mathbf{B}^{-1}\boldsymbol{\Gamma}\boldsymbol{\xi}\boldsymbol{\xi}'\Gamma'\mathbf{B}^{-1'} + \mathbf{B}^{-1}\boldsymbol{\zeta}\boldsymbol{\zeta}'\mathbf{B}^{-1'}]\boldsymbol{\Lambda}_y' + \boldsymbol{\Theta}_\varepsilon\\
&= \boldsymbol{\Lambda}_y(\mathbf{B}^{-1}\boldsymbol{\Gamma}\boldsymbol{\Phi}\boldsymbol{\Gamma}'\mathbf{B}^{-1'}+\mathbf{B}^{-1}\boldsymbol{\Psi}\mathbf{B}^{-1'})\boldsymbol{\Lambda}_y' + \boldsymbol{\Theta}_\varepsilon \qquad (8.34)\\
E[\mathbf{y}\mathbf{x}'] &= E[(\boldsymbol{\Lambda}_y\boldsymbol{\eta}+\boldsymbol{\varepsilon})(\boldsymbol{\Lambda}_x\boldsymbol{\xi}+\boldsymbol{\delta})']\\
&= E[(\boldsymbol{\Lambda}_y\mathbf{B}^{-1}\boldsymbol{\Gamma}\xi + \mathbf{B}^{-1}\zeta + \boldsymbol{\varepsilon})(\boldsymbol{\Lambda}_x\boldsymbol{\xi}+\boldsymbol{\delta})']\\
&= \boldsymbol{\Lambda}_y\mathbf{B}^{-1}\boldsymbol{\Gamma}\boldsymbol{\Phi}\boldsymbol{\Lambda}_x' \qquad (8.35)
\end{aligned}
$$

Equations (8.33) through (8.35) provide the information to complete the covariance matrix in Equation (8.32). In fact, the observed covariance matrix can be computed from the sample of observations:

$$\mathbf{S} = \begin{bmatrix}\mathbf{S}_{\mathbf{yy}} & \mathbf{S}_{\mathbf{yx}}\\ \mathbf{S}_{\mathbf{xy}} & \mathbf{S}_{\mathbf{xx}}\end{bmatrix} \qquad (8.36)$$

8.2.2 Estimation

The estimation consists in finding the parameters of the model which will replicate as closely as possible the observed covariance matrix in Equation (8.36). For the maximum likelihood estimation, the comparison of the matrices $\mathbf{S}$ and $\boldsymbol{\Sigma}$ is made through the following expression:

$$F = \text{Ln}|\boldsymbol{\Sigma}| + \text{tr}(\mathbf{S}\boldsymbol{\Sigma}^{-1}) - \text{Ln}|\mathbf{S}| - (p+q) \qquad (8.37)$$

The expression F is minimized (note that the last term $-\text{Ln}|\mathbf{S}| - (p+q)$ is a constant) by searching over values for each of the parameters. If the observed variables $\begin{pmatrix}\mathbf{y}\\ \mathbf{x}\end{pmatrix}$ are distributed as a multivariate normal distribution, the parameter estimates that minimize the Equation (8.37) are the maximum likelihood estimates.

There are $\frac{1}{2}(p+q)(p+q+1)$ distinct elements which constitute the data (this comes from half of the symmetric matrix to which one needs to add back half of the diagonal in order to count the variances of the variables themselves (i.e., $[(p+q)\times(p+q)/2+(p+q)/2]$). Consequently, the number of degrees of freedom corresponds to the number of distinct data points as defined above minus the number of parameters in the model to estimate.

An example will illustrate the model and the degrees of freedom. MacKenzie, Lutz and Belch (1986) compare several models of the role of attitude toward the ad on brand attitude and purchase intentions. Focusing on their dual mediation hypothesis model (DMH) which they found to be supported by the data, three types of cognitive responses to advertising (about the ad execution, about the source and about repetition) are the three exogenous constructs explaining the attitude toward the ad. Attitude toward the ad, according to that DMH theory, affects the attitude towards the brand not only directly but also indirectly by affecting brand cognitions which, in turn, affect the attitude toward the brand. Purchase intentions are affected by the attitude towards the brand as well as directly by the attitude towards the ad. These relationships between the three exogenous constructs and these four endogenous constructs are drawn in Figure 8.1.

These relationships can be expressed by the system of four equations:

$$\begin{aligned}
\eta_1 &= \beta_{12}\eta_2 + \gamma_{11}\xi_1 + \gamma_{12}\xi_2 + \gamma_{13}\xi_3 + \zeta_1 \\
\eta_2 &= \beta_{21}\eta_1 + \beta_{24}\eta_4 + \zeta_2 \\
\eta_3 &= \beta_{31}\eta_1 + \beta_{32}\eta_2 + \zeta_3 \\
\eta_4 &= \beta_{41}\eta_1 + \zeta_4
\end{aligned} \tag{8.38}$$

or

$$\begin{bmatrix} 1 & \beta_{12} & 0 & 0 \\ -\beta_{21} & 1 & 0 & -\beta_{24} \\ -\beta_{31} & -\beta_{32} & 1 & 0 \\ -\beta_{41} & 0 & 0 & 1 \end{bmatrix} \begin{bmatrix} \eta_1 \\ \eta_2 \\ \eta_3 \\ \eta_4 \end{bmatrix} = \begin{bmatrix} \gamma_{11} & \gamma_{12} & \gamma_{13} \\ 0 & 0 & 0 \\ 0 & 0 & 0 \\ 0 & 0 & 0 \end{bmatrix} \begin{bmatrix} \xi_1 \\ \xi_2 \\ \xi_3 \end{bmatrix} + \begin{bmatrix} \zeta_1 \\ \zeta_2 \\ \zeta_3 \\ \zeta_4 \end{bmatrix} \tag{8.39}$$

In addition, Figure 8.1 indicates that the exogenous constructs are each measured by a single item, x_1 for ξ_1, x_2 for ξ_2 and x_3 for ξ_3. The attitude towards the ad (η_1) is measured by two items y_1 and y_2. The attitude towards the brand (η_2) and purchase intentions (η_3) are both measured by three items, y_3, y_4 and y_5 for η_2, and y_6, y_7 and y_8 for η_3. Finally, the brand cognitions (η_4) are measured by a single indicator y_9. The measurement model for the endogenous constructs can then be represented by Equation (8.40) and the measurement model for the exogenous constructs can be expressed by Equation (8.41):

$$\begin{bmatrix} y_1 \\ y_2 \\ y_3 \\ y_4 \\ y_5 \\ y_6 \\ y_7 \\ y_8 \\ y_9 \end{bmatrix} = \begin{bmatrix} \lambda_{y1} & 0 & 0 & 0 \\ \lambda_{y2} & 0 & 0 & 0 \\ 0 & \lambda_{y3} & 0 & 0 \\ 0 & \lambda_{y4} & 0 & 0 \\ 0 & \lambda_{y5} & 0 & 0 \\ 0 & 0 & \lambda_{y6} & 0 \\ 0 & 0 & \lambda_{y7} & 0 \\ 0 & 0 & \lambda_{y8} & 0 \\ 0 & 0 & 0 & \lambda_{y9} \end{bmatrix} \begin{bmatrix} \eta_1 \\ \eta_2 \\ \eta_3 \\ \eta_4 \end{bmatrix} + \begin{bmatrix} \varepsilon_1 \\ \varepsilon_2 \\ \varepsilon_3 \\ \varepsilon_4 \\ \varepsilon_5 \\ \varepsilon_6 \\ \varepsilon_7 \\ \varepsilon_8 \\ \varepsilon_9 \end{bmatrix} \tag{8.40}$$

and

$$\begin{bmatrix} x_1 \\ x_2 \\ x_3 \end{bmatrix} = \begin{bmatrix} \lambda_{x1} & 0 & 0 \\ 0 & \lambda_{x2} & 0 \\ 0 & 0 & \lambda_{x3} \end{bmatrix} \begin{bmatrix} \xi_1 \\ \xi_2 \\ \xi_3 \end{bmatrix} + \begin{bmatrix} \delta_1 \\ \delta_2 \\ \delta_3 \end{bmatrix} \tag{8.41}$$

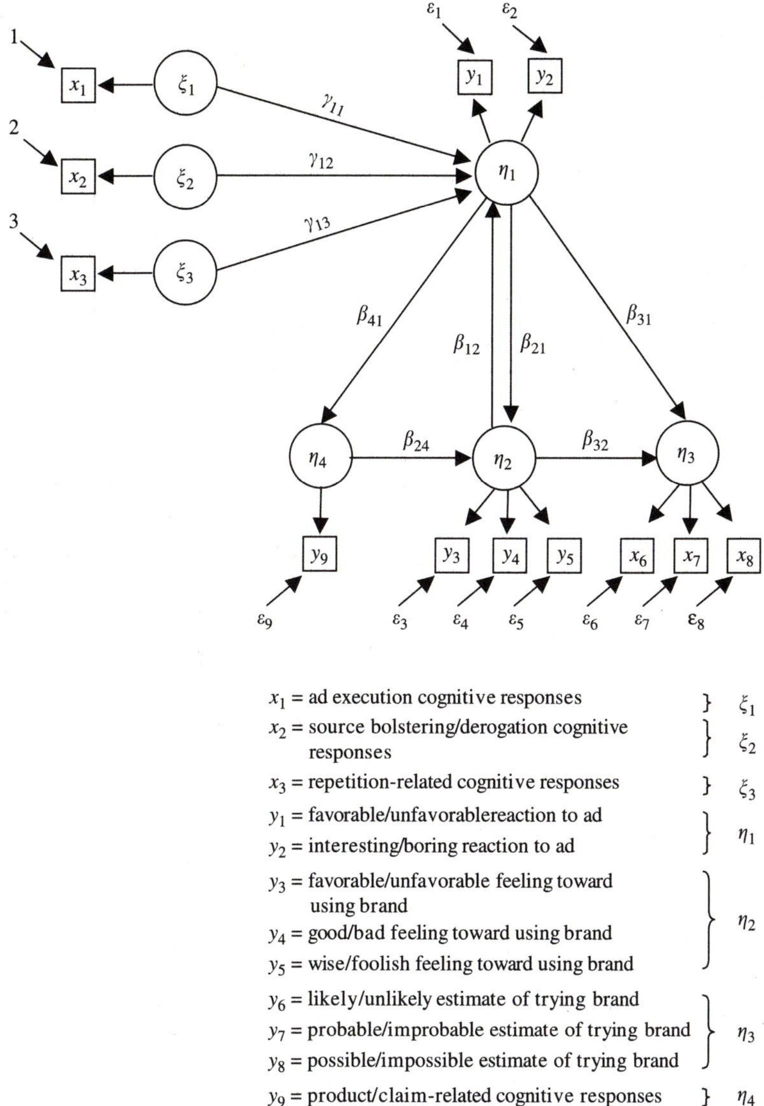

Fig. 8.1 A graphical representation of MacKenzie, Lutz and Belch's Model (1986) of the role of attitude towards the ad. Adapted from MacKenzie, Lutz and Belch (1986).

It should be noted that some restrictions on the measurement model parameters must be made for identification purposes. For each construct, the unit or scale of measurement must be defined. This is accomplished by setting one of the lambdas for a given construct to one; the corresponding variable will then serve as the unit of reference for that construct. For example, we can define $\lambda_{y1} = \lambda_{y3} = \lambda_{y6} = \lambda_{y9} = \lambda_{x1} = \lambda_{x2} = \lambda_{x3} = 1$. Alternatively, especially in the case of confirmatory factor analysis, the variance of the constructs could be set to unity.

We also need to impose some restrictions on some parameters in the cases where the constructs are measured by a single item. In such cases indeed, the loading parameter is set to one, as discussed above and the error term is necessarily equal to zero. This means that the variance of the error term of that measurement equation must be constrained to be zero. This is the case for the example with $\theta_{\varepsilon 9}$, $\theta_{\delta 1}$, $\theta_{\delta 2}$ and $\theta_{\delta 3}$. Normally, the covariance matrices $\boldsymbol{\theta}_\delta$ and $\boldsymbol{\theta}_\varepsilon$ are assumed to be diagonal. Exceptionally, a few of the correlations between error terms of measurement equations can be estimated. This was the case in the example reported above from MacKenzie, Lutz and Belch (1986). However, it should only be done with great care, as the interpretation may be difficult.

The covariance matrix of the exogenous constructs can be symmetric or, with orthogonal factors it can be defined as diagonal with zero covariances. With orthogonal factors in the example, three variances $\boldsymbol{\Psi}$ must be estimated.

Finally, the covariance matrix $\boldsymbol{\Phi}$ must be specified. It can be symmetric in the general case where the error terms of the structural equations are correlated. In this example, there would be four variances and six covariances to estimate. The matrix is often assumed to be diagonal, in which case only four parameters (four variances) need to be estimated.

The equations described and the restrictions applied above indicate that 29 parameters must be estimated: there are 5 lambdas, 6 betas, 3 gammas, 8 thetas, 4 phis and 3 psis. Given that with twelve observed variables the covariance matrix consists of 78 different data points (i.e., $(12 \times 13)/2$), this leaves 49 degrees of freedom.

8.2.3 Model Fit

The measure of the fit of the model to the data corresponds to the criterion which was minimized, i.e., a measure of the extent to which the model, given the best possible values of the parameters, can lead to a covariance matrix of the observed variables that is sufficiently similar to the actually observed covariance matrix. We first present and discuss the basic chi-squared test of the fit of the model. We then introduce a number of measures of fit that are typically reported and which alleviate the problems inherent to the chi-squared test. We finally discuss how modification indices can be used as diagnostics for model improvement.

8.2.3.1 Chi-square tests

Based on large sample distribution theory, $v = (N - 1)\hat{F}$ (where N is the sample size used to generate the covariance matrix of the observed variables and $\hat{F}$ is the minimum value of the expression F as defined by Equation (8.37) is distributed as a chi-squared with the number of degrees of freedom corresponding to the number of data points minus the number of estimated parameters, as computed in the example above. If the value of v is significantly greater than zero, the model is rejected; this means that the theoretical model is unable to generate data with a covariance matrix close enough to the one obtained from the actual data.

One problem with that expression v is due to the fact that it contains N, the sample size, in the numerator. This means that as the sample size increases, it becomes less likely that one will fail to reject the model. This is why several other measures of fit have been developpped. They are discussed below. Another problem inherent to the methodology is the fact that the hypothesis which the researcher would like to get support for is the null hypothesis that there is no difference between the observed covariance matrix and the matrix that can be generated by the model. Failure to reject the hypothesis, and therefore "accepting" the model, can, therefore, be due to the lack of power of the test. This is clearly apparent in the issue mentionned above concerning the sample size. A small enough sample size can contribute to finding fitting models based on chi-squared tests.

It should be noted that the sample size problem disappears when two nested models are compared. Indeed, the test of a restriction of a subset of the parameters implies the comparison of two of the measures of fit v, each distributed as a chi-squared. Consequently, the difference between the value v_r of a restricted model and v_u, the unrestricted model, follows a chi-squared distribution with a number of degrees of freedom corresponding to the number of restrictions. This, in fact, is the basis for most of the goodness of fit measures that have been proposed.

8.2.3.2 *Other goodness of fit measures*

Of all the models possible, one extreme case is when there is no relationship postulated between any pair of the constructs. This model of statistical independence can be considered the null model. At the other extreme, it is possible to consider the model where all the relationships are estimated (a "saturated model"), in which case there are zero degrees of freedom. These two models provide the extreme values of the chi-squares and the difference between these chi-squares is the largest one possible: any other model which is a restricted version of the "saturated" model will have a better fit than the null model but worse than the saturated one. It is then possible to use an index of fit based on these ideas. One measure, the Bentler and Bonnet (1980) goodness-of-fit index (GFI) is the percentage improvement over the null model relative to the largest possible improvement that would be realized with a saturated model. This index is a pseudo R squared and is similar to an R squared in the sense that it varies between 0 and 1 and that approaching 1 means a better fit versus approching 0 means a bad fit; however, it cannot be interpreted as a percentage of variance explained. Another GFI is provided in the LISREL output; it is a more direct measure of the fit between the theoretical and observed covariance matrices following from the fit criterion of Equation (8.37) and it is defined as

$$\mathrm{GFI} = 1 - \frac{\mathrm{tr}[(\hat{\boldsymbol{\Sigma}}^{-1}\mathbf{S} - \mathbf{I})^2]}{\mathrm{tr}[(\hat{\boldsymbol{\Sigma}}^{-1}\mathbf{S})^2]} \tag{8.42}$$

From this equation, it is clear that if the estimated and the observed variances are identical, the numerator of the expression substracted from 1 is 0 and, therefore, GFI $= 1$. To correct for the fact that the GFI is affected by the number of indicators, an adjusted Goodness of Fit Index (AGFI) is also proposed. This measure of fit corrects the GFI for the degrees of freedom, just like an adjusted R squared would in a regression context:

$$\mathrm{AGFI} = 1 - \left[\frac{(p+q)(p+q+1)}{(p+q)(p+q+1) - 2t}\right][1 - \mathrm{GFI}] \tag{8.43}$$

where t is the number of estimated parameters.

As the number of estimated parameters increases, holding everything else constant, the adjusted GFI decreases.

A threshold value of 0.9 (either for the GFI or AGFI) has become a norm for the acceptability of the model fit (Bagozzi and Yi 1988, Baumgartner and Homburg 1996, Kuester, Homburg and Robertson 1999).

8.2.3.3 *Modification indices*

The solution obtained for the parameter estimates uses the derivatives of the objective function relative to each parameter. This means that for a given solution, it is possible to know the direction in which a parameter should change in order to improve the fit and how steeply it should change. As a result, the modification indices indicate the expected gains in fit which would be obtained if a particular coefficient should become unconstrained (holding all other parameters fixed at their estimated value). Although not a substitute for theory, this modification index can be useful to analyze structural relationships and in particular to refine the correlational assumptions of random terms and for the modeling of control factors.

8.2.4 Test of Significance of Model Parameters

Because of the maximum likelihood properties of the estimates, the significance of each parameter can be tested using the standard t statistics formed by the ratio of the parameter estimate and its standard deviation.

8.2.5 Simultaneous Estimation of Measurement Model Parameters with Structural Relationship Parameters Versus Sequential Estimation

It can be noted that in the estimation method described above, the measurement model parameters are estimated at the same time as the structural model parameters. This means that the fit of the structural model and the structural model parameters are affected by the measurement model parameters. The motivation of the approach was to correct the bias produced by errors in measurement. However, the simultaneity of the estimation of all the parameters (measurement model and structural model) implies that a trade off is made between the values estimated for the measurement model and those for the structural model. In order to avoid this problem, it is a better practice to estimate first the measurement model and then estimate the structural model parameters in a fully specified model (i.e., with the measurement model) but where the parameters of the measurement model are fixed to the values estimated when this measurement model is estimated alone (Anderson and Gerbing 1988). This procedure does take into account the fact that the variables in the structural model are measured with error in order to estimate the structural model parameters, but does not let the estimation of the measurement model interfere with the estimation of the structural model and vice-versa.

8.2.6 Identification

As discussed earlier in Chapter 5, a model is identified if its parameters are identified, which means that there is only one set of values of the parameters that generate the covariance matrix. Although there is no general necessary and sufficient conditions for the general model discussed here to be identified, if the information matrix is not positive definite, the model is not identified. Furthermore, it appears logical that the structural model be identified on its own. The order and rank conditions presented in Chapter 5 should consequently be used to verify the identification of the structural relationships in an analysis of covariance structure model.

8.3 Examples

We now present examples of analysis of covariance structure using LISREL8 for Windows or AMOS. These examples include the test of a single factor analytic structure, the estimation of a factor analytic structure with two correlated factors and a full structural model with error in measurement.

8.3.1 Example of Confirmatory Factor Analysis

The following example in Figure 8.2 shows the input file for LISREL8 for Windows:

An exclamation mark indicates that what follows is a comment and is not part of the LISREL8 commands. Therefore, the first real input line in Figure 8.2 starts with DA which stands for data. On that line, NI indicates the number of input (observed) variables (6 in this example), MA = KM indicates the type of matrix to be modeled, KM for correlation or CV for covariance.

The second line of input is used to specify how to read the data. RA indicates that the raw data will be read (from which the correlation matrix will be automatically computed) and FI = *filename* indicates the name of the file containing that data, where *filename* is the Windows file name including the full path.

The third line, with LA, indicates that next come the labels of the indicator (input) variables. These are shown as Q5, Q7, etc. on the following line.

The next line specifies the model, as indicated by the code MO at the beginning of that line. NX indicates the number of indicators corresponding to the exogenous constructs (here, there are six). NK stands for the number of ksi constructs (we have a unique factor in this example). PH = ST indicates that the covariance matrix phi is specified here as a standardized matrix, i.e., a correlation matrix with 1's in the diagonal and 0's off-diagonal. The covariance matrix of the measurement model error terms, theta delta, is specified as a symmetric matrix (TD = SY). A diagonal matrix (TD = DI) could have presented a simpler model where all covariances are zero. However, this example illustrates how some of these parameters can be estimated.

```
!Examp8-1.spl
!Raw Data From File: Examp8-1.txt

DA NI=6 MA = KM XM = 9
RA FI=C:\SAMD\Chapter8\Examples\Examp8-1.txt
LA
Q5 Q7 Q8 Q12 Q13 Q14
MO NX = 6 NK = 1 PH = ST TD = SY
LK
FactorOne                                                  !The First Factor
FR LX(1,1) LX(2,1) LX(3,1) LX(4,1) LX(5,1) LX(6,1) TD(3,2) TD(6,5)
Path Diagram
OU SE TV AD = 50 MI
```

Fig. 8.2 LISREL input example for confirmatory factor analytic model (examp8-1.spl).

LK, on the next line, stands for the label of the ksi constructs, although there is only one of them in this example. That label "FactorOne" follows on the next line.

The following line starting with FR is the list of the parameters that are estimated where LX stands for lambda x and TD for theta delta. Each are followed by the row and column of the corresponding matrix, as defined in the model specification in Equations (8.26) and (8.30). The line "Path Diagram" indicates that a graphical representation of the model is requested. The last line of the input file describes the output (OU) requested. SE means standard errors, TV their t-values and MI the modification indices.

The LISREL8 output of such a model is given in Figure 8.3. In the output, as shown in Figure 8.3, after listing the instruction commands described earlier

```
                         DATE:  1/ 8/2001
                          TIME: 10:20


                         L I S R E L  8.30

                               BY

                   Karl G. Jöreskog & Dag Sörbom


             This program is published exclusively by
             Scientific Software International, Inc.
                7383 N. Lincoln Avenue, Suite 100
                 Chicago, IL 60646-1704, U.S.A.
     Phone: (800)247-6113, (847)675-0720, Fax: (847)675-2140
  Copyright by Scientific Software International, Inc., 1981-99
    Use of this program is subject to the terms specified in the
                 Universal Copyright Convention.
                   Website: www.ssicentral.com

The following lines were read from file C:\SAMD\CHAPTER8\EXAMPLES\EXAMP8-1.SPL:

!Examp8-1.spl
!Raw Data From File: Examp8-1.txt

DA NI=6 MA = KM XM = 9
RA FI=C:\SAMD\Chapter8\Examples\Examp8-1.txt
LA
Q5 Q7 Q8 Q12 Q13 Q14
MO NX = 6 NK = 1 PH = ST TD = SY
LK
FactorOne       !The First Factor
FR LX(1,1) LX(2,1) LX(3,1) LX(4,1) LX(5,1) LX(6,1) TD(3,2) TD(6,5)
Path Diagram
OU SE TV AD = 50 MI
```

```
!Examp8-1.spl

                          Number of Input Variables  6
                          Number of Y - Variables    0
                          Number of X - Variables    6
                          Number of ETA - Variables  0
                          Number of KSI - Variables  1
                          Number of Observations   138

!Examp8-1.spl

        Covariance Matrix to be Analyzed

                Q5         Q7         Q8        Q12        Q13        Q14
          --------   --------   --------   --------   --------   --------
     Q5       1.00
     Q7       0.47       1.00
     Q8       0.58       0.75       1.00
    Q12       0.55       0.60       0.65       1.00
    Q13       0.44       0.40       0.51       0.50       1.00
    Q14       0.39       0.44       0.57       0.55       0.59       1.00


!Examp8-1.spl


Parameter Specifications

        LAMBDA-X

           FactorOn
          --------
     Q5          1
     Q7          2
     Q8          3
    Q12          4
    Q13          5
    Q14          6


        THETA-DELTA

                Q5         Q7         Q8        Q12        Q13        Q14
          --------   --------   --------   --------   --------   --------
     Q5          7
     Q7          0          8
     Q8          0          9         10
    Q12          0          0          0         11
    Q13          0          0          0          0         12
    Q14          0          0          0          0         13         14
```

```
!Examp8-1.spl

Number of Iterations =  7


LISREL Estimates (Maximum Likelihood)

        LAMBDA-X

           FactorOn
           --------
      Q5       0.68
             (0.08)
               8.45

      Q7       0.71
             (0.08)
               8.69

      Q8       0.83
             (0.08)
              11.01

     Q12       0.81
             (0.08)
              10.64

     Q13       0.62
             (0.08)
               7.46

     Q14       0.66
             (0.08)
               8.07

        PHI

           FactorOn
           --------
               1.00

        THETA-DELTA

                 Q5         Q7         Q8        Q12        Q13        Q14
           --------   --------   --------   --------   --------   --------
      Q5       0.54
             (0.08)
               7.09

      Q7        - -       0.50
                        (0.08)
                          6.44
```

```
Q8          - -       0.16       0.31
                     (0.06)     (0.06)
                      2.81       4.99

Q12         - -        - -        - -       0.35
                                           (0.06)
                                            5.54

Q13         - -        - -        - -        - -       0.62
                                                      (0.08)
                                                       7.36

Q14         - -        - -        - -        - -       0.18       0.57
                                                      (0.06)     (0.08)
                                                       2.89       7.17

   Squared Multiple Correlations for X - Variables

              Q5         Q7         Q8        Q12        Q13        Q14
        --------   --------   --------   --------   --------   --------
            0.46       0.50       0.69       0.65       0.38       0.43

                        Goodness of Fit Statistics

                          Degrees of Freedom = 7
              Minimum Fit Function Chi-Square = 6.61 (P = 0.47)
   Normal Theory Weighted Least Squares Chi-Square = 6.27 (P = 0.51)
                Estimated Non-centrality Parameter (NCP) = 0.0
            90 Percent Confidence Interval for NCP = (0.0 ; 9.27)

                     Minimum Fit Function Value = 0.048
              Population Discrepancy Function Value (F0) = 0.0
            90 Percent Confidence Interval for F0 = (0.0 ; 0.068)
            Root Mean Square Error of Approximation (RMSEA) = 0.0
           90 Percent Confidence Interval for RMSEA = (0.0 ; 0.098)
             P-Value for Test of Close Fit (RMSEA < 0.05) = 0.71

                Expected Cross-Validation Index (ECVI) = 0.26
           90 Percent Confidence Interval for ECVI = (0.26 ; 0.32)
                      ECVI for Saturated Model = 0.31
                     ECVI for Independence Model = 3.02

  Chi-Square for Independence Model with 15 Degrees of Freedom = 402.09
                         Independence AIC = 414.09
                             Model AIC = 34.27
                           Saturated AIC = 42.00
                         Independence CAIC = 437.65
                             Model CAIC = 89.26
                          Saturated CAIC = 124.47

                   Root Mean Square Residual (RMR) = 0.020
                          Standardized RMR = 0.020
                     Goodness of Fit Index (GFI) = 0.98
```

```
              Adjusted Goodness of Fit Index (AGFI) = 0.95
             Parsimony Goodness of Fit Index (PGFI) = 0.33

                    Normed Fit Index (NFI) = 0.98
                  Non-Normed Fit Index (NNFI) = 1.00
               Parsimony Normed Fit Index (PNFI) = 0.46
                  Comparative Fit Index (CFI) = 1.00
                  Incremental Fit Index (IFI) = 1.00
                   Relative Fit Index (RFI) = 0.96

                      Critical N (CN) = 383.87

!Examp8-1.spl

Modification Indices and Expected Change

No Non-Zero Modification Indices for LAMBDA-X

No Non-Zero Modification Indices for PHI

        Modification Indices for THETA-DELTA

                 Q5         Q7         Q8        Q12        Q13        Q14
            --------   --------   --------   --------   --------   --------
     Q5        - -
     Q7       0.50        - -
     Q8       1.00        - -        - -
    Q12       0.00       3.20       3.82        - -
    Q13       0.96       0.43       0.00       0.00        - -
    Q14       2.38       0.54       1.23       0.33        - -        - -

        Expected Change for THETA-DELTA

                 Q5         Q7         Q8        Q12        Q13        Q14
            --------   --------   --------   --------   --------   --------
     Q5        - -
     Q7      -0.03        - -
     Q8       0.04        - -        - -
    Q12       0.00       0.08      -0.09        - -
    Q13       0.05      -0.03       0.00       0.00        - -
    Q14      -0.08      -0.03       0.04       0.03        - -        - -

Maximum Modification Index is    3.82 for Element ( 4, 3) of THETA-DELTA

         The Problem used     6608 Bytes (=  0.0% of Available Workspace)

                     Time used:     0.172 Seconds
```

Fig. 8.3 LISREL8 for Windows output example for confirmatory factor analytic model (examp8-1.out).

according to the model specified in the input file shown in Figure 8.2, the observed covariance matrix (in this case a correlation matrix) to be modeled is printed.

The "Parameter Specifications" section indicates the list and number of parameters to be estimated, with a detail of all the matrices containing the parameters. The value zero indicates that the corresponding parameter is fixed and is not to be estimated. Unless specified otherwise, the default value of these fixed parameters is set to zero.

The number of iterations shows the number which was necessary to obtain convergence and the parameter estimates follow. Below each parameter estimate value, its standard error is shown in parentheses and the t-value below it.

Then follow the Goodness of Fit Statistics among which those described earlier can be found. This example run in Figure 8.3 shows that the single factor model represents well the observed correlation matrix since the chi squared is not statistically significant and the GFI is high with a value of 0.98.

The modification indices are reasonably small, which indicates that freeing additional parameters would not lead to a big gain in fit. The diagram of such a confirmatory factor analytic model is shown in Figure 8.4 below.

8.3.2 Example of Model to Test Discriminant Validity Between Two Constructs

The following example is typical of an analysis where the goal is to assess the validity of a construct. A construct must be different from other constructs (discriminant validity) but are nevertheless mutually conceptually related (convergent validity). The discriminant validity of the constructs is ascertained by comparing measurement models where the correlations between the construct is estimated with one where the correlation is constrained to be

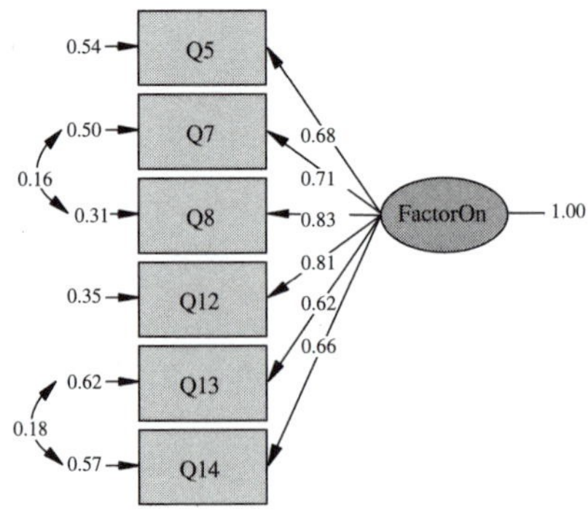

Fig. 8.4 Path diagram of confirmatory factor analytic model (examp8-1.pth).

one (whereby assuming a single factor structure). The discriminant validity of the constructs is examined for each pair at a time. This procedure, proposed by Bagozzi, Yi and Phillips (1991) indicates that, if the model where the correlation is not equal to one improves significantly the fit, the two constructs are distinct from each other, although they can possibly be significantly correlated. The convergent validity of the constructs is assessed by comparing a measurement model where the correlation between the two constructs is estimated with a model where the correlation is constrained to be equal to zero. A significant improvement in fit indicates that the two constructs are indeed related, which confirms convergence validity. Combining the two tests (that the correlation is different from one and different from zero) demonstrates that the two constructs are different (discriminant validity) although related with a significantly different from zero correlation (convergent validity).

Figure 8.5 shows the input file to estimate a two factor model (such analyses are usually performed two factors at a time because the modeling of all the factors at once typically involves problems too big to obtain satisfactory fits). The commands are identical to those described with Figure 8.2, except that now two constructs, "FactorOne" and "FactorTwo", are specified.

The LISREL8 ouput corresponding to this two-factor confirmatory factor structure is shown in Figure 8.6. The description of this output is similar to the one described above involving a single factor. The major difference is the estimate of the correlation between the two factors, which is shown to

```
!Examp8-2.spl
!Raw Data From File: Examp8-2.txt

DA NI=12 MA = KM XM = 9
RA FI=C:\SAMD\Chapter8\Examples\Examp8-2.txt
LA
Q5 Q7 Q8  Q12 Q13 Q14
Q6 Q9 Q10 Q11 Q17 Q18

MO NX = 12 NK = 2 PH = ST TD = SY              !CORR = Free
LK
FactorOne                                      !Competence Destroying
FactorTwo                                      !Competence Enhancing
FR LX(1,1) LX(2,1) LX(3,1) LX(4,1) LX(5,1) LX(6,1)        C
   LX(7,2) LX(8,2) LX(9,2) LX(10,2) LX(11,2) LX(12,2)    C
   TD(3,2) TD(6,5) TD(8,7) TD(10,8) TD(10,7)
Path Diagram
OU SE TV RS MR FS AD = 50 MI
```

Fig. 8.5 LISREL8 for Windows input for model with two factors (examp8-2.spl).

```
                              DATE:  1/ 8/2001
                                TIME: 11:04

                              L I S R E L  8.30

                                     BY

                         Karl G. Jöreskog & Dag Sörbom


                    This program is published exclusively by
                    Scientific Software International, Inc.
                       7383 N. Lincoln Avenue, Suite 100
                        Chicago, IL 60646-1704, U.S.A.
            Phone: (800)247-6113, (847)675-0720, Fax: (847)675-2140
        Copyright by Scientific Software International, Inc., 1981-99
          Use of this program is subject to the terms specified in the
                        Universal Copyright Convention.
                          Website: www.ssicentral.com

 The following lines were read from file C:\SAMD\CHAPTER8\EXAMPLES\EXAMP8-2.SPL:


 !Examp8-2.spl
!Raw Data From File: Examp8-2.txt


 DA NI=12 MA = KM XM = 9
 RA FI=C:\SAMD\Chapter8\Examples\Examp8-2.txt
 LA
 Q5 Q7 Q8  Q12 Q13 Q14
 Q6 Q9 Q10 Q11 Q17 Q18


 MO NX = 12 NK = 2 PH = ST TD = SY  !CORR = Free
 LK
 FactorOne      !Competence Destroying
 FactorTwo     !Competence Enhancing
 FR LX(1,1) LX(2,1) LX(3,1) LX(4,1) LX(5,1) LX(6,1) LX(7,2) LX(8,2) LX(9,2) LX(10,2) C
 LX(11,2) LX(12,2) TD(3,2) TD(6,5) TD(8,7) TD(10,8) TD(10,7)
 Path Diagram
 OU SE TV RS MR FS AD = 50 MI


 !Examp8-2.spl
                          Number of Input Variables 12
                          Number of Y - Variables    0
                          Number of X - Variables   12
                          Number of ETA - Variables  0
                          Number of KSI - Variables  2
                          Number of Observations   134
```

!Examp8-2.spl

Covariance Matrix to be Analyzed

	Q5	Q7	Q8	Q12	Q13	Q14
Q5	1.00					
Q7	0.46	1.00				
Q8	0.57	0.74	1.00			
Q12	0.53	0.60	0.64	1.00		
Q13	0.43	0.40	0.51	0.49	1.00	
Q14	0.40	0.44	0.58	0.56	0.59	1.00
Q6	-0.13	-0.27	-0.20	-0.36	-0.06	-0.19
Q9	-0.17	-0.26	-0.18	-0.38	-0.08	-0.11
Q10	-0.13	-0.27	-0.22	-0.40	-0.19	-0.26
Q11	-0.26	-0.25	-0.23	-0.36	-0.18	-0.19
Q17	-0.19	-0.29	-0.32	-0.34	-0.26	-0.32
Q18	-0.20	-0.27	-0.21	-0.40	-0.10	-0.22

Covariance Matrix to be Analyzed

	Q6	Q9	Q10	Q11	Q17	Q18
Q6	1.00					
Q9	0.56	1.00				
Q10	0.36	0.33	1.00			
Q11	0.58	0.70	0.41	1.00		
Q17	0.38	0.41	0.44	0.43	1.00	
Q18	0.40	0.38	0.47	0.42	0.47	1.00

!Examp8-2.spl

Parameter Specifications

LAMBDA-X

	FactorOn	FactorTw
Q5	1	0
Q7	2	0
Q8	3	0
Q12	4	0
Q13	5	0
Q14	6	0
Q6	0	7
Q9	0	8
Q10	0	9
Q11	0	10
Q17	0	11
Q18	0	12

```
         PHI

            FactorOn   FactorTw
            --------   --------
FactorOn           0
FactorTw          13          0

         THETA-DELTA

                  Q5         Q7         Q8        Q12        Q13        Q14
            --------   --------   --------   --------   --------   --------
      Q5          14
      Q7           0         15
      Q8           0         16         17
     Q12           0          0          0         18
     Q13           0          0          0          0         19
     Q14           0          0          0          0         20         21
      Q6           0          0          0          0          0          0
      Q9           0          0          0          0          0          0
     Q10           0          0          0          0          0          0
     Q11           0          0          0          0          0          0
     Q17           0          0          0          0          0          0
     Q18           0          0          0          0          0          0


         THETA-DELTA

                  Q6         Q9        Q10        Q11        Q17        Q18
            --------   --------   --------   --------   --------   --------
      Q6          22
      Q9          23         24
     Q10           0          0         25
     Q11          26         27          0         28
     Q17           0          0          0          0         29
     Q18           0          0          0          0          0         30


!Examp8-2.spl
Number of Iterations = 10

LISREL Estimates (Maximum Likelihood)

         LAMBDA-X

            FactorOn   FactorTw
            --------   --------
      Q5        0.65       - -
              (0.08)
                7.92

      Q7        0.70       - -
              (0.08)
                8.59
```

```
      Q8        0.80        - -
              (0.08)
               10.35

     Q12        0.84        - -
              (0.08)
               11.06

     Q13        0.60        - -
              (0.08)
                7.14

     Q14        0.67        - -
              (0.08)
                8.18


      Q6        - -         0.57
                          (0.09)
                            6.22

      Q9        - -         0.56
                          (0.09)
                            6.12

     Q10        - -         0.65
                          (0.09)
                            7.48

     Q11        - -         0.62
                          (0.09)
                            6.99

     Q17        - -         0.69
                          (0.09)
                            8.01

     Q18        - -         0.69
                          (0.09)
                            8.01


         PHI

            FactorOn    FactorTw
            --------    --------
FactorOn        1.00

FactorTw       -0.56        1.00
              (0.08)
               -6.93
```

THETA-DELTA

	Q5	Q7	Q8	Q12	Q13	Q14
Q5	0.58 (0.08) 7.19					
Q7	- -	0.51 (0.08) 6.60				
Q8	- -	0.18 (0.06) 3.21	0.36 (0.06) 5.65			
Q12	- -	- -	- -	0.30 (0.06) 5.01		
Q13	- -	- -	- -	- -	0.64 (0.09) 7.35	
Q14	- -	- -	- -	- -	0.19 (0.06) 3.01	0.55 (0.08) 7.04
Q6	- -	- -	- -	- -	- -	- -
Q9	- -	- -	- -	- -	- -	- -
Q10	- -	- -	- -	- -	- -	- -
Q11	- -	- -	- -	- -	- -	- -
Q17	- -	- -	- -	- -	- -	- -
Q18	- -	- -	- -	- -	- -	- -

THETA-DELTA

	Q6	Q9	Q10	Q11	Q17	Q18
Q6	0.68 (0.10) 7.00					
Q9	0.25 (0.08) 3.27	0.69 (0.10) 7.04				

```
Q10        - -       - -       0.58
                              (0.09)
                               6.51

Q11       0.23      0.35       - -       0.61
         (0.07)    (0.08)               (0.09)
          3.13      4.48                 6.67

Q17        - -       - -       - -       - -       0.52
                                                  (0.09)
                                                   6.13

Q18        - -       - -       - -       - -       - -       0.52
                                                            (0.09)
                                                             6.12


   Squared Multiple Correlations for X - Variables

            Q5        Q7        Q8       Q12       Q13       Q14
      --------  --------  --------  --------  --------  --------
          0.42      0.49      0.64      0.70      0.36      0.45

   Squared Multiple Correlations for X - Variables

            Q6        Q9       Q10       Q11       Q17       Q18
      --------  --------  --------  --------  --------  --------
          0.32      0.31      0.42      0.39      0.48      0.48


                     Goodness of Fit Statistics

                       Degrees of Freedom = 48
            Minimum Fit Function Chi-Square = 54.78 (P = 0.23)
  Normal Theory Weighted Least Squares Chi-Square = 55.76 (P = 0.21)
             Estimated Non-centrality Parameter (NCP) = 7.76
         90 Percent Confidence Interval for NCP = (0.0 ; 30.50)


                  Minimum Fit Function Value = 0.41
            Population Discrepancy Function Value (F0) = 0.058
           90 Percent Confidence Interval for F0 = (0.0 ; 0.23)
        Root Mean Square Error of Approximation (RMSEA) = 0.035
        90 Percent Confidence Interval for RMSEA = (0.0 ; 0.069)
           P-Value for Test of Close Fit (RMSEA < 0.05) = 0.73


            Expected Cross-Validation Index (ECVI) = 0.87
        90 Percent Confidence Interval for ECVI = (0.81 ; 1.04)
                   ECVI for Saturated Model = 1.17
                  ECVI for Independence Model = 5.81
```

```
Chi-Square for Independence Model with 66 Degrees of Freedom = 748.31
                  Independence AIC = 772.31
                      Model AIC = 115.76
                    Saturated AIC = 156.00
                  Independence CAIC = 819.08
                     Model CAIC = 232.69
                   Saturated CAIC = 460.03


          Root Mean Square Residual (RMR) = 0.048
                  Standardized RMR = 0.048
             Goodness of Fit Index (GFI) = 0.93
        Adjusted Goodness of Fit Index (AGFI) = 0.89
       Parsimony Goodness of Fit Index (PGFI) = 0.58


               Normed Fit Index (NFI) = 0.93
             Non-Normed Fit Index (NNFI) = 0.99
          Parsimony Normed Fit Index (PNFI) = 0.67
             Comparative Fit Index (CFI) = 0.99
             Incremental Fit Index (IFI) = 0.99
               Relative Fit Index (RFI) = 0.90

                  Critical N (CN) = 179.90


!Examp8-2.spl
        Fitted Covariance Matrix

                Q5          Q7          Q8         Q12         Q13         Q14
          --------    --------    --------    --------    --------    --------
      Q5      1.00
      Q7      0.46        1.00
      Q8      0.52        0.74        1.00
     Q12      0.54        0.59        0.67        1.00
     Q13      0.39        0.42        0.48        0.50        1.00
     Q14      0.44        0.47        0.53        0.56        0.59        1.00
      Q6     -0.21       -0.22       -0.25       -0.26       -0.19       -0.21
      Q9     -0.20       -0.22       -0.25       -0.26       -0.19       -0.21
     Q10     -0.24       -0.26       -0.29       -0.30       -0.22       -0.24
     Q11     -0.23       -0.24       -0.28       -0.29       -0.21       -0.23
     Q17     -0.25       -0.27       -0.31       -0.32       -0.23       -0.26
     Q18     -0.25       -0.27       -0.31       -0.32       -0.23       -0.26


        Fitted Covariance Matrix

                Q6          Q9         Q10         Q11         Q17         Q18
          --------    --------    --------    --------    --------    --------
      Q6      1.00
      Q9      0.56        1.00
     Q10      0.37        0.36        1.00
```

```
    Q11        0.58       0.70       0.40       1.00
    Q17        0.39       0.38       0.45       0.43       1.00
    Q18        0.39       0.38       0.45       0.43       0.48       1.00


       Fitted Residuals

                 Q5         Q7         Q8        Q12        Q13        Q14
           --------   --------   --------   --------   --------   --------
     Q5        0.00
     Q7        0.00       0.00
     Q8        0.05       0.00       0.00
    Q12       -0.01       0.01      -0.03       0.00
    Q13        0.04      -0.02       0.03      -0.01       0.00
    Q14       -0.04      -0.03       0.04       0.00       0.00       0.00
     Q6        0.07      -0.05       0.05      -0.09       0.13       0.02
     Q9        0.03      -0.04       0.07      -0.12       0.11       0.10
    Q10        0.11      -0.01       0.07      -0.09       0.03      -0.01
    Q11       -0.04      -0.01       0.05      -0.07       0.02       0.04
    Q17        0.06      -0.02      -0.01      -0.02      -0.03      -0.06
    Q18        0.05       0.00       0.10      -0.08       0.13       0.04


       Fitted Residuals

                 Q6         Q9        Q10        Q11        Q17        Q18
           --------   --------   --------   --------   --------   --------
     Q6        0.00
     Q9        0.00       0.00
    Q10       -0.01      -0.03       0.00
    Q11        0.00       0.00       0.00       0.00
    Q17       -0.01       0.03      -0.01       0.00       0.00
    Q18        0.01       0.00       0.02      -0.01       0.00       0.00


Summary Statistics for Fitted Residuals


Smallest Fitted Residual =   -0.12
  Median Fitted Residual =    0.00
 Largest Fitted Residual =    0.13


Stemleaf Plot

- 1|2
- 0|998765
- 0|4443333222111111111100000000000000000000000
  0|1122233334444
  0|55556777
  1|001133
```

Standardized Residuals

	Q5	Q7	Q8	Q12	Q13	Q14
Q5	- -					
Q7	-0.02	- -				
Q8	1.81	- -	- -			
Q12	-0.47	0.64	-2.05	- -		
Q13	0.92	-0.57	0.85	-0.45	- -	
Q14	-0.99	-0.85	1.65	-0.12	- -	- -
Q6	1.05	-0.80	0.83	-1.62	1.88	0.26
Q9	0.49	-0.58	1.12	-1.97	1.52	1.43
Q10	1.71	-0.16	1.34	-1.76	0.45	-0.21
Q11	-0.59	-0.14	0.79	-1.22	0.36	0.66
Q17	1.00	-0.30	-0.20	-0.36	-0.49	-0.96
Q18	0.77	0.05	1.83	-1.57	2.05	0.68

Standardized Residuals

	Q6	Q9	Q10	Q11	Q17	Q18
Q6	- -					
Q9	- -	- -				
Q10	-0.19	-0.83	- -			
Q11	- -	- -	0.13	- -		
Q17	-0.19	0.74	-0.29	-0.02	- -	
Q18	0.32	0.00	0.57	-0.33	-0.10	- -

Summary Statistics for Standardized Residuals

```
Smallest Standardized Residual =   -2.05
  Median Standardized Residual =    0.00
 Largest Standardized Residual =    2.05
```

Stemleaf Plot

```
- 2|00
- 1|866
- 1|200
- 0|98866655
- 0|4433322222111000000000000000000000
  0|1334
  0|556677788899
  1|01134
  1|577889
  2|0
```

```
!Examp8-2.spl

                        Qplot of Standardized Residuals

 3.5...........................................................................
    .                                                                        ..
    .                                                                       . .
    .                                                                     .   .
    .                                                                   .     .
    .                                                                  .      .
    .                                                                .        .
    .                                                              .          .
    .                                                             .           .
    .                                                          x.             .
    .                                                         .               .
    .                                                        x                .
    .                                                      . x                .
    .                                                    .  x                 .
    .                                                   .  *                  .
N   .                                                 . xx                    .
o   .                                               .x x                      .
r   .                                              x*                         .
m   .                                            .x                           .
a   .                                          .x*x                           .
l   .                                         .*x                             .
    .                                       x*x                               .
Q   .                                    x*x                                  .
u   .                                   *x                                    .
a   .                                  xx                                     .
n   .                                .x*                                      .
t   .                               .xx                                       .
i   .                             . *x                                        .
l   .                           .x *                                          .
e   .                          . *                                            .
s   .                        . *                                              .
    .                   x . x                                                 .
    .                   x.                                                    .
    .                 x.                                                      .
    .               x.                                                        .
    .               .                                                         .
    .             .x                                                          .
    .           .                                                             .
    .          .                                                              .
    .        .                                                                .
    .      .                                                                  .
    .     .                                                                   .
    .   .                                                                     .
    . .                                                                       .
-3.5...........................................................................
  -3.5                                                                       3.5
                            Standardized Residuals
```

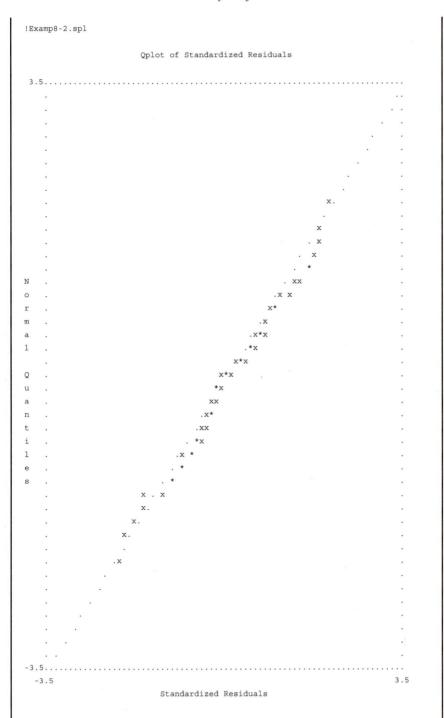

```
!Examp8-2.spl
Modification Indices and Expected Change
        Modification Indices for LAMBDA-X

           FactorOn   FactorTw
           --------   --------
     Q5        - -       2.14
     Q7        - -       1.44
     Q8        - -       4.74
    Q12        - -       9.41
    Q13        - -       1.70
    Q14        - -       0.09
     Q6       0.00        - -
     Q9       0.01        - -
    Q10       0.00        - -
    Q11       0.08        - -
    Q17       0.11        - -
    Q18       0.29        - -

        Expected Change for LAMBDA-X

           FactorOn   FactorTw
           --------   --------
     Q5        - -       0.15
     Q7        - -      -0.10
     Q8        - -       0.17
    Q12        - -      -0.29
    Q13        - -       0.13
    Q14        - -      -0.03
     Q6       0.00        - -
     Q9       0.01        - -
    Q10       0.00        - -
    Q11      -0.02        - -
    Q17      -0.04        - -
    Q18       0.06        - -

No Non-Zero Modification Indices for PHI
        Modification Indices for THETA-DELTA

                 Q5         Q7         Q8        Q12        Q13        Q14
           --------   --------   --------   --------   --------   --------
     Q5        - -
     Q7       0.48        - -
     Q8       3.12        - -        - -
    Q12       0.22       1.53       4.28        - -
    Q13       1.54       0.20       0.24       0.16        - -
    Q14       1.72       1.35       2.58       0.00        - -        - -
     Q6       1.47       1.03       0.39       1.11       3.57       0.95
     Q9       0.46       1.00       1.30       4.69       0.66       1.61
    Q10       2.69       0.25       1.55       2.84       0.00       0.13
    Q11       3.77       0.73       0.17       1.55       1.97       0.26
    Q17       0.53       0.36       2.02       2.86       1.18       0.89
    Q18       0.02       0.37       2.27       3.02       3.07       0.00
```

```
        Modification Indices for THETA-DELTA

                  Q6         Q9        Q10        Q11        Q17        Q18
            --------   --------   --------   --------   --------   --------
      Q6        - -
      Q9        - -        - -
     Q10       0.00       0.86        - -
     Q11        - -        - -       0.39        - -
     Q17       0.13       0.73       0.09       0.15        - -
     Q18       0.15       0.01       0.33       0.17       0.01        - -

        Expected Change for THETA-DELTA

                  Q5         Q7         Q8        Q12        Q13        Q14
            --------   --------   --------   --------   --------   --------
      Q5        - -
      Q7      -0.03        - -
      Q8       0.08        - -        - -
     Q12      -0.03       0.06      -0.10        - -
     Q13       0.07      -0.02       0.02      -0.02        - -
     Q14      -0.07      -0.05       0.06       0.00        - -        - -
      Q6       0.06      -0.04       0.02      -0.05       0.10      -0.05
      Q9       0.03      -0.04       0.04      -0.09       0.04       0.05
     Q10       0.09      -0.02       0.05      -0.08       0.00      -0.02
     Q11      -0.09       0.03      -0.01       0.05      -0.06       0.02
     Q17       0.04       0.03      -0.06       0.08      -0.06      -0.05
     Q18      -0.01      -0.03       0.06      -0.08       0.09       0.00

        Expected Change for THETA-DELTA

                  Q6         Q9        Q10        Q11        Q17        Q18
            --------   --------   --------   --------   --------   --------
      Q6        - -
      Q9        - -        - -
     Q10       0.00      -0.05        - -
     Q11        - -        - -       0.03        - -
     Q17      -0.02       0.04      -0.02      -0.02        - -
     Q18       0.02       0.00       0.04      -0.02      -0.01        - -

Maximum Modification Index is    9.41 for Element ( 4, 2) of LAMBDA-X

!Examp8-2.spl

Covariances

        X - KSI

                  Q5         Q7         Q8        Q12        Q13        Q14
            --------   --------   --------   --------   --------   --------
FactorOn       0.65       0.70       0.80       0.84       0.60       0.67
FactorTw      -0.36      -0.39      -0.45      -0.47      -0.34      -0.37
```

```
        X - KSI

                     Q6         Q9        Q10        Q11        Q17        Q18
               --------   --------   --------   --------   --------   --------
 FactorOn         -0.32      -0.31      -0.36      -0.35      -0.38      -0.38
 FactorTw          0.57       0.56       0.65       0.62       0.69       0.69

 !Examp8-2.spl

 Factor Scores Regressions


        KSI

                     Q5         Q7         Q8        Q12        Q13        Q14
               --------   --------   --------   --------   --------   --------
 FactorOn          0.15       0.10       0.25       0.37       0.09       0.13
 FactorTw         -0.03      -0.02      -0.04      -0.06      -0.01      -0.02


        KSI

                     Q6         Q9        Q10        Q11        Q17        Q18
               --------   --------   --------   --------   --------   --------
 FactorOn         -0.01      -0.01      -0.03      -0.01      -0.03      -0.03
 FactorTw          0.11       0.06       0.24       0.14       0.28       0.28


         The Problem used     22936 Bytes (=  0.0% of Available Workspace)

                             Time used:     0.230 Seconds
```

Fig. 8.6 LISREL8 for Windows output for model with two factors (examp8-2.out).

be −0.56 in this particular example. The diagram representing that factor analytic structure is shown in Figure 8.7.

Figures 8.8 and 8.9 show respectively the input and output files for a factor analytic structure where a single factor is assumed to be reflected by all the items. The resulting chi squared ($\chi^2 = 126.75$ in Figure 8.9) can be compared with the chi-squared resulting from a model with a correlation between the two factors ($\chi^2 = 54.78$ in Figure 8.6). The χ^2 difference (126.75 − 54.78) has one degree of freedom and its significance indicates that there are indeed two different constructs (factors), i.e., demonstrating the discriminant validity of the constructs.

Next, in order to assess the convergent validity, one needs to compare the fit of a model with zero correlation between the factors with a model where the factors are correlated (as in Figure 8.6). The input and output files for a model with independent factors (zero correlation) are shown respectively in Figures 8.10 and 8.11. The independent factor model has a chi squared

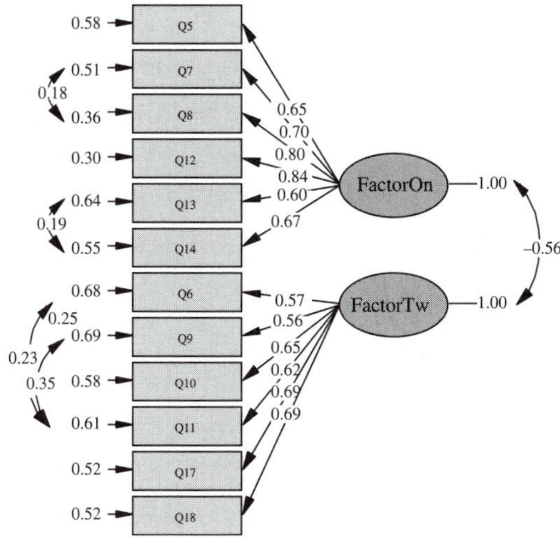

Fig. 8.7 LISREL8 for Windows path diagram for model with two factors (examp8-2.pth).

```
!Examp8-3.spl
!Raw Data From File: Examp8-2.txt

DA NI=12 MA = KM XM = 9
RA FI=C:\SAMD\Chapter8\Examples\Examp8-2.txt
LA
Q5 Q7 Q8  Q12 Q13 Q14
Q6 Q9 Q10 Q11 Q17 Q18

MO NX = 12 NK = 1 PH = ST TD = SY
LK
FactOne

FR LX(1,1) LX(2,1) LX(3,1) LX(4,1) LX(5,1) LX(6,1)          C
   LX(7,1) LX(8,1) LX(9,1) LX(10,1) LX(11,1) LX(12,1)       C
   TD(3,2) TD(6,5) TD(8,7) TD(10,8) TD(10,7)
Path Diagram
OU SE TV RS MR FS AD = 50 MI
```

Fig. 8.8 LISREL8 for Windows input for model with single factor (examp8-3.spl)

of 84.34 (Figure 8.11), which when compared with the chi squared of the model estimating a correlation between the two constructs (Figure 8.6) shows a chi squared difference of 29.56. This difference being significant (with one degree of freedom at the 0.05 level), this indicates that the constructs are not independent, i.e., showing convergent validity of the two constructs.

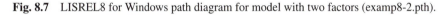

```
                                   DATE:  1/ 8/2001
                                     TIME: 11:14


                                   L I S R E L  8.30

                                          BY

                             Karl G. Jöreskog & Dag Sörbom



                        This program is published exclusively by
                        Scientific Software International, Inc.
                           7383 N. Lincoln Avenue, Suite 100
                            Chicago, IL 60646-1704, U.S.A.
                Phone: (800)247-6113, (847)675-0720, Fax: (847)675-2140
            Copyright by Scientific Software International, Inc., 1981-99
              Use of this program is subject to the terms specified in the
                            Universal Copyright Convention.
                              Website: www.ssicentral.com


The following lines were read from file C:\SAMD\CHAPTER8\EXAMPLES\EXAMP8-3.SPL:



!Examp8-3.spl
!Raw Data From File: Examp8-2.txt

DA NI=12 MA = KM XM = 9
RA FI=C:\SAMD\Chapter8\Examples\Examp8-2.txt
LA
Q5 Q7 Q8  Q12 Q13 Q14
Q6 Q9 Q10 Q11 Q17 Q18

MO NX = 12 NK = 1 PH = ST TD = SY
LK
FactOne      !Competence Destroying
FR LX(1,1) LX(2,1) LX(3,1) LX(4,1) LX(5,1) LX(6,1) C
LX(7,1) LX(8,1) LX(9,1) LX(10,1) LX(11,1) LX(12,1) C
TD(3,2) TD(6,5) TD(8,7) TD(10,8) TD(10,7)
Path Diagram
OU SE TV RS MR FS AD = 50 MI

!Examp8-3.spl
                          Number of Input Variables 12
                          Number of Y - Variables    0
                          Number of X - Variables   12
                          Number of ETA - Variables  0
                          Number of KSI - Variables  1
                          Number of Observations   134
```

```
!Examp8-3.spl
         Covariance Matrix to be Analyzed

                  Q5         Q7         Q8        Q12        Q13        Q14
            --------   --------   --------   --------   --------   --------
      Q5        1.00
      Q7        0.46       1.00
      Q8        0.57       0.74       1.00
     Q12        0.53       0.60       0.64       1.00
     Q13        0.43       0.40       0.51       0.49       1.00
     Q14        0.40       0.44       0.58       0.56       0.59       1.00
      Q6       -0.13      -0.27      -0.20      -0.36      -0.06      -0.19
      Q9       -0.17      -0.26      -0.18      -0.38      -0.08      -0.11
     Q10       -0.13      -0.27      -0.22      -0.40      -0.19      -0.26
     Q11       -0.26      -0.25      -0.23      -0.36      -0.18      -0.19
     Q17       -0.19      -0.29      -0.32      -0.34      -0.26      -0.32
     Q18       -0.20      -0.27      -0.21      -0.40      -0.10      -0.22


         Covariance Matrix to be Analyzed

                  Q6         Q9        Q10        Q11        Q17        Q18
            --------   --------   --------   --------   --------   --------
      Q6        1.00
      Q9        0.56       1.00
     Q10        0.36       0.33       1.00
     Q11        0.58       0.70       0.41       1.00
     Q17        0.38       0.41       0.44       0.43       1.00
     Q18        0.40       0.38       0.47       0.42       0.47       1.00


!Examp8-3.spl


Parameter Specifications


         LAMBDA-X

             FactOne
            --------
      Q5           1
      Q7           2
      Q8           3
     Q12           4
     Q13           5
     Q14           6
      Q6           7
      Q9           8
     Q10           9
     Q11          10
     Q17          11
     Q18          12
```

```
        THETA-DELTA

                  Q5         Q7         Q8        Q12        Q13        Q14
            --------   --------   --------   --------   --------   --------
      Q5          13
      Q7           0         14
      Q8           0         15         16
     Q12           0          0          0         17
     Q13           0          0          0          0         18
     Q14           0          0          0          0         19         20
      Q6           0          0          0          0          0          0
      Q9           0          0          0          0          0          0
     Q10           0          0          0          0          0          0
     Q11           0          0          0          0          0          0
     Q17           0          0          0          0          0          0
     Q18           0          0          0          0          0          0


        THETA-DELTA

                  Q6         Q9        Q10        Q11        Q17        Q18
            --------   --------   --------   --------   --------   --------
      Q6          21
      Q9          22         23
     Q10           0          0         24
     Q11          25         26          0         27
     Q17           0          0          0          0         28
     Q18           0          0          0          0          0         29



!Examp8-3.spl

Number of Iterations = 18

LISREL Estimates (Maximum Likelihood)

        LAMBDA-X

             FactOne
            --------
      Q5        0.61
              (0.08)
                7.37

      Q7        0.68
              (0.08)
                8.35

      Q8        0.75
              (0.08)
                9.48
```

```
Q12         0.85
           (0.07)
           11.50


Q13         0.57
           (0.09)
            6.66


Q14         0.65
           (0.08)
            7.85


 Q6        -0.40
           (0.09)
           -4.54


 Q9        -0.40
           (0.09)
           -4.50


Q10        -0.46
           (0.09)
           -5.27


Q11        -0.45
           (0.09)
           -5.08


Q17        -0.48
           (0.09)
           -5.57


Q18        -0.47
           (0.09)
           -5.34


   PHI

         FactOne
        --------
            1.00
```

```
         THETA-DELTA

                  Q5          Q7          Q8         Q12         Q13         Q14
            --------    --------    --------    --------    --------    --------
       Q5       0.62
              (0.08)
                7.41

       Q7        - -        0.54
                          (0.08)
                            6.96

       Q8        - -        0.24        0.44
                          (0.06)      (0.07)
                            4.00        6.51

      Q12        - -         - -         - -        0.27
                                                  (0.06)
                                                    4.83

      Q13        - -         - -         - -         - -        0.68
                                                              (0.09)
                                                                7.54

      Q14        - -         - -         - -         - -        0.23        0.58
                                                              (0.07)      (0.08)
                                                                3.48        7.24

       Q6        - -         - -         - -         - -         - -         - -

       Q9        - -         - -         - -         - -         - -         - -

      Q10        - -         - -         - -         - -         - -         - -

      Q11        - -         - -         - -         - -         - -         - -

      Q17        - -         - -         - -         - -         - -         - -

      Q18        - -         - -         - -         - -         - -         - -


         THETA-DELTA

                  Q6          Q9         Q10         Q11         Q17         Q18
            --------    --------    --------    --------    --------    --------
       Q6       0.84
              (0.11)
                7.91

       Q9       0.40        0.84
              (0.08)      (0.11)
                4.80        7.92
```

```
Q10          - -        - -      0.79
                                (0.10)
                                  7.83

Q11        0.40       0.52        - -      0.80
          (0.08)     (0.09)               (0.10)
           4.88       5.95                  7.85

Q17          - -        - -        - -        - -      0.77
                                                      (0.10)
                                                        7.78

Q18          - -        - -        - -        - -        - -      0.78
                                                                 (0.10)
                                                                   7.82


   Squared Multiple Correlations for X - Variables

             Q5         Q7         Q8        Q12        Q13        Q14
       --------   --------   --------   --------   --------   --------
           0.38       0.46       0.56       0.73       0.32       0.42


   Squared Multiple Correlations for X - Variables

             Q6         Q9        Q10        Q11        Q17        Q18
       --------   --------   --------   --------   --------   --------
           0.16       0.16       0.21       0.20       0.23       0.22


                       Goodness of Fit Statistics

                         Degrees of Freedom = 49
              Minimum Fit Function Chi-Square = 126.75 (P = 0.00)
  Normal Theory Weighted Least Squares Chi-Square = 158.94 (P = 0.00)
               Estimated Non-centrality Parameter (NCP) = 109.94
           90 Percent Confidence Interval for NCP = (75.53 ; 151.95)

                       Minimum Fit Function Value = 0.95
               Population Discrepancy Function Value (F0) = 0.83
             90 Percent Confidence Interval for F0 = (0.57 ; 1.14)
             Root Mean Square Error of Approximation (RMSEA) = 0.13
            90 Percent Confidence Interval for RMSEA = (0.11 ; 0.15)
              P-Value for Test of Close Fit (RMSEA < 0.05) = 0.00

                Expected Cross-Validation Index (ECVI) = 1.63
            90 Percent Confidence Interval for ECVI = (1.37 ; 1.95)
                       ECVI for Saturated Model = 1.17
                       ECVI for Independence Model = 5.81
```

```
Chi-Square for Independence Model with 66 Degrees of Freedom = 748.31
                    Independence AIC = 772.31
                           Model AIC = 216.94
                       Saturated AIC = 156.00
                   Independence CAIC = 819.08
                          Model CAIC = 329.97
                      Saturated CAIC = 460.03

           Root Mean Square Residual (RMR) = 0.10
                          Standardized RMR = 0.10
               Goodness of Fit Index (GFI) = 0.83
     Adjusted Goodness of Fit Index (AGFI) = 0.74
    Parsimony Goodness of Fit Index (PGFI) = 0.52

                   Normed Fit Index (NFI) = 0.83
              Non-Normed Fit Index (NNFI) = 0.85
         Parsimony Normed Fit Index (PNFI) = 0.62
              Comparative Fit Index (CFI) = 0.89
              Incremental Fit Index (IFI) = 0.89
                 Relative Fit Index (RFI) = 0.77

                        Critical N (CN) = 79.62


!Examp8-3.spl

        Fitted Covariance Matrix

                Q5         Q7         Q8        Q12        Q13        Q14
          --------   --------   --------   --------   --------   --------
     Q5       1.00
     Q7       0.42       1.00
     Q8       0.46       0.74       1.00
    Q12       0.52       0.58       0.64       1.00
    Q13       0.35       0.39       0.42       0.48       1.00
    Q14       0.40       0.44       0.48       0.55       0.59       1.00
     Q6      -0.25      -0.27      -0.30      -0.34      -0.23      -0.26
     Q9      -0.25      -0.27      -0.30      -0.34      -0.23      -0.26
    Q10      -0.28      -0.31      -0.34      -0.39      -0.26      -0.30
    Q11      -0.27      -0.30      -0.33      -0.38      -0.25      -0.29
    Q17      -0.30      -0.33      -0.36      -0.41      -0.27      -0.31
    Q18      -0.29      -0.32      -0.35      -0.40      -0.26      -0.30

        Fitted Covariance Matrix

                Q6         Q9        Q10        Q11        Q17        Q18
          --------   --------   --------   --------   --------   --------
     Q6       1.00
     Q9       0.56       1.00
    Q10       0.19       0.18       1.00
    Q11       0.58       0.70       0.21       1.00
    Q17       0.20       0.19       0.22       0.22       1.00
    Q18       0.19       0.19       0.22       0.21       0.23       1.00
```

Fitted Residuals

	Q5	Q7	Q8	Q12	Q13	Q14
Q5	0.00					
Q7	0.04	0.00				
Q8	0.11	0.00	0.00			
Q12	0.01	0.02	0.01	0.00		
Q13	0.09	0.01	0.08	0.01	0.00	
Q14	0.00	0.00	0.10	0.01	0.00	0.00
Q6	0.11	0.00	0.10	-0.01	0.17	0.07
Q9	0.08	0.02	0.12	-0.04	0.15	0.15
Q10	0.16	0.05	0.13	0.00	0.07	0.04
Q11	0.01	0.05	0.10	0.02	0.07	0.10
Q17	0.11	0.04	0.04	0.07	0.01	0.00
Q18	0.08	0.05	0.14	0.00	0.17	0.09

Fitted Residuals

	Q6	Q9	Q10	Q11	Q17	Q18
Q6	0.00					
Q9	0.00	0.00				
Q10	0.17	0.14	0.00			
Q11	0.00	0.00	0.20	0.00		
Q17	0.19	0.22	0.22	0.21	0.00	
Q18	0.21	0.20	0.25	0.21	0.25	0.00

```
Summary Statistics for Fitted Residuals

Smallest Fitted Residual =   -0.04
  Median Fitted Residual =    0.05
 Largest Fitted Residual =    0.25

Stemleaf Plot
- 0|4100000000000000000000000
  0|11111112224444
  0|555777788899
  1|00001112344
  1|5567779
  2|0011122
  2|55
```

Standardized Residuals

	Q5	Q7	Q8	Q12	Q13	Q14
Q5	- -					
Q7	0.92	- -				
Q8	3.04	- -	- -			
Q12	0.45	0.95	0.37	- -		
Q13	1.71	0.32	2.15	0.38	- -	

```
      Q14      -0.01       0.00       2.76       0.28        - -        - -
       Q6       1.95       0.00       2.15      -0.48       2.77       1.20
       Q9       1.30       0.29       2.56      -1.16       2.37       2.63
      Q10       2.79       0.97       2.91      -0.14       1.22       0.77
      Q11       0.15       1.00       2.27       0.80       1.14       1.83
      Q17       1.98       0.84       1.00       2.58       0.18      -0.08
      Q18       1.50       1.00       3.13      -0.08       2.81       1.61

         Standardized Residuals

                  Q6         Q9        Q10        Q11        Q17        Q18
            --------   --------   --------   --------   --------   --------
       Q6        - -
       Q9        - -        - -
      Q10       2.57       2.12        - -
      Q11        - -        - -       3.08        - -
      Q17       2.81       3.28       3.37       3.26        - -
      Q18       3.17       2.93       3.88       3.18       3.86        - -

Summary Statistics for Standardized Residuals

Smallest Standardized Residual =   -1.16
  Median Standardized Residual =    0.98
 Largest Standardized Residual =    3.88

Stemleaf Plot

- 1|2
- 0|5111000000000000000000000
  0|2233344488899
  1|0000122356789
  2|01113466668888899
  3|0112233499
Largest Positive Standardized Residuals
Residual for       Q8 and       Q5   3.04
Residual for      Q14 and       Q8   2.76
Residual for       Q6 and      Q13   2.77
Residual for       Q9 and      Q14   2.63
Residual for      Q10 and       Q5   2.79
Residual for      Q10 and       Q8   2.91
Residual for      Q11 and      Q10   3.08
Residual for      Q17 and      Q12   2.58
Residual for      Q17 and       Q6   2.81
Residual for      Q17 and       Q9   3.28
Residual for      Q17 and      Q10   3.37
Residual for      Q17 and      Q11   3.26
Residual for      Q18 and       Q8   3.13
Residual for      Q18 and      Q13   2.81
Residual for      Q18 and       Q6   3.17
Residual for      Q18 and       Q9   2.93
Residual for      Q18 and      Q10   3.88
Residual for      Q18 and      Q11   3.18
Residual for      Q18 and      Q17   3.86
```

```
!Examp8-3.spl


                        Qplot of Standardized Residuals

 3.5..........................................................................
    .                                                                       ..
    .                                                                      . .
    .                                                                    .   .
    .                                                                  .     .
    .                                                                 .      .
    .                                                               .        .
    .                                                             .          .
    .                                                            .           .
    .                                                          .             x
    .                                                        .               .
    .                                                       .                x
    .                                                     .                 x.
    .                                                   .                  x .
    .                                                  .                  *  .
N   .                                                .                   xx  .
o   .                                              .                    xx   .
r   .                                             .                   x*     .
m   .                                           .                    x*      .
a   .                                         .                    *xx       .
l   .                                        .                  xx x         .
    .                                      .                 x x             .
Q   .                                    .               xx xx               .
u   .                                   .            xx x                    .
a   .                                 .            *xx                       .
n   .                               .             x*                         .
t   .                              .             xx                          .
i   .                            .          *x                               .
l   .                          .           *x                                .
e   .                         .           *                                  .
s   .                       .           *                                    .
    .                     .             *                                    .
    .                    .              x                                    .
    .                  .               x                                     .
    .                .              x                                        .
    .               .                                                        .
    .             .         x                                                .
    .           .                                                            .
    .          .                                                             .
    .        .                                                               .
    .      .                                                                 .
    .     .                                                                  .
    .   .                                                                    .
    . .                                                                      .
-3.5..........................................................................
  -3.5                                                                      3.5
                            Standardized Residuals
```

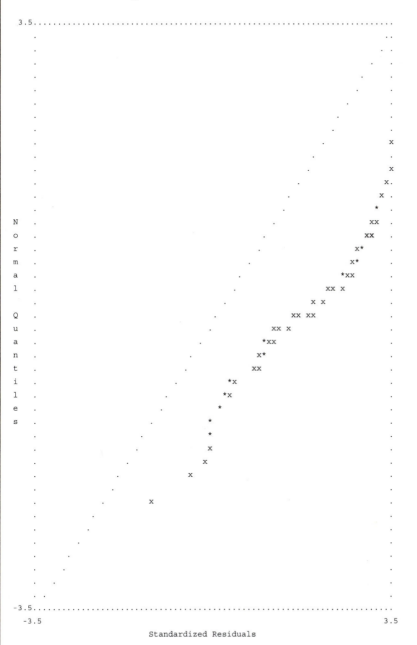

```
!Examp8-3.spl

Modification Indices and Expected Change

No Non-Zero Modification Indices for LAMBDA-X

No Non-Zero Modification Indices for PHI

         Modification Indices for THETA-DELTA

                  Q5          Q7          Q8         Q12         Q13         Q14
            --------    --------    --------    --------    --------    --------
       Q5       - -
       Q7      0.27         - -
       Q8      7.37         - -         - -
      Q12      0.20        0.61        0.02         - -
      Q13      3.16        0.06        1.25        0.08         - -
      Q14      0.45        1.24        4.69        0.02         - -         - -
       Q6      3.20        0.84        1.33        0.21        4.75        0.83
       Q9      1.10        0.86        2.05        3.59        0.84        1.78
      Q10      7.77        0.17        6.68        0.02        0.99        0.11
      Q11      1.76        0.88        0.00        3.90        1.32        0.39
      Q17      3.93        0.16        0.37        6.64        0.05        0.02
      Q18      2.25        0.24        7.86        0.01        5.50        0.35

         Modification Indices for THETA-DELTA

                  Q6          Q9         Q10         Q11         Q17         Q18
            --------    --------    --------    --------    --------    --------
       Q6       - -
       Q9       - -         - -
      Q10      1.41        0.01         - -
      Q11       - -         - -        3.21         - -
      Q17      1.05        1.58       11.37        1.29         - -
      Q18      2.51        0.55       15.04        1.36       14.90         - -

         Expected Change for THETA-DELTA

                  Q5          Q7          Q8         Q12         Q13         Q14
            --------    --------    --------    --------    --------    --------
       Q5       - -
       Q7     -0.02         - -
       Q8      0.12         - -         - -
      Q12      0.02        0.03       -0.01         - -
      Q13      0.10       -0.01        0.05        0.01         - -
      Q14     -0.04       -0.05        0.09        0.01         - -         - -
       Q6      0.10       -0.04        0.05       -0.02        0.11       -0.05
       Q9      0.05       -0.04        0.05       -0.08        0.04        0.06
      Q10      0.18       -0.02        0.13       -0.01        0.06        0.02
      Q11     -0.06        0.04        0.00        0.08       -0.05        0.03
      Q17      0.13        0.02        0.03        0.14        0.01       -0.01
      Q18      0.10       -0.03        0.14        0.00        0.14        0.03
```

```
        Expected Change for THETA-DELTA

                 Q6         Q9        Q10        Q11        Q17        Q18
            --------   --------   --------   --------   --------   --------
      Q6        - -
      Q9        - -        - -
     Q10       0.07       0.00        - -
     Q11        - -        - -       0.09        - -
     Q17       0.06       0.07       0.24       0.06        - -
     Q18       0.10       0.04       0.28       0.06       0.27        - -

Maximum Modification Index is   15.04 for Element (12, 9) of THETA-DELTA

!Examp8-3.spl

Covariances

        X - KSI

                 Q5         Q7         Q8        Q12        Q13        Q14
            --------   --------   --------   --------   --------   --------
 FactOne       0.61       0.68       0.75       0.85       0.57       0.65

        X - KSI

                 Q6         Q9        Q10        Q11        Q17        Q18
            --------   --------   --------   --------   --------   --------
 FactOne      -0.40      -0.40      -0.46      -0.45      -0.48      -0.47

!Examp8-3.spl

Factor Scores Regressions

        KSI

                 Q5         Q7         Q8        Q12        Q13        Q14
            --------   --------   --------   --------   --------   --------
 FactOne       0.13       0.09       0.17       0.40       0.07       0.12

        KSI

                 Q6         Q9        Q10        Q11        Q17        Q18
            --------   --------   --------   --------   --------   --------
 FactOne      -0.03      -0.02      -0.08      -0.04      -0.08      -0.08


         The Problem used    21704 Bytes (=  0.0% of Available Workspace)

                           Time used:    0.211 Seconds
```

Fig. 8.9 LISREL8 for Windows output of model with single factor (examp8-3.out).

```
!Examp8-4.spl
!Raw Data From File: Examp8-2.txt

DA NI=12 MA = KM XM = 9
RA FI=C:\SAMD\Chapter8\Examples\Examp8-2.txt
LA
Q5 Q7 Q8  Q12 Q13 Q14
Q6 Q9 Q10 Q11 Q17 Q18

MO NX = 12 NK = 2 PH = DI TD = SY           !CORR = 0
LK
FactOne                                              !Competence Destroying
FactTwo                                     !Competence Enhancing
FR LX(1,1) LX(2,1) LX(3,1) LX(4,1) LX(5,1) LX(6,1)   C
   LX(7,2) LX(8,2) LX(9,2) LX(10,2) LX(11,2) LX(12,2)      C
   TD(3,2) TD(6,5) TD(8,7) TD(10,8) TD(10,7)
Path Diagram
OU SE TV RS MR FS AD = 50 MI
```

Fig. 8.10 LISREL8 for Windows input for model with two independent factors (examp8-4.spl).

```
                         DATE:  1/ 8/2001
                           TIME: 11:17


                         L I S R E L  8.30

                                BY

                   Karl G. Jöreskog & Dag Sörbom



                This program is published exclusively by
                Scientific Software International, Inc.
                   7383 N. Lincoln Avenue, Suite 100
                    Chicago, IL 60646-1704, U.S.A.
        Phone: (800)247-6113, (847)675-0720, Fax: (847)675-2140
     Copyright by Scientific Software International, Inc., 1981-99
       Use of this program is subject to the terms specified in the
                    Universal Copyright Convention.
                      Website: www.ssicentral.com
```

```
The following lines were read from file C:\SAMD\CHAPTER8\EXAMPLES\EXAMP8-4.SPL:

!Examp8-4.spl

!Raw Data From File: Examp8-2.txt

DA NI=12 MA = KM XM = 9
RA FI=C:\SAMD\Chapter8\Examples\Examp8-2.txt
LA
Q5 Q7 Q8  Q12 Q13 Q14
Q6 Q9 Q10 Q11 Q17 Q18


MO NX = 12 NK = 2 PH = DI TD = SY  !CORR = 0
LK
FactOne       !Competence Destroying
FactTwo      !Competence Enhancing
FR LX(1,1) LX(2,1) LX(3,1) LX(4,1) LX(5,1) LX(6,1) C
LX(7,2) LX(8,2) LX(9,2) LX(10,2) LX(11,2) LX(12,2) C
TD(3,2) TD(6,5) TD(8,7) TD(10,8) TD(10,7)
Path Diagram
OU SE TV RS MR FS AD = 50 MI


!Examp8-4.spl

                          Number of Input Variables 12
                          Number of Y - Variables    0
                          Number of X - Variables   12
                          Number of ETA - Variables  0
                          Number of KSI - Variables  2
                          Number of Observations   134


!Examp8-4.spl

        Covariance Matrix to be Analyzed

                 Q5         Q7         Q8        Q12        Q13        Q14
           --------   --------   --------   --------   --------   --------
      Q5       1.00
      Q7       0.46       1.00
      Q8       0.57       0.74       1.00
     Q12       0.53       0.60       0.64       1.00
     Q13       0.43       0.40       0.51       0.49       1.00
     Q14       0.40       0.44       0.58       0.56       0.59       1.00
      Q6      -0.13      -0.27      -0.20      -0.36      -0.06      -0.19
      Q9      -0.17      -0.26      -0.18      -0.38      -0.08      -0.11
     Q10      -0.13      -0.27      -0.22      -0.40      -0.19      -0.26
     Q11      -0.26      -0.25      -0.23      -0.36      -0.18      -0.19
     Q17      -0.19      -0.29      -0.32      -0.34      -0.26      -0.32
     Q18      -0.20      -0.27      -0.21      -0.40      -0.10      -0.22
```

```
         Covariance Matrix to be Analyzed

                   Q6         Q9        Q10        Q11        Q17        Q18
             --------   --------   --------   --------   --------   --------
       Q6        1.00
       Q9        0.56       1.00
      Q10        0.36       0.33       1.00
      Q11        0.58       0.70       0.41       1.00
      Q17        0.38       0.41       0.44       0.43       1.00
      Q18        0.40       0.38       0.47       0.42       0.47       1.00


!Examp8-4.spl


Parameter Specifications

         LAMBDA-X

              FactOne    FactTwo
             --------   --------
       Q5           1          0
       Q7           2          0
       Q8           3          0
      Q12           4          0
      Q13           5          0
      Q14           6          0
       Q6           0          7
       Q9           0          8
      Q10           0          9
      Q11           0         10
      Q17           0         11
      Q18           0         12


         THETA-DELTA

                   Q5         Q7         Q8        Q12        Q13        Q14
             --------   --------   --------   --------   --------   --------
       Q5          13
       Q7           0         14
       Q8           0         15         16
      Q12           0          0          0         17
      Q13           0          0          0          0         18
      Q14           0          0          0          0         19         20
       Q6           0          0          0          0          0          0
       Q9           0          0          0          0          0          0
      Q10           0          0          0          0          0          0
      Q11           0          0          0          0          0          0
      Q17           0          0          0          0          0          0
      Q18           0          0          0          0          0          0
```

```
        THETA-DELTA

                 Q6         Q9        Q10        Q11        Q17        Q18
            --------   --------   --------   --------   --------   --------
      Q6          21
      Q9          22         23
     Q10           0          0         24
     Q11          25         26          0         27
     Q17           0          0          0          0         28
     Q18           0          0          0          0          0         29


!Examp8-4.spl


Number of Iterations = 29


LISREL Estimates (Maximum Likelihood)


        LAMBDA-X

             FactOne    FactTwo
            --------   --------
      Q5        0.67       - -
              (0.08)
                8.11

      Q7        0.71       - -
              (0.08)
                8.50

      Q8        0.83       - -
              (0.08)
               10.76

     Q12        0.80       - -
              (0.08)
               10.31

     Q13        0.62       - -
              (0.08)
                7.29

     Q14        0.67       - -
              (0.08)
                8.19

      Q6         - -       0.56
                         (0.09)
                           6.08
```

```
      Q9          - -       0.56
                           (0.09)
                             5.97

     Q10          - -       0.65
                           (0.09)
                             7.35

     Q11          - -       0.62
                           (0.09)
                             6.78

     Q17          - -       0.68
                           (0.09)
                             7.75

     Q18          - -       0.70
                           (0.09)
                             7.97


        PHI
        Note: This matrix is diagonal.

             FactOne    FactTwo
            --------   --------
                1.00       1.00


        THETA-DELTA

                  Q5         Q7         Q8        Q12        Q13        Q14
            --------   --------   --------   --------   --------   --------
      Q5        0.56
              (0.08)
                7.04

      Q7         - -       0.50
                         (0.08)
                           6.32

      Q8         - -       0.16       0.32
                         (0.06)     (0.06)
                           2.74       4.91

     Q12         - -        - -        - -       0.36
                                               (0.07)
                                                 5.55

     Q13         - -        - -        - -        - -       0.62
                                                          (0.09)
                                                            7.22
```

```
 Q14       - -       - -       - -       - -      0.18      0.55
                                                (0.06)    (0.08)
                                                  2.83      6.92

  Q6       - -       - -       - -       - -       - -       - -

  Q9       - -       - -       - -       - -       - -       - -

 Q10       - -       - -       - -       - -       - -       - -

 Q11       - -       - -       - -       - -       - -       - -

 Q17       - -       - -       - -       - -       - -       - -

 Q18       - -       - -       - -       - -       - -       - -


   THETA-DELTA

              Q6        Q9       Q10       Q11       Q17       Q18
          --------  --------  --------  --------  --------  --------
  Q6        0.68
          (0.10)
            6.87

  Q9        0.25      0.69
          (0.08)    (0.10)
            3.21      6.91

 Q10       - -       - -        0.57
                              (0.09)
                                6.31

 Q11        0.24      0.36       - -      0.62
          (0.08)    (0.08)              (0.10)
            3.08      4.40                6.53

 Q17       - -       - -       - -       - -      0.53
                                                (0.09)
                                                  5.96

 Q18       - -       - -       - -       - -       - -      0.51
                                                          (0.09)
                                                            5.74

   Squared Multiple Correlations for X - Variables

              Q5        Q7        Q8       Q12       Q13       Q14
          --------  --------  --------  --------  --------  --------
            0.44      0.50      0.68      0.64      0.38      0.45
```

```
 Squared Multiple Correlations for X - Variables

           Q6          Q9         Q10         Q11         Q17         Q18
     --------    --------    --------    --------    --------    --------
         0.32        0.31        0.43        0.38        0.47        0.49


                         Goodness of Fit Statistics

                          Degrees of Freedom = 49
              Minimum Fit Function Chi-Square = 84.34 (P = 0.0013)
      Normal Theory Weighted Least Squares Chi-Square = 77.75 (P = 0.0055)
                Estimated Non-centrality Parameter (NCP) = 28.75
           90 Percent Confidence Interval for NCP = (8.62 ; 56.81)

                       Minimum Fit Function Value = 0.63
             Population Discrepancy Function Value (F0) = 0.22
            90 Percent Confidence Interval for F0 = (0.065 ; 0.43)
           Root Mean Square Error of Approximation (RMSEA) = 0.066
          90 Percent Confidence Interval for RMSEA = (0.036 ; 0.093)
             P-Value for Test of Close Fit (RMSEA < 0.05) = 0.16

                Expected Cross-Validation Index (ECVI) = 1.02
           90 Percent Confidence Interval for ECVI = (0.87 ; 1.23)
                        ECVI for Saturated Model = 1.17
                       ECVI for Independence Model = 5.81

 Chi-Square for Independence Model with 66 Degrees of Freedom = 748.31
                          Independence AIC = 772.31
                              Model AIC = 135.75
                            Saturated AIC = 156.00
                          Independence CAIC = 819.08
                             Model CAIC = 248.79
                           Saturated CAIC = 460.03

                    Root Mean Square Residual (RMR) = 0.17
                           Standardized RMR = 0.17
                    Goodness of Fit Index (GFI) = 0.91
               Adjusted Goodness of Fit Index (AGFI) = 0.86
              Parsimony Goodness of Fit Index (PGFI) = 0.57



                       Normed Fit Index (NFI) = 0.89
                     Non-Normed Fit Index (NNFI) = 0.93
                  Parsimony Normed Fit Index (PNFI) = 0.66
                     Comparative Fit Index (CFI) = 0.95
                     Incremental Fit Index (IFI) = 0.95
                       Relative Fit Index (RFI) = 0.85

                          Critical N (CN) = 119.15
```

```
!Examp8-4.spl


        Fitted Covariance Matrix

                   Q5         Q7         Q8        Q12        Q13        Q14
             --------   --------   --------   --------   --------   --------
       Q5        1.00
       Q7        0.47       1.00
       Q8        0.55       0.74       1.00
      Q12        0.53       0.56       0.66       1.00
      Q13        0.41       0.43       0.51       0.49       1.00
      Q14        0.45       0.48       0.56       0.54       0.59       1.00
       Q6         - -        - -        - -        - -        - -        - -
       Q9         - -        - -        - -        - -        - -        - -
      Q10         - -        - -        - -        - -        - -        - -
      Q11         - -        - -        - -        - -        - -        - -
      Q17         - -        - -        - -        - -        - -        - -
      Q18         - -        - -        - -        - -        - -        - -


        Fitted Covariance Matrix

                   Q6         Q9        Q10        Q11        Q17        Q18
             --------   --------   --------   --------   --------   --------
       Q6        1.00
       Q9        0.56       1.00
      Q10        0.37       0.36       1.00
      Q11        0.58       0.70       0.40       1.00
      Q17        0.38       0.38       0.45       0.42       1.00
      Q18        0.39       0.39       0.46       0.43       0.48       1.00


        Fitted Residuals

                   Q5         Q7         Q8        Q12        Q13        Q14
             --------   --------   --------   --------   --------   --------
       Q5        0.00
       Q7       -0.01       0.00
       Q8        0.02       0.00       0.00
      Q12        0.00       0.03      -0.02       0.00
      Q13        0.02      -0.03       0.00       0.00       0.00
      Q14       -0.05      -0.04       0.02       0.02       0.00       0.00
       Q6       -0.13      -0.27      -0.20      -0.36      -0.06      -0.19
       Q9       -0.17      -0.26      -0.18      -0.38      -0.08      -0.11
      Q10       -0.13      -0.27      -0.22      -0.40      -0.19      -0.26
      Q11       -0.26      -0.25      -0.23      -0.36      -0.18      -0.19
      Q17       -0.19      -0.29      -0.32      -0.34      -0.26      -0.32
      Q18       -0.20      -0.27      -0.21      -0.40      -0.10      -0.22
```

Fitted Residuals

	Q6	Q9	Q10	Q11	Q17	Q18
Q6	0.00					
Q9	0.00	0.00				
Q10	-0.01	-0.03	0.00			
Q11	0.00	0.00	0.01	0.00		
Q17	0.00	0.03	-0.01	0.01	0.00	
Q18	0.01	0.00	0.01	-0.01	-0.01	0.00

Summary Statistics for Fitted Residuals

```
Smallest Fitted Residual =   -0.40
  Median Fitted Residual =   -0.03
 Largest Fitted Residual =    0.03
```

Stemleaf Plot

```
- 4|00
- 3|866
- 3|422
- 2|977766665
- 2|322100
- 1|9999887
- 1|3310
- 0|865
- 0|4332111110000000000000000000000
  0|1111222233
```

Standardized Residuals

	Q5	Q7	Q8	Q12	Q13	Q14
Q5	- -					
Q7	-0.39	- -				
Q8	0.89	- -	- -			
Q12	0.04	1.59	-1.65	- -		
Q13	0.56	-0.90	-0.10	0.01	- -	
Q14	-1.38	-1.05	1.00	0.77	- -	- -
Q6	-1.54	-3.17	-2.33	-4.13	-0.66	-2.23
Q9	-1.95	-2.97	-2.07	-4.34	-0.92	-1.28
Q10	-1.45	-3.06	-2.48	-4.58	-2.17	-2.96
Q11	-3.05	-2.91	-2.66	-4.11	-2.13	-2.18
Q17	-2.16	-3.32	-3.67	-3.92	-3.04	-3.66
Q18	-2.33	-3.08	-2.42	-4.62	-1.13	-2.49

```
        Standardized Residuals

                  Q6        Q9       Q10       Q11       Q17       Q18
            --------  --------  --------  --------  --------  --------
      Q6        - -
      Q9        - -       - -
     Q10       -0.18     -0.83       - -
     Q11        - -       - -       0.23       - -
     Q17       -0.06      0.92     -0.19      0.22       - -
     Q18        0.23     -0.11      0.41     -0.44     -0.22       - -


Summary Statistics for Standardized Residuals

Smallest Standardized Residual =   -4.62
  Median Standardized Residual =   -0.87
 Largest Standardized Residual =    1.59


Stemleaf Plot

- 4|66311
- 3|97732111000
- 2|9755433222211
- 1|96554311
- 0|998744222111000000000000000000
  0|22246899
  1|06


Largest Negative Standardized Residuals
Residual for      Q6 and       Q7  -3.17
Residual for      Q6 and      Q12  -4.13
Residual for      Q9 and       Q7  -2.97
Residual for      Q9 and      Q12  -4.34
Residual for     Q10 and       Q7  -3.06
Residual for     Q10 and      Q12  -4.58
Residual for     Q10 and      Q14  -2.96
Residual for     Q11 and       Q5  -3.05
Residual for     Q11 and       Q7  -2.91
Residual for     Q11 and       Q8  -2.66
Residual for     Q11 and      Q12  -4.11
Residual for     Q17 and       Q7  -3.32
Residual for     Q17 and       Q8  -3.67
Residual for     Q17 and      Q12  -3.92
Residual for     Q17 and      Q13  -3.04
Residual for     Q17 and      Q14  -3.66
Residual for     Q18 and       Q7  -3.08
Residual for     Q18 and      Q12  -4.62
```

```
!Examp8-4.spl


                        Qplot of Standardized Residuals

 3.5...........................................................................
    .                                                                        ..
    .                                                                       . .
    .                                                                     .   .
    .                                                                   .     .
    .                                                                  .      .
    .                                                                .        .
    .                                                              .          .
    .                                                             .           .
    .                                                     x     .             .
    .                                                         .               .
    .                                               x        .                .
    .                                              x       .                  .
    .                                              x     .                    .
    .                                          x  x     .                     .
N   .                                       x x       .                       .
o   .                                       *       .                         .
r   .                                    x*        .                          .
m   .                                   x        .                            .
a   .                                * xx      .                              .
l   .                         xx  x          .                                .
    .                      x xxx           .                                  .
Q   .                  xxxx               .                                   .
u   .             xxx                    .                                    .
a   .            xx                    .                                      .
n   .          x*                    .                                        .
t   .      x  x *                   .                                         .
i   .    x*                       .                                           .
l   .   x*                      .                                             .
e   . xx                       .                                              .
s   *                        .                                                .
    *                      .                                                  .
    x                     .                                                   .
    x                   .                                                     .
    x                 .                                                       .
    .                .                                                        .
    x              .                                                          .
    .            .                                                            .
    .           .                                                             .
    .         .                                                               .
    .       .                                                                 .
    .      .                                                                  .
    .    .                                                                    .
    .  .                                                                      .
-3.5...........................................................................
   -3.5                                                                      3.5
                             Standardized Residuals
```

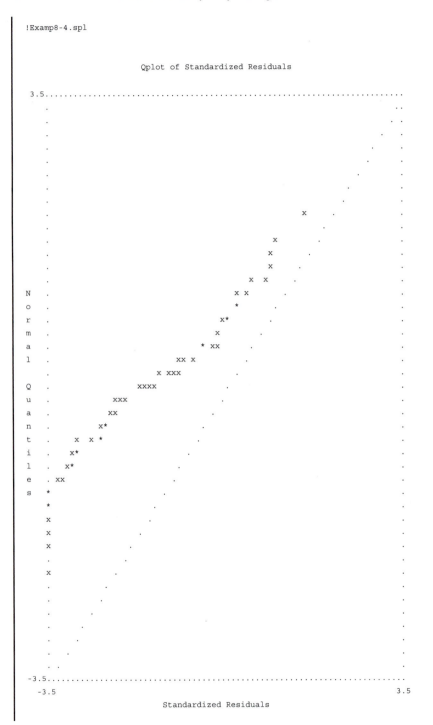

```
!Examp8-4.spl


Modification Indices and Expected Change

        Modification Indices for LAMBDA-X

            FactOne    FactTwo
            --------   --------
      Q5       - -       0.20
      Q7       - -       2.35
      Q8       - -       1.02
     Q12       - -      15.73
     Q13       - -       0.49
     Q14       - -       0.89
      Q6      0.20        - -
      Q9      0.00        - -
     Q10      1.35        - -
     Q11      0.82        - -
     Q17      3.42        - -
     Q18      0.78        - -

        Expected Change for LAMBDA-X

            FactOne    FactTwo
            --------   --------
      Q5       - -       0.03
      Q7       - -      -0.10
      Q8       - -       0.06
     Q12       - -      -0.27
     Q13       - -       0.05
     Q14       - -      -0.07
      Q6     -0.03        - -
      Q9      0.00        - -
     Q10     -0.09        - -
     Q11     -0.06        - -
     Q17     -0.14        - -
     Q18     -0.07        - -

        Modification Indices for PHI

            FactOne    FactTwo
            --------   --------
 FactOne       - -
 FactTwo     25.54        - -

        Expected Change for PHI

            FactOne    FactTwo
            --------   --------
 FactOne       - -
 FactTwo     -0.54        - -
```

Modification Indices for THETA-DELTA

	Q5	Q7	Q8	Q12	Q13	Q14
Q5	- -					
Q7	0.42	- -				
Q8	0.99	- -	- -			
Q12	0.00	3.59	4.40	- -		
Q13	0.94	0.21	0.01	0.04	- -	
Q14	2.41	1.07	1.55	0.52	- -	- -
Q6	1.18	1.09	0.17	1.21	3.24	1.12
Q9	0.27	1.11	0.94	4.50	0.55	1.37
Q10	1.81	0.33	0.80	3.39	0.09	0.33
Q11	4.05	0.76	0.19	1.19	2.12	0.24
Q17	0.35	0.37	2.98	1.85	1.56	1.03
Q18	0.34	0.47	1.19	3.71	2.34	0.04

Modification Indices for THETA-DELTA

	Q6	Q9	Q10	Q11	Q17	Q18
Q6	- -					
Q9	- -	- -				
Q10	0.00	0.94	- -			
Q11	- -	- -	0.52	- -		
Q17	0.10	0.78	0.03	0.06	- -	
Q18	0.12	0.00	0.16	0.19	0.05	- -

Expected Change for THETA-DELTA

	Q5	Q7	Q8	Q12	Q13	Q14
Q5	- -					
Q7	-0.03	- -				
Q8	0.05	- -	- -			
Q12	0.00	0.09	-0.10	- -		
Q13	0.05	-0.02	0.00	-0.01	- -	
Q14	-0.08	-0.05	0.05	0.04	- -	- -
Q6	0.06	-0.05	0.02	-0.05	0.09	-0.05
Q9	0.02	-0.04	0.03	-0.09	0.03	0.05
Q10	0.08	-0.03	0.04	-0.09	-0.02	-0.03
Q11	-0.09	0.03	-0.01	0.04	-0.06	0.02
Q17	0.03	0.03	-0.07	0.07	-0.07	-0.05
Q18	-0.03	-0.03	0.04	-0.09	0.08	-0.01

Expected Change for THETA-DELTA

	Q6	Q9	Q10	Q11	Q17	Q18
Q6	- -					
Q9	- -	- -				
Q10	0.00	-0.05	- -			
Q11	- -	- -	0.04	- -		

```
     Q17      -0.02      0.05     -0.01     -0.01       - -
     Q18       0.02      0.00      0.03     -0.02     -0.02       - -

Maximum Modification Index is   25.54 for Element ( 2, 1) of PHI


!Examp8-4.spl

Covariances

        X - KSI

                 Q5        Q7        Q8       Q12       Q13       Q14
           --------  --------  --------  --------  --------  --------
 FactOne       0.67      0.71      0.83      0.80      0.62      0.67
 FactTwo        - -       - -       - -       - -       - -       - -

        X - KSI

                 Q6        Q9       Q10       Q11       Q17       Q18
           --------  --------  --------  --------  --------  --------
 FactOne        - -       - -       - -       - -       - -       - -
 FactTwo       0.56      0.56      0.65      0.62      0.68      0.70


!Examp8-4.spl

Factor Scores Regressions

        KSI

                 Q5        Q7        Q8       Q12       Q13       Q14
           --------  --------  --------  --------  --------  --------
 FactOne       0.17      0.10      0.32      0.31      0.10      0.14
 FactTwo        - -       - -       - -       - -       - -       - -

        KSI

                 Q6        Q9       Q10       Q11       Q17       Q18
           --------  --------  --------  --------  --------  --------
 FactOne        - -       - -       - -       - -       - -       - -
 FactTwo       0.11      0.07      0.26      0.14      0.29      0.31

         The Problem used    23472 Bytes (=  0.0% of Available Workspace)
                                  Time used:     0.207 Seconds
```

Fig. 8.11 LISREL8 for Windows output of model with two independent factors (examp8-4.out).

Instead of defining the variances of the unobserved constructs to unity, the result would have been the same if one lambda for each construct had been fixed to one but the variances of these constructs had been estimated. This is illustrated with the input which would be needed for running this model with AMOS (although it can been done easily with LISREL8 following the principles described above, this example uses AMOS to introduce its commands.

The input of the corresponding two factor confirmatory factor model with AMOS is shown below:

In AMOS, such as shown in Figure 8.12, each equation for the measurement model (as well as for structural relationships) can be represented with a variable on the left side of an equation and a linear combination of other variables on the right hand side. These equations correspond to the equations as specified by Equations (8.22), (8.25) and (8.26). Inserting "(1)" before a variable on the right hand side indicates that the coefficient is fixed to that

```
! FactorOne vs. FactorTwo in AMOS with non-zero Theta-Deltas
$Standardized
$Smc

$Structure
Q5  = ( 1 )     FactorOne + (1) eps5
Q7  =   FactorOne + (1) eps7
Q8  =   FactorOne + (1) eps8
Q12 =   FactorOne + (1) eps12
Q13 =   FactorOne + (1) eps13
Q14 =   FactorOne + (1) eps14

Q6  = ( 1 )     FactorTwo + (1) eps6
Q9  =   FactorTwo + (1) eps9
Q10 =   FactorTwo + (1) eps10
Q11 =   FactorTwo + (1) eps11
Q17 =   FactorTwo + (1) eps17
Q18 =   FactorTwo + (1) eps18

eps8  <> eps7
eps13 <> eps14
eps6  <> eps9
eps6  <> eps11
eps9  <> eps11

$Include = Examp8-5.amd
```

Fig. 8.12 AMOS input example for confirmatory factor analytic model (examp8-5.ami).

value and that the corresponding parameters will not be estimated. The program recognizes automatically which variables are observed and which ones are unobserved.

Correlations are indicated by "*variable1* <> *variable2*", where *variable1* and *variable2* are the labels of observed variables or of hypothetical constructs. The output provides similar information as available in LISREL8.

8.3.3 Example of Structural Model with Measurement Models

The examples above were concerned exclusively with a measurement model or confirmatory factor analysis. As introduced earlier in this chapter, this is only one component of Analysis of Covariance Structures. The full model contains structural relationships among the unobserved constructs that need to be estimated. An example is provided below, where two characteristics of innovations (the extent to which an innovation is radical and the extent to which it is competence enhancing) are hypothesized to affect two constructs, one being changes in the management of the organization and the other being the success of that organization. Figure 8.13 presents the LISREL8 input file for the first step in the analysis, i.e., the measurement model for all the constructs (including both the exogenous and endogenous constructs, although it would be feasible to estimate a separate measurement model for each). The

```
!Examp8-6.spl
!Raw Data From File: Examp8-6.txt
!Path Diagram

DA NI=19 MA = KM
RA FI=C:\SAMD\Chapter8\Examples\Examp8-6.txt
MO NX = 19 NK = 4 PH = SY TD = SY
FI   LX(1,1) LX(4,2) LX(9,3) LX(15,4)
VA 1 LX(1,1) LX(4,2) LX(9,3) LX(15,4)
LA
Q46 Q47 Q48 Q40 Q42 Q43 Q44 Q45 Q5 Q7 Q8 Q12 Q13 Q14 Q19r Q20 Q21 Q22 Q23
LK
Success Org2 CompEnh Radical
FR             LX(2,1)  LX(3,1)                                   C
   LX(5,2)  LX(6,2)  LX(7,2)  LX(8,2)                             C
               LX(10,3) LX(11,3) LX(12,3) LX(13,3) LX(14,3)       C
               LX(16,4) LX(17,4) LX(18,4) LX(19,4)                C
   TD(14,11)
Path Diagram
OU SE TV AD = 50 MI
```

Fig. 8.13 Step 1: LISREL8 input of measurement model for exogenous and endogenous constructs (examp8-6.spl).

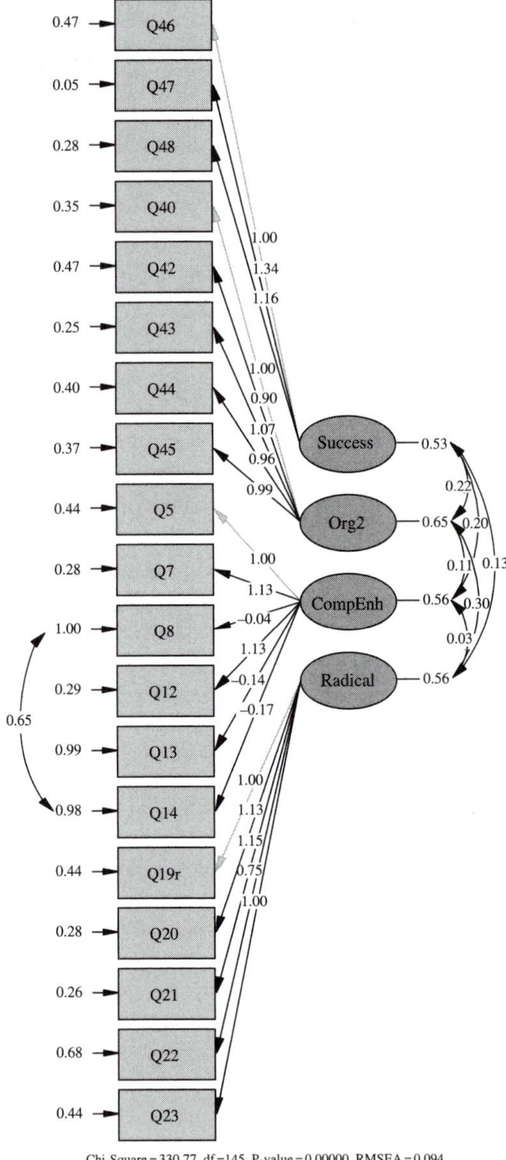

Fig. 8.14 Step 1: graphical representation of measurement model for exogenous and endogenous constructs (examp8-6.pth).

results obtained and shown in Figure 8.15 (and represented graphically in Figure 8.14) are then used as input for step 2, which consists in estimating the structural model parameters with the measurement parameters fixed to the values obtained in step 1. This LISREL8 input file is shown in Figure 8.16.

```
                              DATE: 12/ 7/1999
                                TIME: 17:49


                              L I S R E L  8.30

                                     BY

                        Karl G. Jöreskog & Dag Sörbom


                    This program is published exclusively by
                    Scientific Software International, Inc.
                       7383 N. Lincoln Avenue, Suite 100
                        Chicago, IL 60646-1704, U.S.A.
            Phone: (800)247-6113, (847)675-0720, Fax: (847)675-2140
        Copyright by Scientific Software International, Inc., 1981-99
          Use of this program is subject to the terms specified in the
                        Universal Copyright Convention.
                          Website: www.ssicentral.com

The following lines were read from file C:\SAMD\CHAPTER8\EXAMPLES\Examp8-6.SPL:

!Examp8-6.spl
!Raw Data From File: Examp8-6.txt
!Path Diagram

DA NI=19 MA = KM
RA FI=C:\SAMD\Chapter8\Examples\Examp8-6.txt
MO NX = 19 NK = 4 PH = SY TD = SY
FI LX(1,1) LX(4,2) LX(9,3) LX(15,4)
VA 1 LX(1,1) LX(4,2) LX(9,3) LX(15,4)
LA
Q46 Q47 Q48 Q40 Q42 Q43 Q44 Q45 Q5 Q7 Q8 Q12 Q13 Q14 Q19r Q20 Q21 Q22 Q23
LK
Success Org2 CompEnh Radical
FR       LX(2,1)  LX(3,1)           C
LX(5,2)  LX(6,2)  LX(7,2)  LX(8,2)        C
LX(10,3) LX(11,3) LX(12,3) LX(13,3) LX(14,3)     C
LX(16,4) LX(17,4) LX(18,4) LX(19,4)   C
TD(14,11)         !LX(1,1) LX(4,2) LX(9,3) LX(15,4)
Path Diagram
OU SE TV AD = 50 MI

!Examp8-6.spl

                         Number of Input Variables 19
                         Number of Y - Variables    0
                         Number of X - Variables   19
                         Number of ETA - Variables  0
                         Number of KSI - Variables  4
                         Number of Observations   146
```

!Examp8-6.spl

Covariance Matrix to be Analyzed

	Q46	Q47	Q48	Q40	Q42	Q43
Q46	1.00					
Q47	0.71	1.00				
Q48	0.60	0.83	1.00			
Q40	0.25	0.26	0.24	1.00		
Q42	0.31	0.30	0.25	0.59	1.00	
Q43	0.29	0.27	0.21	0.72	0.60	1.00
Q44	0.32	0.36	0.27	0.60	0.59	0.67
Q45	0.26	0.31	0.25	0.63	0.56	0.70
Q5	0.28	0.30	0.25	0.22	0.05	0.20
Q7	0.26	0.32	0.30	0.19	0.06	0.17
Q8	0.18	0.15	0.11	0.26	0.37	0.36
Q12	0.22	0.26	0.25	0.11	-0.02	0.08
Q13	0.26	0.14	0.09	0.28	0.39	0.32
Q14	0.17	0.11	0.11	0.28	0.41	0.31
Q19r	0.26	0.21	0.15	0.29	0.38	0.32
Q20	0.30	0.19	0.18	0.40	0.42	0.39
Q21	0.18	0.11	0.09	0.32	0.39	0.33
Q22	0.22	0.23	0.20	0.16	0.28	0.18
Q23	0.33	0.23	0.21	0.31	0.35	0.28

Covariance Matrix to be Analyzed

	Q44	Q45	Q5	Q7	Q8	Q12
Q44	1.00					
Q45	0.63	1.00				
Q5	0.18	0.19	1.00			
Q7	0.13	0.15	0.62	1.00		
Q8	0.35	0.36	-0.03	0.01	1.00	
Q12	0.08	0.11	0.63	0.72	-0.06	1.00
Q13	0.21	0.26	-0.10	-0.08	0.56	-0.08
Q14	0.31	0.32	-0.12	-0.07	0.65	-0.13
Q19r	0.28	0.34	0.00	0.00	0.35	-0.09
Q20	0.30	0.32	0.00	0.01	0.47	-0.03
Q21	0.24	0.35	0.07	0.02	0.36	0.03
Q22	0.15	0.17	0.12	0.21	0.29	0.15
Q23	0.20	0.16	0.23	0.20	0.24	0.16

Covariance Matrix to be Analyzed

	Q13	Q14	Q19r	Q20	Q21	Q22
Q13	1.00					
Q14	0.60	1.00				
Q19r	0.48	0.38	1.00			
Q20	0.55	0.47	0.60	1.00		
Q21	0.43	0.35	0.63	0.77	1.00	

```
    Q22        0.29       0.32       0.48       0.40       0.45       1.00
    Q23        0.40       0.26       0.61       0.60       0.61       0.59

       Covariance Matrix to be Analyzed

                Q23
            --------
    Q23        1.00


!Examp8-6.spl

Parameter Specifications

        LAMBDA-X

             Success       Org2    CompEnh    Radical
            --------   --------   --------   --------
    Q46            0          0          0          0
    Q47            1          0          0          0
    Q48            2          0          0          0
    Q40            0          0          0          0
    Q42            0          3          0          0
    Q43            0          4          0          0
    Q44            0          5          0          0
    Q45            0          6          0          0
     Q5            0          0          0          0
     Q7            0          0          7          0
     Q8            0          0          8          0
    Q12            0          0          9          0
    Q13            0          0         10          0
    Q14            0          0         11          0
   Q19r            0          0          0          0
    Q20            0          0          0         12
    Q21            0          0          0         13
    Q22            0          0          0         14
    Q23            0          0          0         15

        PHI

             Success       Org2    CompEnh    Radical
            --------   --------   --------   --------
 Success          16
    Org2          17         18
 CompEnh          19         20         21
 Radical          22         23         24         25

        THETA-DELTA

                 Q46        Q47        Q48        Q40        Q42        Q43
            --------   --------   --------   --------   --------   --------
    Q46           26
    Q47            0         27
```

Q48	0	0	28			
Q40	0	0	0	29		
Q42	0	0	0	0	30	
Q43	0	0	0	0	0	31
Q44	0	0	0	0	0	0
Q45	0	0	0	0	0	0
Q5	0	0	0	0	0	0
Q7	0	0	0	0	0	0
Q8	0	0	0	0	0	0
Q12	0	0	0	0	0	0
Q13	0	0	0	0	0	0
Q14	0	0	0	0	0	0
Q19r	0	0	0	0	0	0
Q20	0	0	0	0	0	0
Q21	0	0	0	0	0	0
Q22	0	0	0	0	0	0
Q23	0	0	0	0	0	0

THETA-DELTA

	Q44	Q45	Q5	Q7	Q8	Q12
Q44	32					
Q45	0	33				
Q5	0	0	34			
Q7	0	0	0	35		
Q8	0	0	0	0	36	
Q12	0	0	0	0	0	37
Q13	0	0	0	0	0	0
Q14	0	0	0	0	39	0
Q19r	0	0	0	0	0	0
Q20	0	0	0	0	0	0
Q21	0	0	0	0	0	0
Q22	0	0	0	0	0	0
Q23	0	0	0	0	0	0

THETA-DELTA

	Q13	Q14	Q19r	Q20	Q21	Q22
Q13	38					
Q14	0	40				
Q19r	0	0	41			
Q20	0	0	0	42		
Q21	0	0	0	0	43	
Q22	0	0	0	0	0	44
Q23	0	0	0	0	0	0

THETA-DELTA

	Q23
Q23	45

```
!Examp8-6.spl

Number of Iterations = 10

LISREL Estimates (Maximum Likelihood)


        LAMBDA-X

                Success      Org2   CompEnh   Radical
               --------  --------  --------  --------
      Q46          1.00       - -       - -       - -

      Q47          1.34       - -       - -       - -
                 (0.12)
                  10.86

      Q48          1.16       - -       - -       - -
                 (0.11)
                  10.37

      Q40           - -      1.00       - -       - -

      Q42           - -      0.90       - -       - -
                           (0.10)
                             9.43

      Q43           - -      1.07       - -       - -
                           (0.09)
                            11.74

      Q44           - -      0.96       - -       - -
                           (0.09)
                            10.17

      Q45           - -      0.99       - -       - -
                           (0.09)
                            10.58

       Q5           - -       - -      1.00       - -

       Q7           - -       - -      1.13       - -
                                     (0.12)
                                       9.48

       Q8           - -       - -     -0.04       - -
                                     (0.12)
                                      -0.31

      Q12           - -       - -      1.13       - -
                                     (0.12)
                                       9.47
```

```
        Q13        - -        - -      -0.14        - -
                                      (0.12)
                                       -1.16

        Q14        - -        - -      -0.17        - -
                                      (0.12)
                                       -1.46

       Q19r        - -        - -        - -       1.00

        Q20        - -        - -        - -       1.13
                                                  (0.11)
                                                   10.18

        Q21        - -        - -        - -       1.15
                                                  (0.11)
                                                   10.36

        Q22        - -        - -        - -       0.75
                                                  (0.11)
                                                    6.63

        Q23        - -        - -        - -       1.00
                                                  (0.11)
                                                    8.93
         PHI

               Success       Org2    CompEnh    Radical
              --------   --------   --------   --------
    Success       0.53
                (0.11)
                  4.95

       Org2       0.22       0.65
                (0.06)     (0.11)
                  3.71       5.70

    CompEnh       0.20       0.11       0.56
                (0.06)     (0.06)     (0.11)
                  3.47       1.86       4.96

    Radical       0.13       0.30       0.03       0.56
                (0.05)     (0.07)     (0.05)     (0.11)
                  2.49       4.41       0.59       5.10

         THETA-DELTA

                   Q46        Q47        Q48        Q40        Q42        Q43
              --------   --------   --------   --------   --------   --------
        Q46       0.47
                (0.06)
                  7.71
```

```
   Q47        - -     0.05
                     (0.04)
                      1.09

   Q48        - -      - -      0.28
                               (0.05)
                                5.95

   Q40        - -      - -      - -      0.35
                                        (0.05)
                                         6.80

   Q42        - -      - -      - -      - -      0.47
                                                 (0.06)
                                                  7.49

   Q43        - -      - -      - -      - -      - -      0.25
                                                          (0.04)
                                                           5.80

   Q44        - -      - -      - -      - -      - -      - -

   Q45        - -      - -      - -      - -      - -      - -

    Q5        - -      - -      - -      - -      - -      - -

    Q7        - -      - -      - -      - -      - -      - -

    Q8        - -      - -      - -      - -      - -      - -

   Q12        - -      - -      - -      - -      - -      - -

   Q13        - -      - -      - -      - -      - -      - -

   Q14        - -      - -      - -      - -      - -      - -

  Q19r        - -      - -      - -      - -      - -      - -

   Q20        - -      - -      - -      - -      - -      - -

   Q21        - -      - -      - -      - -      - -      - -

   Q22        - -      - -      - -      - -      - -      - -

   Q23        - -      - -      - -      - -      - -      - -


         THETA-DELTA

               Q44      Q45       Q5       Q7       Q8      Q12
          -------- -------- -------- -------- -------- --------
   Q44        0.40
             (0.06)
              7.17

   Q45        - -     0.37
                     (0.05)
                      6.93
```

```
 Q5        - -       - -      0.44
                             (0.07)
                              6.74

 Q7        - -       - -       - -      0.28
                                       (0.06)
                                        4.69

 Q8        - -       - -       - -       - -      1.00
                                                 (0.12)
                                                  8.51

Q12        - -       - -       - -       - -       - -      0.29
                                                           (0.06)
                                                            4.79

Q13        - -       - -       - -       - -       - -       - -

Q14        - -       - -       - -       - -      0.65       - -
                                                 (0.10)
                                                  6.59

Q19r       - -       - -       - -       - -       - -       - -

Q20        - -       - -       - -       - -       - -       - -

Q21        - -       - -       - -       - -       - -       - -

Q22        - -       - -       - -       - -       - -       - -

Q23        - -       - -       - -       - -       - -       - -


    THETA-DELTA

              Q13       Q14      Q19r       Q20       Q21       Q22
          --------  --------  --------  --------  --------  --------
Q13           0.99
            (0.12)
              8.50

Q14            - -      0.98
                      (0.12)
                        8.49

Q19r           - -       - -      0.44
                                (0.06)
                                  7.22

Q20            - -       - -       - -      0.28
                                          (0.05)
                                            5.92
```

```
Q21         - -        - -        - -        - -       0.26
                                                      (0.05)
                                                       5.53

Q22         - -        - -        - -        - -        - -       0.68
                                                                 (0.08)
                                                                  8.05
Q23         - -        - -        - -        - -        - -        - -

   THETA-DELTA

              Q23
         --------
Q23          0.44
           (0.06)
             7.24

   Squared Multiple Correlations for X - Variables

              Q46        Q47        Q48        Q40        Q42        Q43
         --------   --------   --------   --------   --------   --------
             0.53       0.95       0.72       0.65       0.53       0.75

   Squared Multiple Correlations for X - Variables

              Q44        Q45         Q5         Q7         Q8        Q12
         --------   --------   --------   --------   --------   --------
             0.60       0.63       0.56       0.72       0.00       0.71

   Squared Multiple Correlations for X - Variables

              Q13        Q14       Q19r        Q20        Q21        Q22
         --------   --------   --------   --------   --------   --------
             0.01       0.02       0.56       0.72       0.74       0.32

   Squared Multiple Correlations for X - Variables

              Q23
         --------
             0.56

                          Goodness of Fit Statistics

                            Degrees of Freedom = 145
              Minimum Fit Function Chi-Square = 332.35 (P = 0.00)
      Normal Theory Weighted Least Squares Chi-Square = 330.77 (P = 0.00)
               Estimated Non-centrality Parameter (NCP) = 185.77
          90 Percent Confidence Interval for NCP = (136.72 ; 242.54)

                       Minimum Fit Function Value = 2.29
               Population Discrepancy Function Value (F0) = 1.28
             90 Percent Confidence Interval for F0 = (0.94 ; 1.67)
```

```
Root Mean Square Error of Approximation (RMSEA) = 0.094
90 Percent Confidence Interval for RMSEA = (0.081 ; 0.11)
P-Value for Test of Close Fit (RMSEA < 0.05) = 0.00

Expected Cross-Validation Index (ECVI) = 2.90
90 Percent Confidence Interval for ECVI = (2.56 ; 3.29)
ECVI for Saturated Model = 2.62
ECVI for Independence Model = 12.01

Chi-Square for Independence Model with 171 Degrees of Freedom = 1702.81
Independence AIC = 1740.81
Model AIC = 420.77
Saturated AIC = 380.00
Independence CAIC = 1816.49
Model CAIC = 600.03
Saturated CAIC = 1136.89

Root Mean Square Residual (RMR) = 0.17
Standardized RMR = 0.17
Goodness of Fit Index (GFI) = 0.81
Adjusted Goodness of Fit Index (AGFI) = 0.75
Parsimony Goodness of Fit Index (PGFI) = 0.62

Normed Fit Index (NFI) = 0.80
Non-Normed Fit Index (NNFI) = 0.86
Parsimony Normed Fit Index (PNFI) = 0.68
Comparative Fit Index (CFI) = 0.88
Incremental Fit Index (IFI) = 0.88
Relative Fit Index (RFI) = 0.77

Critical N (CN) = 82.82

!Examp8-6.spl

Modification Indices and Expected Change

Modification Indices for LAMBDA-X

        Success      Org2   CompEnh   Radical
       --------  --------  --------  --------
Q46        - -       2.36      0.26      6.54
Q47        - -       0.16      0.40      1.64
Q48        - -       0.40      0.14      0.09
Q40       0.76       - -       0.87      0.08
Q42       0.57       - -       3.71      6.56
Q43       2.02       - -       0.00      0.26
Q44       2.65       - -       0.02      1.94
Q45       0.18       - -       0.22      0.27
Q5        0.76       3.01      - -       0.94
Q7        0.48       0.87      - -       0.47
Q8        0.87       5.43      - -       5.36
Q12       1.04       2.45      - -       0.22
Q13       6.24      22.55      - -      44.94
```

Q14	1.22	5.46	- -	7.33
Q19r	0.73	0.53	2.85	- -
Q20	0.01	1.56	2.90	- -
Q21	6.79	0.59	0.36	- -
Q22	2.45	0.52	5.18	- -
Q23	2.10	0.71	10.40	- -

Expected Change for LAMBDA-X

	Success	Org2	CompEnh	Radical
Q46	- -	0.13	0.05	0.22
Q47	- -	-0.03	-0.05	-0.09
Q48	- -	-0.04	0.03	-0.02
Q40	-0.07	- -	0.08	0.03
Q42	0.07	- -	-0.17	0.26
Q43	-0.11	- -	0.00	-0.04
Q44	0.14	- -	0.01	-0.13
Q45	0.04	- -	0.04	-0.05
Q5	0.08	0.14	- -	0.08
Q7	0.06	0.07	- -	0.06
Q8	0.09	0.19	- -	0.20
Q12	-0.09	-0.12	- -	-0.04
Q13	0.32	0.52	- -	0.78
Q14	0.11	0.19	- -	0.24
Q19r	0.07	0.07	-0.14	- -
Q20	0.01	0.10	-0.13	- -
Q21	-0.20	-0.06	-0.04	- -
Q22	0.16	-0.08	0.23	- -
Q23	0.13	-0.08	0.28	- -

No Non-Zero Modification Indices for PHI

Modification Indices for THETA-DELTA

	Q46	Q47	Q48	Q40	Q42	Q43
Q46	- -					
Q47	0.05	- -				
Q48	0.97	3.24	- -			
Q40	0.14	1.68	1.11	- -		
Q42	0.64	0.04	0.01	0.02	- -	
Q43	0.79	0.47	0.58	2.47	2.32	- -
Q44	0.00	2.28	0.53	1.34	1.17	0.03
Q45	1.10	0.62	0.01	0.43	0.40	0.46
Q5	1.34	0.01	0.49	0.77	1.31	0.30
Q7	0.00	0.01	0.15	0.58	0.15	0.17
Q8	0.19	0.15	0.60	1.69	0.01	0.82
Q12	0.02	0.34	0.22	0.17	0.48	0.24
Q13	7.38	0.24	0.65	0.02	5.51	0.21
Q14	0.73	0.77	0.50	0.36	3.35	0.60
Q19r	0.02	1.95	0.92	1.43	0.19	0.17
Q20	2.17	1.17	0.45	2.24	0.00	0.72

Q21	0.86	0.33	0.15	0.57	0.08	0.27
Q22	0.18	0.56	0.03	0.91	1.23	0.44
Q23	2.78	0.71	0.26	1.70	0.85	0.01

Modification Indices for THETA-DELTA

	Q44	Q45	Q5	Q7	Q8	Q12
Q44	- -					
Q45	0.32	- -				
Q5	0.13	0.07	- -			
Q7	0.32	0.32	1.58	- -		
Q8	0.60	0.69	0.11	0.18	- -	
Q12	0.04	0.36	0.03	1.10	0.60	- -
Q13	1.26	0.04	0.19	0.04	7.22	0.01
Q14	0.02	0.00	0.38	0.27	- -	0.00
Q19r	0.28	2.10	0.02	0.33	0.02	3.81
Q20	0.00	1.58	1.51	0.02	2.41	0.07
Q21	1.30	5.34	0.26	2.95	0.11	2.23
Q22	0.03	0.09	0.68	3.25	0.04	0.24
Q23	0.15	10.86	2.80	0.42	1.17	0.11

Modification Indices for THETA-DELTA

	Q13	Q14	Q19r	Q20	Q21	Q22
Q13	- -					
Q14	13.55	- -				
Q19r	2.45	0.33	- -			
Q20	7.22	1.08	2.97	- -		
Q21	0.20	0.55	0.70	17.27	- -	
Q22	0.04	1.50	1.75	8.00	1.82	- -
Q23	0.31	0.02	2.32	2.20	3.37	18.40

Modification Indices for THETA-DELTA

	Q23
Q23	- -

Expected Change for THETA-DELTA

	Q46	Q47	Q48	Q40	Q42	Q43
Q46	- -					
Q47	-0.02	- -				
Q48	-0.06	0.23	- -			
Q40	-0.01	-0.03	0.03	- -		
Q42	0.03	0.01	0.00	0.01	- -	
Q43	0.03	-0.02	-0.02	0.06	-0.06	- -
Q44	0.00	0.04	-0.02	-0.05	0.05	-0.01
Q45	-0.04	0.02	0.00	-0.03	-0.03	0.03
Q5	0.05	0.00	-0.02	0.03	-0.05	0.02

```
       Q7      0.00      0.00      0.01      0.03      0.02      0.01
       Q8      0.02      0.01     -0.03     -0.05      0.00      0.03
      Q12      0.00     -0.02      0.01     -0.01     -0.03     -0.02
      Q13      0.16     -0.02     -0.04      0.01      0.14      0.02
      Q14      0.04     -0.03      0.02      0.02      0.08     -0.03
     Q19r      0.01      0.04     -0.03     -0.05      0.02     -0.01
      Q20      0.05     -0.03      0.02      0.05      0.00      0.03
      Q21     -0.03     -0.01     -0.01     -0.02      0.01     -0.02
      Q22     -0.02      0.03      0.01     -0.04      0.06     -0.03
      Q23      0.07     -0.02      0.02      0.05      0.04      0.00

   Expected Change for THETA-DELTA

              Q44        Q45        Q5         Q7         Q8        Q12
           --------   --------   --------   --------   --------   --------
      Q44      - -
      Q45      0.02       - -
       Q5      0.01      0.01       - -
       Q7     -0.02     -0.02     -0.13       - -
       Q8      0.03      0.03      0.02      0.02       - -
      Q12     -0.01      0.02      0.02      0.15     -0.03       - -
      Q13     -0.06     -0.01     -0.03      0.01      0.17      0.00
      Q14     -0.01      0.00     -0.03      0.02       - -      0.00
     Q19r      0.02      0.06     -0.01      0.02      0.01     -0.08
      Q20      0.00     -0.04     -0.05      0.00      0.06     -0.01
      Q21     -0.04      0.08      0.02     -0.06      0.01      0.05
      Q22     -0.01     -0.01     -0.04      0.08     -0.01      0.02
      Q23     -0.02     -0.13      0.07      0.03     -0.05      0.01

   Expected Change for THETA-DELTA

              Q13        Q14       Q19r        Q20        Q21        Q22
           --------   --------   --------   --------   --------   --------
      Q13      - -
      Q14      0.23       - -
     Q19r      0.09      0.03       - -
      Q20      0.14      0.04     -0.08       - -
      Q21     -0.02     -0.03     -0.04      0.20       - -
      Q22      0.01      0.06      0.07     -0.13     -0.06       - -
      Q23      0.03      0.01      0.07     -0.07     -0.08      0.22

   Expected Change for THETA-DELTA

              Q23
           --------
      Q23      - -

Maximum Modification Index is   44.94 for Element (13, 4) of LAMBDA-X
         The Problem used    52512 Bytes (=  0.1% of Available Workspace)
                          Time used:     0.340 Seconds
```

Fig. 8.15 Step 1: the measurement model results – LISREL8 output (examp8-6.out).

```
!Examp8-7.spl
!Raw Data From File: Examp8-6.txt
!Path Diagram

DA NI=19 MA = KM XM = 9
RA FI=C:\SAMD\Chapter8\Examples\Examp8-6.txt
MO NY = 8 NX = 11 NE = 2 NK = 2 PH = SY TD = SY

FI LY(1,1) LY( 2,1) LY(3,1)                                                C
   LY(4,2) LY( 5,2) LY(6,2) LY(7,2)  LY(8,2)                               C
   LX(1,1) LX( 2,1) LX(3,1) LX(4,1)  LX(5,1) LX(6,1)                       C
   LX(7,2) LX( 8,2) LX(9,2) LX(10,2) LX(11,2)                              C
   TE(1,1) TE( 2,2) TE(3,3) TE(4 ,4) TE( 5,5) TE(6,6) TE(7,7)              C
   TE(8,8)                                                                 C
   TD(1,1) TD( 2,2) TD(3,3) TD(4 ,4) TD( 5,5) TD(6,6) TD(7,7)              C
   TD(8,8) TD( 9,9) TD(10,10) TD(11,11)                                    C
   PH(1,1) PH( 2,1) PH( 2, 2)

VA  1        LY( 1,1) LX(1,1) LY(4,2)  LX(7,2)
VA  1.34   LY( 2,1)
VA  1.16   LY( 3,1)
VA  0.90   LY( 5,2)
VA  1.07   LY( 6,2)
VA  0.96   LY( 7,2)
VA  0.99   LY( 8,2)
VA  1.13   LX( 2,1)
VA -0.04   LX( 3,1)
VA  1.13   LX( 4,1)
VA -0.14   LX( 5,1)
VA -0.17   LX( 6,1)
VA  1.13   LX( 8,2)
VA  1.15   LX( 9,2)
VA  0.75   LX(10,2)
VA  1.00   LX(11,2)

VA  0.47   TE( 1,1)
VA  0.05   TE( 2,2)
VA  0.28   TE( 3,3)
VA  0.35   TE( 4,4)
VA  0.47   TE( 5,5)
VA  0.25   TE( 6,6)
VA  0.40   TE( 7,7)
VA  0.37   TE( 8,8)

VA  0.44   TD( 1,1)
VA  0.28   TD( 2,2)
VA  1.00   TD( 3,3)
VA  0.29   TD( 4,4)
VA  0.99   TD( 5,5)
VA  0.98   TD( 6,6)
VA  0.44   TD( 7,7)
VA  0.28   TD( 8,8)
```

```
VA  0.26   TD( 9,9)
VA  0.68   TD(10,10)
VA  0.44   TD(11,11)
VA  0.65   TD( 6,3)

VA  0.56   PH( 1,1)
VA  0.03   PH( 2,1)
VA  0.56   PH( 2,2)

LA
Q46 Q47 Q48 Q40 Q42 Q43 Q44 Q45  Q5 Q7 Q8 Q12 Q13 Q14 Q19r Q20 Q21 Q22 Q23
LE
Success Org2
LK
CompEnh Radical

Path Diagram
OU SE TV AD = 50 MI
```

Fig. 8.16 Step 2: LISREL8 input of full structural model (examp8-7.spl).

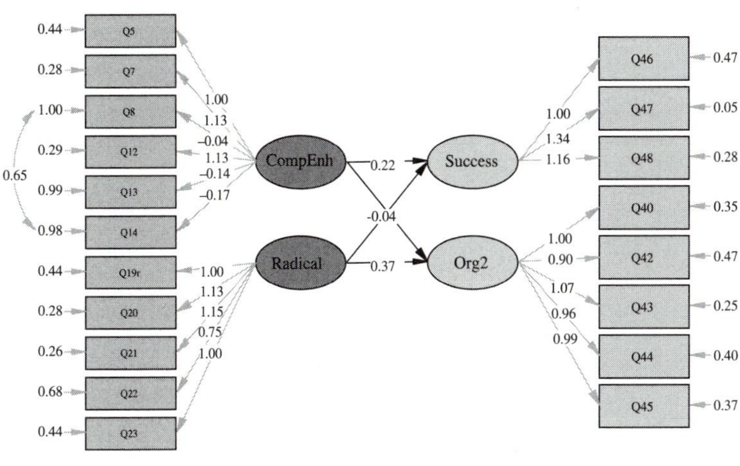

Fig. 8.17 Step 2: graphical representation of full structural model (examp8-7.pth).

The estimation of the model presented in that Figure leads to maximum likelihood structural parameter estimates which take into consideration the fact that the constructs are measured with error. These parameter estimates are shown graphically in Figure 8.17 and the full LISREL8 output is listed in Figure 8.18. These examples are given for illustrative purposes; the model shown here could be improved, as its fit to the data is not as high as would be desirable.

```
                              DATE:  1/ 8/2001
                                TIME:  9:51


                              L I S R E L  8.30

                                     BY

                       Karl G. Jöreskog & Dag Sörbom



                 This program is published exclusively by
                 Scientific Software International, Inc.
                    7383 N. Lincoln Avenue, Suite 100
                     Chicago, IL 60646-1704, U.S.A.
          Phone: (800)247-6113, (847)675-0720, Fax: (847)675-2140
      Copyright by Scientific Software International, Inc., 1981-99
        Use of this program is subject to the terms specified in the
                     Universal Copyright Convention.
                       Website: www.ssicentral.com


The following lines were read from file C:\SAMD\CHAPTER8\EXAMPLES\EXAMP8-7.SPL:

!Examp8-7.spl
!Raw Data From File: Examp8-6.txt
!Path Diagram

DA NI=19 MA = KM XM = 9
RA FI=C:\SAMD\Chapter8\Examples\Examp8-6.txt
MO NY = 8 NX = 11 NE = 2 NK = 2 PH = SY TD = SY

FI LY(1,1) LY( 2,1) LY(3,1)                  C
LY(4,2) LY( 5,2) LY(6,2) LY(7,2)  LY(8,2)      C
LX(1,1) LX( 2,1) LX(3,1) LX(4,1)  LX(5,1) LX(6,1)        C
LX(7,2) LX( 8,2) LX(9,2) LX(10,2) LX(11,2)          C
TE(1,1) TE( 2,2) TE(3,3) TE(4 ,4) TE( 5,5) TE(6,6) TE(7,7)  C
TE(8,8)         C
TD(1,1) TD( 2,2) TD(3,3) TD(4 ,4) TD( 5,5) TD(6,6) TD(7,7)  C
TD(8,8) TD( 9,9) TD(10,10) TD(11,11)     C
PH(1,1) PH( 2,1) PH( 2, 2)

VA  1     LY( 1,1) LX(1,1) LY(4,2)  LX(7,2)
VA  1.34   LY( 2,1)
VA  1.16   LY( 3,1)
VA  0.90   LY( 5,2)
VA  1.07   LY( 6,2)
VA  0.96   LY( 7,2)
VA  0.99   LY( 8,2)
VA  1.13   LX( 2,1)
VA -0.04   LX( 3,1)
```

```
VA  1.13   LX( 4,1)
VA -0.14   LX( 5,1)
VA -0.17   LX( 6,1)
VA  1.13   LX( 8,2)
VA  1.15   LX( 9,2)
VA  0.75   LX(10,2)
VA  1.00   LX(11,2)

VA  0.47   TE( 1,1)
VA  0.05   TE( 2,2)
VA  0.28   TE( 3,3)
VA  0.35   TE( 4,4)
VA  0.47   TE( 5,5)
VA  0.25   TE( 6,6)
VA  0.40   TE( 7,7)
VA  0.37   TE( 8,8)

VA  0.44   TD( 1,1)
VA  0.28   TD( 2,2)
VA  1.00   TD( 3,3)
VA  0.29   TD( 4,4)
VA  0.99   TD( 5,5)
VA  0.98   TD( 6,6)
VA  0.44   TD( 7,7)
VA  0.28   TD( 8,8)
VA  0.26   TD( 9,9)
VA  0.68   TD(10,10)
VA  0.44   TD(11,11)
VA  0.65   TD( 6,3)

VA  0.56   PH( 1,1)
VA  0.03   PH( 2,1)
VA  0.56   PH( 2,2)

LA
Q46 Q47 Q48 Q40 Q42 Q43 Q44 Q45  Q5 Q7 Q8 Q12 Q13 Q14 Q19r Q20 Q21 Q22 Q23
LE
Success Org2
LK
CompEnh Radical

Path Diagram
OU SE TV AD = 50 MI

!Examp8-7.spl

                          Number of Input Variables 19
                          Number of Y - Variables    8
                          Number of X - Variables   11
                          Number of ETA - Variables  2
                          Number of KSI - Variables  2
                          Number of Observations    96
```

```
!Examp8-7.spl

        Covariance Matrix to be Analyzed

                 Q46        Q47        Q48        Q40        Q42        Q43
              --------   --------   --------   --------   --------   --------
      Q46       1.00
      Q47       0.75       1.00
      Q48       0.73       0.84       1.00
      Q40       0.04       0.09       0.16       1.00
      Q42       0.20       0.25       0.31       0.41       1.00
      Q43       0.09       0.11       0.16       0.57       0.54       1.00
      Q44       0.17       0.21       0.21       0.52       0.59       0.73
      Q45       0.00       0.18       0.28       0.49       0.55       0.57
       Q5       0.21       0.13       0.13       0.11      -0.13       0.03
       Q7       0.26       0.20       0.25       0.10      -0.07       0.00
       Q8      -0.11      -0.04       0.05       0.21       0.19       0.26
      Q12       0.23       0.20       0.24       0.05      -0.09      -0.03
      Q13       0.06       0.06       0.04       0.07       0.12       0.14
      Q14       0.01      -0.02       0.05       0.11       0.25       0.15
     Q19r       0.19       0.17       0.12       0.05       0.26       0.14
      Q20       0.13       0.08       0.08       0.20       0.15       0.21
      Q21       0.08       0.07       0.04       0.17       0.22       0.24
      Q22       0.28       0.34       0.31       0.07       0.24       0.14
      Q23       0.33       0.17       0.13       0.12       0.14       0.16

        Covariance Matrix to be Analyzed

                 Q44        Q45         Q5         Q7         Q8        Q12
              --------   --------   --------   --------   --------   --------
      Q44       1.00
      Q45       0.59       1.00
       Q5       0.04       0.00       1.00
       Q7      -0.04      -0.03       0.55       1.00
       Q8       0.19       0.22      -0.37      -0.31       1.00
      Q12      -0.09      -0.02       0.69       0.77      -0.41       1.00
      Q13       0.12       0.13      -0.25      -0.30       0.38      -0.32
      Q14       0.29       0.20      -0.37      -0.32       0.45      -0.37
     Q19r       0.19       0.27      -0.03      -0.06      -0.01      -0.19
      Q20       0.19       0.17       0.00      -0.01       0.23      -0.05
      Q21       0.18       0.30       0.17       0.14       0.02       0.13
      Q22       0.23       0.10       0.09       0.19      -0.01       0.08
      Q23       0.21       0.00       0.22       0.16      -0.08       0.08

        Covariance Matrix to be Analyzed

                 Q13        Q14       Q19r        Q20        Q21        Q22
              --------   --------   --------   --------   --------   --------
      Q13       1.00
      Q14       0.38       1.00
     Q19r       0.23       0.10       1.00
      Q20       0.15       0.16       0.35       1.00
```

```
    Q21      -0.03      -0.03       0.42       0.61       1.00
    Q22       0.06       0.09       0.39       0.24       0.39       1.00
    Q23       0.12      -0.05       0.48       0.49       0.56       0.47

       Covariance Matrix to be Analyzed

               Q23
          --------
    Q23       1.00


!Examp8-7.spl

Parameter Specifications

        GAMMA

            CompEnh    Radical
          --------   --------
 Success          1          2
    Org2          3          4

        PSI
        Note: This matrix is diagonal.

            Success       Org2
          --------   --------
                 5          6



!Examp8-7.spl

Number of Iterations = 12

LISREL Estimates (Maximum Likelihood)


        LAMBDA-Y

            Success       Org2
          --------   --------
    Q46       1.00        - -

    Q47       1.34        - -

    Q48       1.16        - -

    Q40        - -       1.00

    Q42        - -       0.90

    Q43        - -       1.07
```

```
     Q44          - -        0.96

     Q45          - -        0.99


        LAMBDA-X

               CompEnh    Radical
              --------   --------
      Q5        1.00        - -

      Q7        1.13        - -

      Q8       -0.04        - -

     Q12        1.13        - -

     Q13       -0.14        - -

     Q14       -0.17        - -

    Q19r        - -        1.00

     Q20        - -        1.13

     Q21        - -        1.15

     Q22        - -        0.75

     Q23        - -        1.00


        GAMMA

               CompEnh    Radical
              --------   --------
 Success        0.22       0.18
               (0.11)     (0.10)
                2.06       1.73

    Org2       -0.04       0.37
               (0.11)     (0.11)
               -0.36       3.31


        Covariance Matrix of ETA and KSI

               Success       Org2    CompEnh    Radical
              --------   --------   --------   --------
 Success        0.54
    Org2        0.04       0.60
```

```
CompEnh       0.13      -0.01       0.56
Radical       0.11       0.21       0.03       0.56

       PHI

           CompEnh    Radical
          --------   --------
CompEnh       0.56

Radical       0.03       0.56

       PSI
       Note: This matrix is diagonal.

           Success       Org2
          --------   --------
              0.49       0.52
            (0.08)     (0.09)
              6.50       5.98


       Squared Multiple Correlations for Structural Equations

           Success       Org2
          --------   --------
              0.09       0.13

       THETA-EPS

               Q46        Q47        Q48        Q40        Q42        Q43
          --------   --------   --------   --------   --------   --------
              0.47       0.05       0.28       0.35       0.47       0.25


       THETA-EPS

               Q44        Q45
          --------   --------
              0.40       0.37


       Squared Multiple Correlations for Y - Variables

               Q46        Q47        Q48        Q40        Q42        Q43
          --------   --------   --------   --------   --------   --------
              0.53       0.95       0.72       0.63       0.51       0.73

       Squared Multiple Correlations for Y - Variables

               Q44        Q45
          --------   --------
              0.58       0.61
```

THETA-DELTA

	Q5	Q7	Q8	Q12	Q13	Q14
Q5	0.44					
Q7	- -	0.28				
Q8	- -	- -	1.00			
Q12	- -	- -	- -	0.29		
Q13	- -	- -	- -	- -	0.99	
Q14	- -	- -	0.65	- -	- -	0.98
Q19r	- -	- -	- -	- -	- -	- -
Q20	- -	- -	- -	- -	- -	- -
Q21	- -	- -	- -	- -	- -	- -
Q22	- -	- -	- -	- -	- -	- -
Q23	- -	- -	- -	- -	- -	- -

THETA-DELTA

	Q19r	Q20	Q21	Q22	Q23
Q19r	0.44				
Q20	- -	0.28			
Q21	- -	- -	0.26		
Q22	- -	- -	- -	0.68	
Q23	- -	- -	- -	- -	0.44

Squared Multiple Correlations for X - Variables

Q5	Q7	Q8	Q12	Q13	Q14
0.56	0.72	0.00	0.71	0.01	0.02

Squared Multiple Correlations for X - Variables

Q19r	Q20	Q21	Q22	Q23
0.56	0.72	0.74	0.32	0.56

```
                      Goodness of Fit Statistics

                        Degrees of Freedom = 184
          Minimum Fit Function Chi-Square = 324.49 (P = 0.00)
  Normal Theory Weighted Least Squares Chi-Square = 375.12 (P = 0.00)
           Estimated Non-centrality Parameter (NCP) = 191.12
       90 Percent Confidence Interval for NCP = (139.61 ; 250.40)

                   Minimum Fit Function Value = 3.42
           Population Discrepancy Function Value (F0) = 2.01
         90 Percent Confidence Interval for F0 = (1.47 ; 2.64)
         Root Mean Square Error of Approximation (RMSEA) = 0.10
       90 Percent Confidence Interval for RMSEA = (0.089 ; 0.12)
         P-Value for Test of Close Fit (RMSEA < 0.05) = 0.00

             Expected Cross-Validation Index (ECVI) = 4.07
        90 Percent Confidence Interval for ECVI = (3.53 ; 4.70)
                    ECVI for Saturated Model = 4.00
                  ECVI for Independence Model = 10.79

   Chi-Square for Independence Model with 171 Degrees of Freedom = 987.42
                       Independence AIC = 1025.42
                           Model AIC = 387.12
                         Saturated AIC = 380.00
                       Independence CAIC = 1093.14
                           Model CAIC = 408.50
                         Saturated CAIC = 1057.23

                 Root Mean Square Residual (RMR) = 0.13
                         Standardized RMR = 0.13
                     Goodness of Fit Index (GFI) = 0.75
              Adjusted Goodness of Fit Index (AGFI) = 0.74
             Parsimony Goodness of Fit Index (PGFI) = 0.72

                      Normed Fit Index (NFI) = 0.67
                    Non-Normed Fit Index (NNFI) = 0.84
                 Parsimony Normed Fit Index (PNFI) = 0.72
                    Comparative Fit Index (CFI) = 0.83
                    Incremental Fit Index (IFI) = 0.83
                     Relative Fit Index (RFI) = 0.69

                         Critical N (CN) = 68.79

!Examp8-7.spl

Modification Indices and Expected Change
        Modification Indices for LAMBDA-Y

            Success       Org2
           --------   --------
     Q46       0.46       0.17
     Q47       0.36       0.15
```

```
Q48         0.05        3.16
Q40         0.72        1.28
Q42         3.70        0.01
Q43         1.03        0.23
Q44         1.31        1.27
Q45         0.58        0.14

   Expected Change for LAMBDA-Y

          Success        Org2
         --------    --------
Q46         0.07       -0.04
Q47        -0.05       -0.03
Q48         0.02        0.14
Q40        -0.08       -0.10
Q42         0.20       -0.01
Q43        -0.09        0.04
Q44         0.11        0.11
Q45         0.07       -0.04

   Modification Indices for LAMBDA-X

          CompEnh     Radical
         --------    --------
  Q5        0.18        0.77
  Q7        0.06        0.34
  Q8        6.10        0.16
 Q12        0.20        0.86
 Q13        5.29        1.50
 Q14        0.20        0.10
Q19r        7.40        1.82
 Q20        3.70        0.24
 Q21        4.57        0.17
 Q22        1.64        0.07
 Q23        2.92        0.07

   Expected Change for LAMBDA-X

          CompEnh     Radical
         --------    --------
  Q5       -0.05        0.09
  Q7       -0.02        0.06
  Q8       -0.27        0.04
 Q12        0.04       -0.09
 Q13       -0.34        0.18
 Q14       -0.05        0.03
Q19r       -0.29       -0.14
 Q20       -0.18       -0.04
 Q21        0.19        0.04
 Q22        0.16       -0.03
 Q23        0.18        0.03

No Non-Zero Modification Indices for GAMMA
```

Modification Indices for PHI

	CompEnh	Radical
CompEnh	0.03	
Radical	0.07	1.14

Expected Change for PHI

	CompEnh	Radical
CompEnh	0.02	
Radical	0.02	-0.10

Modification Indices for PSI

	Success	Org2
Success	- -	
Org2	2.67	- -

Expected Change for PSI

	Success	Org2
Success	- -	
Org2	0.09	- -

Modification Indices for THETA-EPS

	Q46	Q47	Q48	Q40	Q42	Q43
Q46	1.20					
Q47	0.16	0.09				
Q48	2.98	0.07	0.29			
Q40	0.05	0.55	0.12	12.82		
Q42	0.46	0.00	1.11	3.94	1.04	
Q43	0.85	0.50	0.18	1.48	1.43	2.58
Q44	0.67	0.99	0.98	2.66	0.98	5.32
Q45	8.88	0.21	4.00	1.21	1.09	4.51

Modification Indices for THETA-EPS

	Q44	Q45
Q44	0.62	
Q45	0.00	3.34

Expected Change for THETA-EPS

	Q46	Q47	Q48	Q40	Q42	Q43
Q46	-0.08					
Q47	-0.01	0.01				
Q48	0.07	-0.01	-0.02			
Q40	-0.01	-0.02	0.01	0.22		
Q42	0.04	0.00	0.04	-0.10	0.08	
Q43	0.04	-0.02	-0.01	-0.05	-0.05	0.08
Q44	0.04	0.03	-0.04	-0.07	0.05	0.09
Q45	-0.14	0.02	0.08	-0.05	0.05	-0.08

Expected Change for THETA-EPS

	Q44	Q45
Q44	-0.05	
Q45	0.00	0.12

Modification Indices for THETA-DELTA-EPS

	Q46	Q47	Q48	Q40	Q42	Q43
Q5	0.58	0.01	0.79	0.33	4.75	0.17
Q7	0.55	0.92	0.92	1.17	0.08	0.02
Q8	3.69	0.01	1.32	1.35	1.25	5.03
Q12	0.06	0.03	0.43	0.02	0.06	0.01
Q13	0.12	0.26	0.01	0.25	0.01	0.31
Q14	2.46	0.53	0.06	2.15	3.19	4.43
Q19r	0.07	1.10	0.31	5.93	3.86	2.20
Q20	0.00	0.70	0.28	4.10	2.55	0.28
Q21	2.26	0.01	0.45	0.27	0.14	0.02
Q22	0.05	1.12	0.54	1.02	2.52	0.09
Q23	10.55	1.01	0.41	0.54	0.00	0.50

Modification Indices for THETA-DELTA-EPS

	Q44	Q45
Q5	1.64	0.06
Q7	0.12	0.72
Q8	3.41	0.00
Q12	1.07	0.65
Q13	0.03	0.19
Q14	7.70	0.23
Q19r	0.08	6.86
Q20	0.26	1.21

Q21	3.48	8.04
Q22	2.52	1.24
Q23	2.76	16.59

Expected Change for THETA-DELTA-EPS

	Q46	Q47	Q48	Q40	Q42	Q43
Q5	0.04	0.00	-0.04	0.03	-0.12	0.02
Q7	0.04	-0.03	0.04	0.05	0.01	-0.01
Q8	-0.10	0.00	0.05	0.06	-0.06	0.10
Q12	-0.01	-0.01	0.02	-0.01	0.01	0.00
Q13	0.03	0.03	-0.01	-0.03	0.01	0.03
Q14	0.08	-0.03	0.01	-0.07	0.10	-0.10
Q19r	0.01	0.04	-0.02	-0.12	0.10	-0.06
Q20	0.00	-0.03	0.02	0.08	-0.07	0.02
Q21	-0.07	0.00	-0.02	-0.02	-0.02	0.00
Q22	-0.01	0.05	0.04	-0.06	0.10	-0.02
Q23	0.17	-0.04	-0.03	0.04	0.00	0.03

Expected Change for THETA-DELTA-EPS

	Q44	Q45
Q5	0.07	-0.01
Q7	-0.02	-0.04
Q8	-0.10	0.00
Q12	-0.05	0.04
Q13	0.01	0.03
Q14	0.15	0.02
Q19r	0.01	0.13
Q20	-0.02	-0.05
Q21	-0.08	0.12
Q22	0.09	-0.06
Q23	0.08	-0.20

Modification Indices for THETA-DELTA

	Q5	Q7	Q8	Q12	Q13	Q14
Q5	0.20					
Q7	6.16	0.03				
Q8	0.43	0.03	12.62			
Q12	2.93	1.86	3.30	3.81		
Q13	0.02	0.46	2.99	0.90	0.11	
Q14	0.36	0.01	20.67	0.28	1.38	10.70
Q19r	0.03	0.13	3.70	5.56	4.21	2.83
Q20	1.00	0.27	9.50	0.04	1.08	0.29
Q21	0.25	0.37	0.08	3.18	7.15	2.06
Q22	0.64	2.64	2.28	0.15	0.01	2.62
Q23	3.22	0.34	2.28	0.80	0.64	0.00

Modification Indices for THETA-DELTA

	Q19r	Q20	Q21	Q22	Q23
Q19r	12.84				
Q20	14.36	21.95			
Q21	7.22	0.20	6.99		
Q22	2.87	13.48	0.25	0.58	
Q23	1.44	3.37	0.55	4.76	0.89

Expected Change for THETA-DELTA

	Q5	Q7	Q8	Q12	Q13	Q14
Q5	0.03					
Q7	-0.12	0.01				
Q8	-0.04	0.01	0.29			
Q12	0.08	0.05	-0.09	-0.12		
Q13	-0.01	-0.05	0.13	-0.06	-0.05	
Q14	-0.03	0.00	-0.22	0.03	0.09	0.27
Q19r	0.01	0.02	-0.11	-0.11	0.15	0.09
Q20	-0.05	-0.02	0.15	0.01	0.07	-0.03
Q21	0.02	-0.02	0.01	0.07	-0.17	-0.07
Q22	-0.05	0.09	-0.10	-0.02	0.01	0.10
Q23	0.10	0.03	-0.08	-0.04	0.06	0.00

Expected Change for THETA-DELTA

	Q19r	Q20	Q21	Q22	Q23
Q19r	0.26				
Q20	-0.17	0.26			
Q21	-0.12	-0.02	0.14		
Q22	0.10	-0.19	-0.03	0.08	
Q23	0.06	-0.08	-0.03	0.13	0.07

```
Maximum Modification Index is   21.95 for Element ( 8, 8) of THETA-DELTA

          The Problem used    34008 Bytes (=  0.1% of Available Workspace)

                          Time used:    0.320 Seconds
```

Fig. 8.18 Step 2: LISREL8 output of full structural model (examp8-7.out).

8.4 Assignment

Using the SURVEY data, develop a model that specifies structural relationships between unobservable constructs measured with multiple items. Develop a model with multiple equations and verify the identification of the structural model. Estimate first the measurement model corresponding to a confirmatory factor analysis (including convergent and discriminant validity) and then estimate the structural model parameters.

References

Basic Technical Readings

Anderson, J. C. and D. W. Gerbing (1988), "Structural Equation Modeling in Practice: A Review and Recommended Two-Step Approach," *Psychological Bulletin*, 103, 3, 411–423.

Bagozzi, R. P. and Y. Yi (1988), "On the Evaluation of Structural Equation Models," *Journal of the Academy of Marketing Science*, 16 (Spring), 74–94.

Bagozzi, R. P., Y. Yi and L. W. Phillips (1991), "Assessing Construct Validity in Organizational Research," *Administrative Science Quarterly*, 36, 421–458.

Baumgartner, H. and C. Homburg (1996), "Applications of Structural Equation Modeling in Marketing and Consumer Research: A Review," *International Journal of Research in Marketing*, 13 (April), 139–161.

Bearden, W. O., S. Sharma and J. E. Teel (1982), "Sample Size Effects on Chi Square and Other Statistics Used in Evaluating Causal Models," *Journal of Marketing Research*, 19 (November), 425–430.

Bentler, P. M. (1980), "Multivariate Analysis with Latent Variables: Causal Modeling," *Annual Review of Psychology*, 31, 419–456.

Bentler, P. M. and D. G. Bonett (1980), "Significance Tests and Goodness of Fit in the Analysis of Covariance Structures," *Psychological Bulletin*, 88, 3, 588–606.

Gerbin, D. W. and J. C. Anderson (1987), "Improper Solutions in the Analysis of Covariance Structures: Their Interpretability and a Comparison of Alternate Respecifications," *Psychometrika*, 52, 1, 99–111.

Gerbing, D. W. and J. C. Anderson (1988), "An Updated Paradigm for Scale Development Incorporating Unidimensionality and its Assessment," *Journal of Marketing Research*, 25, 2, 186–192.

Joreskog, K. G. (1973), "A General Method for Estimating a Linear Structural Equation System," in Goldberger and Duncan, eds., *Structural Equation Models in the Social Sciences*, NY: Seminar Press, pp. 85, 85–112.

Application Readings

Ahearne, M., T. W. Gruen, C. B. Jarvis (1999), "If Looks Could Sell: Moderation and Mediation of the Attractiveness Effect on Salesperson Performance," *International Journal of research in Marketing*, 16, 4, 269–284.

Anderson, J. C. (1987), "An Approach for Confirmatory Measurement and Structural Equation Modeling of Organizational Properties," *Management Science*, 33, 4 (April), 525–541.

Anderson, J. C. and J. A. Narus (1990), "A Model of Distributor Firm and Manufacturer Firm Working Partnerships," *Journal of Marketing*, 54 (January), 42–58.

Capron, L. (1999), "The Long-Term Performance of Horizontal Acquisitions," *Strategic Management Journal*, Forthcoming.

Cudeck, R. (1989), "Analysis of Correlation Matrices Using Covariance Structure Models," *Psychological Bulletin*, 105, 2, 317–327.

Gilbert, F. W. and W. E. Warren (1995), "Psychographic Constructs and Demographic Segments", *Psychology and Marketing*, 12, 3 (May), 223–237.

Kuester, S., C. Homburg and T. S. Robertson (1999), "Retaliatory Behavior to New Product Entry," *Journal of Marketing*, 63, 4 (October), 90–106.

MacKenzie, S. B., R. J. Lutz and G. E. Belch (1986), "The Role of Attitude Toward the Ad as a Mediator of Advertising Effectiveness: A Test of Competing Explanations," *Journal of Marketing Research*, 23, 2 (May), 130–143.

Murtha, T. P., S. A. Lenway and R. P. Bagozzi. (1998), "Global Mind-sets and Cognitive Shift in a Complex Multinational Corporation," *Strategic Management Journal*, 19, 97–114.

Philips, L. W. (1981), "Assessing Measurement Error in Key Informant Reports: A Methodological Note on Organizational Analysis in Marketing," *Journal of Marketing Research*, 18, 4 (November), 395–415.

Philips, L. W., D. R. Chang and R. D. Buzzell (1983), "Product Quality, Cost Position and Business Performance," *Journal of Marketing*, 47, 2, 26–43.

Reddy, S. K. and P. A. LaBarbera (1985), "Hierarchical models of Attitude," *Multivariate Behavioral Research*, 20, 451–471.

Stimpert, J. L. and I. M. Duhaime (1997), "In the Eyes of the Beholder: Conceptualizations of the Relatedness Held by the Managers of Large Diversified Firms," *Strategic Management Journal* 18, 2, 111–125.

Titman, S. and R. Wessels (1988), "The Determinants of Capital Structure Choice," *The Journal of Finance*, XLIII, 1 (March), 1–19.

Trieschmann, J. S., A. R. Dennis, G. B. Northcraft and A. W. Niemi, Jr. (2000), "Serving Multiple Constituencies in Business Schools: M.B.A. Program Versus Research Performance," *Academy of Management Journal*, 43, 6, 1130–1141.

Vanden, A. P. (1989), "Comment on 'An Investigation of the Structure of Expectancy-Value Attitude and its Implications'," *International Journal of Research in Marketing*, 6, 85–87.

Venkatraman, N. and V. Ramanujam (1987), "Planning System Success: A Conceptualization and an Operational Model," *Management Science* 33, 6 (June), 687–705.

Walters, R. G. and S. B. MacKenzie (1988), "A Structural Equations Analysis of the Impact of Price Promotions on Store Performance," *Journal of Marketing Research*, 25 (February), 51–63.

Yi, Y. (1989), "An Investigation of the Structure of Expectancy-Value Attitude and its Implications," *International Journal of Research in Marketing*, 6, 71–83.

Yi, Y. (1989), "Rejoinder to 'An Investigation of the Structure of Expectancy-Value Attitude and its Implications'," *International Journal of Research in Marketing*, 6, 89–94.

9. *Analysis of Similarity and Preference Data*

Similarity data in management research are typically collected in order to understand the underlying dimensions determining perceptions of stimuli such as brands or companies. One advantage of such data is that it is cognitively easier for respondents to provide subjective assessments of the similarity between objects than to rate these objects on a number of attributes. Furthermore, when asking respondents to rate objects on attributes, the selection of the attributes proposed may influence the results while, in fact, it is not clear that these attributes are the relevant ones. In Multidimensional Scaling, the methodology allows one to infer the structure of perceptions by enabling the researcher to make inferences regarding the number of dimensions necessary to fit the similarity data. In this chapter, we first describe the type of data collected to perform multidimensional scaling and we then present metric and non-metric methods of multidimensional scaling. Multidimensional Scaling explains the similarity of objects. We then turn to the analysis of preference data, where the objective is to model and explain preferences for objects. These explanations are based on the underlying dimensions of preferences that are discovered through the methodology.

9.1 Proximity Matrices

The input data for multidimensional scaling correspond to proximity or distance measures. Several possibilities exist, especially metric versus non-metric and conditional versus unconditional.

9.1.1 Metric versus Non-metric Data

The data which serve as input to similarity analysis can be metric or non-metric. Metric measures of proximity are ratio scales where zero indicates perfect similarity of two objects. The scale measures the extent to which the objects differ from each other. This measure of *dis*similarity between objects is used as input to the method which will consist in finding the underlying dimensions that discriminate between the objects to reproduce the dissimilarities (or similarities) between objects. In effect, these measures are distance measures (dissimilarity) or proximity measures (similarity), and the objective is to produce the map underlying the distances between the objects.

Non-metric data reflects also these proximity measures; however, only information about the rank order of the distances is available. As discussed in Chapter 7, special care must be taken with such data because most standard statistics such as means, standard deviations and correlations are inappropriate.

9.1.2 Unconditional versus Conditional Data

With unconditional data, all entries in the rows and columns are comparable, i.e., each stimulus is ranked relative to *all* other stimuli in the matrix (a number from 1 to $n(n-1)/2$ for non-metric data).

If only the entries within a particular row are comparable, i.e., each of the n column stimuli is ranked relative to one row stimulus (a number from 1 to n for non-metric data), the data are said to be conditional. In this case, the data matrix consists of $n-1$ objects ranked in terms of similarity relative to the row stimulus. Even though it is less cognitively complex for respondents to provide conditional data, unconditional data are frequent.

9.1.3 Derived Measures of Proximity

It should be noted that it may be possible to derive distance measures from data of the evaluation of stimuli on attributes. However, it is not clear what attributes should be used and why some other relevant ones may be missing. Furthermore, if the objective is to assess the underlying dimensions behind these attributes, multidimensional scaling will use the computed proximities as input and will ignore some of the information contained in the original attribute level information. Consequently, the use of such a procedure will lose information relative to, for example, principal component analysis. It therefore appears more effective to reserve multidimensional scaling for direct measures of similarity rather than similarity measures derived from attribute level data.

9.1.4 Alternative Proximity Matrices

Apart from these two broad categories of proximity data, the matrix can take several specific forms.

9.1.4.1 Symmetric (half) matrix – missing diag. (=0)

When dealing with distance measures, it is clear that the distance between objects A and B is the same as the distance between objects B and A. Therefore, when concerned with pure distance or proximity data, the full data are contained in half of the matrix, where the rows and the columns denote the objects and the cells represent the distance between these two objects. This matrix is symmetric. Furthermore, the diagonal represents the distance between an object and itself, and, consequently, the elements of the diagonal are zeros (often they are not even included in the input).

9.1.4.2 Nonsymmetric matrix – missing diag. (=0)

In some cases, the matrix may not be symmetric. This is the case for confusion data, which consists of having each cell represent the frequency with which object i is matched with object j (for example with morse codes, the percentage of times that a code of a particular letter is understood to be some other letter) or one minus that percentage. The greater the confusion, the greater the similarity between the two objects.

9.1.4.3 Nonsymmetric matrix – diag. present ($\neq$0)

In the case of confusion data, the diagonal may not be zeros because a particular stimulus (e.g., a letter) may not be recognized all the time.

9.2 Problem Definition

In defining the problem, we consider non-metric dissimilarity measures among n stimuli. This is the basic problem such as defined for the KYST algorithm.

Let the table or matrix of dissimilarity (input data) be represented by

$$\underset{n\times n}{\boldsymbol{\Delta}} = \{\delta(j,k)\} \tag{9.1}$$

where $\boldsymbol{\Delta}$ is symmetric and the diagonal cells are zero ($\delta(j,j)=0$, for all j's).

Although we do not know the dimensions of perceptions underlying these distance measures, let us assume there are r such dimensions and that the stimuli are rated on these dimensions. Let $\underset{r\times 1}{\boldsymbol{x}_j}$ be the vector of coordinates of object j in the r-dimensional space. If, indeed, we knew these values $\underset{r\times 1}{\boldsymbol{x}_j}$ and r, then we would be able to compute the Euclidean distance between each pair of objects j and k:

$$\underset{1\times 1}{\boldsymbol{d}^2}(j,k) = (x_j - x_k)'(x_j - x_k) = \sum_{\ell=1}^{r}(x_{j\ell} - x_{k\ell})^2 \tag{9.2}$$

The problem is then defined as finding x_j's such that the $\boldsymbol{d}^2(j,k)$'s for all pairs are closest to the actual dissimilarities $\delta(j,k)$'s.

9.2.1 Objective Function

Because the input data about the dissimilarities are not metric, the basic concept used here is to transform the rank-ordered dissimilarities through a monotonic function:

$$f(\delta_{ij}) = d_{ij} \tag{9.3}$$

To reproduce the original dissimilarity data, the calculated Euclidean distance should lead to a rank order of these similarities as close as possible to the original or, equivalently, there should be a monotonic transformation of the rank-ordered dissimilarities that are as similar as possible to the computed distances. The differences between the monotonic transformation of the rank-ordered dissimilarities and the calculated dissimilarities are the error in the fit for each pair i, j:

$$f(\delta_{ij}) - d_{ij} \tag{9.4}$$

which, for all the pairs, gives the function to minimize:

$$\sum_i \sum_j [f(\delta_{ij}) - d_{ij}]^2 \tag{9.5}$$

This quantity above is divided by a scaling factor, usually $\left(\sum_i \sum_j d_{ij}^2\right)$, in order to interpret the objective function relative to the distance values:

$$\frac{\sum_i \sum_j [f(\delta_{ij}) - d_{ij}]^2}{\text{scale factor}} \tag{9.6}$$

9.2.2 Stress as an Index of Fit

Equation (9.6) provides the basis of the measure or index of fit of the model at the optimal level. This measure is called the stress and is obtained as

$$\text{Stress} = \sqrt{\frac{\sum_{M=1}^{MM} [DIST(M) - DHAT(M)]^2}{\sum_{M=1}^{MM} [DIST(M) - DBAR]^2}} \tag{9.7}$$

Where M = index for each object pair from 1 to MM $(= n^2)$, $DIST(M)$ = computed distances from the solution of $\mathbf{x}_j$'s, $DHAT$ = predicted distances obtained from the monotonic regression of $DIST$ on the rank-ordered dissimilarity data, $DBAR$ = arithmetic average of the values of variable $DIST$.

The denominator enables the comparison across solutions with a different number of dimensions r.

Equation (9.7) can be rewritten as

$$\text{Stress} = \sqrt{\frac{\sum_{M=1}^{MM}[d_M - \hat{d}_M]^2}{\sum_{M=1}^{MM}[d_M - \bar{d}]^2}} \tag{9.8}$$

where

$$d_M = DIST(M)$$

$$\hat{\mathbf{d}}_M = \hat{\boldsymbol{\beta}}_0 + \hat{\boldsymbol{\beta}}_1 \delta_M \tag{9.9}$$

$$\bar{\mathbf{d}} = \frac{1}{MM} \sum_{M}^{MM} d_M \tag{9.10}$$

It is clear from Equations (9.7) or (9.8) that a stress of 0 indicates a perfect fit.

9.2.3 Metric

The discussion above used Euclidean distance measures

$$d_{ij} = \left[\sum_{k=1}^{r} (x_{ik} - x_{jk})^2 \right]^{1/2} \tag{9.11}$$

This is the most commonly used metric. However, it is possible also to use the Minkowski p-metric:

$$d_{ij}(p) = \left[\sum_{k=1}^{r} |x_{ik} - x_{jk}|^p \right]^{1/p} \qquad p \geq 1 \tag{9.12}$$

The easiest case to interpret is for $p = 1$, which represents the city block metric. For $p = 2$, it is the Euclidean distance.

9.2.4 Minimum Number of Stimuli

A minimum number of data points (distances) is needed to be able to derive a space that can reproduce the distances. This number has been empirically assessed to be between 4 and 6 objects per dimension. Even though the researcher does not know a priori the number of dimensions, that means that a significant number of objects are needed to implement the methodology successfully. However, because the most typical solutions involve two or three dimensions, a dozen to eighteen objects should be sufficient in most cases.

9.2.5 Dimensionality

Because the number of dimensions r is not known a priori, and because the solution for the x_j's depends on the number of dimensions, the dimensionality must be inferred from the results obtained for different values of r. Three criteria can be used together: The stress levels under different dimensionality assumptions, the stability of the results, and the interpretability of these solutions.

The goodness of fit or stress values can be plotted as a function of the number of dimensions (scree plot) to identify the elbow where adding dimensions produces little marginal gain in stress levels:

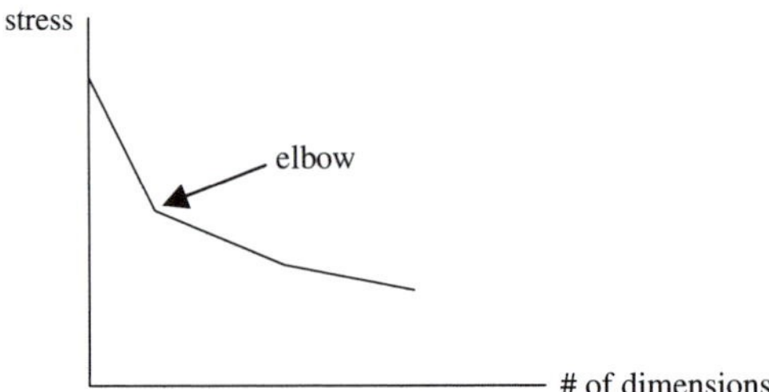

The stability of the results is typically assessed by splitting the sample in two and verifying that the results are similar for each subsample.

The interpretability of the results concerns the meaning of the dimensions of perception uncovered by the procedure. Although subjective, this is the most critical for the research to be meaningful.

9.2.6 Interpretation of MDS Solution

The interpretation of the dimensions is mostly the fruit of the researcher's expertise. However, this expertise can benefit from a complementary data analysis when the objects have also been rated on a number of attributes (although this does lengthen considerably the task for the respondents). This analysis consists of property (attribute) fitting procedures. Three possibilities are available:

(a) Maximum r procedure
This is based on the bivariate correlation coefficient of each attribute with a particular dimension. A high value of the correlation indicates a strong linear relationship between that attribute and the dimension. Consequently, this attribute would provide a significant input in the identification of the dimension.

(b) Monotone multiple regressions
A combination of attributes can explain the dimension in a non-linear fashion. The R^2's provide a measure of the explanatory power.

(c) Property Fitting (PROFIT)
This analysis provides for the possibility of non-monotonous relationships. The objective is to obtain a fit so that the stimulus projections are correlated with the scale.

9.2.7 The KYST Algorithm

Finding a solution, as described above, involves finding an initial configuration from which to start an iterative process and then determining the process by which to move from an iteration to the next.

Step 1: Finding Initial Configuration
Assume that the coordinates x_j's are centered at the origin (the means are zero). Let the n objects be identified by their coordinates in the p-dimensional space:

$$\underset{r\times n}{\mathbf{X}} = (x_1, x_2, \ldots, x_j, \ldots, x_n) \tag{9.13}$$

$$\underset{n\times n}{\mathbf{B}} = X'X = \begin{pmatrix} x_1' \\ x_2' \\ \vdots \\ x_j' \\ \vdots \\ x_n' \end{pmatrix} (x_1 x_2 \cdots x_j \cdots x_n) \tag{9.14}$$

$$= \begin{bmatrix} x_1'x_1 & x_1'x_2 & \cdots & x_1'x_n \\ \vdots & & \ddots & \\ x_n'x_1 & \cdots & \cdots & x_n'x_n \end{bmatrix} \tag{9.15}$$

$$x_j'x_k = \sum_{\ell=1}^{r} x_{j\ell}x_{k\ell} \tag{9.16}$$

The principal component decomposition of $\mathbf{\Delta}$ can provide the initial configuration with r eigenvectors or orthogonal dimensions.

Step 2: Configuration Improvement
In this step, the gradient of the stress provides the direction in which the solution should be changed to improve its value. For that purpose, the disparities between the actual dissimilarities and the predicted dissimilarities computed from the current iteration solution are calculated and the stress S is computed according to the equations above. The gradient is computed from the changes in the stress from one iteration to the next relative to the changes in the coordinate values from

the prior to the current iteration:

$$\frac{\delta S}{\delta x_{tn}} \quad \text{for } t = 1, \ldots, r \tag{9.17}$$

The coordinate values x_{tj}'s are then modified in the direction of the gradient.

9.3 Individual Differences in Similarity Judgments

One way to recognize individual differences in perceptions is to allow all m subjects to share a common space, but to permit each individual to weight differently the dimensions of this space (which corresponds to stretching and shrinking of the axes). This assumption is reflected in the INDSCAL algorithm.

Consequently, we denote the matrix of dissimilarities between objects for individual i as:

$$\mathbf{\Delta}^{(i)} = \{\delta^{(1)}(j,k)\} \quad \text{for } i = 1, \ldots, m \tag{9.18}$$

Each individual has a different weight for each dimension. These weights are represented by the diagonal matrix.

Let

$$\underset{r \times r}{\mathbf{W}^{(i)}} = \text{diag}\{w_t^{(i)}\} \tag{9.19}$$

The problem consists now of finding not only the coordinates of points in the common space but also the weights of each dimension for each individual so as to reproduce as much as possible the original dissimilarities:

$$\delta^{(i)^2}(j,k) \approx (x_j - x_k)'\mathbf{W}^{(i)}(x_j - x_k) \tag{9.20}$$

Wold's non-linear iterative least squares procedure is used where, at each iteration, either $\mathbf{X}$ or $\mathbf{W}^{(i)}$ is fixed to the last iteration estimate.

9.4 Analysis of Preference Data

In this section we do not refer any longer to modeling for the purpose of understanding the underlying dimensions of *perceptions*. Now the objective is to represent preferences for some stimili over others.

Preferences follow from two basic models. One model predicts that more of any dimension is always preferred to less. This is the Vector model of preference. Another model assumes that the more the better is true up to a certain point, from which too much is as bad as not enough. This assumption corresponds to the Ideal Point model of preference.

9.4.1 Vector Model of preferences

MDPREF is a model which derives the space where stimuli are represented in terms of preferences, as well as the individual differences in preference. Individuals are represented in a preference space by different vectors. Each vector is defined so that the projections of the brands/stimuli on this vector correspond to this individual's preferences such that the more the projection falls in the direction of the vector, the more preferred the stimulus. The stimuli are represented in the space by points such that the projections on the individual vector correspond the closest possible to the stated preferences. In MDPREF, both the individual vectors and the stimuli points are inferred simultaneously from the preference data.

9.4.2 Ideal Point Model of Preference

PREFMAP differs in two major ways from MDPREF. First, while the individual vectors of preferences and the stimuli points are derived simultaneously from the preference data, this is not the case in PREFMAP. In this program, the stimuli configuration is provided externally. This configuration is obtained from the other methods we described above to derive a perceptual map from similarity data. The results of KYST or INSCAL can be used as input in this analysis of preferences. The second difference comes from the possibility of analysing a vector model of preference as well as ideal point models.

Indeed, PREFMAP offers two models of preferences. The vector model is similar to the model described above in the context of MDPREF. However, the difference is, as discussed above, due to the fact that the stimuli points are externally supplied. The interpretation of the individual vectors is similar to what is described above. However, the interpretation of the stimuli configuration is more easily done, as the configuration corresponds to perceptions and not preferences. The joint space for representing perceptions and preferences facilitates also the interpretation of the individual vectors since the dimensions are those derived from the perceptual analysis.

The ideal point model of preferences is such that preferences for an individual are also represented as a point in the perceptual space. The preferences for stimuli are such that the most preferred are the stimuli that are the closest in that space to the point representing the individual ideal preference. The further away the stimuli are from the ideal point, the less preferred they are. PREFMAP derives the ideal points for each individual that best represent his/her preference. It should be noted that the vector model is a particular case of the ideal point model where the ideal point is located at infinity.

9.5 Examples

Examples of the various algorithms described above are now given using the PC-MDS software.

9.5.1 Example of KYST

Rank-ordered measures of dissimilarity between brands are the major input of KYST. The example input file is shown in Figure 9.1.

The first line of the input file contains three numbers. The first number is the number of stimuli (here, 10 brands). The second number and the third number are for the number of replications and the number of groups (usually 1 each).

The second line is the format (Fortran style) in which the data will be read. The data matrix is then shown with 9 rows and 9 columns of the bottom half of a symmetric matrix without the diagonal (assumed to be zeros). Finally, the stimuli (here, brands) labels are written on separate lines.

The output of KYST with this particular problem is shown in Figure 9.2. A two-dimensional solution was requested during the interactive dialog while running the software by indicating a minimum and a maximum number of dimensions of 2. The output shows the results by providing the stress obtained from that solution (a stress value of 0.266) and the coordinates in that two-dimensional space for the ten brands. The Shepard diagram represents the plot of the pairs of brands with the actual dissimilarity data on the y axis and the computed distances (before and after transformation through monotone regression). This shows how well the model replicates each of the pairs of

```
  10 1 1
  (9f3.0)
 22
 13 26
 01 25 36
 31 32 23 16
 44 18 14 02 30
 04 24 40 35 17 05
 07 27 38 42 19 06 34
 09 28 39 41 21 08 33 45
 37 20 15 03 29 43 12 10 11
sama
salt
semi
self
sibi
siro
sono
sold
suli
susi
```

Fig. 9.1 Example of PC-MDS input file for KYST (examp9-1.dat).

```
                    K Y S T   MULTIDIMENSIONAL  SCALING
    WRITTEN BY  JOSEPH B. KRUSKAL, FOREST W. YOUNG, WITH JUDITH SEERY
                            PC-MDS  VERSION

ANALYSIS START:  DATE  05/07/2002,  TIME  17:17:50

ANALYSIS TITLE: KYST Rankings
DATA IS READ FROM FILE: ex_kystr.dat
OUTPUT FILE IS: ex_kystr.out

INPUT PARAMETERS:

MAXIMUM DIMENSIONS                                      2
MINIMUM DIMENSIONS                                      2
DIMENSION DECREMENT                                     1
MINIMUM STRESS                                           .01000
SCALE FACTOR GRADIENT                                    .00000
STRESS STEP RATIO                                        .99900
MAXIMUM ITERATIONS                                     50
COSINE OF ANGLE BETWEEN GRADIENTS                        .66000
AVERAGE COSINE OF ANGLE                                  .66000
NUMBER OF PRE-ITERATIONS                                1
THE NUMBER OF DATA POINTS TO BE FIXED IS:                0
EUCLIDEAN DISTANCE
STRESS FORMULA 1
TIES PRIMARY
LOWER HALF MATRIX
NOT BLOCK DIAGONAL
DIAGONAL ABSENT
SPLIT BY DECK
TORSCA INITIAL CONFIGURATION
NO WEIGHTS AFTER DATA
MONOTONE MODEL
ASCENDING DATA
ALL PLOTS OF FINAL CONFIGURATION
ALL SCATTER PLOTS OF DIST VS DHAT
ROTATE FINAL CONFIG. COORDINATES

PARAMETERS:  10  1  1
TITLE:   (9f3.0)

DATA FOR RECORD:    10
 .37E+02 .20E+02 .15E+02 .30E+01 .29E+02 .43E+02 .12E+02 .10E+02 .11E+02

ON THE SHEPARD DIAGRAM THE ORIGINAL DATA (DATA) ARE PLOTTED;
ON THE Y AXIS AND DISTANCES (DIST,0) AND ESTIMATED DISTANCES
(DHAT,X) ON THE X AXIS. A ; INDICATES TWO VALUES ARE PLOTTED
ON TOP OF EACH OTHER AND A > INDICATES POINT NUMBERS GREATER
THAN 50.  IDENTIFIERS FOR THE CONFIGURATION PLOT IN 2 DIMENSIONS ARE:
```

```
*****IDENTIFICATION KEY FOR PLOTS WITH IDENTIFIED POINTS*****

PT #   1   2   3   4   5   6   7   8   9  10  11  12  13  14  15
CHAR   1   2   3   4   5   6   7   8   9   A   B   C   D   E   F

PT #  16  17  18  19  20  21  22  23  24  25  26  27  28  29  30
CHAR   G   H   I   J   K   L   M   N   O   P   Q   R   S   T   U

PT #  31  32  33  34  35  36  37  38  39  40  41  42  43  44  45
CHAR   V   W   X   Y   Z   +   /   =   *   &   $   @   ]   -   <

PT #  46  47  48  49  50
CHAR   (   )   "   #   '


TITLE: KYST Rankings

INITIAL CONFIGURATION COMPUTATION   NO. PTS.=  10    DIM=   2

STRESS STARTING TO INCREASE  BEST VALUE ACHIEVED ON PRE-ITERATION NUMBER  0

THE BEST INITIAL CONFIGURATION OF  10 POINTS IN   2 DIMENSIONS
HAS A STRESS OF    .401.  STRESS FORMULA 1 WAS USED.

TITLE: KYST Rankings

HISTORY OF COMPUTATION:
N=  10 THERE ARE    45 DATA VALUES, SPLIT INTO   1 LIST(S).
DIMENSION(S) =   2


MINIMUM WAS ACHIEVED

THE FINAL CONFIGURATION HAS BEEN ROTATED TO PRINCIPAL COMPONENTS.


THE FINAL CONFIGURATION OF  10 POINTS IN  2 DIMENSIONS HAS STRESS OF  .266
FORMULA 1 WAS USED.  THE FINAL CONFIGURATION APPEARS:

       1       2
  1 -1.007  -.210
  2   .162   .728
  3   .194  -.726
  4  -.992   .175
  5  -.030  -.009
  6  1.036   .854
  7   .715   .020
  8  1.055  -.830
  9  -.586  1.012
 10  -.546 -1.014
```

```
DATA GROUP(S)
SERIAL  COUNT STRESS REGRESSION COEFFICIENTS (FROM DEGREE 0 TO MAX OF 4)
    1     45   .266  ASCENDING

**********************************************************************
KYST Rankings


DIST AND DHAT VERSES DATA FOR   2 DIMENSION(S)
STRESS =     .2662


               .    .5095.    .9675.   1.4255.   1.8835.   2.3415.
               .2805      .7385     1.1965     1.6545     2.1125     2.5705
             *.****.****.****.****.****.****.****.****.****.****.*
     47.20 ..                                                    .. 47.20
     45.41 ..                                               X    .. 45.41
     43.61 ..                                           0 X0     .. 43.61
     41.82 ..            0        X                     X        .. 41.82
     40.03 ..            0        X                              .. 40.03
S    38.24 ..           0         X           0                  .. 38.24
H    36.44 ..            0        X  0                           .. 36.44
E    34.65 ..            0        X       0                      .. 34.65
P    32.86 ..        0            X      0                       .. 32.86
A    31.07 ..              0      X                              .. 31.07
R    29.27 ..                 0   X0                             .. 29.27
D    27.48 ..         0           X         0                    .. 27.48
     25.69 ..                    0X  0                           .. 25.69
     23.90 ..           0         X                              .. 23.90
     22.10 ..        0            X   0                          .. 22.10
     20.31 ..                 0   X           0                  .. 20.31
D    18.52 ..           0         X0                             .. 18.52
I    16.73 ..        0    0       X                              .. 16.73
A    14.93 ..         0           X                              .. 14.93
G    13.14 ..                    0X         0                    .. 13.14
R    11.35 ..                     X     0        0               .. 11.35
A     9.56 ..                    0X     0                        ..  9.56
M     7.76 ..                     X     0           0            ..  7.76
      5.97 ..                     X       0                      ..  5.97
      4.18 ..           0         X        0                     ..  4.18
      2.39 ..                    0X                 0            ..  2.39
       .59 ..  X                                                 ..   .59
     -1.20 ..                                                    .. -1.20
             *.****.****.****.****.****.****.****.****.****.****.*
               .    .5095.    .9675.   1.4255.   1.8835.   2.3415.
               .2805      .7385     1.1965     1.6545     2.1125     2.5705
```

```
CONFIGURATION PLOT  DIMENSION   2 (Y-AXIS) VS. DIMENSION   1 (X-AXIS)
KYST Rankings
           .*....*....*....*....*....*....*....*....*....*....*....*....*
 3.000**                                                          ** 3.000
 2.769**                                                          ** 2.769
 2.538**                                                          ** 2.538
 2.308**                                                          ** 2.308
 2.077**                                                          ** 2.077
 1.846**                                                          ** 1.846
 1.615**                                                          ** 1.615
 1.385**                                                          ** 1.385
 1.154**                                                          ** 1.154
  .923**                        9           6                     **  .923
  .692**                             2                            **  .692
  .462**                                                          **  .462
  .231**                     4                                    **  .231
  .000**-----------------------------5----7-----------------------**  .000
 -.231**                    1                                     ** -.231
 -.462**                                                          ** -.462
 -.692**                             3                            ** -.692
 -.923**                        A           8                     ** -.923
-1.154**                                                          **-1.154
-1.385**                                                          **-1.385
-1.615**                                                          **-1.615
-1.846**                                                          **-1.846
-2.077**                                                          **-2.077
-2.308**                                                          **-2.308
-2.538**                                                          **-2.538
-2.769**                                                          **-2.769
-3.000**                                                          **-3.000
           .*....*....*....*....*....*....*....*....*....*....*....*....*
           .  -3.3333.  -2.0000.   -.6667.    .6667.   2.0000.   3.3333.
       -4.0000    -2.6667   -1.3333     .0000    1.3333    2.6667    4.0000

ANALYSIS END:  DATE  05/07/2002,  TIME  17:18:13
```

Fig. 9.2 PC-MDS output of KYST (examp9-1.out).

stimuli. The plot of the brands in the two-dimensional space is shown, where the brands are numbered in the order of the input. The interpretation can be inferred from the knowledge about the brands according to the attributes that appear to discriminate these brands along the two dimensions found (here, an economy and a performance dimension). An example of PROFIT analysis to help interpret the meaning of the dimensions is shown below.

9.5.2 Example of INDSCAL

In INDSCAL, the data for several individuals are analyzed. The input file of an example is shown in Figure 9.3.

```
  3   2   2   2  25   1   0   1   0   0  '12345677'  0   0   1   0  .001
  4 10 10
(2X,9F5.2)
01 4.88
01 4.07 0.93
01 5.33 0.62 1.27
01 2.89 1.99 1.24 2.47
01 0.51 5.38 4.56 5.83 3.39
01 3.67 1.37 0.44 1.69 0.94 4.16
01 5.40 0.61 1.34 0.13 2.53 5.90 1.77
01 5.38 0.59 1.33 0.13 2.51 5.88 1.76 0.02
01 0.69 5.56 4.73 5.99 3.57 0.19 4.32 6.06 6.05
02 5.65
02 6.37 2.98
02 7.84 3.52 1.54
02 3.28 2.38 3.97 5.16
02 0.63 6.10 6.58 8.08 3.77
02 6.74 3.95 0.99 1.87 4.70 6.86
02 7.42 2.78 1.48 0.77 4.57 7.70 2.17
02 7.36 2.71 1.47 0.84 4.51 7.65 2.19 0.07
02 1.18 6.18 6.35 7.87 3.93 0.65 6.54 7.55 7.51
03 4.34
03 5.08 2.45
03 6.22 2.92 1.19
03 2.51 1.84 3.27 4.20
03 0.49 4.67 5.21 6.37 2.88
03 5.44 3.25 0.80 1.42 3.90 5.49
03 5.84 2.30 1.13 0.64 3.69 6.03 1.68
03 5.79 2.24 1.12 0.69 3.64 5.98 1.70 0.06
03 0.95 4.71 4.98 6.16 2.99 0.54 5.20 5.87 5.83
04 2.42
04 4.86 2.89
04 5.63 3.56 0.80
04 1.27 1.17 3.86 4.59
04 0.34 2.33 4.63 5.41 1.25
04 5.68 3.79 0.90 0.60 4.73 5.43
04 4.91 2.78 0.46 0.78 3.83 4.70 1.15
04 4.84 2.71 0.47 0.85 3.76 4.64 1.20 0.07
04 0.96 2.04 4.06 4.85 1.19 0.64 4.84 4.16 4.10
sama
salt
semi
self
sibi
siro
sono
sold
suli
susi
```

Fig. 9.3 Example of PC-MDS input file for INSCAL (examp9-2.dat).

The first line of the input file contains the following information:

- Number of ways of the data (3-way data)
- Maximum number of dimensions (2 in this example)
- Minimum number of dimensions (2 in this example)
- Type of input data (2 means lower-half dissimilarity matrix with no diagonal; other possibilities include a value of 1 for a lower-half similarity matrix without diagonal)
- Maximum number of iterations (25 were defined in this example).

The remaining codes on this first line correspond to more advanced options. The second line contains a number for each way. The first one is the number of subjects and the other two give the number of stimuli. The third line shows the format (Fortran-style) in which the data will be inputed. The dissimilarity data are then shown for each individual (it is good practice to show first the subject number, although, as indicated by the format statement, this number is not read in). Finally, the objects labels (brand names) are listed, one per line. The results of INDSCAL are shown in Figure 9.4.

```
                              I N D S C A L
                        INDIVIDUAL  DIFFERENCES  SCALING
                     BY DR. J. D. CARROLL AND JIH JIE CHANG
                              PC-MDS VERSION




ANALYSIS TITLE:             INDSCAL Example
DATA IS READ FROM FILE:     ex_inds.dat
OUTPUT FILE IS:             ex_inds.out


ANALYSIS START:  DATE  05/07/2002,  TIME  16:09:04

INDIFF- INDIVIDUAL DIFFERENCES ANALYSIS USING CANONICAL DECOMPOSITION
OF   3 WAY TABLE IN   2 DIMENSIONS

TITLE: INDSCAL Example
******************************************************************************

PARAMETERS

NF        DIMENSION OF SOLUTION                                  2

N         NO. OF WAYS OR MATRICES                                3
MAXDIM    MAXIMUM NO. OF DIMENSIONS                              2
MINDIM    MINIMUM NO. OF DIMENSIONS                              2
IRDATA    TYPE OF DATA INPUT                                     2
ITMAX     MAXIMUM NO. OF ITERATIONS                             25
```

```
ISET      OPTION TO SET MATRIX 2 EQUAL TO MATRIX 3               1
IOY       SELECT SIMULTANEOUS SOLUTION                           0
IDR       CORRELATIONS FOR EACH SUBJECT                          1
ISAM      SOLVE FOR ALL MATRICES                                 0
IPUNSP    PUNCH SCALAR PRODUCT MATRICES                          0
IRN       RANDOM NUMBER GENERATOR START SET               12345677
CRIT      CRITERION FOR QUITTING ITERATION                        .001
IVEC      MATRIX OR VECTOR FORM FOR DATA                         0
IP        OUTPUT NORMALIZED A-MATRIX                             0
IA        PRINT ORIGINAL DATA MATRICES                           1
IS        PRINT INTERMEDIATE ITERATIVE MATRICES                  0

MATRIX SIZES     4  10  10
******************************************************************************


   *****IDENTIFICATION KEY FOR PLOTS WITH IDENTIFIED POINTS*****

PT #   1   2   3   4   5   6   7   8   9  10  11  12  13  14  15
CHAR   1   2   3   4   5   6   7   8   9   A   B   C   D   E   F

PT #  16  17  18  19  20  21  22  23  24  25  26  27  28  29  30
CHAR   G   H   I   J   K   L   M   N   O   P   Q   R   S   T   U

PT #  31  32  33  34  35  36  37  38  39  40  41  42  43  44  45
CHAR   V   W   X   Y   Z   +   /   =   *   &   $   @   [   ?   <

PT #  46  47  48  49  50
CHAR   (   )   "   ;   ]

POINT NUMBERS ABOVE 50 IDENTIFIED AS  > MULTIPLE POINTS IDENTIFIED AS  #

SUBJECT    1
    4.88
    4.07     .93
    5.33     .62    1.27
    2.89    1.99    1.24    2.47
     .51    5.38    4.56    5.83    3.39
    3.67    1.37     .44    1.69     .94    4.16
    5.40     .61    1.34     .13    2.53    5.90    1.77
    5.38     .59    1.33     .13    2.51    5.88    1.76     .02
     .69    5.56    4.73    5.99    3.57     .19    4.32    6.06    6.05

SUBJECT    4
    2.42
    4.86    2.89
    5.63    3.56     .80
    1.27    1.17    3.86    4.59
     .34    2.33    4.63    5.41    1.25
    5.68    3.79     .90     .60    4.73    5.43
    4.91    2.78     .46     .78    3.83    4.70    1.15
    4.84    2.71     .47     .85    3.76    4.64    1.20     .07
     .96    2.04    4.06    4.85    1.19     .64    4.84    4.16    4.10
```

```
INITIAL A MATRICES

MATRIX 1
 1      1.0000      1.0000      1.0000      1.0000
 2      1.0000      1.0000      1.0000      1.0000
MATRIX 2
 1       .4257      -.0724      -.1040       .4653      -.1853
        -.3849      -.0541       .3826      -.0469      -.3351

 2       .3026       .1942      -.3516      -.2383       .2954
         .3221       .3436      -.4229       .1126      -.3603
MATRIX 3
 1       .4448       .3780       .4900       .0394      -.4308
        -.2456      -.2815      -.4792      -.4867       .2676

 2      -.2278      -.4010      -.2592      -.1818       .3562
        -.1681       .1906      -.4663      -.3248       .2688


HISTORY OF COMPUTATION

ITERATION        CORRELATIONS BETWEEN
                  Y(DATA) AND YHAT          (R**2)              (1-R**2)
     0               -.021067              .000444              .999556
     1                .953993              .910103              .089897
     2                .984229              .968707              .031293
     3                .986800              .973774              .026226
     4                .990679              .981445              .018555
     5                .995783              .991585              .008415
     6                .998820              .997641              .002359
     7                .999428              .998857              .001143
     8                .999591              .999182              .000818
     9                .999690              .999380              .000620
*******************************************************************************

EQUATE MATRIX 2 AND MATRIX 3, ITERATE AGAIN


INITIAL A MATRICES


MATRIX 1
 1      -.1499      -.1080      -.1020      -.0334
 2      -.0194       .1066       .1212       .2540


MATRIX 2
 1      1.1527      -.6224      -.4095      -.8760       .1087
        1.3216      -.2866      -.8801      -.8722      1.3638

 2       .3719       .1729      -.2487      -.3310       .2871
         .3238      -.3798      -.2185      -.2089       .2312
```

```
MATRIX 3
 1      1.1527      -.6224      -.4095      -.8760       .1087
        1.3216      -.2866      -.8801      -.8722      1.3638

 2       .3719       .1729      -.2487      -.3310       .2871
         .3238      -.3798      -.2185      -.2089       .2312

HISTORY OF COMPUTATION

ITERATION        CORRELATIONS BETWEEN
                  Y(DATA) AND YHAT          (R**2)            (1-R**2)
     0              -.795407              .632673             .367327
     1               .999731              .999463             .000537

INDSCAL Example

NORMALIZED A MATRICES

MATRIX   1
 1         1.03187     -.05535
 2          .73697      .36435
 3          .69485      .41314
 4          .21598      .85421

MATRIX   2
 1          .41044      .41167
 2         -.22162      .19138
 3         -.14581     -.27529
 4         -.31193     -.36649
 5          .03871      .31787
 6          .47060      .35844
 7         -.10205     -.42043
 8         -.31338     -.24193
 9         -.31057     -.23122
10          .48561      .25599

MATRIX   3
 1          .41044      .41167
 2         -.22162      .19138
 3         -.14581     -.27529
 4         -.31193     -.36649
 5          .03871      .31787
 6          .47060      .35844
 7         -.10205     -.42043
 8         -.31338     -.24193
 9         -.31057     -.23122
10          .48561      .25599

MATRIX   1

SUMS OF PRODUCTS
 1         2.13736      .68297
 2          .68297     1.03618
```

```
SUM OF SQUARES =        3.17353

MATRIX   2

SUMS OF PRODUCTS
 1        1.00000       .77684
 2         .77684      1.00000

SUM OF SQUARES =        2.00000

MATRIX   3

SUMS OF PRODUCTS
 1        1.00000       .77684
 2         .77684      1.00000

SUM OF SQUARES =        2.00000


         THIS IS PLOT OF DIMENSION  1 VS.DIMENSION  2 FOR TABLE NO.  1

         +....+....+....+....+....+....+....+....+....+....+....+....+
    1.20+                              |                              +
        .                              |                              .
        .                              |                              .
     .92+                              |                              +
        .                              |    4                         .
        .                              |                              .
     .65+                              |                              +
        .                              |                              .
        .                              |                              .
     .37+                              |                32            +
        .                              |                              .
        .                              |                              .
     .09+                              |                              +
        .------------------------------0------------------------------.
        .                              |                        1     .
    -.18+                              |                              +
        .                              |                              .
        .                              |                              .
    -.46+                              |                              +
        .                              |                              .
        .                              |                              .
    -.74+                              |                              +
        .                              |                              .
        .                              |                              .
   -1.02+                              |                              +
        .                              |                              .
        .                              |                              .
         +....+....+....+....+....+....+....+....+....+....+....+....+
       -1.2 -1.0  -.8  -.6  -.4  -.2   .0   .2   .4   .6   .8  1.0  1.2
```

```
     THIS IS PLOT OF DIMENSION  1 VS.DIMENSION  2 FOR TABLE NO.  2

     +....+....+....+....+....+....+....+....+....+....+....+....+
1.20+                              |                              +
    .                              |                              .
    .                              |                              .
 .92+                              |                              +
    .                              |                              .
    .                              |                              .
 .65+                              |                              +
    .                              |                              .
    .                              |                              .
 .37+                              |         1 6                  +
    .                              |5          A                  .
    .                        2     |                              .
 .09+                              |                              +
    .------------------------------0------------------------------.
    .                              |                              .
-.18+                              |                              +
    .                      #   3   |                              .
    .                      4       |                              .
-.46+                          7   |                              +
    .                              |                              .
    .                              |                              .
-.74+                              |                              +
    .                              |                              .
    .                              |                              .
-1.02+                             |                              +
    .                              |                              .
    .                              |                              .
     +....+....+....+....+....+....+....+....+....+....+....+....+
   -1.2 -1.0  -.8  -.6  -.4  -.2   .0   .2   .4   .6   .8  1.0  1.2
```

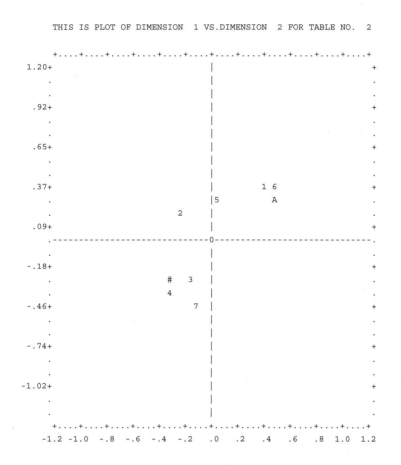

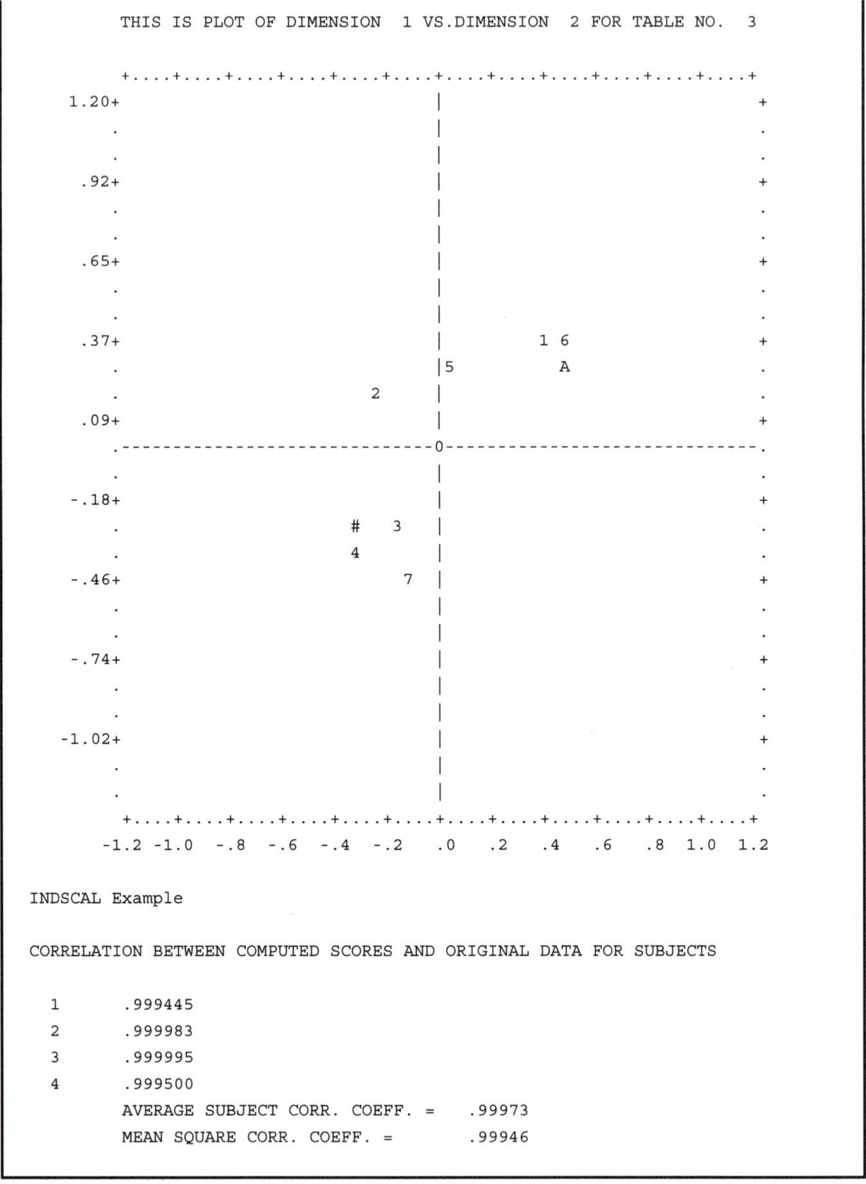

```
        THIS IS PLOT OF DIMENSION  1 VS.DIMENSION  2 FOR TABLE NO.  3

        +....+....+....+....+....+....+....+....+....+....+....+....+
   1.20+                             |                              +
       .                             |                              .
       .                             |                              .
    .92+                             |                              +
       .                             |                              .
       .                             |                              .
    .65+                             |                              +
       .                             |                              .
       .                             |                              .
    .37+                             |         1 6                  +
       .                             |5          A                  .
       .                        2    |                              .
    .09+                             |                              +
       .-----------------------------0------------------------------.
       .                             |                              .
   -.18+                             |                              +
       .                      #   3  |                              .
       .                      4      |                              .
   -.46+                           7 |                              +
       .                             |                              .
       .                             |                              .
   -.74+                             |                              +
       .                             |                              .
       .                             |                              .
  -1.02+                             |                              +
       .                             |                              .
       .                             |                              .
        +....+....+....+....+....+....+....+....+....+....+....+....+
      -1.2 -1.0  -.8  -.6  -.4  -.2   .0   .2   .4   .6   .8  1.0  1.2

INDSCAL Example

CORRELATION BETWEEN COMPUTED SCORES AND ORIGINAL DATA FOR SUBJECTS

  1        .999445
  2        .999983
  3        .999995
  4        .999500
           AVERAGE SUBJECT CORR. COEFF. =    .99973
           MEAN SQUARE CORR. COEFF. =        .99946
```

Fig. 9.4 Output example for INDSCAL (examp9-2.out).

The output, under the title "history of computation," shows the fit measure at each iteration. Because INDSCAL is a metric model, the fit measure is the correlation between the input dissimilarity data and the predicted dissimilarity from the model parameter values at that iteration. The value of 0.999 obtained in the example is excellent.

Under the title "Normalized A Matrices" matrix 1 lists the individual weights for each of the 4 individuals. Matrix 2 lists the coordinates of the objects in the common object space.

The individual weights shown in Matrix 1 are plotted along the two dimensions in the first plot. Plot No. 2 represents the brands corresponding to the coordinates listed in matrix 2.

9.5.3 Example of PROFIT (Property Fitting) Analysis

In the example below, we use the configuration (coordinates) obtained from the KYST analysis described earlier in section 9.5.1. (It is possible to use the output configuration of other models such as INSCAL). The relationships of the two dimensions corresponding to these perceptions of the ten brands with five characteristics of the brands (i.e., weight, design, volume, maximum frequency and power) are analysed in this run of PROFIT. Therefore, the ratings of these brands on these characteristics are matched as well as possible with the ratings obtained from the KYST configuration. Each characteristic is represented in the perceptual space by a vector so that the fit with the perceptions of the brands is maximized. For rating data on the properties (brand characteristics), the correlation between these ratings and the projection of the brand perceptions on that vector is maximized.

The input file shown in Figure 9.5 provides the information necessary to run the program. The first line of input indicates the basic parameters of the problem. The first number (1 in Figure 9.5) indicates that a linear relationship between properties and perceptions will be evaluated. The second number (10 in Figure 9.5) indicates the number of stimuli (brands). The third number (2 in Figure 9.5) shows the number of dimensions in the perceptual space used as input. The fourth number (5 in Figure 9.5) is the number of properties to be analyzed. The other numbers correspond to more advanced options.

The second line is the Fortran-style format in which the data for the stimuli (brands) coordinates are read. Then follow the perception coordinates, one line for each stimulus (brand). In this example, the stimulus number (1 to 10) is shown to better visualize the input, but this information is not read by the program, as the format above indicates that the first two columns are skipped ("2X"). After the perceptual coordinates, the data on the properties are shown. First, the format in which the data are to be read is indicated in the ususal Fortran-style format. Then, for each of the properties, the label of the property is shown on a line and on a separate line the values of the property on all the ten stimuli are shown. The first number indicates the property number but is not used, as shown by the format of the input which skips the first two columns of data ("2X"). Finally, the last ten lines correspond to the labels of the ten stimuli, in this case the names of the brands.

```
1 10 2 5 0    0    2   0.0
(2X,2F7.3)
 1 -1.007  -.210
 2    .162   .728
 3    .194  -.726
 4   -.992   .175
 5   -.030  -.009
 6   1.036   .854
 7    .715   .020
 8   1.055  -.830
 9   -.586  1.012
10   -.546 -1.014
(2X,10F3.0)
Weight
01 10 12 17 15 11 10 10 17 10 15
Design
02 08 09 07 05 09 03 03 07 03 06
Volume
03 30 37 50 60 35 50 70 50 50 40
Max Frequency
04 25 25 30 40 25 20 20 30 25 20
Power
05 10 30 80 90 20 10 90 70 20 70
sama
salt
semi
self
sibi
siro
sono
sold
suli
susi
```

Fig. 9.5 Example of PC-MDS input file for PROFIT (examp9-3.dat).

Figure 9.6 shows the output of the PROFIT analysis. First, for each property, the correlations between the the original and the fitted vectors are shown, followed by the corresponding plot of the stimuli.

The last graph shows the perceptions of the stimuli (the ten brands) numbered from 1 to 9, plus the letter *A* to represent the tenth brand. The points labeled *B* to *F* represent the end points of the property vectors that maximize the correlation with the projections of the brands on this vector with the original property values. The vectors have been added in Figure 9.6 and do not appear on the original computer output. *B* represents the weight property, *C* represents the design, *D* the volume, *E* the maximum frequency, and *F* the power of the brands.

```
                         P R O F I T
                  PROPERTY FITTING ANALYSIS
      PROGRAM WRITTEN BY DR. J. D. CARROLL AND JIH JIE CHANG
                        PC-MDS VERSION



 ANALYSIS START:  DATE  05/15/2002,  TIME  18:43:07

 ANALYSIS TITLE: Profit test
 DATA IS READ FROM FILE: ex_prof.dat
 OUTPUT FILE IS: ex_prof.out
 LANA (REGRESSION OPTION):                                    1
 N    NO. OF STIMULI    (400 MAX)                            10
 K    NO. OF DIMENSIONS (10 MAX)                              2
 M    NO. OF PROPERTIES (60 MAX)                              5
 IRX  0 = N X K INPUT; 1 = K X N INPUT                        0
 IWGT 0 = RATIO OF ERROR VAR. TO TRUE VAR. (USUAL OPTION)     0
      1 = RATIO OF MEAN SQ. SUCCESSIVE DIFFERENCE TO VARIANCE
IPLOT 0 = PROPERTIES ONLY                                     2
      1 = PLOT PROPERTIES AND FUNCTIONS
      2 = DO ALL PLOTS
 BCO (FLOATING POINT NUMBER FOR NON LINEAR REG.)              0.


 DATA FOR RECORD:     1
 -.10E+01-.21E+00


 DATA FOR RECORD:    10
 -.55E+00-.10E+01

 LINEAR REGRESSION

 NORMALIZED CONFIGURATION
   1       -1.0071      .1619      .1939     -.9921     -.0301
            1.0359      .7149     1.0549     -.5861     -.5461

   2        -.2100      .7280     -.7260      .1750     -.0090
             .8540      .0200     -.8300     1.0120    -1.0140


 COVARIANCE MATRIX
   1      5.4020    -.0008
   2      -.0008    4.6028

 X*(X''X) INVERSE
   1      -.1864     .0300     .0359    -.1837    -.0056     .1918     .1323
           .1953    -.1085    -.1011
   2      -.0457     .1582    -.1577     .0380    -.0020     .1856     .0044
          -.1803     .2198    -.2203
```

```
          PROPERTY  1

INTERMEDIATE SUMS BEFORE SQUARING:        .2484      -2.9634

SSQ =        8.84321    XL =        2.97375

ORIGINAL VALUES ON PROPERTY  1
          10.0000      12.0000      17.0000      15.0000      11.0000
          10.0000      10.0000      17.0000      10.0000      15.0000

PROJECTIONS ON FITTED VECTORS
            .1251       -.7119        .7397       -.2573        .0065
           -.7645        .0398        .9152      -1.0574        .9648

 PLOT OF ORIGINAL (X-AXIS) VERSUS OBTAINED (Y-AXIS) FOR PROPERTY VECTOR NO.  1

         +.........+.........+.........+.........+.........+.........+
   1.066+                                                              +
        .                                        A                     .
        .                                                       8      .
    .819+                                                              +
        .                                                       3      .
        .                                                              .
    .572+                                                              +
        .                                                              .
        .                                                              .
    .324+                                                              +
        .                                                              .
        .   1                                                          .
    .077+   7                                                          +
        .           5                                                  .
        .                                                              .
   -.170+                                                              +
        .                                        4                     .
        .                                                              .
   -.417+                                                              +
        .                                                              .
        .                                                              .
   -.664+                                                              +
        .   6              2                                           .
        .                                                              .
   -.911+                                                              +
        .                                                              .
        .   9                                                          .
  -1.159+                                                              +
         +.........+.........+.........+.........+.........+.........+
       9.6510.2910.9311.5712.2212.8613.5014.1414.7815.4216.0716.7117.35


CORRELATION BETWEEN ORIGINAL AND FITTED VECTORS FOR PROPERTY   1 IS:

         R =      .713 , RSQ =      .509
```

```
          PROPERTY  2

INTERMEDIATE SUMS BEFORE SQUARING:      -.5318     -1.2280

SSQ =       1.79091    XL =       1.33825

ORIGINAL VALUES ON PROPERTY  2
           8.0000       9.0000       7.0000       5.0000       9.0000
           3.0000       3.0000       7.0000       3.0000       6.0000

PROJECTIONS ON FITTED VECTORS
            .5929       -.7324        .5891        .2337        .0202
          -1.1953       -.3025        .3424       -.6957       1.1475


 PLOT OF ORIGINAL (X-AXIS) VERSUS OBTAINED (Y-AXIS) FOR PROPERTY VECTOR NO.  2

        +.........+.........+.........+.........+.........+.........+
  1.265+                                                               +
       .                              A                                .
       .                                                               .
   .978+                                                               +
       .                                                               .
       .                                                               .
   .692+                                                               +
       .                                       3        1              .
       .                                                               .
   .406+                                                               +
       .                                       8                       .
       .                   4                                           .
   .119+                                                               +
       .                                                         5     .
       .                                                               .
  -.167+                                                               +
       .   7                                                           .
       .                                                               .
  -.453+                                                               +
       .                                                               .
       .                                                               .
  -.740+   9                                                     2     +
       .                                                               .
       .                                                               .
 -1.026+                                                               +
       .                                                               .
       .   6                                                           .
 -1.312+                                                               +
        +.........+.........+.........+.........+.........+.........+
     2.70 3.25 3.80 4.35 4.90 5.45 6.00 6.55 7.10 7.65 8.20 8.75 9.30


CORRELATION BETWEEN ORIGINAL AND FITTED VECTORS FOR PROPERTY   2 IS:

         R =     .404 , RSQ =     .163
```

```
          PROPERTY  3

INTERMEDIATE SUMS BEFORE SQUARING:       5.2440       1.5567

SSQ =       29.92298    XL =        5.47019

ORIGINAL VALUES ON PROPERTY  3
          30.0000      37.0000      50.0000      60.0000      35.0000
          50.0000      70.0000      50.0000      50.0000      40.0000

PROJECTIONS ON FITTED VECTORS
          -1.0252        .3624       -.0207       -.9013       -.0314
           1.2361        .6910        .7751       -.2739       -.8121


 PLOT OF ORIGINAL (X-AXIS) VERSUS OBTAINED (Y-AXIS) FOR PROPERTY VECTOR NO.  3

          +.........+.........+.........+.........+.........+.........+
   1.349+                                                              +
        .                             6                                .
        .                                                              .
   1.073+                                                              +
        .                                                              .
        .                                                              .
    .796+                             8                                +
        .                                                          7   .
        .                                                              .
    .520+                                                              +
        .                                                              .
        .           2                                                  .
    .244+                                                              +
        .                                                              .
        .                                                              .
   -.033+         5                   3                                +
        .                                                              .
        .                                                              .
   -.309+                             9                                +
        .                                                              .
        .                                                              .
   -.586+                                                              +
        .                                                              .
        .               A                                              .
   -.862+                                           4                  +
        .                                                              .
        .  1                                                           .
  -1.138+                                                              +
          +.........+.........+.........+.........+.........+.........+
     28.0031.6735.3339.0042.6746.3350.0053.6757.3361.0064.6768.3372.00


 CORRELATION BETWEEN ORIGINAL AND FITTED VECTORS FOR PROPERTY   3 IS:

          R =      .348 , RSQ =      .121
```

```
          PROPERTY  4

INTERMEDIATE SUMS BEFORE SQUARING:     -2.7142       -.9683

SSQ =        8.30432    XL =        2.88172

ORIGINAL VALUES ON PROPERTY  4
          25.0000      25.0000      30.0000      40.0000      25.0000
          20.0000      20.0000      30.0000      25.0000      20.0000

PROJECTIONS ON FITTED VECTORS
           1.0191      -.3971        .0613        .8756        .0314
          -1.2626      -.6801       -.7147        .2120        .8551

 PLOT OF ORIGINAL (X-AXIS) VERSUS OBTAINED (Y-AXIS) FOR PROPERTY VECTOR NO.  4

         +.........+.........+.........+.........+.........+.........+
   1.133+                                                              +
        .             1                                                .
        .                                                              .
    .854+  A                                                       4   +
        .                                                              .
        .                                                              .
    .575+                                                              +
        .                                                              .
        .                                                              .
    .297+                                                              +
        .             9                                                .
        .                                                              .
    .018+             5             3                                  +
        .                                                              .
        .                                                              .
   -.261+                                                              +
        .             2                                                .
        .                                                              .
   -.540+                                                              +
        .                                                              .
        .  7                        8                                  .
   -.819+                                                              +
        .                                                              .
        .                                                              .
  -1.098+                                                              +
        .                                                              .
        .  6                                                           .
  -1.377+                                                              +
         +.........+.........+.........+.........+.........+.........+
      19.0020.8322.6724.5026.3328.1730.0031.8333.6735.5037.3339.1741.00

CORRELATION BETWEEN ORIGINAL AND FITTED VECTORS FOR PROPERTY   4 IS:

        R =     .360 , RSQ =     .130
```

```
        PROPERTY  5

INTERMEDIATE SUMS BEFORE SQUARING:       3.5137     -26.3463

SSQ =       706.47380    XL =       26.57957

ORIGINAL VALUES ON PROPERTY  5
          10.0000      30.0000      80.0000      90.0000      20.0000
          10.0000      90.0000      70.0000      20.0000      70.0000

PROJECTIONS ON FITTED VECTORS
            .0750       -.7002        .7453       -.3046        .0049
           -.7096        .0747        .9622      -1.0806        .9329


 PLOT OF ORIGINAL (X-AXIS) VERSUS OBTAINED (Y-AXIS) FOR PROPERTY VECTOR NO.  5

        +.........+.........+.........+.........+.........+.........+
   1.064+                                                            +
        .                                           8                .
        .                                           A                .
    .815+                                                            +
        .                                                 3          .
        .                                                            .
    .565+                                                            +
        .                                                            .
        .                                                            .
    .315+                                                            +
        .                                                            .
        .                                                            .
    .066+   1                                                  7     +
        .         5                                                  .
        .                                                            .
   -.184+                                                            +
        .                                                      4     .
        .                                                            .
   -.434+                                                            +
        .                                                            .
        .                                                            .
   -.683+   6           2                                            +
        .                                                            .
        .                                                            .
   -.933+                                                            +
        .                                                            .
        .         9                                                  .
  -1.183+                                                            +
        +.........+.........+.........+.........+.........+.........+
      6.0013.3320.6728.0035.3342.6750.0057.3364.6772.0079.3386.6794.00

CORRELATION BETWEEN ORIGINAL AND FITTED VECTORS FOR PROPERTY    5 IS:

        R =      .563 , RSQ =      .317
```

TABLE 1. THE MAXIMUM CORRELATION BETWEEN THE PROPERTY AND THE PROJECTIONS ON FITTED VECTOR

	RHO	PROPERTY
1	.7133	Weight
2	.4035	Design
3	.3484	Volume
4	.3602	Max Frequency
5	.5630	Power

TABLE 2. DIRECTION COSINES OF FITTED VECTORS IN NORMALIZED SPACE

	DIMENSION	
VECTOR	1	2
1	.0835	-.9965
2	-.3974	-.9176
3	.9587	.2846
4	-.9419	-.3360
5	.1322	-.9912

TABLE 3. COSINE OF ANGLES BETWEEN VECTORS

VECTOR:	1	2	3	4
2	.881			
3	-.203	-.642		
4	.256	.683	-.999	
5	.999	.857	-.155	.209

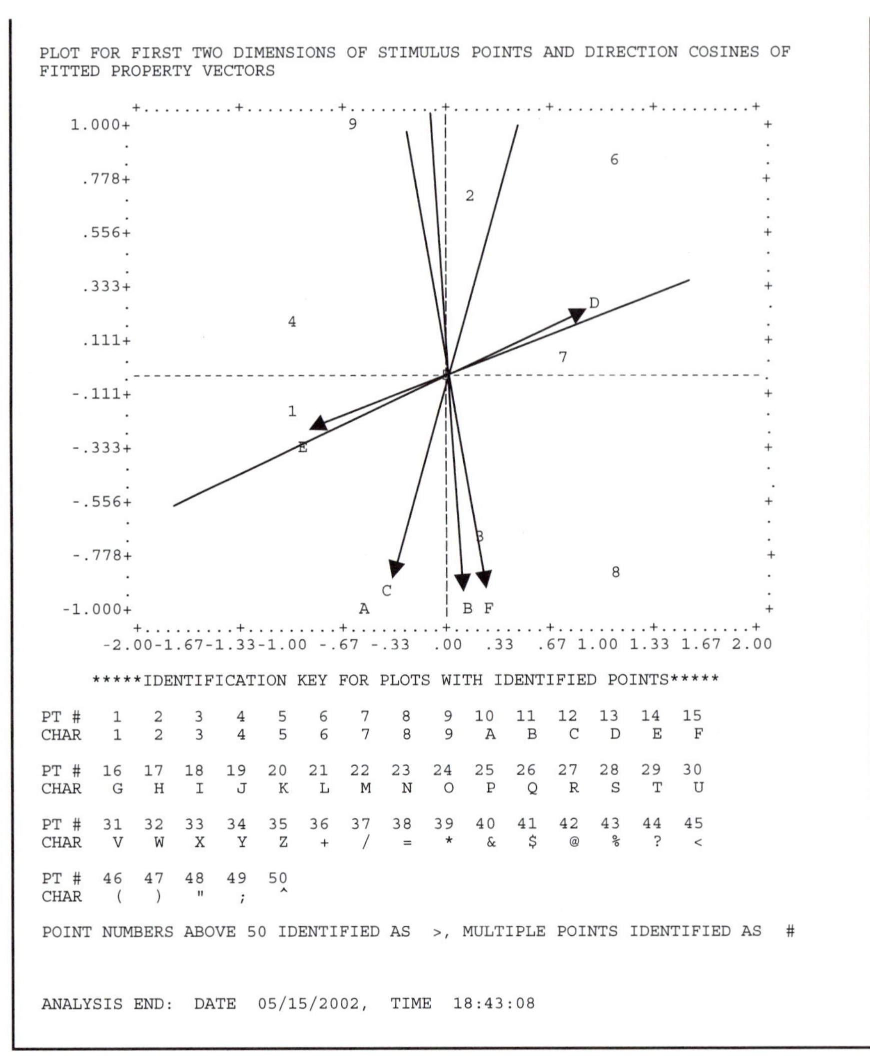

```
PLOT FOR FIRST TWO DIMENSIONS OF STIMULUS POINTS AND DIRECTION COSINES OF
FITTED PROPERTY VECTORS
```



```
*****IDENTIFICATION KEY FOR PLOTS WITH IDENTIFIED POINTS*****

PT #    1   2   3   4   5   6   7   8   9  10  11  12  13  14  15
CHAR    1   2   3   4   5   6   7   8   9   A   B   C   D   E   F

PT #   16  17  18  19  20  21  22  23  24  25  26  27  28  29  30
CHAR    G   H   I   J   K   L   M   N   O   P   Q   R   S   T   U

PT #   31  32  33  34  35  36  37  38  39  40  41  42  43  44  45
CHAR    V   W   X   Y   Z   +   /   =   *   &   $   @   %   ?   <

PT #   46  47  48  49  50
CHAR    (   )   "   ;   ^

POINT NUMBERS ABOVE 50 IDENTIFIED AS  >, MULTIPLE POINTS IDENTIFIED AS  #


ANALYSIS END:  DATE  05/15/2002,  TIME  18:43:08
```

Fig. 9.6 Output example for INDSCAL (examp9-3.out).

This plot indicates that the *Y* dimension (dimension 2) is closely related to Weight and Power and also, although not as strongly, to Design (the higher the values of the properties, the lower the perceptions on that dimension). The *X* dimension (dimension 1) reflects more the volume, which appears to be negatively correlated with the maximum frequency. Therefore, generally, the higher the perceptual value on dimension 1, the higher the volume but the lower the maximum frequency. It should be noted that these can be used only to help the interpretation of the dimensions. However, the dimensions and the properties do not coincide perfectly. For example, although the vectors *B* and *F* are particularly close to axis *Y*, Axis *X* is not very close to either vector

D or *E*. Consequently, the property fitting analysis will not be as useful to interpret the *X* axis as it will be for the *Y* axis.

9.5.4 Example of MDPREF

The first row in the input file shown in Figure 9.7 defines:

- the number of rows in the data matrix, or number of subjects (there are 5 subjects in this example);
- the number of columns in the data matrix, or number of stimuli (there are 10 brands shown in Figure 9.7);
- number of dimensions (2 in this example);
- number of dimensions to be plotted (2);
- a code to normalize by subtracting the row mean (= 1) or to normalize and divide by the standard deviation (= 2);
- a dummy code to normalize subject vectors (= 1; 0 otherwise).

The second line defines the format in which the preference data are read, followed by the data themselves. The first number of each row is the subject number, which is not read by the program, as indicated by the format statement starting with 2*X*. For each row (subject), the ten numbers indicate the values given by the subject to each of the 10 brands.

```
5 10 2 2 1 0
(2X,10F3.0)
01 41 39 62 47 46 40 68 43 43 26
02 70 38 47 28 59 70 46 28 28 67
03 30 72 95 78 58 25 84 81 81 02
04 30 83 84 76 66 24 73 81 82 00
05 78 16 18 00 41 84 17 00 00 87
subj1
subj2
subj3
subj4
subj5
sama
salt
semi
self
sibi
siro
sono
sold
suli
susi
```

Fig. 9.7 Example of PC-MDS input file for MDPREF (examp9-4.dat).

The following lines are used for the labels of the subjects and then of the stimuli.

The first graph in the output file maps the subject vectors starting at the origin with the end point at the location of the number corresponding to the subject. The second graph maps the stimuli according to their preferences, while the third graph shows both the subject vectors and the stimuli points at the same time. Given that the sole input concerns preferences, this plot of the brands should be carefully interpreted, as it does not correspond to perceptual data but is only derived from preferences.

On the graphs shown in Figure 9.8, the vectors have been added to the original output. The projections of the stimuli on a particular subject vector indicate the preferences of that individual subject. For example, subject 1 (indicated by the letter B on Figure 9.8) has a preference for brands 3 (SEMI) and 7 (SONO). Subject 5 (letter F on Figure 9.8) prefers brand 10 (SUSI; indicated by the letter A) and then brands 1 (SAMA) and 6 (SIRO), both confounded on the map and represented by the symbol "#". The least preferred brands for this subject are brands 2 (SALT), 8 (SOLD) and 9 (SULI), these last two brands being confounded on the map and represented by the # sign in the lower right quadrant.

```
                          M D P R E F
            MULTIDIMENSIONAL ANALYSIS OF PREFERENCE DATA
      PROGRAM WRITTEN BY DR. J. D. CARROLL AND JIH JIE CHANG
                       PC - MDS VERSION




. ANALYSIS START:  DATE  07/04/2002,  TIME  10:56:38

 ANALYSIS TITLE: MDPref example, Chapter 9
 DATA IS READ FROM FILE: mdprf_t.dat
 OUTPUT FILE IS: mdprf_t.out


 NP (NO. OF VECTORS (SUBJECTS))                                    5
 NS (NO. OF POINTS  (STIMULI))                                    10
 NF (NO. OF DIMENSIONS)                                            2
 NFP (NO. OF DIMENSIONS PLOTTED)                                   2

 IREAD  1=NP X NS SCORE MATRIX WITH ROW MEAN SUBTRACTED            1
        2=SAME AS 1 WITH SCORES DIVIDED BY ROW S. D.

 NORP   0=NORMALIZE SUBJ. VECTORS                                  0
        1=DO NOT
```

```
INPUT FORMAT = (2X,10F3.0)

DATA FOR RECORD:      1
.41E+02 .39E+02 .62E+02 .47E+02 .46E+02 .40E+02 .68E+02 .43E+02 .43E+02 .26E+02

DATA FOR RECORD:      5
.78E+02 .16E+02 .18E+02 .00E+00 .41E+02 .84E+02 .17E+02 .00E+00 .00E+00 .87E+02

                        MEAN OF THE RAW SCORES  (BY SUBJECT)

         45.5000     48.1000     60.6000     59.9000     34.1000

                        FIRST SCORE MATRIX   (SUBJECT  BY  STIMULUS)

   1     -4.5000     -6.5000     16.5000      1.5000       .5000     -5.5000
         22.5000     -2.5000     -2.5000    -19.5000

   2     21.9000    -10.1000     -1.1000    -20.1000     10.9000     21.9000
         -2.1000    -20.1000    -20.1000     18.9000

   3    -30.6000     11.4000     34.4000     17.4000     -2.6000    -35.6000
         23.4000     20.4000     20.4000    -58.6000

   4    -29.9000     23.1000     24.1000     16.1000      6.1000    -35.9000
         13.1000     21.1000     22.1000    -59.9000

   5     43.9000    -18.1000    -16.1000    -34.1000      6.9000     49.9000
        -17.1000    -34.1000    -34.1000     52.9000

                        CROSS PRODUCT MATRIX OF SUBJECTS

   1   1266.5000   -511.5000   2419.0000   1961.5000  -1913.5000

   2   -511.5000   2754.9000  -3957.6000  -3985.9000   5421.9000

   3   2419.0000  -3957.6000   8640.4000   8247.6000  -9382.6010

   4   1961.5000  -3985.9000   8247.6000   8286.9000  -9282.8990

   5  -1913.5000   5421.9000  -9382.6010  -9282.8990  11630.9000

                        CORRELATION MATRIX OF SUBJECTS

   1      1.0000     -.2738       .7313       .6055      -.4986

   2      -.2738     1.0000      -.8112      -.8342       .9578

   3       .7313     -.8112      1.0000       .9747      -.9359

   4       .6055     -.8342       .9747      1.0000      -.9455

   5      -.4986      .9578      -.9359      -.9455      1.0000
```

CROSS PRODUCT MATRIX OF STIMULI

```
 1   4257.4400  -2026.0600  -2578.3600  -2957.7600    436.5401   4857.7400
    -2005.6600  -3181.0600  -3210.9600   6408.1400

 2  -2026.0600   1135.4400   1144.1400   1380.7400   -126.9600  -2323.7600
      753.8400   1556.4400   1579.5400  -3073.3600

 3  -2578.3600   1144.1400   2296.8400   1582.4400    -57.2600  -3008.0600
     1769.5400   1740.1400   1764.2400  -4653.6600

 4  -2957.7600   1380.7400   1582.4400   2131.0400   -400.6601  -3347.4600
     1277.1400   2257.7400   2273.8400  -4197.0600

 5    436.5401   -126.9600    -57.2600   -400.6601    210.6400    453.8401
     -110.5600   -379.9601   -373.8600    348.2401

 6   4857.7400  -2323.7600  -3008.0600  -3347.4600    453.8401   5556.0400
    -2326.3600  -3611.7600  -3647.6600   7397.4400

 7  -2005.6600    753.8400   1769.5400   1277.1400   -110.5600  -2326.3600
     1522.2400   1322.8400   1335.9400  -3538.9600

 8  -3181.0600   1556.4400   1740.1400   2257.7400   -379.9601  -3611.7600
     1322.8400   2434.4400   2455.5400  -4594.3600

 9  -3210.9600   1579.5400   1764.2400   2273.8400   -373.8600  -3647.6600
     1335.9400   2455.5400   2477.6400  -4654.2600

10   6408.1400  -3073.3600  -4653.6600  -4197.0600    348.2401   7397.4400
    -3538.9600  -4594.3600  -4654.2600  10557.8400
```

ROOTS OF THE FIRST SCORE MATRIX

```
    30298.1700   1799.9580    417.2757     50.7452     13.4566
```

PROPORTION OF VARIANCE ACCOUNTED FOR BY EACH FACTOR

```
        1            2            3            4            5
     .9300        .0552        .0128        .0016        .0004
```

CUMULATIVE PROPORTION OF VARIANCE ACCOUNTED FOR

```
        1            2            3            4            5
     .9300        .9852        .9980        .9996       1.0000
```

SECOND SCORE MATRIX (SUBJECT BY STIMULUS)

```
 1       -.0914       -.0220        .5479       -.0747        .1387       -.1508
          .4424       -.0662       -.0610       -.6630

 2        .4172       -.2344       -.0098       -.3569        .1138        .4534
          .0036       -.3786       -.3794        .3712
```

```
  3      -.3292       .1409       .3360       .1897       .0086      -.3888
          .2637       .2091       .2128      -.6428

  4      -.3536       .1610       .2882       .2241      -.0125      -.4107
          .2243       .2444       .2477      -.6129

  5       .3972      -.2029      -.1602      -.2976       .0631       .4460
         -.1191      -.3193      -.3215       .5143


POPULATION MATRIX (VECTORS)

FACTOR

  1       .6395       .7688
  2      -.9089       .4171
  3       .9821       .1882
  4       .9961       .0877
  5      -.9872       .1593


NORMALIZED STIMULUS MATRIX (POINTS)

FACTOR

  1      -.3717       .1903
  2       .1771      -.1759
  3       .2445       .5093
  4       .2519      -.3067
  5      -.0307       .2059
  6      -.4262       .1583
  7       .1883       .4189
  8       .2729      -.3131
  9       .2758      -.3087
 10      -.5820      -.3783


STIMULUS MATRIX (STRETCHED BY SQ. ROOT OF THE EIGENVALUES)

FACTOR

  1    -64.6951      8.0733
  2     30.8328     -7.4634
  3     42.5580     21.6070
  4     43.8507    -13.0122
  5     -5.3419      8.7374
  6    -74.1819      6.7176
  7     32.7685     17.7715
  8     47.4974    -13.2833
  9     48.0113    -13.0977
 10   -101.2998    -16.0502
```

```
*****IDENTIFICATION KEY FOR PLOTS WITH IDENTIFIED POINTS*****
```

PT #	1	2	3	4	5	6	7	8	9	10	11	12	13	14	15
CHAR	1	2	3	4	5	6	7	8	9	A	B	C	D	E	F
PT #	16	17	18	19	20	21	22	23	24	25	26	27	28	29	30
CHAR	G	H	I	J	K	L	M	N	O	P	Q	R	S	T	U
PT #	31	32	33	34	35	36	37	38	39	40	41	42	43	44	45
CHAR	V	W	X	Y	Z	+	/	=	*	&	$	@	%	?	<
PT #	46	47	48	49	50										
CHAR	(	)	"	;	@										

```
POINT NUMBERS ABOVE 50 IDENTIFIED AS  >, MULTIPLE POINTS IDENTIFIED AS  #

IN JOINT SPACE PLOTS, THE FIRST  10 POINTS ARE STIMULI AND THE NEXT   5
ARE VECTOR (SUBJECT) END POINTS.
```

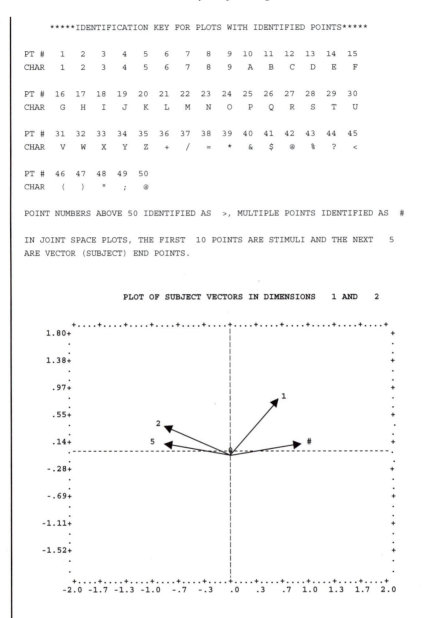

PLOT OF SUBJECT VECTORS IN DIMENSIONS 1 AND 2

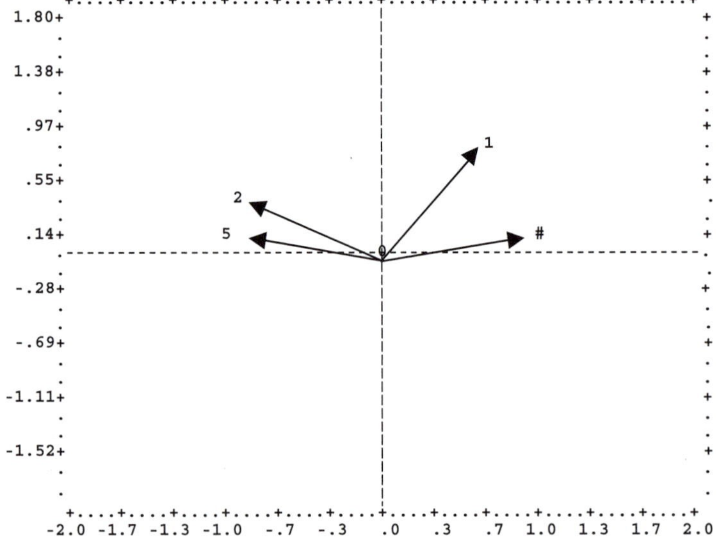

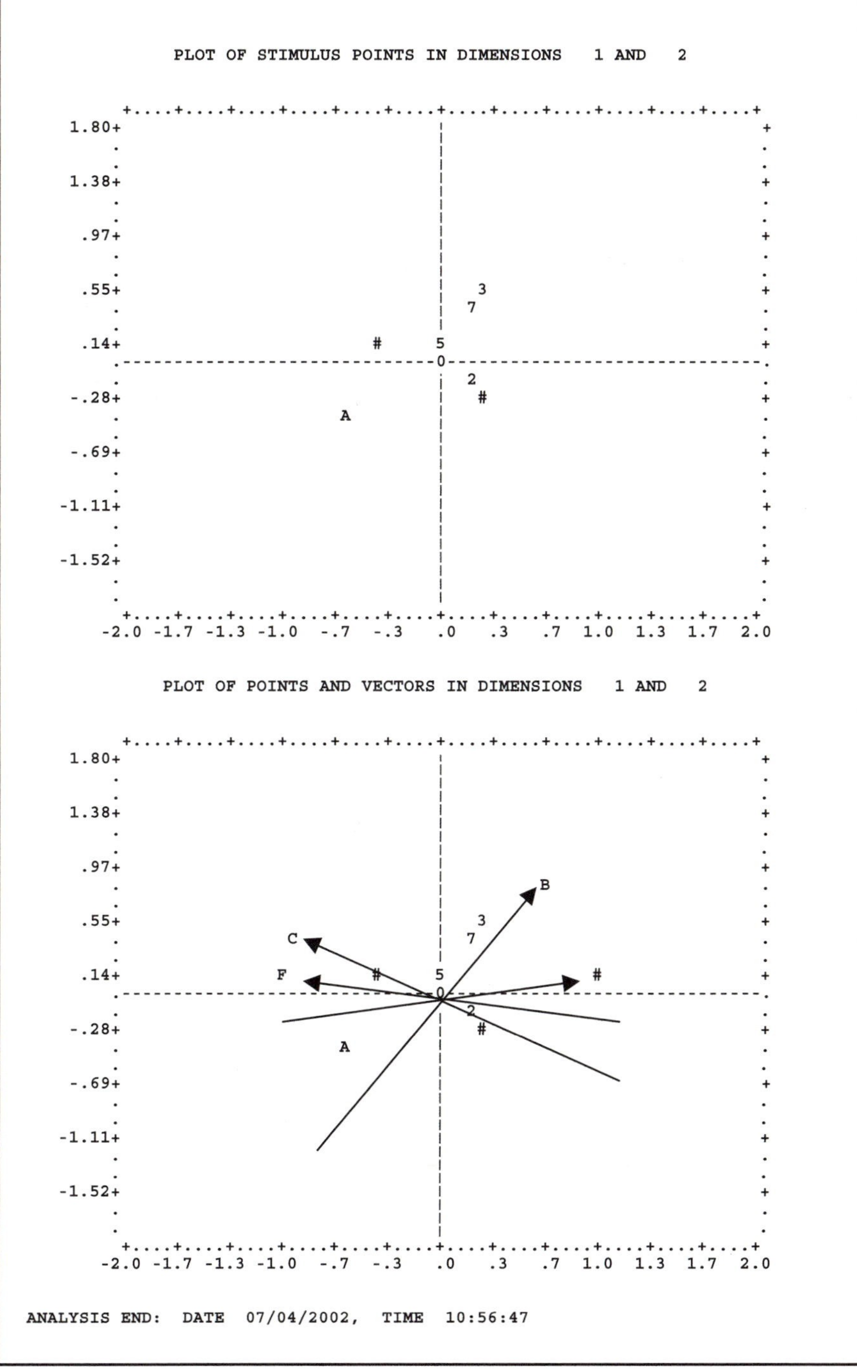

Fig. 9.8 Output example for MDPREF (examp9-4.out).

9.5.5 Example of PREFMAP

In the example provided in Figure 9.9, the external source of the perceptual space configuration has been taken from the INDSCAL run. The first line of input in that file allows the user to define the various parameters concerning the data and the analysis to be done:

- the number of stimuli (here 10 brands)
- the number of dimensions of the externally supplied perceptual space (here 2)
- the number of subjects for which preferences are being modeled (here 5)

```
  10   2   5   0   1   0   2   4   0   1   1  15   0   0  1
 (2X,2F8.3)
 1    0.410    0.412  sama
 2   -0.222    0.191  salt
 3   -0.146   -0.275  semi
 4   -0.312   -0.366  self
 5    0.039    0.318  sibi
 6    0.471    0.358  siro
 7   -0.102   -0.420  sono
 8   -0.313   -0.242  sold
 9   -0.311   -0.231  suli
10    0.486    0.256  susi
(2X,10F4.0)
01 059 061 038 053 054 060 032 057 057 074
02 030 062 053 072 041 030 054 072 072 033
03 070 028 005 022 042 075 016 019 019 098
04 070 017 016 024 034 076 027 019 018 100
05 022 084 082 100 059 016 083 100 100 013
sama
salt
semi
self
sibi
siro
sono
sold
suli
susi
SUBJ1
SUBJ2
SUBJ3
SUBJ4
SUBJ5
```

Fig. 9.9 Example of PC-MDS input file for PREFMAP (examp9-5.dat).

– a code to indicate that the higher the score of a brand in the data, the higher the preference for that brand (code = 1) or that the higher the score, the lower the preference (code = 0); in the example, preferences are decreasing with the ratings and, therefore, a code 0 has been entered.

These numbers are followed by additional codes corresponding to advanced setting options.

The second line of input gives the format in which the coordinates in the perceptual space will be read. Then follow these coordinates for the ten stimuli/brands. Note that, given the format provided, the stimulus number (the first number on each of the line for the coordinates) is not read by the program.

Then follows the format in which the preference data will be read. These preference data correspond to the ones described for the input of MDPREF. Therefore, the preference ratings of the ten brands are shown for each of the four subjects studied. Finally, the stimuli labels (brand names) are indicated.

The results are shown in Figure 9.10. Phase 1 corresponds to the general unfolding model where the axes may be rotated differently for each subject and where each subject can weight each axis differently. Although it makes the visualization difficult, due to the different rotation of the axes, this is the most flexible model. It should be noted that there is one more point for subjects than there are subjects. This last point corresponds to the average preference (average ratings) across all the subjects.

Phase 2 corresponds to the weighted unfolding model wherein all subjects share the same configuration without rotation but each subject is allowed to weight each dimension differently. The preferences of each subject are shown by his/her ideal point in that common perceptual space.

In Phase 3, each subject uses the same perceptual space configuration with no axis rotation and no differential weighting of the dimensions.

Finally, Phase 4 corresponds to the vector model of preferences, similarly to MDPREF, except for the fact that the perceptual configuration is externally provided. Here is an example from the INDSCAL analysis.

The plot resulting from the analysis of Phase 3 provides the ideal points of the five subjects, as well as that of the average subject. This plot shows that subject 4 (represented by the letter D) prefers brands 2 (SALT), 3 (SEMI), 8 (SOLD) or 9 (SULI) best (the closests to his/her ideal brand). This fits the preference data used as input, where these brands have a low score value (most preferred).

For the vector model of preferences, the last graph shows the end points of the individual vectors. The vectors drawn on Figure 9.10 have been added to the original output, showing the differences in preferences across individuals according to the projections of the stimuli on their respective vectors. For example, the projections of the brands on the vectors of subjects 2 (C) and 5 (F), indicate that brands 1 (SAMA), 6 (SIRO) and 10 (SUSI; indicated by the letter A on the plot) are the prefered ones. These correspond indeed to the lowest scores (most preferred) in the input data.

```
                              P R E F M A P
          MDSCALING VIA A GENERALIZATION OF COOMBS UNFOLDING MODEL
                  BY DR. J. D. CARROLL AND JIH JIE CHANG
                            PC - MDS VERSION

ANALYSIS START:  DATE  07/03/2002,  TIME  18:37:47

ANALYSIS TITLE: Prefmap example, Chapter 9
DATA IS READ FROM FILE: prefv_t.dat
OUTPUT FILE IS: prefv_t.out

******************************************************************************

 N         NO. OF STIMULI                                          10
 K         NO. OF DIMENSIONS                                        2
 NSUB      NO. OF SUBJECTS                                          5
 ISV     0=SMALL SCALE VALUE REPRESENTS GREATER PREF.               0
 NORS    1=NORMALIZE SCALE VALUES                                   1
 IRX     0=STIMULUS COORDINATES N BY K, OR 1 = K BY N               0
 IPS       STARTING PHASE                                           2
 IPE       ENDING PHASE                                             4
 IRWT    1=READ IN WEIGHTS,  0=NO WEIGHTS READ IN                   0
 LFITSW    HOW D**2 IS RELATED TO SCALE VALUES                      1
         0=LINEARLY,
         1=MONOTONE WITH NO TIES,
         2=BLOCK MONOTONE WITH ORDERING IN BLOCKS
         3=BLOCK MONOTONE WITH EQUALITY IN BLOCKS
 IAV     0=AVERAGE SUBJECTS COMPUTED ONCE FOR ALL PHASES,           1
         1=CALCULATE EACH PHASE
 MAXIT     MAXIMUM ITERATIONS, WHEN 0 IT IS SET TO 15              15
 ISHAT   0=USE SCALE VALUES FROM PREVIOUS PHASE,                    0
         1=USE ORIG VALUES
 IPLOT   0=AVERAGE SUBJECTS,                                        0
         1=AVERAGE SUBJECTS & SUBJECT FUNCTIONS,
         2=ALL PLOTS
 CRIT      CRITERIA FOR STOPPING MONOTONE FIT                       .0010

******************************************************************************

   *****IDENTIFICATION KEY FOR PLOTS WITH IDENTIFIED POINTS*****

PT #   1   2   3   4   5   6   7   8   9  10  11  12  13  14  15
CHAR   1   2   3   4   5   6   7   8   9   A   B   C   D   E   F

PT #  16  17  18  19  20  21  22  23  24  25  26  27  28  29  30
CHAR   G   H   I   J   K   L   M   N   O   P   Q   R   S   T   U

PT #  31  32  33  34  35  36  37  38  39  40  41  42  43  44  45
CHAR   V   W   X   Y   Z   +   /   =   *   &   $   @   %   ?   <

PT #  46  47  48  49  50
CHAR   (   )   "   #   @
```

```
POINT NUMBERS ABOVE 50 IDENTIFIED AS  >, MULTIPLE POINTS IDENTIFIED AS  ;


POINTS 1 TO 10 ARE STIMULI AND POINTS  11 TO   15 ARE IDEAL POINTS

VARIABLE FORMAT (STIMULUS COORDINATES)  =  (2X,2F8.3)

ORIGINAL CONFIGURATION  (X MATRIX)


    1    .41000    .41200
    2  -.22200    .19100
    3  -.14600   -.27500
    4  -.31200   -.36600
    5    .03900    .31800
    6    .47100    .35800
    7  -.10200   -.42000
    8  -.31300   -.24200
    9  -.31100   -.23100
   10    .48600    .25600

VARIABLE FORMAT  (SCALE VALUES) = (2X,10F4.0)

PHASE  2

X MATRIX, (INPUT CONFIGURATION AFTER NORMALIZATION)
  1       .4100      -.2220      -.1460      -.3120       .0390       .4710
         -.1020      -.3130      -.3110       .4860
  2       .4120       .1910      -.2750      -.3660       .3180       .3580
         -.4200      -.2420      -.2310       .2560

PHASE  2

SUBJECT   1

SCALE VALUES BEFORE NORMALIZATION FOR SUBJECT    1
      59.00000    61.00000    38.00000    53.00000    54.00000    60.00000
      32.00000    57.00000    57.00000    74.00000

S (VECTOR OF SCALE VALUES, E.G. PREFERENCES)
        .12645      .18265     -.46364     -.04215     -.01405      .15455
       -.63224      .07025      .07025      .54794

BEGIN ITERATION ON MONOTONE FIT
END OF ITERATION, REACHED CRITERION

BETA VALUES  (IN THE MOST GENERAL CASE THERE ARE (2K + K(K-1)/2 + 1) TERMS -
QUADRATIC, LINEAR, THEN A CONSTANT TERM)
       -.13961     -.72085      .81888     3.30984    -1.91886

(CORRELATION)=      .99947
```

```
SIGNED DSQ, (SIGNED DISTANCE SQUARED FROM STIMULI TO IDEAL)
      .22438      .36144      -.24263      -.05777      -.00483      .39385
     -.62257      .19123       .20465       .46720

******************************************************************************

SUBJECT     1

COORDINATES OF IDEAL POINT WITH RESPECT TO OLD AXES
            .10889           .21338

IMPORTANCES OF NEW AXES
           3.30984         -1.91886

******************************************************************************

SUBJECT   2

SCALE VALUES BEFORE NORMALIZATION FOR SUBJECT     2
     30.00000    62.00000    53.00000    72.00000    41.00000    30.00000
     54.00000    72.00000    72.00000    33.00000

S (VECTOR OF SCALE VALUES, E.G. PREFERENCES)
      -.41725      .19243      .02096      .38295      -.20767      -.41725
       .04001      .38295      .38295     -.36009

BEGIN ITERATION ON MONOTONE FIT
END OF ITERATION, REACHED CRITERION

BETA VALUES  (IN THE MOST GENERAL CASE THERE ARE (2K + K(K-1)/2 + 1) TERMS -
QUADRATIC, LINEAR, THEN A CONSTANT TERM)
      -.17419    -1.21683     -.04638     1.55564      .18543

(CORRELATION)=        .99931

SIGNED DSQ, (SIGNED DISTANCE SQUARED FROM STIMULI TO IDEAL)
       .01582      .58556      .47845      .81375      .19976      .01999
       .43334      .79621      .79036      .01719

******************************************************************************

SUBJECT     2

COORDINATES OF IDEAL POINT WITH RESPECT TO OLD AXES
            .39110           .12507

IMPORTANCES OF NEW AXES
           1.55564           .18543

******************************************************************************
```

```
SUBJECT   3

SCALE VALUES BEFORE NORMALIZATION FOR SUBJECT    3
      70.00000      28.00000       5.00000      22.00000      42.00000      75.00000
      16.00000      19.00000      19.00000      98.00000

S (VECTOR OF SCALE VALUES, E.G. PREFERENCES)
        .32920       -.12264       -.37008       -.18719        .02797        .38299
       -.25174       -.21946       -.21946        .63042

BEGIN ITERATION ON MONOTONE FIT
END OF ITERATION, REACHED CRITERION

BETA VALUES  (IN THE MOST GENERAL CASE THERE ARE (2K + K(K-1)/2 + 1) TERMS -
QUADRATIC, LINEAR, THEN A CONSTANT TERM)
       -.15664        .48421        .24583       1.52976        .03537

(CORRELATION)=        .99909

SIGNED DSQ, (SIGNED DISTANCE SQUARED FROM STIMULI TO IDEAL)
       1.02841        .48159        .36244        .37805        .56841       1.12542
        .33497        .40634        .40792       1.12735

********************************************************************************

SUBJECT     3

COORDINATES OF IDEAL POINT WITH RESPECT TO OLD AXES
            -.15826       -3.47505

IMPORTANCES OF NEW AXES
            1.52976         .03537

********************************************************************************

SUBJECT   4

SCALE VALUES BEFORE NORMALIZATION FOR SUBJECT    4
      70.00000      17.00000      16.00000      24.00000      34.00000      76.00000
      27.00000      19.00000      18.00000     100.00000

S (VECTOR OF SCALE VALUES, E.G. PREFERENCES)
        .32845       -.25376       -.26474       -.17686       -.06701        .39437
       -.14390       -.23179       -.24277        .65801

BEGIN ITERATION ON MONOTONE FIT
END OF ITERATION, REACHED CRITERION

BETA VALUES  (IN THE MOST GENERAL CASE THERE ARE (2K + K(K-1)/2 + 1) TERMS -
QUADRATIC, LINEAR, THEN A CONSTANT TERM)
       -.12124        .76701       -.06093       1.39435       -.18300

(CORRELATION)=        .99917
```

```
SIGNED DSQ, (SIGNED DISTANCE SQUARED FROM STIMULI TO IDEAL)
        .59310      -.01946       .02106      -.00538       .09456       .72572
        .02999       .00097       .00104       .77492

******************************************************************************


SUBJECT     4

COORDINATES OF IDEAL POINT WITH RESPECT TO OLD AXES
           -.27504        -.16648

IMPORTANCES OF NEW AXES
           1.39435        -.18300

******************************************************************************


SUBJECT   5

SCALE VALUES BEFORE NORMALIZATION FOR SUBJECT    5
      22.00000     84.00000     82.00000    100.00000     59.00000     16.00000
      83.00000    100.00000    100.00000     13.00000

S (VECTOR OF SCALE VALUES, E.G. PREFERENCES)
       -.40706       .16783       .14929       .31619      -.06398      -.46269
        .15856       .31619       .31619      -.49051

BEGIN ITERATION ON MONOTONE FIT

AVERAGE SUBJECT

S (VECTOR OF SCALE VALUES, E.G. PREFERENCES)
        .02086       .05391      -.12695       .02712      -.11193       .08604
       -.19693       .06852       .06852       .11084

BETA VALUES  (IN THE MOST GENERAL CASE THERE ARE (2K + K(K-1)/2 + 1) TERMS -
QUADRATIC, LINEAR, THEN A CONSTANT TERM)
       -.13147      -.34136       .18293      1.57832      -.26520

(CORRELATION)=         .99884

SIGNED DSQ, (SIGNED DISTANCE SQUARED FROM STIMULI TO IDEAL)
        .14262       .16575       .00004       .14458       .00735       .20777
       -.08546       .18859       .18933       .22325

******************************************************************************


SUBJECT     6

COORDINATES OF IDEAL POINT WITH RESPECT TO OLD AXES
            .10814         .34488
```

```
IMPORTANCES OF NEW AXES
           1.57832        -.26520

*****************************************************************************

PHASE  3

X MATRIX, (INPUT CONFIGURATION AFTER NORMALIZATION)
  1       .5151      -.2789      -.1834      -.3920       .0490       .5917
         -.1281      -.3932      -.3907       .6106
  2       .2122       .0984      -.1416      -.1885       .1638       .1844
         -.2163      -.1246      -.1190       .1318

PHASE  3

SUBJECT   1

S (VECTOR OF SCALE VALUES, E.G. PREFERENCES)
       .13300       .28639      -.33440      -.14939      -.09641       .28639
      -.71466       .10653       .10653       .37602


BEGIN ITERATION ON MONOTONE FIT
END OF ITERATION, REACHED CRITERION

BETA VALUES  (IN THE MOST GENERAL CASE THERE ARE (2K + K(K-1)/2 + 1) TERMS -
QUADRATIC, LINEAR, THEN A CONSTANT TERM)
      -.31127      -.83629      1.99854      2.36724

(CORRELATION)=         .99951

SIGNED DSQ, (SIGNED DISTANCE SQUARED FROM STIMULI TO IDEAL)
       .16681       .24310      -.44543      -.11724      -.11944       .27404
      -.74493       .06110       .06892       .24625

*****************************************************************************

SUBJECT     1

COORDINATES OF IDEAL POINT WITH RESPECT TO OLD AXES
            .17664         .42212

IMPORTANCES OF NEW AXES
           2.36724       -2.36724

*****************************************************************************

SUBJECT   2

S (VECTOR OF SCALE VALUES, E.G. PREFERENCES)
      -.39970       .17073       .04090       .39919      -.21554      -.39693
       .04090       .37870       .37870      -.39693
```

```
BEGIN ITERATION ON MONOTONE FIT
END OF ITERATION, REACHED CRITERION

BETA VALUES  (IN THE MOST GENERAL CASE THERE ARE (2K + K(K-1)/2 + 1) TERMS -
QUADRATIC, LINEAR, THEN A CONSTANT TERM)
       -.11185      -.87503      -.23917       .85102

(CORRELATION)=        .99876

SIGNED DSQ, (SIGNED DISTANCE SQUARED FROM STIMULI TO IDEAL)
       -.10586       .48661       .41405       .69670       .10530      -.08470
        .34614       .70038       .69633      -.05521

******************************************************************************


SUBJECT     2

COORDINATES OF IDEAL POINT WITH RESPECT TO OLD AXES
             .51410        -.14052

IMPORTANCES OF NEW AXES
             .85102        -.85102

******************************************************************************


SUBJECT   3

S (VECTOR OF SCALE VALUES, E.G. PREFERENCES)
        .40689      -.14069      -.27377      -.22496      -.05375       .50402
       -.27377      -.22496      -.22496       .50596

BEGIN ITERATION ON MONOTONE FIT

SUBJECT   4

S (VECTOR OF SCALE VALUES, E.G. PREFERENCES)
        .37192      -.22229      -.22229      -.22229      -.12725       .50470
       -.19190      -.22229      -.22229       .55396

BEGIN ITERATION ON MONOTONE FIT

SUBJECT   5

S (VECTOR OF SCALE VALUES, E.G. PREFERENCES)
       -.40780       .17542       .15478       .33307      -.06671      -.46796
        .15478       .30461       .30461      -.48483

BEGIN ITERATION ON MONOTONE FIT

AVERAGE SUBJECT
```

```
S (VECTOR OF SCALE VALUES, E.G. PREFERENCES)
       .02402        .05482       -.13502        .03375       -.10786        .08389
      -.19180        .06715        .06715        .10390

BETA VALUES  (IN THE MOST GENERAL CASE THERE ARE (2K + K(K-1)/2 + 1) TERMS -
QUADRATIC, LINEAR, THEN A CONSTANT TERM)
      -.12947       -.27321        .36106        .98483

(CORRELATION)=        .99713

SIGNED DSQ, (SIGNED DISTANCE SQUARED FROM STIMULI TO IDEAL)
       .13869        .16465       -.00178        .14122        .00755        .20210
      -.08713        .18528        .18606        .21666

*******************************************************************************


SUBJECT     6

COORDINATES OF IDEAL POINT WITH RESPECT TO OLD AXES
             .13871         .18331

IMPORTANCES OF NEW AXES
             .98483        -.98483

*******************************************************************************

STIMULI COORDINATES
DIMENSION        1              2
STIMULI
  1             .51509         .21217
  2           -.27890          .09836
  3           -.18342        -.14162
  4           -.39197        -.18848
  5             .04900         .16376
  6             .59172         .18436
  7           -.12814        -.21629
  8           -.39323        -.12463
  9           -.39071        -.11896
 10             .61057         .13183


COORDINATES OF IDEAL POINTS

DIMENSION        1              2
SUBJECTS
  1             .17664         .42212
  2             .51410        -.14052
  3           -.24813          .22016
  4           -.33261         -.04437
  5          -7.43571         2.44479
  6             .13871         .18331
```

```
SUBJECT   6 IS THE AVERAGE SUBJECT

WEIGHTS OF AXES
DIMENSION        1             2
SUBJECTS
  1          2.36724      -2.36724
  2           .85102       -.85102
  3           .89211       -.89211
  4           .89720       -.89720
  5          -.04765        .04765
  6           .98483       -.98483

SUBJECT   6 IS THE AVERAGE SUBJECT



    STIMULI AND IDEAL POINTS:  Prefmap example, Chapter 9

        .*....*....*....*....*....*....*....*....*....*....*....*....*
    1.50**                             |                             **
    1.38**                             |                             **
    1.27**                             |                             **
    1.15**                             |                             **
    1.04**                             |                             **
     .92**                             |                             **
     .81**                             |                             **
     .69**                             |                             **
     .58**                             |                             **
     .46**                             |  B                          **
     .35**                             |                             **
     .23**                        D    | G     16                    **
     .12**                        2    |5       A                    **
     .00**----------------------E----0---------------------------**
    -.12**                      ;  3   |       C                     **
    -.23**                      4    7 |                             **
    -.35**                             |                             **
    -.46**                             |                             **
    -.58**                             |                             **
    -.69**                             |                             **
    -.81**                             |                             **
    -.92**                             |                             **
   -1.04**                             |                             **
   -1.15**                             |                             **
   -1.27**                             |                             **
   -1.38**                             |                             **
   -1.50**                             |                             **
        .*....*....*....*....*....*....*....*....*....*....*....*....*
        .   -1.6667.  -1.0000.   -.3333.    .3333.   1.0000.   1.6667.
       -2.0000   -1.3333    -.6667     .0000     .6667    1.3333    2.0000
```

```
PHASE  4

X MATRIX, (INPUT CONFIGURATION AFTER NORMALIZATION)
  1       .5151      -.2789      -.1834      -.3920        .0490        .5917
        -.1281      -.3932      -.3907       .6106
  2       .2122       .0984      -.1416      -.1885        .1638        .1844
        -.2163      -.1246      -.1190       .1318

PHASE  4

SUBJECT   1

S (VECTOR OF SCALE VALUES, E.G. PREFERENCES)
       -.20366      -.29138       .40907       .08173       .08173      -.29138
        .70881      -.10177      -.10177      -.29138

BEGIN ITERATION ON MONOTONE FIT
END OF ITERATION, REACHED CRITERION

BETA VALUES  (IN THE MOST GENERAL CASE THERE ARE (2K + K(K-1)/2 + 1) TERMS -
QUADRATIC, LINEAR, THEN A CONSTANT TERM)
        .00010       .11482     -1.90631

(CORRELATION)=       .87383

PROJECTIONS ON THE FITTED VECTOR
       -.18082      -.11495       .13034       .16458      -.16052      -.14845
        .20820       .10076       .09525      -.09489

SUBJECT   2

S (VECTOR OF SCALE VALUES, E.G. PREFERENCES)
        .42686      -.16703      -.06027      -.37874       .21519       .40565
       -.06027      -.37874      -.37874       .37609

BEGIN ITERATION ON MONOTONE FIT
END OF ITERATION, REACHED CRITERION

BETA VALUES  (IN THE MOST GENERAL CASE THERE ARE (2K + K(K-1)/2 + 1) TERMS -
QUADRATIC, LINEAR, THEN A CONSTANT TERM)
       -.00002       .68450       .33335

(CORRELATION)=       .99939

PROJECTIONS ON THE FITTED VECTOR
        .55599      -.20768      -.22691      -.43493       .11575       .61271
       -.20991      -.40810      -.40336       .60666

SUBJECT   3

S (VECTOR OF SCALE VALUES, E.G. PREFERENCES)
       -.39168       .14174       .26475       .23034       .05320      -.50049
        .26475       .23034       .23034      -.52329
```

```
BEGIN ITERATION ON MONOTONE FIT
END OF ITERATION, REACHED CRITERION

BETA VALUES  (IN THE MOST GENERAL CASE THERE ARE (2K + K(K-1)/2 + 1) TERMS -
QUADRATIC, LINEAR, THEN A CONSTANT TERM)
        .00004      -.48253      -.86681

(CORRELATION) =       .99356

PROJECTIONS ON THE FITTED VECTOR
       -.43592       .04971       .21295       .35533      -.16692      -.44889
        .25131       .30015       .29398      -.41216

SUBJECT   4


S (VECTOR OF SCALE VALUES, E.G. PREFERENCES)
       -.37048       .22038       .22038       .22038       .12371      -.50450
        .20456       .22038       .22038      -.55519

BEGIN ITERATION ON MONOTONE FIT
END OF ITERATION, REACHED CRITERION

BETA VALUES  (IN THE MOST GENERAL CASE THERE ARE (2K + K(K-1)/2 + 1) TERMS -
QUADRATIC, LINEAR, THEN A CONSTANT TERM)
       -.00000      -.80876       .07031

(CORRELATION) =       .98856

PROJECTIONS ON THE FITTED VECTOR
       -.49478       .28637       .17047       .37417      -.03463      -.57353
        .10893       .38095       .37894      -.59685

SUBJECT   5

S (VECTOR OF SCALE VALUES, E.G. PREFERENCES)
        .41885      -.17783      -.15883      -.32247       .06547       .47127
       -.15883      -.30594      -.30594       .47426

BEGIN ITERATION ON MONOTONE FIT

AVERAGE SUBJECT

S (VECTOR OF SCALE VALUES, E.G. PREFERENCES)
       -.06377      -.07260       .11979       .05698      -.00084      -.06240
        .11541      -.01085      -.01085      -.07087

BETA VALUES  (IN THE MOST GENERAL CASE THERE ARE (2K + K(K-1)/2 + 1) TERMS -
QUADRATIC, LINEAR, THEN A CONSTANT TERM)
        .00002       .04867      -.43837

(CORRELATION) =       .81988
```

```
PROJECTIONS ON THE FITTED VECTOR
      -.15404      -.12854       .12052       .14408      -.15736      -.11795
       .20083       .08047       .07512      -.06366
```

```
STIMULI COORDINATES
DIMENSION        1              2
STIMULI
  1            .51509         .21217
  2           -.27890         .09836
  3           -.18342        -.14162
  4           -.39197        -.18848
  5            .04900         .16376
  6            .59172         .18436
  7           -.12814        -.21629
  8           -.39323        -.12463
  9           -.39071        -.11896
 10            .61057         .13183
```

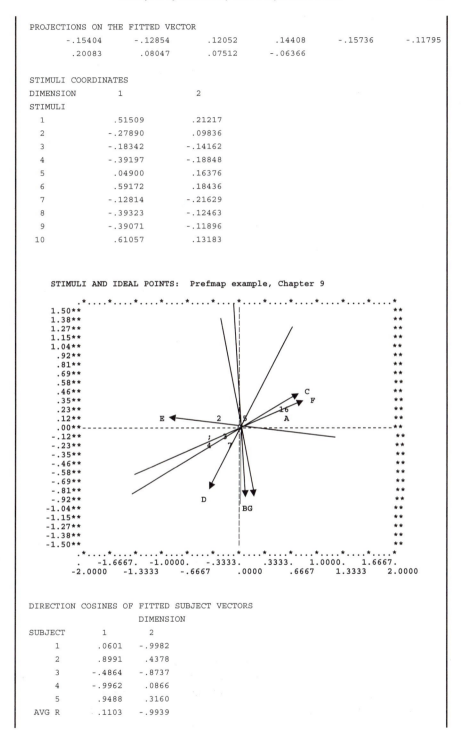

STIMULI AND IDEAL POINTS: Prefmap example, Chapter 9

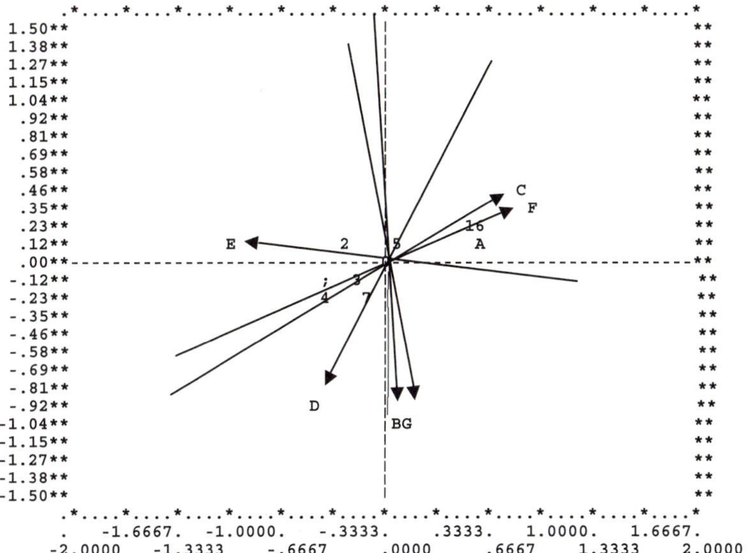


```
DIRECTION COSINES OF FITTED SUBJECT VECTORS
                    DIMENSION
SUBJECT        1         2
     1       .0601    -.9982
     2       .8991     .4378
     3      -.4864    -.8737
     4      -.9962     .0866
     5       .9488     .3160
 AVG R       .1103    -.9939
```

```
          CORRELATION (PHASE)                         F RATIO (PHASE)

          R1        R2        R3        R4        F1        F2        F3        F4

DF                                                5 4       4 5       3 6       2 7
SUBJ
 1         .000      .999     1.000      .874      .000 1177.124 1000.000    11.304
 2         .000      .999      .999      .999      .000  904.412  803.281 2889.408
 3         .000      .999      .998      .994      .000  682.663  642.385  269.136
 4         .000      .999     1.000      .989      .000  752.687 1000.000   150.310
 5         .000      .999     1.000     1.000      .000  765.898 1000.000 1000.000
AVG        .000      .999      .997      .820      .000  537.822  347.263     7.177

          F RATIO (BETWEEN PHASE)
          F12       F13       F14       F23       F24       F34
DF        1 4       2 4       3 4       1 5       2 5       1 6
SUBJ
 1         .000      .000      .000     -.409   554.674 1000.000
 2         .000      .000      .000     3.997     -.309   -3.077
 3         .000      .000      .000     3.491    15.060   18.817
 4         .000      .000      .000    -2.871    31.812 1000.000
 5         .000      .000      .000    -3.122    -1.820 1000.000
AVG        .000      .000      .000     7.348   350.915  337.465

ROOT MEAN SQUARE
PHASE
 1         .000
 2         .999
 3         .999
 4         .972


    AN F - VALUE OF 1000.0 IN THE ABOVE TABLE INDICATES
    A POSSIBLE DIVISION BY ZERO. I.E. R IS VERY CLOSE TO 1.00


NORMAL END OF PROGRAM


ANALYSIS END:  DATE  07/03/2002,  TIME  18:37:48
```

Fig. 9.10 Output example for PREFMAP (examp9-5.out).

9.6 Assignment

Collect proximity data about a set of brands of your choice and determine the dimensions used in the perception of these brands. Gather data about characteristics of these brands to help you interpret the underlying perceptual dimensions. For these same brands, obtain preferences of the respondents in order to develop a map of subject preferences and stimuli.

References

Basic Technical Readings

Carroll, J. D. and P. Arabie (1980), "Multidimensional Scaling," *Annual Review of Psychology*, 31: 607–649.
Kruskal, J. B. and M. Wish (1978), *Multidimensional Scaling*, Beverly Hills, CA: Sage Publications.
Shepard, R. N. (1980), "Multidimensional Scaling, Tree-Fitting, and Clustering," *Science*, 210, 24 (October), 390–398.
Ward, J. (1963), "Hierarchical Grouping to Optimize an Objective Function," *Journal of the American Statistical Association*, 58, 236–244.

Application Readings

Bijmolt, T. H. A. and M. Wedel (1999), "A Comparison of Multidimensional Scaling Methods for Perceptual Mapping," *Journal of Marketing Research*, 36, May, 277–285.
Cooper, L. G. (1983), "A Review of Multidimensional Scaling in Marketing Research," *Applied Psychological Measurement*, 7, 4 (Fall).
DeSarbo, W. S. and G. De Soete (1984), "On the Use of Hierarchical Clustering for the Analysis of Nonsymmetric Proximities," *Journal of Consumer Research*, June, 601–610.
DeSarbo, W. S., M. R. Young and A. Rangaswamy (1997), "A Parametric Multidimensional Unfolding Procedure for Incomplete Nonmetric Preference/Choice Set Data in Marketing Research," *Journal of Marketing Research*, 34, 4 (November), 499–516.
Green, P. E. (1975), "Marketing Applications of MDS: Assessment and Outlook," *Journal of Marketing*, 39 (January), 24–31.
Green, P. E. and F. J. Carmone (1989), "Multidimensional Scaling: An Introduction and Comparison of Nonmetric Unfolding Techniques," *Journal of Marketing Research*, 6 (August), 330–341.
Helsen, K. and P. E. Green (1991), "A Computational Study of Replicated Clustering With an Application to Market Segmentation," *Decision Sciences*, 22, 1124–1141.
Johnson, R. M. (1971), "Market Segmentation: A Strategic Management Tool," *Journal of Marketing Research*, (February), 13–18.
Neidell, L. A. (1969), "The Use of Nonmetric Multidimensional Scaling in Marketing Analysis," *Journal of Marketing*, 33 (October), 37–43.
Sexton, D. E. Jr. (1974), "A Cluster Analytic Approach to Market Response Functions," *Journal of Marketing Research*, February, 109–.
Srivatsava, R. K., R. P. Leone and A. D. Shocker (1981), "Market Structure Analysis: Hierarchical Clustering of Products based on Substitution in Use," *Journal of Marketing*, Summer, 38–48.

Appendices

Appendix A: Rules in Matrix Algebra

Vector and Matrix Differentiation

$$\frac{\partial \mathbf{a}'\mathbf{v}}{\partial \mathbf{v}} = \mathbf{a} \tag{A.1}$$

$$\frac{\partial \mathbf{v}'\mathbf{A}\mathbf{v}}{\partial \mathbf{v}} = (\mathbf{A} + \mathbf{A}')\mathbf{v} \tag{A.2}$$

Kronecker Products

$$\mathbf{A} \otimes \mathbf{B} \tag{A.3}$$

$$\mathbf{A} = \begin{bmatrix} a_{11} & a_{12} \\ a_{21} & a_{22} \end{bmatrix} \tag{A.4}$$

$$\mathbf{A} \otimes \mathbf{B} = \begin{bmatrix} a_{11}\mathbf{B} & a_{12}\mathbf{B} \\ a_{21}\mathbf{B} & a_{22}\mathbf{B} \end{bmatrix} \tag{A.5}$$

$$(\mathbf{A} \otimes \mathbf{B})^{-1} = \mathbf{A}^{-1} \otimes \mathbf{B}^{-1} \tag{A.6}$$

APPENDIX B: Statistical Tables

Cumulative Normal Distribution

z	0.00	0.01	0.02	0.03	0.04	0.05	0.06	0.07	0.08	0.09
0.0	.5000	.5040	.5080	.5120	.5160	.5199	.5239	.5279	.5319	.5359
0.1	.5398	.5438	.5478	.5517	.5557	.5596	.5636	.5675	.5714	.5753
0.2	.5793	.5832	.5871	.5910	.5948	.5987	.6026	.6064	.6103	.6141
0.3	.6179	.6217	.6255	.6293	.6331	.6368	.6406	.6443	.6480	.6517
0.4	.6554	.6591	.6628	.6664	.6700	.6736	.6772	.6808	.6844	.6879
0.5	.6915	.6950	.6985	.7019	.7054	.7088	.7123	.7157	.7190	.7224
0.6	.7257	.7291	.7324	.7357	.7389	.7422	.7454	.7486	.7517	.7549
0.7	.7580	.7611	.7642	.7673	.7704	.7734	.7764	.7794	.7823	.7852
0.8	.7881	.7910	.7939	.7967	.7995	.8023	.8051	.8078	.8106	.8133
0.9	.8159	.8186	.8212	.8238	.8264	.8289	.8315	.8340	.8365	.8389
1.0	.8413	.8438	.8461	.8485	.8508	.8531	.8554	.8577	.8599	.8621
1.1	.8643	.8665	.8686	.8708	.8729	.8749	.8770	.8790	.8810	.8830
1.2	.8849	.8869	.8888	.8907	.8925	.8944	.8962	.8980	.8997	.9015
1.3	.9032	.9049	.9066	.9082	.9099	.9115	.9131	.9147	.9162	.9177
1.4	.9192	.9027	.9222	.9236	.9251	.9265	.9279	.9292	.9306	.9319
1.5	.9332	.9345	.9357	.9370	.9382	.9394	.9406	.9418	.9429	.9441
1.6	.9452	.9463	.9474	.9484	.9495	.9505	.9515	.9525	.9535	.9545
1.7	.9554	.9564	.9573	.9582	.9591	.9599	.9608	.9616	.9625	.9633
1.8	.9641	.9649	.9656	.9664	.9671	.9678	.9686	.9693	.9699	.9706
1.9	.9713	.9719	.9726	.9732	.9738	.9744	.9750	.9756	.9761	.9767
2.0	.9772	.9778	.9783	.9788	.9793	.9798	.9803	.9808	.9812	.9817
2.1	.9821	.9826	.9830	.9834	.9838	.9842	.9846	.9850	.9854	.9857
2.2	.9861	.9864	.9868	.9871	.9875	.9878	.9881	.9884	.9887	.9890
2.3	.9893	.9896	.9898	.9901	.9904	.9906	.9909	.9911	.9913	.9916
2.4	.9918	.9920	.9922	.9925	.9927	.9929	.9931	.9932	.9934	.9936
2.5	.9938	.9940	.9941	.9943	.9945	.9946	.9948	.9949	.9951	.9952
2.6	.9953	.9955	.9956	.9957	.9959	.9960	.9961	.9962	.9963	.9964
2.7	.9965	.9966	.9967	.9968	.9969	.9970	.9971	.9972	.9973	.9974
2.8	.9974	.9975	.9976	.9977	.9977	.9978	.9979	.9979	.9980	.9981
2.9	.9981	.9982	.9982	.9983	.9984	.9984	.9985	.9985	.9986	.9986
3.0	.9987	.9987	.9987	.9988	.9988	.9989	.9989	.9989	.9990	.9990
3.1	.9990	.9991	.9991	.9991	.9992	.9992	.9992	.9992	.9993	.9993
3.2	.9993	.9993	.9994	.9994	.9994	.9994	.9994	.9995	.9995	.9995
3.3	.9995	.9995	.9995	.9996	.9996	.9996	.9996	.9996	.9996	.9997
3.4	.9997	.9997	.9997	.9997	.9997	.9997	.9997	.9997	.9997	.9998

Chi-Squared Distribution

ν	0.005	0.010	0.025	0.050	0.100	0.250	0.500	0.750	0.900	0.950	0.975	0.990	0.995
1	0.00004	0.0002	0.001	0.004	0.02	0.10	0.45	1.32	2.71	3.84	5.02	6.63	7.88
2	0.01	0.02	0.05	0.10	0.21	0.58	1.39	2.77	4.61	5.99	7.38	9.21	10.60
3	0.07	0.11	0.22	0.35	0.58	1.21	2.37	4.11	6.25	7.81	9.35	11.34	12.84
4	0.21	0.30	0.48	0.71	1.06	1.92	3.36	5.39	7.78	9.49	11.14	13.28	14.86
5	0.41	0.55	0.83	1.15	1.61	2.67	4.35	6.63	9.24	11.07	12.83	15.09	16.75
6	0.68	0.87	1.24	1.64	2.20	3.45	5.35	7.84	10.64	12.59	14.45	16.81	18.55
7	0.99	1.24	1.69	2.17	2.83	4.25	6.35	9.04	12.02	14.07	16.01	18.48	20.28
8	1.34	1.65	2.18	2.73	3.49	5.07	7.34	10.22	13.36	15.51	17.53	20.09	21.95
9	1.73	2.09	2.70	3.33	4.17	5.90	8.34	11.39	14.68	16.92	19.02	21.67	23.59
10	2.16	2.56	3.25	3.94	4.87	6.74	9.34	12.55	15.99	18.31	20.48	23.21	25.19
11	2.60	3.05	3.82	4.57	5.58	7.58	10.34	13.70	17.28	19.68	21.92	24.72	26.76
12	3.07	3.57	4.40	5.23	6.30	8.44	11.34	14.85	18.55	21.03	23.34	26.22	28.30
13	3.57	4.11	5.01	5.89	7.04	9.30	12.34	15.98	19.81	22.36	24.74	27.69	29.82
14	4.07	4.66	5.63	6.57	7.79	10.17	13.34	17.12	21.06	23.68	26.12	29.14	31.32
15	4.60	5.23	6.26	7.26	8.55	11.04	14.34	18.25	22.31	25.00	27.49	30.58	32.80
16	5.14	5.81	6.91	7.96	9.31	11.91	15.34	19.37	23.54	26.30	28.85	32.00	34.27
17	5.70	6.41	7.56	8.67	10.09	12.79	16.34	20.49	24.77	27.59	30.19	33.41	35.72
18	6.26	7.01	8.23	9.39	10.86	13.68	17.34	21.60	25.99	28.87	31.53	34.81	37.16
19	6.84	7.63	8.91	10.12	11.65	14.56	18.34	22.72	27.20	30.14	32.85	36.19	38.58
20	7.43	8.26	9.59	10.85	12.44	15.45	19.34	23.83	28.41	31.41	34.17	37.57	40.00
21	8.03	8.90	10.28	11.59	13.24	16.34	20.34	24.93	29.62	32.67	35.48	38.93	41.40

ν	0.005	0.010	0.025	0.050	0.100	0.250	0.500	0.750	0.900	0.950	0.975	0.990	0.995
22	8.64	9.54	10.98	12.34	14.04	17.24	21.34	26.04	30.81	33.92	36.78	40.29	42.80
23	9.26	10.20	11.69	13.09	14.85	18.14	22.34	27.14	32.01	35.17	38.08	41.64	44.18
24	9.89	10.86	12.40	13.85	15.66	19.04	23.34	28.24	33.20	36.42	39.36	42.98	45.56
25	10.52	11.52	13.12	14.61	16.47	19.94	24.34	29.34	34.38	37.65	40.65	44.31	46.93
30	13.79	14.95	16.79	18.49	20.60	24.48	29.34	34.80	40.26	43.77	46.98	50.89	53.67
35	17.19	18.51	20.57	22.47	24.80	29.05	34.34	40.22	46.06	49.80	53.20	57.34	60.27
40	20.71	22.16	24.43	26.51	28.05	33.66	39.34	45.62	51.81	55.76	59.34	63.69	66.77
45	24.31	25.90	28.37	30.61	33.35	38.29	44.64	50.98	57.51	61.66	65.41	69.96	73.17
50	27.99	29.71	32.36	34.76	37.69	42.94	49.33	56.33	63.17	67.50	71.42	76.15	79.49

F Distribution

	ν_1 = Degrees of Freedom for the Numerator								
ν_2	1	2	3	4	5	6	7	8	9
1	161.45	199.50	215.71	224.58	230.16	233.99	236.77	238.88	240.54
2	18.51	19.00	19.16	19.25	19.30	19.33	19.35	19.37	19.38
3	10.13	9.55	9.28	9.12	9.01	8.94	8.89	8.85	8.81
4	7.71	6.94	6.59	6.39	6.26	6.16	6.09	6.04	6.00
5	6.61	5.79	5.41	5.19	5.05	4.95	4.88	4.82	4.77
6	5.99	5.14	4.76	4.53	4.39	4.28	4.21	4.15	4.10
7	5.59	4.74	4.35	4.12	3.97	3.87	3.79	3.73	3.68
8	5.32	4.46	4.07	3.84	3.69	3.58	3.50	3.44	3.39
9	5.12	4.26	3.86	3.63	3.48	3.37	3.29	3.23	3.18
10	4.96	4.10	3.71	3.48	3.33	3.22	3.14	3.07	3.02
15	4.54	3.68	3.29	3.06	2.90	2.79	2.71	2.64	2.59
20	4.35	3.49	3.10	2.87	2.71	2.60	2.51	2.45	2.39
25	4.24	3.39	2.99	2.76	2.60	2.49	2.40	2.34	2.28
30	4.17	3.32	2.92	2.69	2.53	2.42	2.33	2.27	2.21
40	4.08	3.23	2.84	2.61	2.45	2.34	2.25	2.18	2.12
50	4.03	3.18	2.79	2.56	2.40	2.29	2.20	2.13	2.07
70	3.98	3.13	2.74	2.50	2.35	2.23	2.14	2.07	2.02
100	3.94	3.09	2.70	2.46	2.31	2.19	2.10	2.03	1.97
∞	3.84	3.00	2.60	2.37	2.21	2.10	2.01	1.94	1.88

Appendix C: Description of Data Sets

The data sets described below can be downloaded from the web at http://www.insead.edu/~gatignon. Three different kinds of information, which correspond to typically available data about markets, are provided for analysis: industry, panel and survey data. In addition, scanner data is provided for a product category in the form typically available in practice.

The industry dataset includes aggregate product and market data for all of the brands sold in each time period. This type of information is often provided by market research services, trade and business publications, and trade associations, to all of the firms competing in an industry. The other two datasets contain information collected from a sample of consumers rather than from the entire population. The first, panel data, is gathered from a group of consumers who have agreed to periodically record their brand perceptions, preferences, and purchase behavior. This information is often purchased by advertisers from syndicated research services and is useful for tracking changes in consumer behavior over time. The second, survey data, is collected by questionnaire or personal interview from a large group of consumers. Surveys are often conducted by advertising agencies (such as DDB Needham Worldwide, N. W. Ayer, and others), survey research companies, and by the advertisers themselves. These surveys typically measure a broad

	ν_1 = Degrees of Freedom for the Numerator								
ν_2	10	12	15	20	30	40	50	60	∞
1	241.88	243.91	245.95	248.01	250.10	251.14	252.20	252.20	254.19
2	19.40	19.41	19.43	19.45	19.46	19.47	19.48	19.48	19.49
3	8.79	8.74	8.70	8.66	8.62	8.59	8.57	8.57	8.53
4	5.96	5.91	5.86	5.80	5.75	5.72	5.69	5.69	5.63
5	4.74	4.68	4.62	4.56	4.50	4.46	4.43	4.43	4.37
6	4.06	4.00	3.94	3.87	3.81	3.77	3.74	3.74	3.67
7	3.64	3.57	3.51	3.44	3.38	3.34	3.30	3.30	3.23
8	3.35	3.28	3.22	3.15	3.08	3.04	3.01	3.01	2.93
9	3.14	3.07	3.01	2.94	2.86	2.83	2.79	2.79	2.71
10	2.98	2.91	2.85	2.77	2.70	2.66	2.62	2.62	2.54
15	2.54	2.48	2.40	2.33	2.25	2.20	2.16	2.16	2.07
20	2.35	2.28	2.20	2.12	2.04	1.99	1.95	1.95	1.85
25	2.24	2.16	2.09	2.01	1.92	1.87	1.82	1.82	1.72
30	2.16	2.09	2.01	1.93	1.84	1.79	1.74	1.74	1.63
40	2.08	2.00	1.92	1.84	1.74	1.69	1.64	1.64	1.52
50	2.03	1.95	1.87	1.78	1.69	1.63	1.58	1.58	1.45
70	1.97	1.89	1.81	1.72	1.62	1.57	1.50	1.50	1.36
100	1.93	1.85	1.77	1.68	1.57	1.52	1.45	1.45	1.30
∞	1.83	1.75	1.67	1.57	1.46	1.39	1.34	1.31	1.30

range of consumer characteristics, including attitudes, interests, values, and lifestyles. This information is especially useful for selecting target audiences and designing creative appeals.

The MARKSTRAT® market simulation program was used to create the industry and panel datasets. The survey dataset was developed separately to conform to this environment. We first describe the MARKSTRAT® environment and the characteristics of the industry. We then present the three types of data provided with this book and discuss the contents of each dataset.

The MARKSTRAT® Environment

To understand the industry in which competing firms operate, the reader must be familiar with two general dimensions of the MARKSTRAT® environment: (1) the structure of the industry in terms of the products, competition, and market characteristics, and (2) the marketing decisions that each firm can make over time. The discussion which follows concentrates on those aspects which are most relevant to advertising planning decisions.

Competition and market structure

In the MARKSTRAT® environment, five firms compete in a single market with a number of brands. Each firm starts out with a set of brands and has the ability to initiate research and development (R&D) projects to create new brands. If an R&D project is successful, then the sponsoring firm has the option of bringing the new product to market. All new products are introduced with new brand names.

Product Characteristics. The generic products in this industry are consumer durable goods comparable to electronic entertainment products. They are called Sonites. Because these products are durable, each customer win usually purchase only one item over a long period of time. Consequently, there are no issues of repeat purchase, brand loyalty, or brand switching in this market.

The products are characterized by five physical attributes: (1) weight (in kilograms), (2) design (measured on a relative scale), (3) volume (in cubic decimeters), (4) maximum frequency (in kilohertz), and (5) power (in watts). Not all attributes are equally important to consumers. Different segments have different preferences for these product characteristics, although the preferences are expressed in terms of brand image rather than purely physical characteristics. Consumers' brand evaluations are a function of their perceptions of the brands on three general dimensions, roughly corresponding to three of the five physical characteristics listed above. The first and most important characteristic is the perceived price of the product. Next, people consider the product's power (wattage). Finally, consumers evaluate the product's design (aesthetic value). Although less important than the other dimensions, the product's design helps consumers to differentiate between the various competing brands. The design attribute is measured on a scale from 1 to 10 by expert judges. To form an overall evaluation of each brand, consumers compare the brand's performance on each dimension with their preferences for a certain "ideal level" on each of these dimensions.

Because of the durability of the Sonite product and the importance of the purchase, the consumer decision process tends to follow a "high involvement" hierarchy. Measures of brand awareness, perceptions, preferences, and purchase intentions are, therefore, particularly relevant to the advertising decisions.

Consumer Segments. The consumer market for Sonites can be decomposed into five segments with distinguishable preferences. Segment 1 consists primarily of the "buffs," or experts in the product category. They are innovators and have high standards and requirements in terms of the technical quality of the product. Segment 2 is composed of "singles" who are relatively knowledgeable about the product but somewhat price sensitive. "Professionals" are found mostly in segment 3. They are demanding in terms of product quality and are willing to pay a premium price for that quality. "High earners" constitute segment 4. These individuals are also relatively price insensitive. However, they are not as educated as the professionals, and are not particularly knowledgeable about the product category. They buy the product mostly to enhance their social status. The fifth and last segment covers all consumers who cannot be grouped with any of the other four segments. They have used the product less than consumers in other segments and are considered to be late adopters of this product category. Given that this group is defined as a residual, it is very difficult to characterize the members in terms of demographics or lifestyle.

Although the preferences of the five consumer segments may change over time, the composition of each segment does not. Consequently, the survey data collected in the eighth time period (to be described) also describes consumers during the previous seven periods.

Distribution Structure. Sonites are sold through three different channels of distribution. Each channel carries all brands of Sonites, but the potential number of distributors and the characteristics of each channel are different. Channel 1 is made up of specialty retail stores. These stores provide specialized services to customers, and the bulk of their sales come from Sonites. There are 3,000 such outlets. Electric appliance stores are channel number 2. The 35,000 appliance stores carry Sonite products only as an addition to their main lines of electric appliances. Channel 3 is the 4,000 department stores that exist in the MARKSTRAT® world. Department stores sell a broad range of products, including clothing, furniture, housewares, and appliances. The three channels differ in terms of the proportion of the product that they sell and the types of clientele that they attract.

Marketing mix decisions

A product's marketing mix reflects the marketing strategy for the brand. A brand's attributes will influence how the brand is positioned and to whom it is marketed. Its price will affect the advertising budget and the brand image. Its distribution will determine where the brand is advertised, and so on. In this section we review the four main marketing mix variables, price, sales force, advertising, and product, that characterize brands in the MARKSTRAT® environment.

Prices. Each Sonite brand has a recommended retail price. These prices are generally accepted by the distribution channels and are passed on to consumers. As indicated earlier, different consumer segments are more or less sensitive to price differences across brands. A segment's price sensitivity or "elasticity" also depends on the selection of products offered to that segment and on the other marketing mix variables.

Sales Force. The two most important aspects of a firm's sales force are its size and its assignment to the three channels of distribution. Each salesperson carries the entire line of brands produced by his or her company. When a firm changes the number of salespeople it assigns to a particular channel, this is likely to affect the availability or distribution coverage of the firm's brands.

Advertising. Each brand of Sonite is advertised individually. Firms in this industry do not practice umbrella or generic (product category) advertising. However, advertising of specific brands can increase the total market demand for Sonites or affect Sonite demand in one or more segments.

Advertising can serve a number of communication purposes. It can be used to increase top-of-mind brand awareness and inform consumers about a brand's characteristics. Research has revealed that advertising expenditures are strongly positively related to brand awareness. Advertising can also have a substantial persuasive effect on consumers. Advertising can be used to position or reposition a brand so that the brand's image is more closely aligned with consumers' needs.

In addition, it is clear that advertising plays an important competitive role. One cannot consider a brand's advertising in isolation. Instead, the relative advertising weight or "share of voice" is a better predictor of consumers' purchase behavior than absolute advertising expenditures. Share of voice is the ratio of the brand's advertising expenditures to the total industry spending on advertising.

Products. The database reports information on all of the Sonite products that were marketed by firms during an eight-year time period. The names of the brands sold during this period are listed in Table C.1. This table also lists the periods during which each brand was available. The reader should note that some of the brands were introduced after the first time period and/or were discontinued before the last (eighth) period.

The brands of Sonites are named to facilitate identification of the marketing firm. The second letter of each brand name is a vowel that corresponds to one

Table C.1 Names of brands marketed during each period

Firm	Brand	Period of Availability
1	SALT	0–6
1	SAMA	0–6
2	SELF	0–5*
2	SELT	3–6
2	SEMA	4–6
2	SEMI	0–6
2	SEMU	4–6
3	SIBI	0–6
3	SICK	4–6
3	SIRO	0–3*
3	SIRT	4–6
4	SODA	2–6
4	SOLD	0–6
4	SONO	0–5*
5	SULI	0–6
5	SUSI	0–6

*Indicates a discontinued brand.

of the five competing firms. Firm I markets all brands that have an "A" as the second letter of the name, such as SAMA. "E" corresponds to firm 2, "I" to firm 3, "O" to firm 4, and "U" to firm 5.

During the eight time periods, each firm has the opportunity to design and market a portfolio of different brands. In response to consumer or market pressures, companies may change the physical characteristics of each brand over time. Information about brands and their attributes is provided in the industry data set, as described below.

Survey

A mail survey of a group of 300 consumers was conducted in the eighth (most recent) time period. The survey collected a variety of consumer information including demographic data, psychographics, information on product purchase behavior, decision processes, and media habits. These data are particularly useful for segmentation analysis, which is an important precursor to selecting a target market, generating copy appeals, and media selection. A list of the variables from the questionnaire and the coding scheme for the items are provided in Tables C.2 and C.3 respectively.

Indup

The industry dataset provides two types of performance information for each brand and time period: sales figures (in units and dollar sales) and market

Table C.2 Survey questionnaire and scale type

Number	Abbreviation	Question	Scale
Demographics			
1	Age	Age	continuous
2	Marital	Marital status	categorical
3	Income	Total household income	categorical
4	Education	Education	categorical
5	HHSize	Household size	continuous
6	Occupation	Occupation	categorical
7	Location	Geographic location of household	categorical
Psychographics			
8	TryHairdo	I often try the latest hairdo styles.	likert
9	LatestStyle	I usually have one or more outfits that are of the very latest style.	likert
10	DressSmart	An important part of my life and activities is dressing smartly.	likert
11	BlondsFun	I really do believe that blondes have more fun.	likert*
12	LookDif	I want to look a little different from others.	likert
13	LookAftract	Looking attractive is important in keeping your husband (wife).	liked
14	GrocShop	I like grocery shopping.	likert
15	LikeBaking	I love to bake and frequently do.	likert
16	ClothesFresh	Clothes should be dried in the fresh air and out-of-doors.	likert
17	WashHands	It is very important for people to wash their hands before eating every meal	likert
18	Sporting	I would rather go to a sporting event than a dance.	likert
19	LikeColors	I like bright, splashy colors.	likert
20	FeelAffract	I like to feel attractive.	likert
21	TooMuchSex	There is too much emphasis on sex today.	likert
22	Social	I do more things socially than do most of my friends.	likert
23	LikeMaid	I would like to have a maid to do the housework.	likert
24	ServDinners	Ilike to serve unusual dinners.	likert
25	SaveRecipes	I save recipes from newspapers and magazines.	likert
26	LikeKitchen	The kitchen is my favorite room.	likert
27	LoveEat	I love to eat.	likert
28	SpiritualVal	Spiritual values are more important than material things.	likert
29	Mother	If it was good enough for my mother, it's good enough for me.	likert
30	ClassicMusic	Classical music is more interesting than popular music.	likert
31	Children	I try to arrange my home for my children's convenience.	likert

Table C.2 Continued.

Number	Abbreviation	Question	Scale
32	Appliances	It is important to have new appliances.	likert
33	CloseFamily	Our family is a close-knit group.	likert
34	LoveFamily	There is a lot of love in our family.	likert
35	TalkChildren	I spend a lot of time with my children talking about their activities, friends, and problems.	likert
36	Exercise	Everyone should take walks, bicycle, garden, or otherwise exercise several times a week.	likert
37	LikeMyself	I like what I see when I look in the mirror.	likert
38	CareOfSkin	I take good care of my skin.	likert
39	MedCheckup	You should have a medical checkup at least once a year.	likert
40	EveningHome	I would rather spend a quiet evening at home than go out to a party.	likert
41	TripWorld	I would like to take a trip around the world.	likert
42	Homebody	I am a homebody	likert
43	LondonParis	I would like to spend a year in London or Paris.	likert
44	Comfort	I furnish my home for comfort, not for style.	likert
45	Ballet	I like ballet.	likert
46	Parties	I like parties where there is lots of music and talk.	likert
47	WomenNtSmoke	Women should not smoke in public.	likert
48	BrightFun	I like things that are bright, fun, and exciting.	likert
49	Seasoning	I am interested in spices and seasoning.	likert
50	ColorTV	If I had to choose, I would rather have a color television set than a new refrigerator.	likert
51	SloppyPeople	Sloppy people feel terrible.	likert
Purchase bevavior			
52	Smoke	How often do you smoke?	0 to 7
53	Gasoline	How much gasoline do you use?	0 to 7
54	Headache	How much do you use headache remedies?	0 to 7
55	Whiskey	How much do you drink whiskey?	0 to 7
56	Bourbon	How much do you drink bourbon?	0 to 7
57	FastFood	How often do you eat at fast food restaurants?	0 to 7
58	Restaurants	How often do you eat at restaurants with table service?	0 to 7
59	OutForDinner	How often do you go out for dinner?	0 to 7
60	OutForLunch	How often do you go out for lunch?	0 to 7

Table C.2 Continued.

Number	Abbreviation	Question	Scale
61	RentVideo	How often do you rent video tapes?	0 to 7
62	Catsup	How often do you use catsup?	0 to 7
Purchase decision process			
63	KnowledgeSon	How much do you know about the product category of Sonites?	likert
64	PerceiveDif	How large a difference do you perceive between various brands of Sonites?	likert
65	BrandLoyalty	When purchasing a Sonite, how loyal are you to a particular brand name?	likert
66	CategMotiv	What is your primary reason or motivation for purchasing a Sonite (the product category)?	categorical
67	BrandMotiv	What is your primary reason or motivation for purchasing a particular brand of Sonite?	categorical
68	OwnSonite	Do you currently own a Sonite?	0/1
69	NecessSonite	Do you feel that owning a Sonite is a necessity?	0/1
70	Otherinflnc	If you were to purchase a Sonite, would you make the decision about which brand to purchase by yourself or with the help of others?	categorical
71	DecisionTime	If you were to purchase a Sonite, would you make the decision about which brand to purchase before going to the retail store, or would you wait until you were in the store to decide?	categorical
Media habits			
72	ReadWomen	I read Women's magazines.	0/1
73	ReadHomeServ	I read Home Service magazines.	0/1
74	ReadFashion	I read Fashion magazines.	0/1
75	ReadMenMag	I read Men's magazines.	0/1
76	ReadBusMag	I read Business and Financial magazines.	0/1
77	ReadNewsMag	I read News magazines.	0/1
78	ReadGIMag	I read General magazines.	0/1
79	ReadYouthMag	I read Youth magazines.	0/1
80	ReadNwspaper	I read the newspaper.	0/1
81	WtchDayTV	I watch network television during the day time.	0/1
82	WtchEveTV	I watch network television early evening news.	0/1
83	WtchPrmTV	I watch network television during prime time.	0/1
84	WtchLateTV	I watch network television in the late evening.	0/1

Table C.2 Continued.

Number	Abbreviation	Question	Scale
85	WtchWkEndTV	I or my kid(s) watch children's programs on television during the weekend.	0/1
86	WtchCosbyTV	I watch The Cosby Show regularly.	0/1
87	WtchFamTisTV	I watch Family Ties regularly.	0/1
88	WtchCheersTV	I watch Cheers regularly.	0/1
89	WtchMoonTV	I watch Moonlighting regularly.	0/1
90	WtchBossTV	I watch Who's the Boss regularly.	0/1
91	WtchGrwTV	I watch Growing Pains regularly.	0/1
92	WtchMiaVicTV	I watch Miami Vice regularly.	0/1
93	WtchDynasTV	I watch Dynasty regularly.	0/1
94	WtchGoidGTV	I watch Golden Girls regularly.	0/1
95	WtchBowlTV	I watch the Superbowl each year.	0/1

*Likert items are scaled from 1 = Disagree to 7 = Agree.

Table C.3 Coding of variables

Variable	Category	Code
Question #2	Married	1
Marital Status	Widowed	2
	Divorced	3
	Separated	4
	Single	5
Question #3	Less than $4,000	1
Household Income	$4,000 to $5,999	2
	$6,000 to $7,999	3
	$8,000 to $9,999	4
	$10,000 to $11,999	5
	$12,000 to $14,999	6
	$15,000 to $17,499	7
	$17,500 to $19,999	8
	$20,000 to $24,999	9
	$25,000 to $29,999	10
	$30,000 to $49,999	11
	$50,000 and over	12
Question #4	Did not attend school	1
Education Level	Went to elementary or grammar school	2
	Went to high school or trade school for less than four years	3
	Graduated from high school or trade school	4
	Some college, jr. college, or technical school	5
	Graduated from college	6
	Have post-graduate degree	7

Table C.3 Continued.

Variable	Category	Code
Question #6	Professional workers	1
Occupation	Managers & administrators, except farm	2
	Clerical workers	3
	Sales workers	4
	Craftsmen	5
	Operatives, except transport	6
	Transport equipment operators	7
	Laborers, except farm	8
	Farmers, farm managers, laborers & foremen	9
	Service & private household workers	0
Question #7	New York	1
Location	Los Angeles	2
	Chicago	3
	Philadelphia	4
	San Francisco	5
	Boston	6
	Detroit	7
	Dallas	8
	Washington	9
	Houston	10
	Cleveland	11
	Atlanta	12
	Pittsburgh	13
	Miami	14
	Minneapolis-St.Paul	15
	Seaftle-Tacoma	16
	Tampa-St. Petersburg	17
	St. Louis	18
	Denver	19
	Sacramento-Stockton	20
Question #66	To remove a problem	1
Category Purchase	To avoid a problem	2
Motivation	To replace another Sonite	3
	For sensory stimulation	4
	For intellectual stimulation	5
	For social approval	6
	To enhance my self esteem	7
Question #67	To remove a problem	1
Brand Purchase	To avoid a problem	2
Motivation	Because of dissatisfaction with my current brand	3
	For sensory stimulation	4
	For intellectual stimulation	5
	For social approval	6
	To enhance my self esteem	7

Table C.3 Continued.

Variable	Category	Code
Question #70	By myself (individually)	1
Decision Making	With the help of others (as a group)	2
Question #71	Before going to the store	1
Decision Timing	In the store	2

Other Variables:

Questions		Scale
8 to 51	Disagree	1 2 3 4 5 6 7 Agree
63 to 65		
52 to 62	Never/None 0	1 2 3 4 5 6 7 Very Often/A Lot
68 & 69		0 = No 1 = Yes
72 to 95		

share data (based on unit and dollar sales). The dataset also includes information on the values of the marketing mix variables for each competing brand. The data describe each brand's price, advertising expenditures, sales force size (for each channel of distribution), and physical characteristics (i.e., the four Ps). Finally, the dataset reports the variable cost of each brand at each time period. The reader should note that this cost is not the actual current production cost, as this information is typically not available for each competitive brand. The reported cost figures reflect the basic cost of production that can be estimated for a given first batch of 100,000 units at the period of introduction of the brand. A list of the variables in the industry dataset is given in Table C.4.

Panel

The panel dataset provides information that, in many ways, complements the data in the industry dataset. Panel data are available at the level of the individual market segment rather than at the total market level. The panel dataset includes information on the size of each segment (in unit sales of Sonites) and the market share for each brand with each segment. The dataset also provides the results of a panel questionnaire with items on advertising communication, brand perceptions, and preferences. Variables include the extent of brand name awareness, segment preferences in terms of the ideal levels of the three most important attributes (price, power, and design), consumers' brand perceptions on the same three dimensions, and brand purchase intentions. Finally, the dataset reports the shopping habits of each segment in

Table C.4 Variables in industry level data base

Abbreviation	Variable
Period	Period Number
Firm	Firm Number
Brand	Brand Name
Price	Price
Adver	Advertising Expenditures
Char0l	Product Characteristic #1: Weight (Kg)
Char02	Product Characteristic #2: Design (Index)
Char03	Product Characteristic #3: Volume (dM3)
Char04	Product Characteristic #4: Maximum Frequency (khz)
Char05	Product Characteristic #5: Power (W)
Salesmen1	Number of Salesmen-Channel 1
Salesmen2	Number of Salesmen-Channel 2
Salesmen3	Number of Salesmen-Channel 3
Cost	Average Unit Cost of Initial Batch
Dist01	Number of Distributors-Channel 1
Dist02	Number of Distributors-Channel 2
Dist03	Number of Distributors-Channel 3
UnitSales	Total Sales in Units
DolSales	Total Sales in Dollars
UnitShare	Market Share (Based on Units)
DolShare	Market Share (Based on Dollars)
AdShare	Advertising Share (Share of Voice)
RelPrice	Relative Price (Price relative to average market price)

the three channels of distribution. A summary of these variables is provided in Table C.5.

Scan

SCAN.DAT contains a simulated sample of scanner data, similar to the dataset of refrigerated orange juice dataset used in Fader and Lattin (1993); Fader, Lattin and Little (1992); and Hardie, Johnson and Fader (1992). (See these papers for a full description of this dataset, and SCANNER.SAS for the criteria used to create this subset. The six brands along with their brand id codes, are:

1 Brand 1
2 Brand 2
3 Brand 3
4 Brand 4
5 Brand 5
6 Brand 6

This file is set up for estimation of the standard Guadagni and Little (1983) MNL model of brand choice, including their "loyalty" variable. The value of

Table C.5 Variables in panel data base

Abbreviation	Variable
Period	Period Number
Segment	Segment Number
SegSize	Segment Size (Unit Sales in Segment)
Ideal01	Ideal Value of Price (for each segment)
Ideal02	Ideal Value of Power (for each segment)
Ideal03	Ideal Value of Design (for each segment)
Brand	Brand Name
Awareness	Percentage of segment aware of the brand
Intent	Purchase Intent (for each brand and segment)
Shop01	Percentage of segment shopping in Channel 1
Shop02	Percentage of segment shopping in Channel 2
Shop03	Percentage of segment shopping in Channel 3
Perc01	Perception of Price (for each brand)
Perc02	Perception of Power (for each brand)
Perc03	Perception of Design (for each brand)
Dev01	Deviation from Ideal Price (for each brand in each segment)
Dev02	Deviation from Ideal Power (for each brand in each segment)
Dev03	Deviation from Ideal Design (for each brand in each segment)
Share	Segment Share (for each brand)

the smoothing constant is set to 0.8; the loyalty variable is initialized using purchase information for weeks 1–52.

In this dataset, the number of choice alternatives varies over time (due to shopping at different stores, stock-outs, etc). Rather than having one record per purchase occasion, we have one record per choice alternative.

The format of SCAN.DAT is as follows:

panelist id
week of purchase
a dummy variable indicating whether this record is associated with the brand chosen
the number of records (brands available) associated with this purchase occasion
the brand id of this record
regular shelf price for this brand
any price reduction for this brand on this purchase occasion (price paid = price − price cut)
a dummy variable indicating the presence of a feature ad for this brand
the value of the Guadagny and Little loyalty variable for this brand (on this purchase occasion)
a brand-specific constant/dummy for brand 1
a brand-specific constant/dummy for brand 2
a brand-specific constant/dummy for brand 3

a brand-specific constant/dummy for brand 5
a brand-specific constant/dummy for brand 6

The reference brand is, therefore, brand 4, a private label.

This dataset was created specifically for analysis using LIMDEP. The file examp6–2.lim contains a sample "program" for reading this dataset into LIMDEP. Note that other estimation packages may require the data in a slightly different format. Minor formatting changes can easily be accomplished using SAS; for major changes it may make sense to modify the SCANNER.PAS program (or write your own version of this program using your language of choice). An executable file "scanner.exe", is available to create similar data sets using a different constant for building the loyalty variable.

Fader, Lattin, and Little (1992) describe a procedure for estimating non-linear parameters in MNL models using standard MNL estimation routines. The smoothing constant in the G&L loyalty variable is such a nonlinear parameter. The value used in the creation of SCAN.DAT (0.8) is not necessarily optimal. To find the optimal value, you require derivative terms (see Fader, Lattin and Little (1992) for complete details). SCANNER.PAS is the program used to create SCAN.DAT. This program allows you to create a dataset called SCAN.DAT for any value of the smoothing constant (alpha) and gives you the option of including the required derivative terms (which are inserted between the loyalty variable and the brand-specific constant for brand 1; the format is F10.6). The "scanner.exe" program will prompt you for the value to use for the smoothing constant.

The original simulated raw data are contained in the files PURCHASES.DAT and STORE.DAT. PURCHASES.DAT contains the simulated purchase history information for 200 households. The format of this file is as follows:

panelist id   brand id of brand chosen   week of purchase   store id

STORE.DAT contains the store environment information. The format of this file is as follows:

week #   store id   brand id   regular price   price cut   feature dummy

Note that a price (and price cut) of 9.99 indicates brand not available that store/week.

SCANNER.PUR is the subset of PURCHASES.DAT used in the creation of SCAN.DAT. SCANNER.PUR was created using SCANNER.SAS.

Index

ERRATA

The publisher regrets the errors that appear in the first printing of this book. Below please find the corrected text.

Page 60: Equations 4.29 and 4.32: should replace the delta sign with the differentiation operator ∂ both at the denominator and numerator (i.e., correct the sign)

Page 62: Equations after "BLUE (Best Linear Unbiased Estimator)": should have no small "k" but only capital "K" (2 occurences in equation and 2 other occurences in 2 lines above it)

Page 64: Equation 4.54: should have no small "k" but only capital "K"

Page 65: Equation 4.63: should have no small "k" but only capital "K"

Page 86: Equation 5.43: should end with "y" sub "1" (i.e., the sub "1" is missing)

Page 167: Fig. 8.1.: upper left hand corner part of figure: the three numbers "1", "2" and "3" should be preceeded with the delta sign (i.e., this sign is missing); the equation should then read: "delta" sub "1", "delta" sub "2", "delta" sub "3"